Walking in the Way

Walking in the Way

An Introduction to
Christian Ethics

Joe E. Trull

BROADMAN
&HOLMAN
PUBLISHERS

Nashville, Tennessee

0-8054-2082-7

Published by Broadman & Holman Publishers, Nashville, Tennessee
Acquisitions and Development Editor: John Landers
Page Design by Anderson Thomas Design, Nashville, Tennessee
Typography by TF Designs, Mt. Juliet, Tennessee

Dewey Decimal Classification: 241
Subject Heading: CHRISTIAN ETHICS
Library of Congress Card Catalog Number: 95-51903

Library of Congress Cataloging-in-Publication Data
    Trull, Joe E., 1935–
        Walking in the way : an introduction to Christian ethics / Joe E. Trull.
            p. cm.
        Includes bibliographical references.
        ISBN 0-8054-2082-7 (pbk.)
        1. Christian ethics. I. Title.
    BJ1251.T78   1997
    241—dc21
                                                                95-51903
                                                                CIP

Contents

v

129038

PREFACE

Ethics professor Larry Rasmussen recently wrote, "Like a wrinkle in time, we find ourselves, at the close of the second Christian millennium, not far from the terrain of Christians at the beginning of the first. Ours is also a 'hellenistic' era—diverse, cosmopolitan, multilingual, -racial, -cultural, -religious, fragmented, eclectic, riddled by extremes of all kinds. A dislocated world, people then felt and people now feel isolated or off center. . . . And those first Christians, like us, worried about moral deformation everywhere, even as they rejoiced in the coming of a new world."[1]

Walking in the Way is the title of this book because it best defines for me the essence of **Christian ethics**. In one sense, Christian ethics is a study—an academic discipline. But it is much more than that. Ideally and ultimately, *Christian ethics is a way of life.* To be the people of God in the twenty-first century will require us, as it did first-century believers, to be followers of "the Way" (Acts 9:2). Disciples of Jesus are people of "the Way," who walk in the way of the LORD (Ps. 119:1-3).

I discovered this truth in a Christian ethics class taught by my mentor, Thomas Buford Maston.[2] That was a life-changing revelation. For the first time I understood the relevance of the Christian faith to the world in which I lived. This realization, along with the influence of T. B. Maston, convinced me to do graduate studies in Christian ethics during Maston's last years of teaching. To a large degree, this textbook reflects the mind and spirit of my teacher and mentor, one who walked in "the Way," as well as taught it.

vii

This book also shares a special kinship with other colleagues in the field of Christian ethics, whose writings aided me immensely when I "re-entered" academia in 1985. Introductory material in Christian ethics by Henlee Barnette, Guy Greenfield, Ebbie C. Smith, and William M. Tillman Jr. provided basic structure in the development of a course of study, from which this text emerged. I am indebted to many other ethicists, too numerous to name, whose shadows often fall across these pages.

In a practical sense, I am deeply grateful to several persons who have encouraged, enriched, and facilitated the writing of this book. Colleagues Paul Robertson, Fisher Humphreys, and Gary Farley rescued me from numerous near shipwrecks. Because of the constant support and guidance I received from my editor, John Landers, the journey was enjoyable and successful. My graduate student assistant, Mark Sheffield, assisted with many mid-course corrections, as did my multi-talented student secretary, Shannon Hall, whose proofreading and perception kept the project shipshape. Finally, my gratitude for the ethics students at New Orleans Baptist Seminary, who provided the best laboratory for testing this introduction to Christian ethics—the classroom.

During this writing pilgrimage one person has been a constant encourager, a willing reader, a kind inquisitor, and a "minister of miscellaneous." For forty years she has also been my best friend and the love of my life—thank you, Audra.

After eleven years of teaching and writing about Christian ethics, I am acutely aware of the controversial nature of the subject and possible reactions to some proposals. My greatest fear, however, is the view expressed in Abelard's criticism of Anselm: "If any one went to him in uncertainty, he returned more uncertain still. He was wonderful to hear, but at once failed if you questioned him. He kindled a fire, not to give light, but to fill the house with smoke."[3]

My hope for this text is light, not smoke—that Christian ethics will be better understood, or at least, as Kierkegaard once said of his own writing, "to be more passionately misunderstood."[4]

INTRODUCTION

"It's very difficult on a black night in the middle of a sandstorm to sort out good and evil!" These painful words were uttered by an American officer to a television reporter as he tried to explain his action in the Persian Gulf War. The pilot's "friendly" fire upon American tanks had killed two of his fellow soldiers.[1]

Have you ever felt like this Gulf War veteran as you faced a **moral** decision? Each week seems to bring new moral storms, darker nights, and tougher choices. Discerning what is the right thing to do, as well as doing it, is increasingly difficult. How does a Christian live ethically in a world like ours?

This book is an introduction to the study and practice of **Christian ethics.** Both study and practice are important. Knowledge is foundational to doing **ethics,** but putting ethical theory into practice is the proof that ethics works.

In his classical survey of Christian ethics, Edward Leroy Long Jr. began by stressing that Christian ethics is concerned with both theory and practice. Quoting Paul Ramsey and James Gustafson, Long stressed that as a theory Christian ethics always interprets Christian action. Furthermore, as a study, it can never replace the responsibility to act.[2]

So it has been from the earliest days of ethical deliberation. Ancient Greek and Roman philosophers not only taught a way of thinking, they claimed to pursue a *bios*, a "way of life." The Greek philosopher Socrates (470-399 B.C.) spent his life arguing the importance of living virtuously, using debate and dialogue to

1

examine the "good life." The philosophical schools revolved around lifestyle and ethics, "which **philosophy** sought to embody in a life of discipline and virtue. The reference was not so much to the *study* of philosophy as to the *practice* of it *(askesis)*. Socrates was said to have risen above natural human instincts by 'practicing philosophy.'"[3]

So it was for the first Christian community. The earliest disciples of Jesus were called people of "the Way" even before they were called "Christians" (Acts 9:2). The metaphor, common in Greek and Hebrew Scriptures, was used frequently of the people who walked in "God's way" or in the "way of the Lord." Jesus presented Himself as "the Way" (John 14:6) and once spoke of the broad way that leads to destruction and the narrow way that leads to life (Matt. 7:13–14).

"The Way" refers both to the destination of the journey and to the manner of travel. "To walk in 'the Way' involves a moral style so intimately related to the destination itself that to wander from 'the Way' is to miss the goal (a righteous life in a community faithful to God)."[4]

Our approach to the study of Christian ethics will also have this twofold thrust. One major aim will be to understand the cognitive side of Christian ethics, sorting out moral categories and ethical methodologies. But it will not end there. The purpose of our investigation will also be practical—to learn how to live as the people of God, in **character** and in conduct. Christian ethics includes both belief and behavior.

Socrates reportedly began his conversations with his students with the statement, "Before we start talking, let's decide what we are talking about." That is a good way to begin our own conversations about Christian ethics. Let's start our survey by discussing six basic questions: Should **ethics** come first? What is Christian ethics? What is the main **authority** for Christian ethics? Is biblical religion ethical? Why study Christian ethics? Can ethics be taught?

SHOULD ETHICS COME FIRST?

James McClendon Jr. raised this question in the opening pages of his *Systematic Theology: Ethics*. This Baptist theologian began his systematized statement of belief by arguing for the "chronological priority of ethics" in theological scholarship.[5] Quoting Ron Sider,

McClendon noted theologians are forever leaving ethics until last, and at times leaving ethics out altogether.[6]

McClendon believes that Christian ethics comes first in the Christian faith. So do I—not just because I fear leaving it out, but because biblical religion has always been ethical. But the reason for the priority of ethics is that Christianity began that way. The gospel proclaimed by Jesus was foremost a call to become part of God's kingdom, a call to live under God's rule and reign. "Christianity is more than a matter of a new understanding. Christianity is an invitation to be part of an alien people who make a difference because they see something that cannot otherwise be seen without Christ."[7]

The unbelievers who first responded to Christianity did not view it as a new philosophy or another national religion. They saw a new community of people who lived counterculture to the world of that day. The church of the first century was identified not by its theological teachings or its mystical revelations—in the beginning Christianity was a different way of life.[8]

To become a member of the Christian family required a second birth (John 3:3), which created a totally new life (2 Cor. 5:17). Christian conversion meant change, "a redirection of life, characterized by a new allegiance at the center of the personality and by a new direction in social relationships."[9]

When Zaccheus the tax collector was converted, he immediately responded by resolving to distribute his wealth to the poor and to those whom he had cheated. "Today salvation has come to this house" (Luke 19:9), responded Jesus. Salvation was for this publican a radical transformation of life.

In a Graeco-Roman society of vicious immorality, where wealth was worshiped, life was cheap, and purity and chastity were vanishing, came a new moral influence. The extraordinary daily life of Christians was a moral witness that astounded and attracted the first-century world.

A moving description of the ethical lifestyle of the first followers of "the Way" is given in the second-century *Epistle to Diognetus:*

> Christians are distinguished from other men neither by country, nor language, nor the customs which they observe . . . , they display to us their wonderful and confessedly striking method of life. They dwell in their own countries, but simply as sojourners. As citizens they share in all things with others, and yet endure all things as if foreigners. . . . To sum up all in one word—what the soul is in the body, that are Christians in the world . . . they are the preservers of the world.[10]

Perhaps the most striking quality of the followers of Jesus was their *agape* love, especially toward the most neglected of that day—the orphans, the aged, the sick, the prisoners, the slaves, and the abandoned. Tertullian once defended the Christian faith from false accusations in his *Apology* when he wrote, "One in mind and soul, we do not hesitate to share our earthly goods with one another. All things are common among us but our wives."[11]

In the beginning, the Christian faith was profoundly ethical. The earliest community of believers became known for their love for God and for neighbor, just as Jesus had taught them (Matt. 22:37-39). Sadly, this original focus on the ethical life of believers was soon corrupted.

T. B. Maston, my mentor and ethics professor, often emphasized that the outstanding weakness of Christianity has been its ethical deficiency. Christian history is replete with examples of "the Way" interpreted almost exclusively in theological terms, unrelated to life and society.

No study of Christian ethics could overlook this central truth. For the followers of Jesus, Christian ethics comes first—it is primary, not secondary, in importance. That is one reason this introductory survey of Christian ethics intends to stress the primary importance of ethics in the Christian faith.

In light of this biblical and historical truth, how do we then define the subject of our study? This is our next task.

WHAT IS CHRISTIAN ETHICS?

To avoid confusion, let us also be sure we understand what we mean by Christian ethics. As we have just declared, Christian ethics is both a subject to be studied and a way of life. The Danish religious philosopher Søren Kierkegaard wrote in one of his early journals, "I want a truth for which I can live and die."[12] He was asking the ultimate ethical question, "What is worth living for?"

Indeed, this has been the sphinx-like riddle every philosopher has sought to solve: What is the meaning of life? Relying primarily on reason, great thinkers like Socrates, Plato, and Aristotle proposed various answers in their search for the **virtuous** and happy life—the "good" life.

Christian ethics attempts to answer that question also. However, what is right or good for the Christian is not solely determined by human reason. Swiss theologian Emil Brunner defined Christian ethics as "the science of human conduct as determined by Divine conduct."[13] Brunner underscored the main difference between **philosophical ethics** and Christian ethics—each looks to a different authority. For philosophers the *summum bonum* in life is discovered through human wisdom; for Christians the highest good is found in knowing and doing God's will.

Though Brunner's concise definition is accurate as far as it goes, it omits a vital element. Along with the study of human conduct (doing), a complete Christian ethic must also deal with moral character (being). In fact, the Christian must *be* something before he or she can *do* anything. Christian character not only precedes conduct, it is the artesian well from which true goodness flows.

Christian ethics, therefore, deals with "oughtness." What *ought* a Christian "be" (character) and "do" (conduct) which accomplishes God's will in human relationships? In other words, Christian ethics defines how to live and what to live for.

WHAT IS THE MAIN AUTHORITY FOR CHRISTIAN ETHICS?

A third major question in the study of Christian ethics deals with authority—who or what sources determine the virtuous life? Throughout Christian history the Scriptures have occupied a central place of influence, although the nature of biblical authority has always been a matter of debate.

Most evangelical Christians believe the Scriptures to be the main objective revelation of God's will. We describe the Bible as the Word of God because in it we believe God has spoken and continues to speak. Although there are many resources to which we turn for ethical guidance, the Bible remains the major moral compass for Christian ethics.

The apex of God's self-revelation was the incarnation—the life and teachings of Jesus. The Gospels contain the clearest communication of God's moral will because God best revealed His nature and character in and through Jesus of Nazareth. To see Jesus is to see God (2 Cor. 4:6).

The apostle John began his Gospel with the declaration that Jesus is the Word of God in human flesh and "in him was life, and the life was the light of all people" (1:4). The Epistle to the Hebrews (written to convince Jewish believers that Jesus was the Hebrew

Messiah) opens with the same affirmation: "Long ago God spoke to our ancestors in many and various ways by the prophets, but in these last days he has spoken to us by a Son, whom he appointed heir of all things, through whom he also created the worlds. He is the reflection of God's glory and the exact imprint of God's very being" (Heb. 1:1-3).

As Jesus was God incarnate and came to reveal God, what place did ethics have in this "one solitary life"—the historical revelation of God in Christ?

Scholars across the centuries have universally agreed that "whatever else Jesus was, He was a great ethical teacher."[14] The central theme of Jesus' preaching and ministry was the **kingdom of God** (Matt. 4:23; Luke 4:43). The kingdom, the "Reign or Rule of God," was the subject of Jesus' sermons (Mark 1:15), the theme He sent His disciples to preach (Luke 9:2), and the topic of Jesus' last message to His followers after His resurrection (Acts 1:3). L. H. Marshall explained the importance of the kingdom of God in the teaching of Jesus for Christian ethics: "All the ethical teaching of Jesus is simply an exposition of the ethics of the Kingdom of God, of the way in which men inevitably behave when they actually come under the rule of God."[15]

An even greater revelation than Jesus' teachings was the ethical example of Jesus' life. The Scottish theologian R. E. O. White was reluctant to condense the Christian life to one simple **norm**. White admitted, however, that if he were forced to choose, he would have to claim the imitation of Christ as the supreme ethical ideal. "Christian ethics is not Christianity, nor the Christian moral life the whole of the Christian discipleship. The gospel and the moral ideal are separable in thought, not in experience. But when, with whatever qualifications, and only for the sake of study, the separation *is* made, the ultimate word to be spoken about Christian ethics is— the imitation of Christ."[16]

The Bible is also a story—God's story of human history in response to divine revelation. A major role of the Scriptures is the formation of the faith community, the people of God. Although there are many "identity-shaping authorities" for the community of believers, the Bible "is somehow normative for the life of the church and those individuals who identify with that historic community."[17] Moral character is shaped in community; the Christian community is formed and informed by the vision of God in Christ revealed in the biblical narrative.[18]

The Christian can turn to many resources for discovering God's will in human relationships. Yet the one authority that claims universal acceptance as the unequaled source for Christian faith and practice is the Holy Bible. To acknowledge the supremacy of scriptural authority for Christian ethics is to confirm what the Bible itself declares: "All scripture is inspired by God and is useful for teaching, for reproof, for correction, and for training in righteousness, so that everyone who belongs to God may be proficient, equipped for every good work" (2 Tim. 3:16-17).

IS BIBLICAL RELIGION ETHICAL?

Having affirmed the centrality of the Scriptures for Christian ethics, we must now ask to what degree is biblical religion ethical? Most ancient religions worshiped gods who were, by Christian standards, either immoral or amoral. The deities of the Graeco-Roman pantheon were unpredictable; Zeus, the storm god, was as morally chaotic as the weather over which he supposedly reigned. Pagan gods were often anthropomorphic projections of human weaknesses and excesses, such as Bacchus, the Roman god of wine and drunken orgies, and Aphrodite, the Greek goddess of sexual love.

The God of Abraham, Isaac, and Jacob stood in stark contrast to these pagan deities. Jehovah of Israel was a moral Person of consistent ethical character. "What does the LORD require of you," asked the prophet Micah, "but to do justice, and to love kindness, and to walk humbly with your God?" (6:8).

In both the Old and New Testaments, biblical religion stresses the unity of belief and behavior. Faith and works are so permanently bonded that to eliminate one is to lose the other. The Scriptures repeatedly state that a person cannot be spiritually right and at the same time morally wrong. No truth revealed in the Bible is clearer than this one—religion and ethics are inseparable.

For the faithful Hebrew, obedience to God was the basis of the covenant relationship. The psalmist asked, "O LORD, who may abide in your tent? Who may dwell on your holy hill?" (15:1). The answer followed: "Those who walk blamelessly, and do what is right, and speak the truth from their heart" (15:2).

The **Torah** in the Old Testament contained God's requirements for His covenant people. The devout child of Abraham revered the *shema*, which expressed the heart of the Law: "You shall love the

LORD your God with all your heart, and with all your soul, and with all your might" (Deut. 6:5). So venerated was this passage that Hebrew homes enclosed these words on small scrolls in containers attached to door posts. The "Mezuzah" (as it was called) was a constant reminder of the singular moral character of the one and only true God, Jehovah.

One of the most significant ethical passages in the Old Testament is found in the Holiness Code (Lev. 17–26). The ethical nature of "holiness" is uniquely explained and illustrated in chapter 19, which begins with the absolute command: "You shall be holy, for I the LORD your God am holy" (19:2). This injunction is the theological foundation for Christian ethics. The God of Israel is here clearly revealed as a moral deity, the Lord who is "just in all his ways, and kind in all his doings" (Ps. 145:17).

The New Testament scholar C. H. Dodd began his classic work *Gospel and Law* with this affirmation: "The Christian religion, like Judaism (to take another example), is an ethical religion in the specific sense that it recognizes no ultimate separation between the service of God and social behavior. 'Thou shalt love thy God'; 'Thou shalt love thy neighbor as thyself.' The two basic commandments stand together. . . . It is impossible to understand either the ethical content of Christianity or its religious content unless we can in some measure hold the two together and understand them in their true, organic relations within a whole."[19]

Thus far in this introduction to Christian ethics, we have attempted to affirm four fundamental truths: (1) the chronological and theological priority of Christian ethics; (2) the importance of Christian ethics; (3) the centrality of the Bible in Christian ethics; and (4) the ethical nature of biblical religion. Now we turn to a more practical question.

WHY STUDY CHRISTIAN ETHICS?

Students often complain about the requirement in our seminary that every master of divinity student take an introductory course in Christian ethics. The protest often sounds something like this: "Look, I believe the Bible and try to follow its teachings. My life has been dedicated to God's will and to serving Christ. Why should I be required to study Christian ethics?"

Perhaps you feel this way. Let me attempt to explain some major reasons for examining Christian ethics.

Reason 1: Christian Ethics Improves Decision-Making Skills

Ask yourself, what are my own moral **values?** How do I make ethical decisions? How do I develop Christian character? Is my spirituality devoid of moral growth?

Like the American pilot in the Gulf War who accidently killed his comrades, we too face storms in the night—moral storms. And they come in all shapes and sizes. The twenty-first century promises to test our faith as never before. In view of modern moral dilemmas, how does a Christian leader prepare personally to respond to these "storms in the night"?

Doing the right thing has never been easy. One basic ingredient for Christian discernment is moral character. Lack of ethical fiber can be a fatal flaw in moral decision making.

Recently an author who admired Richard Nixon and wrote his three-volume biography was interviewed by a television reporter. When asked what led to Watergate and the former president's downfall, the biographer answered, "He had no moral compass. He could not determine right from wrong. When decision time came, he did what was best for Richard Nixon. He wanted to be Richard the Great, and in some ways he came close."[20]

Ordinary citizens can also lack ethical backbone. Watch almost any afternoon television interview show and you will witness the moral weakness and confusion of the average American.

Add to this weakness of character the complexity of modern issues and the problem is compounded. Look at the moral problems Christians face today—**in vitro fertilization, euthanasia, AIDS, capital punishment, civil disobedience, church-state separation,** and **homosexuality,** to name a few. How does a person begin to deal with such perplexing ethical enigmas?

One way is to improve our decision-making skills.[21] Few of us have ever analyzed the way we make moral decisions. Too often we misuse the Bible, misunderstand the issue, and inconsistently jump from narrow **legalism** on one question to subjective **situationism** on another. Sometimes our motives are less than Christian. A teacher and writer of ethics viewed our modern moral landscape and concluded: "Most moral dilemmas are more like multilemmas—we need to invent a new word!—because there is a variety of choices involved."[22] This is the first reason to study Christian ethics—to help you hone your personal decision-making skills.

Reason 2: Christian Ethics Develops Moral Leadership

Every minister is called to be a moral leader, regardless of the ministry to which he or she is called.[23] Vocational ministry is varied today. God has called some to be military or hospital chaplains. Others testify of a divine direction to serve as a missionary in a foreign country. A large number feel called by God to minister to a congregation as a pastor or other church minister. Whatever your particular Christian vocation, moral leadership is a vital part of your service.

Sociologists sometimes debate whether ministers should be classified as true professionals in the same way as are doctors and lawyers.[24] In some ways, ministers are less than professionals; in other ways they are more. One thing, however, is certain. The minister is a professional in the sense that parishioners expect the clergy to be competent in ministry. When ethical dilemmas confront laypersons, they expect the ordained to help them analyze the issues, interpret biblical teachings, and make responsible Christian decisions.

Not that you as a minister have the answer to every moral question. No one is able to do that, not even an ethics professor! But you should always be able to give moral guidance. Studying Christian ethics should help you in that responsibility.

A deacon in my church has a Ph.D. in microbiology and works with large oil corporations all over the world in ecological concerns. To talk with him about environmental issues is like enrolling in a doctoral seminar on the subject. Yet even he recently confessed a need for greater biblical understanding in determining the ethical actions Christians should take on ecological issues.

In a book on moral leadership, Richard Bondi claims the ministry is inescapably dangerous. Leaders who live only at the edge of the Christian community can become detached and unable to lead. Those who commandeer the center can end up protecting the church from opportunities for ministry at the risky edge. As a faithful and transformative leader, the minister must always live on the "challenging" edge where change occurs, while remaining connected to the "safe" center of ministry where most people live.[25]

Reason 3: Christian Ethics Protects from Common Errors

Any survey of biblical and Christian history will reveal many common errors made in ethical reasoning, as well as in actual behavior. Studying Christian ethics can be like taking a course in defensive driving. If you are made aware of potential dangers, you are less likely to have major accidents.

Likewise, our study of ethics will identify faulty thinking that Christians should avoid. For example, out of a belief that the world lay under Satan's control, the early church developed a rigid, sectarian ethic. Roman rulers were pagan, society was immoral, and the government persecuted those who claimed Jesus was Lord. The solution was to separate from the world and become nonconformist.

This attempt to maintain a pure faith in an evil world led to legalism, the writing of rules for every moral decision. Codes of conduct commanded Christians to abstain not only from gross sins and emperor worship, but also from participation in public office, amusements, and worldly manners.[26] Tertullian (145–220) outlined in meticulous detail every difference between Christians and non-Christians in works like *The Shows*, *On Modesty*, and *On the Apparel of Women*.[27] Legalism became the dominant ethic of the early church.

Although ethical rules have some value and may be appropriate in certain circumstances, as a dominant way to make ethical decisions, legalism has major flaws. The study of ethics will point out the pitfalls of legalism and help you guard against this and other common errors.

Reason 4: Christian Ethics Unifies the Christian Life

Christian ethics is sometimes called a holistic discipline. This description underscores a fourth major value of this study. By "holistic" we simply mean that this exercise unifies many parts of the Christian faith into an organic whole. As a result of your study of Christian ethics, you may see for the first time the whole picture—the way the various parts of your faith contribute to your understanding of God and to your daily life.

Christian ethics utilizes every subject studied in a theological seminary classroom. To understand God's will for human relationships involves a mature faith (theology), a proper use of the Bible (hermeneutics), an ability to discern moral truth (decision making), a recognition of the historical efforts of other Christians to do the truth (tradition), and the ability to think clearly (philosophy).

However, it is never enough just to *know* what is right. The apostle James stressed that faith involves both hearing and doing the Word of God (James 1:22). Discipleship means following Jesus, as well as learning from Him. T. B. Maston titled his last book *To Walk as He Walked*,[28] basing the book's theme on his favorite Scripture passage, 1 John 2:5-6: "By this we may be sure that we are in him: he who says he abides in him ought to walk in the same way in which he walked" (RSV).

The study of Christian ethics will bring unity and harmony to your faith. It will challenge you to develop a belief system and a daily life that is consistent, complete, and Christlike.

So there you have it—four major reasons for studying Christian ethics. I am hopeful these reasons will motivate you to explore the territory with eagerness and expectation. Like the Spanish adventurer Coronado, who searched for treasures in the new world, may your journey into Christian ethics yield valuable discoveries.

CAN ETHICS BE TAUGHT?

One final question needs to be raised at the outset of this inquiry: "Can ethics be taught?" Philosophers, psychologists, and educators have hotly debated this topic. The issue often revolved around the traditional "nature or nurture" debate and whether ethics are "caught" or "taught."

In the late 1980s a number of ethical scandals rocked the American business and economic community. Wall Street reeled from "Greedgate" and widespread charges of insider trading. Legislators in Washington, D.C., and several state governments were convicted of bribery and political corruption. The public added the complaint that too many doctors and lawyers had lost their sense of professionalism and served only their self-interests.

Alarmed by the loss of ethics among many professionals, syndicated columnist Robert C. Maynard suggested that the teaching of ethics become once again a high educational priority: "Whatever else they [corrupt officials] learned, they appear to have had little training in ethics. That, I fear, may be a major contributing factor in these cases. If we stop teaching moral values, as we have in our public schools, can we expect people to know the consequences of corruption?"[29]

The response to a widespread call for teaching ethics in our professional institutions was immediate. Reevaluating their curriculum, many law, business, and medical schools created courses in **professional ethics.** However, this solution to the "ethics problem" by professional schools precipitated another reaction—vigorous debate over the basic question, "Can ethics be taught?"

A *New York Times* column by Michael Levin was boldly titled, "Ethics Courses: Useless." In the essay, Levin called the flood of ethics courses to stem corruption in business and politics "an utterly pointless exercise." He further elaborated that the idea someone can be taught to distinguish right from wrong is a mistake. What makes people good is moral character, "habituating a good child to do the right thing." Through good examples and apt incentives, Levin urged, moral virtues can be caught from parents. Only as honesty, industry, and respect are developed at an early age will individuals be ethical; specific stances on moral issues cannot be taught.[30]

Immediately, teachers of ethics and psychologists disagreed with this controversial article. The first issue of a newsletter from the Center for Applied Ethics at Santa Clara University noted the question was as old as Socrates, who made his position clear. In a debate with his fellow Athenians, the Greek philosopher declared, "Ethics consists of knowing what we ought to do, and such knowledge can be taught."[31]

Another writer added that psychologists have long agreed with Socrates. Contemporary research in the field of moral development by psychologists such as Lawrence Kohlberg of Harvard, Jean Piaget, and James Rest claims that a person's ability to deal with moral issues is not formed all at once but develops in stages.[32] Thus, morality is taught.

A philosophy professor argued with Levin that **moral philosophy** (ethics) involves cognitive elements, which can be explained, memorized, taught, and learned. Even though ethics docs contain an "affective domain," the bioethics teacher insisted that there is a skill component in ethics that can be taught.[33]

What conclusions can we reach on this much-debated question? Let us start by affirming that the ethical life does flow from character, which begins to develop long before persons first make analytical decisions. As Stanley Hauerwas has so well reminded us, Christian ethics germinates in a community of character where our moral identity is formed. Aristotle was correct. Ethics, or right living, has to do first with good habits.

At the same time, we must not divorce reason from emotion—that is, the cognitive from the affective. Christian conduct may begin with character, but the moral life is more than a "good will" or simply being a good person. In our complex world, determining the right thing to do often requires analyzing the facts, considering the consequences, identifying values, and discerning moral principles. These skills can be taught.

What then should you, the student, expect from a decent ethics class? Not moral character. Your basic inner moral orientation has already been shaped in the communities that formed and informed you. Nor will your ethics class simply give you quick answers to every ethical question you will face.

Rather, the study of Christian ethics will build upon your Christian character to strengthen your moral judgments. Christian ethics will stimulate your moral imagination—the ability to see the world through the eyes of others, and especially through Christ's eyes. Christian ethics will hone your skills of analyzing moral issues—the ability to discern the true from the false. Christian ethics will expand your sense of moral obligation—the ability to identify moral **absolutes.**

So, that is our hope and our quest. Let us now begin this challenging task, to understand what Christian ethics means and to apply that knowledge to our own Christian life. Remember that this study is basic, for it explores the very heart of our Christian faith— what we believe, how we behave, and how we treat people.

FOR THOUGHT AND DISCUSSION

1. What did Socrates mean by the "practice of philosophy"?
2. Debate this proposition: "Theology has primary importance in the Christian faith; ethics is secondary."
3. Compare Christianity with other first-century religions, especially noting the differences in ethical teachings.
4. Explain how the study of Christian ethics will benefit you personally.
5. Respond to the statement, "Ethics are caught, not taught."

PART ONE

FOUNDATIONS FOR CHRISTIAN ETHICS

CHAPTER ONE

ORIGINS OF CHRISTIAN ETHICS

When and where did **Christian ethics** begin? The obvious answer would seem to be, "With Christ." Actually, however, Christian ethical thought has both biblical and philosophical legacies that precede the birth of Jesus. To understand the structure of **ethics** and the questions raised by Christian ethics, we must first consider philosophical backgrounds.

Virtually from the beginning, Christian ethical understanding has been influenced by important legacies of Hellenistic **philosophy.**[1] Philosophers like Aristotle, whom Thomas Aquinas revered, made indelible imprints on Christian theology and ethical understanding. Augustine tells in his *Confessions* that his conversion to the Catholic faith was prepared by his readings in **Stoic** and Platonic philosophy.[2]

Various forms of **Gnosticism** (a radical **ascetic** philosophy) confronted the Christian faith for centuries, offering "special knowledge" about God and the world. Though apologists like Irenaeus and Tertullian fought savagely against this heretical system, "the Gnostic movement set in motion ideas and methods of argument that greatly influenced Christianity."[3]

To say that the roots of Christian ethics sink deep into Greek philosophical soil is no exaggeration. Nourishment was there, as well as many destructive organisms. Today, the way we are able to define, study, and organize our thinking about Christian ethics, as well as guard against ethical heresy, is greatly dependent on this ancient ethical heritage.

THE INFLUENCE OF GREEK PHILOSOPHY

Around 600 B.C., ancient scholars developed rational **principles** to support belief in a coherent world and a unified humanity. This was the beginning of ethical inquiry concerning the meaning of life, especially the good life.

Philosophers began to ask, "What sort of life is worth living? What is happiness? What can I do that is meaningful?" Serious ethical thought began with these questions. The most influential thinkers to propose answers were Socrates (469–399 B.C.), Plato (427–347 B.C.), and Aristotle (386–322 B.C.).

Socrates

Even now, almost 2,500 years after he drank the hemlock and died, Socrates remains a leading figure in world history. The most dramatic expression of his ethical conviction came in 399 B.C., when he was in his seventies. Throughout his lifetime Socrates made many enemies by challenging the assumptions of the politicians and leaders of Athens. Accused of "corrupting the minds" of young students, Socrates was tried on several "trumped-up" charges and sentenced to death.

According to Plato's dialogue *Apology* (Socrates left no writings), Socrates continued to defend his teachings, to maintain his innocence, and to point out the injustice of the conviction. His friends had other plans. When they devised a way for him to escape, Socrates refused. Despite the wrong inflicted upon him, the prisoner saw himself as morally bound to do what is right. In this case it meant to obey the laws of the Athenian state, even when they were unjust. "He chose to stay on the grounds that there are matters more important than life itself. That which is most worth living for may also be worth dying for."[4]

Socrates was concerned foremost with the meaning of life and how a person should live. He once said that "the unexamined life is not worth living." The good life, for Socrates, consisted of living morally. His friend Phaedo once told some companions that Socrates was "the best, and also the wisest and the most upright" of all the people they knew.[5]

It is no wonder, then, that Socrates's pupil Plato and Plato's pupil Aristotle, like their mentor, would wrestle with Socrates' fundamental question, "What would a life worth living look like?" These two successors to Socrates spent a good part of their lives developing coherent answers to this inescapable question.

Plato

Disillusioned by the corruptness of the Athenian politicians and the injustice inflicted upon his teacher, Plato withdrew from public life. The rest of his days were devoted to teaching, writing, and the founding of his Academy, which lasted for nine hundred years.

Plato's writings have exerted a profound influence upon philosophy and ethics. Truth, for Plato, is universal, eternal, and rationally comprehensible. Society is mainly composed of three classes of people: the artisans (farmers), the guardians (warriors), and the thinkers (philosophers). These three classes also correspond to the triple aspects of the human faculties, namely the appetitive (need-fulfilling), the spirited (vigorous activity), and the rational (thinking).

In a well-ordered society, the young are educated in all three areas, but eventually each person finds his or her dominant trait and vocation. Interestingly, both men and women possess all of these faculties and reside in all three classes.

Important for ethics is Plato's concept of **virtue** and **vice,** which corresponds to these human traits and social groups. Temperance, or moderation, is the virtue that keeps the appetites in check and guards against the vice of indulgence. Courage addresses the spirited aspect and protects a person from the vice of cowardice. Wisdom, or prudence, is the virtue that rightly controls reason, in contrast to foolishness. The crowning virtue of justice properly orders the three faculties of the individual and the three classes in society.

Plato believed the highest class, the philosophers, should become the rulers; he opposed both the passionate rule of the masses and control by the military. Although his efforts to implement his ideas did not succeed, Plato's concept of society governed by reason, not passion or vested interests, had lasting influence.

Aristotle

The greatest influence upon Western ethical thought came from Plato's outstanding pupil Aristotle. Although inspired in many ways by his teacher, Aristotle deviated from Plato at many points. One important distinction was a reversal of Plato's concept that things are images of ideas. For Aristotle, ideas are a reflection of things.

This distinction between ideas and things had tremendous implications for ethics. Plato felt the moral life consisted in patterning behavior according to universal ideals—moral **absolutes.** Aristotle insisted that morality is achieved by realizing the ends or purposes inherent in one's nature—moral consequences. The Aristotelian analysis of ends led to a rigorous examination of human life, especially life in social, political, and economic institutions.

Aristotle is universally remembered for two contributions to ethics. The first is his oft-quoted observation that human beings are by nature social and political animals.[6] His second significant contribution is his concept of the "golden mean": the idea that the moral life exists between the extremes of excess and deficiency.[7] For example, true courage lies between the extremes of foolhardiness and cowardice.

Stoicism and Epicureanism

Immediately before the time of Christ, several philosophical schools emerged that influenced Christian thought. Two of the most important ones are mentioned in Luke's account of the apostle Paul's discussions in the marketplace in Athens: "Also some Epicurean and Stoic philosophers debated with him" (Acts 17:18).

Stoicism was much more than a "stiff upper lip," although we commonly use the word *stoical* to mean unemotional. Stoicism did emphasize self-discipline and was thoroughly rationalistic in its basic assumptions. Disciples of Stoicism were taught that the cosmos and every human being reflected a rational God who is everywhere and in everyone. Stoics taught that the great danger was to allow the corrupt flesh to turn aside a person from this rational essence, which is God.

For the Stoic, goodness was accepting the will of God—or living according to Nature. The secret of goodness was to learn to want only what you have. The Stoic teaching that all true law must reflect the universal reason of God influenced Roman law. Though civil law enacted by rulers was an imperfect reflection of the **natural law,** the universal law always judged human laws and customs.

Stoics believed all persons were fundamentally equal because all by nature are rational beings. Among Stoic thinkers were the slave Epictetus, the emperor Marcus Aurelius, the writer Seneca, and the orator Cicero.

The Greek philosopher Epicurus founded the movement named after him, which is often defined as pleasure seeking and morally corrupt. This **stereotype** is also misleading. The **Epicureans** believed that humans are chance conglomerations of atoms—that life had no meaning. Thus, the best anyone could hope for was to maximize life's pleasures and minimize life's pains.

Ironically, Epicurus and many of his disciples lived austere lives, believing excess usually led to greater trouble. Nevertheless, for most Epicureans, physical pleasure became the *summum bonum* of life. Most Epicureans avoided social relationships and political responsibilities on the premise that both would probably bring stress and pain. The Epicurean believed in virtue, but only from a selfish point of view—enlightened self-interest was the main motive.

How much influence did the philosophers and philosophies of Greece have upon Christian ethics? In several ways they helped set the agenda for Christian ethical deliberation. Greek philosophers were the first to define categories of moral thought. To determine the good, Plato focused on ethical absolutes, while Aristotle pointed to intentions and consequences. Teachers like Socrates exemplified the importance of **moral character** and living a good life. Basic concepts undergirding present political and social life first appeared in the thoughts and writings of these Hellenistic scholars.

Although the Bible and Christian history clearly evidence the impact of Greek ideas, many scholars believe their role has been overstated.[8] Nevertheless, the fingerprints of Greek thought appear throughout the pages of Christian moral discourse.

As was stated in the beginning, ethics is both a way of life and a discipline of study. Let us now begin the study of the right and the good, the branch of philosophy called ethics.

THE LANGUAGE OF ETHICS

A few years ago, sociologist Raymond Baumhart asked business leaders, "What does ethics mean to you?" Replies were varied:

- "Ethics has to do with what my feelings tell me is right."
- "Ethics has to do with my religious beliefs."
- "Being ethical is doing what the law requires."
- "Ethics consists of the standards of behavior of our society."
- "I don't know what the word means."[9]

Like Baumhart's respondents, many people equate ethics with feelings, religion, the law, or society's standards. Not a few confess with the last person questioned, "I don't know." At this point, some basic definitions are necessary.

Definitions

Every discipline has its own vocabulary. The language of ethics clusters around some key words. The term *ethics (ethica)* was first used by Aristotle in *Nicomachean Ethics*,[10] a compilation of his lecture notes. The Greek word *ethica* meant the science of character and was formed by a slight variation of the cognate *ethos* (habit).[11]

Briefly defined, ethics is the study of the rules of right and wrong behavior, the goals we strive for, the ideals we admire, and the laws we obey. We study ethics to clarify our thinking about the virtues, **values,** precepts, and principles that guide our conduct. For example, a fundamental ethical principle is the basic "right to life." Most of us hold the conviction that people should not be killed, unless there is a very good reason.

But what is a "good reason"? If a person murders someone, does society have the right to punish the murderer by taking his or her life? Is **abortion** always murder, even when the mother's life is threatened? What about war? **Euthanasia?** Suicide? Are these acts ever justified? One aim of ethics is to help persons think clearly about complex issues like these.

Morals is not the same as ethics, though the two terms are often used interchangeably. Taken from the Latin *mores*, the term originally referred to "custom" or "habit." Morality actually refers to the practice of what a person believes to be right, while ethics is the study of the right. In other words, ethics is more theoretical, while morals is more practical. In our approach, morals is concerned with what "is," while ethics is concerned with what "ought" to be. For example, the sexual morals of American teenagers would be determined through a survey of the sexual activity of American youth. Ethics, on the other hand, would not describe actual behavior but would define ideal behavior—what ought to be.

A **norm** is simply a rule for living—a law, a guideline, or a regulation as defined by some recognized **authority.** Norms guide ordinary behavior. Traffic laws, for example, are norms; they are civil statutes that enable citizens to drive safely on public highways.

Value is another important word in our study. Philosophers have traditionally been preoccupied with developing a scale of values. Ordinarily an ethical value is a highly appraised and worthwhile ideal of a person or a society. Most norms are the expression of some value; truth telling is the value behind the biblical norm: "You shall not bear false witness" (Exod. 20:16).

A **principle** is a more general and foundational concept, such as the principles of love and justice. Principles tend to have a more universal quality, often expressed as statements of value, such as "human life is sacred" or Kant's maxim "to treat humanity never only as a means but always also as an end."

Sometimes confused with the word **ethics** is *ethos*, a term which identifies the values of a culture or a group. The Quaker **ethos**, for example, includes a strong commitment to **pacifism.**

One other term often confused with ethics is the idea of *etiquette*. A popular book written in the early part of this century was titled *Ministerial Ethics and Etiquette*. This guidebook for ministers suffered one major flaw: it did not distinguish between a cultural tradition (etiquette) and an ethical obligation.[12] Good manners required ministers to dress in black, but this was not a moral standard.

Understanding the language of ethics is important. These key words will appear many times in the pages to come, for they convey basic concepts in ethical inquiry. Learn them well.

Prescriptive versus Descriptive Ethics

Also important is the distinction between normative and descriptive ethics. Traditionally, ethics refers to well-based standards of right and wrong behavior, often expressed in terms of norms, values, virtues, obligations, and principles. This approach is usually designated normative, or prescriptive, ethics, the attempt to identify norms or standards for the good life.[13] Normative ethics is the endeavor to answer Socrates' basic philosophical query, "What kind of person should I be? What should I do? How should I behave?"

Prescriptive ethics focuses on what ought to be done, the ethical ideals that define moral obligations. This is normative ethics— ethics in the imperative mood, often relying upon terms like *must, should,* and *ought.*

A contrasting category of ethical inquiry seeks to describe the morality of particular societies or groups of people. Sometimes called moral sociology or comparative ethics, **descriptive ethics** aims only to depict what *is*, the moral indicative. When descriptive language is used, the purpose is never to make judgments or issue commands, only to describe.

Ethicists have debated whether it is possible to move from statements of fact to statements of value; that is, can one derive a statement of ought from a statement of is?[14] A fuller discussion of this issue will come later when we consider the concept of natural law.

Ethical Relativism

The study of human cultures by sociologists and anthropologists has heightened belief in **ethical relativism,** the view that all morality is relative. According to this viewpoint, norms vary from one social group to another. "What is moral in India, can get a man hanged in France," wrote one eighteenth-century relativist, who concluded that morals are nothing more than local customs.[15] The relativist does not merely contend that people have different beliefs (descriptive relativism), but that these varied beliefs can all be correct!

Ethical relativism is a popular conviction in the classrooms of major universities and among the general public. A 1994 Barna Research Group Poll reported that 71 percent of all U.S. adults say there is no such thing as absolute truth. In a speech to the National and International Religion Report, George Barna added that four out of ten persons who call themselves evangelicals do not believe in absolute truth.[16]

As a belief system, relativism is subject to two major criticisms.[17] First, it makes meaningful ethical disagreement impossible. If a Chinese bureaucrat states that imprisoning citizens for speaking against the state is legal, and a U.S. official says it is not, they really do not disagree. According to the relativist, each is correctly representing the values of his culture. How then could these two persons ever seriously discuss human rights?

A second major flaw in ethical relativism is that the group cannot give a reason for its belief. Morality is reduced to a statistical count, taking a poll to determine majority opinion. If the claim "smoking marijuana causes no harm" is correct because most people think so, then the only reason that can be given is that the majority's thinking makes it so. Though it appears as a sophisticated belief of the intellectual, relativism is actually a statistical explanation of cultural values.

Freedom and Responsibility

Philosophers commonly agree that moral responsibility requires freedom of action. The person acting, the moral agent, must make a free choice. "The principle involved is: no one is morally guilty for failing to do what he could not do or for doing what he could not fail to do."[18]

Together with the problems of God and immortality, Kant named the problem of the freedom of the will as one of the three great metaphysical issues beyond human comprehension.[19] To believe that moral actions are the result of free rational choice does not imply that the actions are uncaused or originate out of nothing. Moral actions are not chance events. In fact, they are often highly predictable because they flow consistently from stable moral character.

The influence of physical, psychological, and social factors upon behavior is beyond question, yet it is senseless to speak of ethics and moral responsibility at all unless we are free to make decisions. Our judgment must be a free act; otherwise, we are not accountable for our actions.[20]

Motivation

Another key element of ethics is motivation. Why be ethical? The reason behind the moral act, though difficult to determine, is a basic consideration.

Moral philosophers have long debated the reasons and arguments we give for the actions we take. Almost all agree that morality is sharply opposed to selfishness. Morality by nature is "disinterested," while selfishness is devoted to immediate self-interest. Ethical rules are based on some universality that applies to all, while selfishness is concerned only with the individual person—oneself.

How can I be sure my interests are ethical? Motivation is one key factor. To borrow an example from Kant, a grocer who doesn't cheat his customers because he is afraid of getting caught is no paragon of virtue. He just wants to stay in business. Thus, along with correct action, motivation is an essential part of ethical behavior.

What then is essential for a person to be moral as opposed to immoral? Basically, three elements are required: (1) a free moral agent, (2) a right motive, and (3) an ethically right act.[21] In traditional ethical thought, a person is moral when the person acts freely to do the right thing for the right reason.

TRADITIONAL THEORIES OF ETHICS

How then do we determine if our actions are moral or immoral? Across the centuries, three main categories of ethical argument have developed—the **deontological** (absolutist), the **teleological** (consequentialist), and the **relational** (personalist). Each of these approaches is reflected in both moral philosophy and Christian ethics.

The answer of the **absolutist** is that if the moral agent does a morally good act (or refrains from an immoral act), that person is moral. The consequentialist, on the other hand, believes the person acts morally if she or he intends good results from the action; the consequences are the key.

These two traditional answers are both inadequate. The absolutist approach overlooks the role of motivation. A right act done for the wrong reason becomes a wrong act. Likewise, consequentialism falters in assuming right intentions are enough. As an old proverb states, "The road to hell is paved with good intentions."

Repelled by rigid absolutism and dissatisfied with pragmatic consequentialism, recent ethicists have developed a third method. The relational approach focuses on personalist ethical arguments that view morality "not as obedience to absolute principles or as a means to something else, but as an expression of individual feeling, **conscience** or love."[22] The relational response stresses interest in human beings and what happens to human beings as ethical decisions are made.[23]

While this emphasis has much to commend it, a relational approach also has weaknesses. In an effort to avoid the liabilities of **legalism** and **utilitarianism,** the relationalist stresses individual autonomy, which can be very subjective.

Thus each of these traditional ethical arguments has defects. Why then should we study them? Our purpose is to examine the grounds on which our moral beliefs stand and to develop a coherent and consistent system for discerning how we can act ethically. An understanding of these classical methods of moral discernment will aid us in that quest.

Deontological Ethics

The word *deontology* is derived from the Greek *dei,* which means "necessary" or "imperative." Deontological ethics by nature are absolutist—you cannot argue beyond them. Sometimes called the ethics of obligation, this approach asks the question, "What is *right?*" The overriding stress is on duty. "Certain attitudes and actions invariably constitute one's duty; they find expression in laws (e.g., do not commit adultery), principles (faithfulness in marriage), or institutions (marriage itself)."[24]

A deontologist believes goodness or rightness is inherent in the act itself. If one argues that murder is wrong, the reason given might be: "Because it is against God's will," or "Because it is against the law," or even "Because it is just wrong." Such a response simply points to a norm or absolute, beyond which there is no further argument.

Many religious thinkers contend that the deontological absolute is the *will of God*. Not only is this evident in certain strands of Judaism, Christianity, and Islam, but it is also present in ancient Stoicism. With their strong belief in fate and predestination, the Stoics taught that goodness is willingly to accept the will of God by living in harmony with Nature.

Another deontological school is *intuitionism*. Proponents argue that moral duty is revealed directly by human intuition, an inner faculty that bypasses the normal reasoning processes. W. D. Ross, a leading intuitionist philosopher, identified widely recognized obligations, which he termed **prima facie duties.** This phrase means "on first appearance" and defines fundamental duties required of everyone (all other things being equal), such as truth telling, promise keeping, and gratitude.[25]

Traditionalism is a third deontological school. The right or the good is the customary, so say the traditionalists. Morality is rooted in the **mores,** the cultural and religious customs of a particular group. Many modern ethicists view tradition as inessential to ethics or even as morally dangerous.

A fourth ethic of obligation is one grounded in *reason* and best illustrated by a German **Enlightenment** philosopher, Immanuel Kant (1724–1803). Often called the dean of the deontologists, Kant distinguished between two types of moral imperatives: hypothetical imperatives and categorical imperatives. Hypothetical imperatives appeal to consequences: "Be honest in business or you will lose customers." Kant rejected this prudential consideration because it appeals to self-serving interests.

In contrast, **categorical imperatives** appeal to no impure motives; they are purely rational. A categorical imperative is always an end, never a means—an absolute and universally binding moral law.

Kant tested the categorical nature of moral statements in two ways. The first test is universalizability: "Act only according to that maxim by which you can at the same time will that it should become a universal law."[26] In other words, we should always act in a way we would desire all others to behave. An example Kant used was the duty to repay borrowed money.

Kant's second formulation of the categorical imperative stated: "Act so that you treat humanity, whether in your own person or in that of another, always as an end and never as a means only."[27] This principle is very important, for it protects individual human dignity. In marriage, therefore, sexual intercourse should never be used only to satisfy a person's sexual desires, but rather to express love and intimate commitment to a marital partner.

Kant's formulations find connection in their underlying concept of humans as rational beings. It is human reason that gives humans dignity, and human reason that insists people think about situations in universal context, not just individually.[28] For Kant, moral absolutes were discerned through reason and were universally binding, without exception.

Teleological Ethics

A second major category that proposes an approach in ethical arguments is named teleology, from the Greek word *teleos* meaning "end" or "goal." Teleological ethics are consequentialist, claiming good or evil is determined by the end result of an action. Sometimes called the ethics of aspiration, the consequentialist asks, "What is the *good* I seek in this act?" In contrast to the deontologist, morality is not treated as autonomous or an end in itself, but a means to something else.

There is little doubt that consequentialism is the dominant approach to decision making in secularized Western civilization. Although rules have not been discounted, life for moderns is less governed by absolutes—most rules have been relativized.

To return to our former example of why murder is wrong, a consequentialist response might be, "Because murder brings pain and unhappiness," or "Because murder would destroy society." In both responses, murder is immoral, not because it is evil in itself, but because it leads to something undesirable—the absence of happiness or the breakdown of society.

Teleological theories are generally of two types. The first type focuses on good results for the individual (ethical egoism). Aristotle identified the supreme good for humans as "happiness" (*eudaimonia*, or "living well"), which was determined solely by reason. Plato added that anything is good that performs its function; the good student is the one who studies.

Many teleologists have been hedonists, identifying good with pleasure and evil with pain. Aristippus (435–356 B.C.) and the Cyrenaics illustrate the positive side of **hedonism,** for their goal was to enjoy the pleasures of the moment before the opportunity slipped by. "Let us eat and drink, for tomorrow we die" (Isa. 22:13) was a hedonistic life-goal in Isaiah's day.

Epicurus, Aristotle's contemporary, represents the negative form of hedonism, the avoidance of pain and mental anguish. Epicurus was so preoccupied with techniques for confronting pain that he was almost indifferent to the pursuit of pleasure.

Utilitarianism is a second type of teleological theory, emphasizing not the individual but the greatest good for the greatest number (ethical universalism). According to utilitarianism, consequences should be calculated in terms of usefulness or utility. Acts or virtues that bring the most good for the most people are the right moral choices.

Although utilitarianism had been around for a long time, it was Jeremy Bentham (1748–1832) who first argued persuasively for the maximum amount of happiness for the greatest number of people. Bentham even devised a hedonic calculus, or pleasure calculator, which listed all the criteria of pleasure for assessing the consequences of an action. Bentham's contemporary, John Stuart Mill (1806–73), agreed with Bentham but developed a more sophisticated utilitarianism that defined pleasure qualitatively as well as quantitatively.

As has been noted, both deontological and teleological schools of thought have their limitations and inconsistencies. Absolutes must be considered in almost any ethical decision, but if rules and principles alone are followed without concern for consequences, something disastrous may result. Ordinarily, telling the truth is a duty, but when Nazis came to Corrie ten Boom's door searching for Jews, she told a "loving lie" to protect those hiding in her home.[29]

Likewise, utilitarians might justify a morally outrageous deed in the name of an ultimate "good." Terrorist acts have often killed blameless bystanders, in the name of some human liberation movement. Police

officials have sometimes imprisoned innocent citizens in order to
appease a populace angry over terrorism. Utilitarianism tends to justify using morally questionable means to reach good ends.

Because of limitations like these, many ethicists argue for a mix
of the two approaches, believing the moral worth of an act may be
determined by its consequences as much as by deontological
values.[30]

Relational Ethics

In the mid-twentieth century, autonomous reasoning, natural
law, moral philosophy, code morality, and casuistries were under
attack by many well-known voices. Thinking about ethical judgments in relational and personalistic terms became a prominent
method in theological and philosophical circles.[31]

Often called the ethics of responsibility, relationalism asks not
what is right or good, but "What is fitting?" In other words, what
action fits the total situation, especially in light of its effect on
human beings and human covenants?

Exponents of relational and personalist ethics frequently argue
that moral questions cannot be resolved beforehand. To return to
our example of murder, the relationalist asserts it makes no sense
to uphold abstract principles about the wrongness of murder. Only
in particular situations can the individual determine whether ending a human life is right or wrong.

For the personalist, the prospect of murdering a close relative
might be rejected because "I feel it is wrong" or "My conscience
tells me it is wrong" or "It contradicts my love and respect for her
as a person." But the personalist never simply argues that some
authority declared it wrong. The focus is on the individual and the
situation.

The relational approach gained momentum in Protestant circles
with H. Richard Niebuhr's book *The Responsible Self*.[32] According
to Niebuhr, God is sovereign, but God has extended Himself to
humanity for relationship. Niebuhr calls each person to act out of
his or her own character with a strong sense of responsibility and
caring for the relational bonds we have established with others.

At this point you may be saying, "Enough of philosophers and
philosophy—let's get on to Christian ethics!" Your impatience is
understandable. To comprehend Christian ethics, however, this
survey of the history, language, and theories of philiosophical ethics was necessary. Now we shall proceed to look specifically at

what Christianity adds to ethics and how "Christian" qualifies ethics.

THE FRAMEWORK FOR CHRISTIAN ETHICS

What then have we learned from **philosophical ethics** that will help us develop a truly Christian ethic? Do Christians believe in absolute rules, or do they put a premium on human happiness? How important are human relationships? What type of moral thinking is reflected in the Bible and other Christian authorities? We now turn to these questions as we explore the grounds, goals, and guidelines for Christian ethics.

Relation to Philosophical Ethics

Let us begin by asking in what way Christian ethics is different from ethics in general. The question is central to our study. At first glance, many in the Western world would say the two hardly differ. After all, are not Western values largely the product of our Christian past?

However, at a deeper level we discover a variety of answers. Responses range from the near identification of Christian ethics and philosophy by church thinkers like Aquinas (who accepted Aristotle totally), to the complete elimination of philosophy by neoorthodox theologians like Bonhoeffer.

Emil Brunner defined Christian ethics as "the science of human conduct as it is determined by Divine conduct."[33] The first half of his description explains philosophical ethics—"the study of human conduct." Ethics becomes Christian ethics only when the authority for human conduct becomes "divine conduct," the moral character of God.

Both Christian and philosophical ethics search for the *summum bonum*, the highest good. Relying on reason as the ultimate authority, ancient philosophers developed numerous possibilities: pleasure, happiness, power, duty, and self-realization, to name a few. In contrast, Christian ethics proposed the highest good to be the will of God, which was discovered not through human reason but through divine revelation.[34]

This then is the key difference: "All normative ethics attempts to identify the characteristics of a life worth living, and all examines and articulates standards to inform and guide us in shaping our actions and character. Christian ethics undertakes the same task with reference to Jesus of Nazareth."[35]

Christian ethics is ethics based upon the revelation of God in Jesus Christ. To build upon the earlier definition of Emil Brunner, we could state: *Christian ethics is the study and practice of the grounds, the goals, and the guidelines for human character and conduct as determined by the will of God revealed in Jesus Christ and empowered through the Holy Spirit.*

What then is the relationship between Christian ethics and philosophical ethics? Albert C. Knudson has described three historical approaches: elimination, absorption, and supplemental theories.[36]

Thinkers holding the first position believed in *eliminating* or displacing either Christian ethics or philosophy. One segment of this group wished to eliminate Christian ethics. Karl Marx declared Christianity was too otherworldly, promising heavenly reward while ignoring the oppression of the working class. An equal number in this elimination group, mainly Christian theologians, would prefer to displace philosophy. Bonhoeffer, for example, rejected any attempt at natural theology, believing the only truth for the church comes through law and gospel. Both segments saw each other's position as either invalid, unnecessary, or an evil to be eliminated.

A second position, called *absorption* theory, was held by those who recognized a kinship between philosophy and Christian ethics, and who sought to incorporate one into the other. Most in this category believed there was no need for a separate discipline of Christian ethics; it was easily absorbed into philosophy. Wilhelm Herrmann (1846–1932) taught that everything important in Christian ethics was present in philosophical ethics, especially in the teachings of Kant. On the other hand, Anders Nygren and a few other Christian leaders theorized that Christian ethics was the highest and purest form of moral philosophy.

The most common theory for relating philosophy and Christian ethics was the *supplemental* approach, which held that the two are independent of each other and yet essential to each other. Proponents of this view concluded that Christian ethics supplements natural law ethics, a theory dominant in the medieval church and the Roman Catholic tradition.

Both Augustine and Aquinas distinguished between the natural and the supernatural. By discerning natural law (moral laws in nature), all humans could discover the four cardinal virtues: wisdom (prudence), justice, temperance (moderation), and courage. These four virtues formed the basis for the moral life. Added to this quartet must be the Christian virtues of faith, hope, and love, which are perceived only by supernatural revelation.

Augustine believed love *(agape)* was the essence of all virtue and must permeate and transform the Greek cardinal virtues. Aquinas saw the Greek virtues as a preliminary stage of moral development, a foundation on which was built a Christian super-structure—the supernatural supplementing the natural.

In light of these varied views, how should Christian ethics relate to philosophy? The major distinction is that Christian ethics centers in God and revelation, rather than humans and reason. The human problem is not ignorance but sin, and that problem is solved only by God's grace. "In the Christian ethic as in the Christian life in general, the imperative is preceded by the indicative, oughtness by isness. An obligation is placed upon us by what God, through his grace, has done for us. . . . The ethic of the grace or goodness of God also provides a distinctive dynamic or motivation."[37]

At the same time, Christian ethics can and should use the valid wisdom and methodologies of philosophy. As T. B. Maston once observed, "Christian ethics needs the insights of philosophy and science to help fill out its knowledge of the truth and to test and clarify its interpretation of revealed truth."[38]

The Pillars of Christian Ethics

The city of New Orleans, where I live, is a reclaimed swamp. Most of our town is below sea level. When a building is constructed, the first order of business is to drive a number of telephone poles into the soggy soil, and these become the foundation pillars on which the edifice stands. Without these supports a structure will slowly tilt, fracture, and sink into the marshy soil.

Christian ethics is also grounded upon foundational supports — basic theological truths about God, humanity, and society that become the grounds for Christian moral living. The seven pillars listed below are absolutely necessary for an ethic that is biblical and Christian:

1. God is by nature ethical. Jehovah is revealed as a moral God who is concerned about morality among His creation: "You shall be holy, for I the LORD your God am holy" (Lev. 19:2).

2. Humanity is morally responsible. Created in God's image (Gen. 1:27), humans sinned and marred that godlikeness; but defective humanity can be restored through union with Christ (Col. 3:10).

From the beginning God gave each person moral freedom, as well as moral responsibility: "So then, each of us will be accountable to God" (Rom. 14:12).

3. The Bible is the main objective revelation of God's will. Although God has spoken through many sources, the Scriptures remain the primary authority for God's revelation of His ethical will. "Long ago God spoke to our ancestors in many and various ways by the prophets" (Heb. 1:1).

4. Jesus Christ is God's ultimate revelation. "But in these last days he has spoken to us by a Son" (Heb. 1:2). The life and teachings of Jesus are the standard by which all ethical values are judged.

5. The Christian life is by nature ethical. Moral character and ethical conduct are the inevitable result of conversion. An inner relationship with Christ always produces an outer change in attitudes and actions: "So if anyone is in Christ, there is a new creation: everything old has passed away; see, everything has become new!" (2 Cor. 5:17).

6. The church is responsible for influencing the social order. Interaction between the church and the world always creates tension, nevertheless the Christian community is called to be "salt" and "light" in a decaying and dark world (Matt. 5:13-15). Social action and social ministry are important functions of the church.

7. The Holy Spirit is active in the ethical life of the Christian. The Spirit is the Power and Personality living within the believer who produces moral character (Gal. 5:22), provides ethical guidance (John 16:13), and motivates the Christian to live morally (1 Cor. 6:19-20).

These seven theological truths are the grounds upon which our Christian ethical structure is built. To omit any of them is to make the disastrous mistake of the foolish builder in Jesus' miniparable, who saw his foundationless house collapse, "and great was its fall!" (Matt. 7:27).

The Goals of Christian Ethics

As was noted earlier, ethics traditionally has a twofold function: first, to define the "Highest Good," and second, to develop principles of human action necessary to achieve that goal.[39] A study of Christian history reveals a variety of opinions about the goals of ethics.

When medieval mystics asked the teleological question, "What good do we seek?" the monastic answer was, "Seek a vision of God through self-renunciation and contemplation." Pietists proposed a different goal: for them, human perfection was the purpose of the Christian life. At the beginning of this century, social gospel idealists proposed another goal for Christians: work to establish God's kingdom in society. Obviously, each of these groups had a different understanding of Christian ethics.

For other believers, the question of goals was more deontological—"What is the right I am obliged to obey?" The early church, reacting to a pagan environment, codified Christianity into a list of ethical rules. Legalistic obedience to church law was also common in Roman Catholic and Eastern Orthodox traditions. Fundamentalist Protestants interpreted the purpose of the Christian life to be literal obedience to every command of the Bible, while liberal Protestants called for radical obedience to the biblical imperative to love God and neighbor.

More voices have proposed a relational goal for Christian ethics that asks, "What is the fitting response in this situation?" Existential theologians asserted that each moral choice is unique and therefore cannot be prescribed beforehand. The command of God is heard only in a specific context. Some relationalists focused on the human context of ethics; while others pointed toward God's activity in the world to which each Christian must respond.

Salvador Dali once claimed his art was an attempt "to synthesize confusion and discredit reality." This is not our aim. Our purpose in this summary is to clarify. Biblical ethics supports all three responses: ethical commands are found in the Old Testament Law and in the letters of Paul; ethical goals are common in the Book of Proverbs and in Jesus' teachings; **relational ethics** are taught throughout the Scriptures, especially in relation to love and community *(koinonia).*[40]

In sum, a valid Christian ethic includes all three goals. The Christian has an obligation to do the will of God (Matt. 6:10), a purpose to seek the **kingdom of God** (Matt. 6:33), and a responsibility to be in right relationship with God and with others (Matt. 22:37–40).

The Guidelines of Christian Ethics

To what or whom does the Christian look for guidance in ethics? Again we find in Christian history a number of opinions.

Many followers of Jesus have looked within the *individual* for ethical authority. Christian intuitionists have depended on an innate moral sense, a moral gyroscope to point them toward the magnetic north of God's will. Rationalists trusted their minds to reveal moral truth. What about **conscience?** Does it work like

Pinnochio's Jiminy Cricket, always telling us what is right and good? Though we should be true to our conscience, it is not infallible. In simple terms, your conscience is the sum of your moral knowledge—"not a legislator, but a judge."[41]

Tradition is a second option in church history for ethical authority. Social customs may be given divine sanction. Too often cultural loyalties become more important than loyalties to Christ. Every pastor who has put the flags at the wrong place on the podium knows the reaction of "patriots" who remind him that the U.S. flag, not the Christian flag, must have the place of prominence!

One of the most influential ethical authorities in Christian history has been *natural law*. The theory is ancient, articulated in the writings of Aristotle, Plato, and the Stoics. Early church fathers accepted natural law as a major way to discover God's truth. The concept declares that certain discoverable norms (laws) are written into creation. Using reason to reflect on nature and humanity, any person can discover the specific ends and the general purposes for which God created humankind.

Augustine taught that sin so corrupted the image of God in humans, revelation and grace were necessary before reason could properly interpret natural law. Aquinas, however, disagreed. The *imago dei* in humans (rational soul) was not tainted, and thus it was capable of discerning truth. Roman Catholic ethics have been strongly influenced by Aquinas and natural law. For example, since reason dictates that the primary purpose of sexuality is procreation, the Roman church condemns all contraceptives.

The major weaknesses of natural law are its optimistic view of human nature and unrealistic view of sin. Natural law argues from what human beings are to what they ought to be. The moral *ought* must never be derived from the empirical *is*.

From our viewpoint, the authority for Christian ethics is found not in the individual, or tradition, or natural law, but in *revelation*. God has revealed His moral will to His covenant people through the Law, the Prophets, and ultimately through Jesus Christ: "Long ago God spoke to our ancestors in many and various ways by the prophets, but in these last days he has spoken to us by a Son" (Heb. 1:1-2). The Bible is our main objective guideline in Christian ethics because it is God's best and clearest word of revelation.

When discussing major authorities for the Christian faith, Protestants traditionally cite the so-called Wesleyan quadrilateral: Scripture, Tradition, Reason, and Experience.[42] Christians look to these sources for guidance in ethics. In addition, Christians also receive ethical counsel through prayer and the inner witness of the Holy Spirit.

Many other resources are available to assist the Christian in ethical deliberation. Above all, however, the Word of God remains the unique authority and primary source for Christian ethics. In the following chapters we will look more closely at the ethical teachings of the Scriptures.

As we have explored the origins of Christian ethics, we have noted in particular the significant influence of Greek philosophy. Yet we must distinguish between philosophical and Christian ethics. "Whereas secular ethics identifies the primary questions of ethics as 'What is the good life? What is the life worth living?' Christian ethics identifies the primary questions of ethics as 'Who am I as a follower of Jesus? What life is worthy of one who recognizes the authority of Jesus? What sort of people should those who confess Jesus as Christ be?'"[43]

Philosophers note that Jesus resembled Socrates in many ways. Like Socrates, Jesus was primarily a teacher and left no writings. Both were profoundly concerned with the lives of their followers, and both lived morally admirable lives. Like Socrates, Jesus was falsely charged by political enemies; rather than renounce His deepest commitments, Jesus died for His beliefs.

Let us not overlook, however, some profound differences between Jesus and Socrates. After His crucifixion, God raised up Jesus from the dead. After His resurrection, Jesus continues to live in and through all those who believe in Him.

The Christian confession, that Jesus is the Christ, the Son of God, means that God is present in humanity in a special way. This is the difference between ethics in general and Christian ethics; this is the difference between what God has done in human history in Jesus Christ and what God continues to do in the lives and community of those called Christians, the body of Christ in the world.

FOR THOUGHT AND DISCUSSION

1. Which philosopher/philosophy had the greatest influence upon Christianity? Which had the least?
2. Debate this proposition: *Christian ethics* and *biblical ethics* are synonymous terms.

3. If biblical norms are descriptive ethics, what role does the Bible have as an ethical guide today?
4. Read of David's request to Ahimelech (1 Sam. 21:1-6) and Jesus' comments (Matt. 12:3-4), then evaluate David's deception from deontological, teleological, and relational arguments.
5. Write and defend your own definition of Christian ethics.

CHAPTER TWO

THE BIBLE
AND CHRISTIAN ETHICS

Throughout Christian history, the Word of God has occupied a central place in the life of the church. The Bible is the main legacy from which **Christian ethics** has drawn. "With virtually one voice, Christians acknowledge the **authority** of Scripture for the moral life."[1] However, the nature of biblical authority and the interpretation of the Bible for **ethics** have always been matters of deliberation.

Christians normally turn first to the Scriptures for ethical guidance. And rightly so, for the Bible is a builder of **moral character** and a teacher of ethical **values.** However, to use the Bible as a primary source for Christian ethics raises other questions: Is the Bible simply a book of moral rules to be quoted and obeyed? Or does the Bible provide ethical **principles** that navigate the Christian through moral waters? What is the role of biblical **paradigms,** narratives, and other genres in Christian morality? And finally, how do Christians relate ancient biblical precepts, principles, and narratives to twenty-first-century moral questions?

In 1970 James M. Gustafson published a seminal article on Scripture and ethics, which since has become a reference point for discussions of the topic.[2] After outlining how the Bible provides moral rules, ideals, and examples, Gustafson developed a more communal understanding of biblical authority to form a Christian moral perspective.[3]

Since Gustafson's methodological study, ethicists have moved from **Enlightenment** confidence in deductive arguments to a greater emphasis on the role of the Scriptures in the formation of moral communities. At the same time, **postmodern** biblical scholars have become more aware of the social, political, and economic environment of the New Testament world and its impact on Christian communities.[4]

So, how does the Bible shape Christian ethics? Anyone who has read the Bible knows it is quite a diverse book. In fact, within its pages are sixty-six separate books written over a millennium, reflecting different periods of history, different social settings, different types of literature, different writers, and a diversity of ethical perspectives. In such a collection of writings, is a reliable Christian ethic possible? In spite of this variety, theologians and ethicists contend that the Bible contains "an extraordinary mixture of materials with which to think ethically."[5]

Obviously, the Bible discloses ethical ideals in diverse ways. For the Scriptures to occupy a role of prominence and power in ethical deliberation, some core of unity must be found. Otherwise, there would be no basis in the Bible for a consistent Christian ethic that transcends the diversities found there.

From Genesis to Revelation, the one unifying element for ethics in the Bible is God. Distinct from the gods of other ancient religions, the God revealed in the Scriptures is a highly *moral God*: "The personal, living God is set forth as the ground of morals, and all good revolves around Him as the planets around the sun. He is the sublime prototype, the personally holy pattern after which man's life must be shaped."[6]

The Scriptures have great ethical power because they reveal an infinitely moral God. This is the heart of biblical faith—the God of Israel fully revealed in Jesus Christ is the God of "steadfast love" (*hesed*, Deut. 7:9), "righteousness" (*tsedeq*, Ps. 7:9), "holiness" (*qados*, Lev. 19:2), and "justice" (*mishpat*, Deut. 32:4).

Throughout the Bible, God's people are reminded continually to be like Jehovah. "He [God] is a covenant-keeping God; He expects them [Israel] to keep His covenant with them. He is holy; they are to be holy. He loves them; they are to love Him and one another. This idea of likeness to God is more basic and more pervasive than any other moral concept in the Law and elsewhere in the Scriptures."[7]

The Bible's disclosure of God's moral nature moves toward a climax when God fully reveals Himself in Jesus Christ (Heb. 1:1-2). The incarnation is the clearest message about God's nature and God's moral will for humanity: "And the Word became flesh and lived among us, and we have seen his glory, the glory as of a father's only son, full of grace and truth" (John. 1:14).

If the contention that the Bible is the primary source for Christian ethics is accurate, then precisely how does this "Book of books" form and inform the Christian's ethical life? Let us begin by considering the role the Bible plays in shaping our faith and ethics. Once the ethical authority of the Scriptures is established, a second challenge is to develop sound **hermeneutical** principles for correctly interpreting the Bible. One final task in relating the Bible to Christian ethics will be to survey in chapter 3 the major ethical emphases of the Old and New Testaments.

THE ROLE OF THE BIBLE IN CHRISTIAN ETHICS

In 1976 biblical scholars Bruce Birch and Larry Rasmussen pled for a greater use of the Bible in Christian ethics. Both were deeply concerned that Christian ethics and biblical studies had lost touch with each other. In spite of growth in both ethical and biblical scholarship, little material relating the two was available.[8]

A decade later the authors wrote in a revised edition that significant progress had been made in bridging the gap between biblical studies and ethics, but then they added: "Yet, it is not at all clear how the Bible and ethics are properly related. What *is* clear is that it is not a simple matter."[9]

Many conservative Christians have tended to use the Bible as a prescriptive code for moral guidance. Others have looked to the Scriptures for basic moral **principles,** like love and justice, to guide ethical deliberation. Liberal scholars have tended to view biblical ethics as merely a description of how ancient communities developed ethical perspectives. Although theologians disagree about the role of the Bible in ethics, a sadder reality is that so few ethicists utilize the Bible at all. In a day when moral concerns and ethical questions abound, how important it is to reaffirm the importance of the Bible as a primary resource for Christian ethics.

The Relevance of the Bible

The divine-human nature of the Bible affirms its relevance for Christian ethics. "The Bible . . . is in a unique sense a divine-human book. Its twofold nature can be summed up by saying that the Bible is the record of the revelation from God, of God, through men, to men."[10] This concise definition highlights a dual purpose of the Word of God—to reveal God and to disclose God's will for humanity.

The twofold approach of the Holy Scriptures is an important reminder that biblical faith is relevant—the Word of God addresses human life. The Bible is no esoteric book of mystical revelations written by a Tibetan in a cave. It is a divine word from God that relates to humanity and is as relevant as the morning newspaper.

During the Reformation, the recovery of the message of the Bible was enhanced through reading the Scriptures in their original languages. Biblical interpreters were at first perplexed by the ancient Greek manuscripts, which did not read like classical Greek. Some concluded this was a "heavenly language," a special dialect created by God to authenticate this "holy" Book.

However, further investigation uncovered many letters and business transactions of that era written in "*koine* Greek," the language of the marketplace. In other words, when God chose to communicate His most important word to humanity, God spoke not in a language known only to Greek scholars or religious professionals, but in the common dialect of every person. The Bible is relevant because in it God addresses all of humanity.

The Ethical Nature of Biblical Religion

My ethics teacher, T. B. Maston, often used the phrase "abidingly relevant" to describe biblical faith. The Bible recognizes no separation between religion and ethics: "Much of the biblical ethic is just as relevant today as it was in the days in which the books of the Bible were written. A leading English scholar says that the Bible is 'urgently relevant' to our age and it could be added that it is distressingly relevant in some areas."[11]

Belief and behavior are thoroughly integrated in the Bible. The close relationship between religion and ethics is particularly noticeable in the great summaries of the essence of faith, such as the Ten Commandments, the messages of the prophets, and the teachings of Jesus.[12]

For example, when Moses brought the Ten Words down from the mountain, they were inscribed on two tablets, which summarized Israel's basic moral law (Exod. 20:3-17). The **Decalogue** may be logically divided into two parts—duties to God and to others. This division is no coincidence, for it confirms the integral relation between faith and ethics. The first four commandments summarize a person's relation to God, while the second table of six commandments lists a person's basic ethical obligations to others.[13] Israel's basic covenant responsibilities to God included both vertical and horizontal obligations.

One of the clearest statements about the unity of faith and ethics came from Jesus' own lips in response to a lawyer's question: "Teacher, which commandment in the law is the greatest?" (Matt. 22:36). Jesus' answer was twofold. "You shall love the Lord your God with all your heart, and with all your soul, and with all your mind. This is the greatest and first commandment" (Matt. 22:37-38; cf. Deut. 6:5). Jesus quickly added, "And a second is like it: You shall love your neighbor as yourself" (Matt. 22:39; cf. Lev. 19:18).

Although the lawyer requested only one commandment, Jesus felt compelled to give him two. Why? Was it not because love for God never stands alone—it must be reflected in love for others? These two commandments, said Jesus, are alike. Because religion and ethics are inseparable, they are alike in importance. Because love for God and neighbor arise from the same source, they are also alike in kind.[14]

Jesus concluded, "On these two commandments hang all the law and the prophets" (Matt. 22:40). In other words, these two not only summarize the Old Testament, but they fulfill the demands of the Law: "The two *agapes*—to God and to our fellow-Christians—are as convex is to concave—two aspects of a single **virtue**. It is impossible to have the one without the other."[15]

The Authority of the Bible

As a source of authority, what role does the Bible play in Christian ethics? "In biblical Christianity, as in the Old Testament, authority belongs to God the Creator, and therefore to his Word—that is, his communication to his rational creatures, verbalized in both the indicative and the imperative moods, and particularized in relation to each person to whom it is sent."[16]

The Bible is the primary authority for Christian ethics. Although it is not the only avenue for discovering the will of God, the Holy

Scriptures constitute a unique and unrivaled position of influence. "Christians cannot escape the question of biblical authority because it is inherent in the claim that the Bible constitutes Scripture for the church. It is not possible to regard the Bible as simply one of many possible influences or sources of insight in ethical matters. Scripture is understood as somehow normative for the life of the church and those individuals who identify with that historic community."[17]

The Gospels often say that Jesus spoke "with authority." The Greek word used, *exousia*, literally means "out of being," and is sometimes translated "power." Jesus' authority issued "out of His being," and Christ challenged believers to discover "power" in their own "beings," their new spiritual lives.[18]

The Christian community over the centuries has acknowledged the Bible as the normative authority for the Christian life. The Scriptures are the main source of empowerment for the church in the world. Though not the only source of revelation (for God speaks in many ways through many means), the Bible is nevertheless "a unique deposit of divine revelation—a deposit whose special qualities are due to its inspired origins, and which is to be handed down through the ages by an authoritative teaching tradition."[19]

The ultimate authority of God's revelation in the Bible is Jesus Christ, the Word incarnate, who is both revealed in Scripture and whose life and teachings interpret all the words of Scripture. Christ is the Divine Person who gave birth to the Bible and has authority prior to the Bible (John 1:1–3). As Martin Luther put it, the Bible is the cradle in which Christ lies.

Let us never forget that although the Bible is a totally and thoroughly reliable revelation of God, it is never meant to be a substitute for God. Because the Scriptures are our main source of knowledge about God, it is very easy to confuse the medium of revelation with the Source. The Bible itself instructs us to distinguish between God the Revealer and the various means through which God chooses to make Himself known. Whether we realize it or not, if we give attributes to the Bible that belong only to God, we may be guilty of idolatry.[20]

Although we may find affirming the authority of the Bible for Christian ethics relatively easy, it is much more difficult to demonstrate the Bible's relevance. The Bible contains many commands that seem to be irrelevant to modern life, such as laws about proper clothing (Deut. 22:5), unclean foods (Lev. 11), and meat offered to idols (1 Cor. 8). Culturally conditioned **norms** like these should not be casually discarded, for they often express values and principles that are eternally relevant.

The authority of the Bible, then, is expressed in various ways. In the Scriptures are direct commands ("give up stealing," Eph. 4:28), general principles (the value of work, Gen. 2:15), specific principles (honest labor and just wages, Eph. 6:5), positive and negative moral examples (the kings of Israel), and narratives that shape moral character (the parables of Jesus).

The most important test for determining the ethical authority of biblical materials is to ask the question, "Does the ethical teaching reflect the character and nature of God?" Whether expressed in precept or in principle, as narrative or as example, the moral truth gleaned must never contradict the integrity of God. The authority of the Bible is derived from God, who is truly absolute.

Authority Supplemental to the Bible

The Bible has a primary role in shaping the decision maker and in guiding ethical choices. However, we also need the additional insights gained from nonbiblical sources, especially for analyzing contemporary moral issues.

One of the central, yet neglected, resources for Christian ethics is the *Holy Spirit*.[21] The Spirit's role in Christian morality will be discussed later. For now let us affirm that the Holy Spirit is the main inner source for the knowledge of God, whom Jesus promised would guide Christians "into all the truth"(John 16:13). When Jesus promised the disciples a Counselor who would live within each believer, this inner Light was named the "Spirit of truth" (John 14:17). The word *truth* presumably includes the idea of moral truth.[22]

Christian *tradition* is another source, a heritage rich in wisdom and insight for ethics. God speaks not only to the individual, but also to and through the community of Christians, the church. Some Christians believe the final word from God resides in the church, contending that the Bible came after and was the product of the church. While it is true that the church did decide which writings were inspired, it was the divine event of Christ's life, death, and resurrection recorded in the Bible that gave birth to the church.[23]

Although the Bible remains the standard and norm for the church, the history of Christianity and the writings of great Christian leaders like Augustine, Calvin, Luther, and others inform and inspire us. Christian ethics is indebted to the community of believers and their legacy of ethical deliberation. Though not an infallible authority, the church is always a hermeneutical community in which the Bible is interpreted and applied.

Along with the Bible and tradition, the Wesleyan quadrilateral suggests two other major authorities for Christians—*reason* and *experience*. God does speak through our rational deliberations and our experiences to help us discern right from wrong. Thomas Aquinas was one of many theologians who depended almost exclusively upon his "rational soul" for divine truth. The atrocities of this century have reminded us, however, that cultured and intelligent human beings are capable of grave errors and horrendous sins against humanity. Reason and experience are great assets in ethical understanding, as long as we recognize their limitations.

The *social sciences* and other disciplines provide factual data, causes, and valuable insights for Christian ethics. A Christian response to current ethical issues often requires information from biology, sociology, psychology, medical science, and related studies.

Nonbiblical material always must be evaluated in light of the theological and ethical truth revealed in God's Word. Insights derived from supplemental resources may force us to reexamine our interpretations of biblical truth, but they must never take the place of the unique revelation of God's will in the Bible.

BIBLICAL INTERPRETATION AND CHRISTIAN ETHICS

Some years ago I visited Israel with fifteen other ministers, as guests of the government. Jewish families and rabbis from America accompanied us. One evening at our hotel in Safed, we enjoyed a Kosher dinner—mutton steak, a baked potato, vegetables, bread, and coffee, but absolutely no butter, sour cream, cheese, or milk! Even though I explained I was not a Jew, the hostess refused to give me milk products. "These plates are evening dishes which cannot be contaminated," she exclaimed.

The next day as we journeyed from Galilee into southern Lebanon, I had a chance to ask a rabbi from Cleveland the question I had long reserved for that moment: "Where did this Jewish practice of not mixing milk and meat originate?" "It's in the Bible," he said. "Have you not read, 'You shall not boil a kid in its mother's milk' [Exod. 23:19]? What else could it mean?" he asked. "It's as plain as the nose on your face—mixing milk and meat is forbidden by the Law of God!"

Before we ridicule the rabbi for his interpretation, let us remember that Christians have at one time or another used the Bible to defend slavery and emancipation, monogamy and polygamy, gender equality and male dominance, **pacifism** and holy wars! The ethical interpretation of the Bible is no easy task.

This difficulty has led many outside the conservative Christian tradition to propose an illuminative rather than a normative use of the Scriptures, believing the Bible does not *prescribe* moral **absolutes,** but only *describes* the moral pilgrimage of biblical communities. Although evangelical scholars uniformly resist this weakening of biblical authority, they warn that "a simplistic transfer of biblical statements to present situations, without regard for the literary genre of the writing or the specific intention of the author, is unwise."[24]

Another concern calls for Christians to move away from a highly individualistic study of Scripture toward a more communal approach. Ethicist Stanley Hauerwas acknowledges the importance of biblical imperatives, but He proposes that the real value of Scripture for ethics is its community-shaping role: "I am impressed by those who live as if such commands should directly govern their affairs. . . . Yet I contend that [narrative ethics] keeps us from turning commands found there into isolated rules or principles that are assumed to have special status because they are in the Bible. Rather it proposes that Christians (and we hope others) take them to heart (and mind) because they have been found to be crucial to a people formed by the story of God."[25]

One thing is certain. For our ethics to be truly biblical, we must first hear the Word of God in its original context, asking, "What did this passage mean to the recipients in the day in which it was given?" Until the interpreter clearly understands the message God spoke to the communities who first heard the revelation, it is more difficult to hear God speak today.

Principles of Interpretation

At a conference on biblical interpretation, Regent College professor J. I. Packer stated, "Holy Scripture is totally trustworthy but it must be interpreted." After elaborating on the hermeneutical process, the British scholar concluded with three basic questions to raise in the interpretive task: (1) the exegetical question—what did the writer mean? (2) the hermeneutical question—what does the message mean today? (3) the practical question—how does the passage change the Christian today?[26]

To begin, let us establish five *general principles* that are fundamental for the correct interpretation of the ethical teachings of the Scriptures:[27]

1. Affirm your personal conviction in the authority, inspiration, validity, and relevance of the Bible.
2. Use every proper technique for interpreting the Bible.
3. Examine each text exegetically,[28] avoiding common mistakes of interpretation such as extreme literalism (prooftexting), wrongful allegorizing and typologizing, and the "magical" use of the Bible for ethical guidance.[29]
4. Determine the meaning of the passage for those to whom it was originally intended—the "Then and There" principle.
5. Translate biblical teachings into contemporary applications—the "Here and Now" principle.

Although there may be only one interpretation of what the passage meant to the original hearers, there may be many applications to modern life. One key to contemporizing Scripture is finding the "point of contact"—the biblical principle behind the norms and values in the original meaning of the text.

Additional hermeneutical help is provided in Bernard Ramm's classic work, *Protestant Biblical Interpretation*, where he discussed *specific principles* that are of particular value in the ethical interpretation of the Bible.[30]

Never distort the original meaning of the text. To support a position on an ethical issue, zealous Christians may read into the text a meaning not there. A pastor once used the text "Do not handle, Do not taste, Do not touch" (Col. 2:21) as the basis for a sermon on alcohol abuse, although the passage is actually addressing **Gnostic** heresies.

Give attention to specific ethical norms. Although biblical ethics is more than a list of laws to obey, moral imperatives in the Scriptures must always be taken seriously. When Paul wrote to the Christians at Rome, "Pay to all what is due them—taxes to whom taxes are due, revenue to whom revenue is due"(13:7), the apostle used Greek words that meant "tribute to a foreign power" *(phoros)* and "duties on goods" *(telos)*. This specific norm gave clear guidance to early Christians about paying taxes.

Identify the biblical principle behind a specific norm. A basic premise of a **principlist** approach to biblical ethics is that every precept in the Bible is an expression of a value or principle. If the principle is congruent with the moral character of God, then that principle is relevant in every generation. In the passage above (Rom. 13:7), Paul spoke not just to first-century Christians in the Roman Empire. The transcultural principle in the text might be stated: Christians should support their government by paying taxes.

Rely primarily on the locus classicus (classic text). The Mosaic laws concerning marriage and divorce (Deut. 24:1–5) contain many important insights, but the primary passage for this issue is Jesus' dialogue with the Pharisees in which Jesus interprets the Mosaic commandments (Matt. 19:3–12).

Understand the relationship between biblical principles and specific commandments. The Bible contains many detailed imperatives—if not, it would be difficult to know how biblical principles worked in a specific culture. However, the thrust of the Scriptures moves beyond time-bound rules and regulations to values and principles, which make clear God's intent and give direction on issues not covered by biblical laws. The prohibition against eating meat with blood in it (Gen. 9:4) speaks more to respect for life than to consuming a rare steak.

The emphasis of the Bible, therefore, is on principles rather than laws. Nevertheless, the inclusion of both principles and precepts verifies the relevance of the Holy Scriptures.

Biblical laws have a legitimate role. For one thing, they give detailed guidance about everyday decisions, which is especially helpful for new Christians. A rules approach to Christian ethics, however, often leads to provincialism, self-righteousness, and **legalism**. Focusing on ethical principles can help us avoid these potential pitfalls. More importantly, a principle-based ethic moves us toward a deeper understanding of God's moral will and a personal commitment to it.

Emphasize the inner spirit more than outer obedience. In His confrontation with legalistic Pharisees, Jesus often made the point that morality and spirituality are inward. Outwardly these religious zealots appeared to be as pure as "whitewashed tombs," but inwardly, in Jesus' words, they were full of "filth . . . hypocrisy and lawlessness" (Matt. 23:27–28).

The Bible does condemn external acts like gluttony, drunkenness, and adultery, as well as inner motives. But the emphasis of the gospel is undoubtedly on the inner spiritual life from which all external behavior flows (Matt. 15:18–19). Spiritual maturity centers on correct attitudes, proper motives, and cultivating the inner fruit of the Spirit (Gal. 5:22–23).

Translate commands addressed to ancient cultures into language relevant to contemporary cultures. When biblical authors communicated God's message to Israel and other nations, they used terms familiar to those cultures. Paul's words to the Christian women of Corinth about not cutting their hair and wearing a veil (1 Cor. 11:2–16) must be restated for our culture. Some churches have tried to apply these literally. Most Christians have discovered in them a principle related to social customs and their impact on the witness and work of the church.

Cultural Interpretation

The previous specific principle brings before us a topic that must not be avoided in our discussion of biblical interpretation and Christian ethics—the cultural interpretation of Scripture. In a widely used hermeneutics text, Gordon Fee and Douglas Stuart address the question of cultural relativity, noting that this "is the place where the problem of God's *eternal Word* having been given in *historical particularity* comes most sharply into focus."[31] All biblical texts are culture conditioned, but some texts are culture-bound and cannot be directly transferred to the present.

Nearly all Christians do translate ancient biblical texts into contemporary settings. Twentieth-century evangelicals leave to the biblical world the laws that prohibit contact with a corpse (Lev. 5:2), eating pork (Deut. 14:8), touching a woman during menstruation or after childbirth (Lev. 12:4–5), and mixed gender dressing (Deut. 22:5). Few congregations today refuse to serve ham at the annual picnic or prohibit females from dressing in blue jeans or males in kilts. However, many evangelical churches struggle with the idea of women teaching men, serving communion, or even ushering.

A few churches have tried to reject the idea of cultural relativity altogether, seeking to reproduce first-century culture as the divine norm. Others have rejected all cultural expressions of the Christian faith, striving for a "culture-free" Christianity. Certainly both extremes are impossible, for no divinely ordained culture exists. Every generation must relate to its own culture.

Perhaps the answer lies in the recognition that the Bible is a historical document, conditioned by the language and culture of its setting, and it needs to be translated into new settings. But it is essential that for such translation to be valid, it must operate within legitimate hermeneutical guidelines.

Fee and Stuart suggest seven guidelines for distinguishing between items that are culturally relative and those that are transcultural and normative for all Christians of all times:[32]

1. Distinguish between the central core of the message of the Bible and what is peripheral to it. This principle will safeguard the gospel from the insertion of custom and culture as God's law. The "holy kiss" is not a central moral obligation.

2. Distinguish between what the New Testament itself sees as inherently moral and what is not. Inherently moral items are ethical absolutes in every culture; those not innately moral change from culture to culture. The sexual sins Paul lists in 1 Corinthians 6:9-10 are always immoral, but the practice of footwashing was a custom of the early church.

3. Distinguish between items about which the New Testament has a consistent witness and issues that reflect differences. The Christian practices of love, nonretaliation, and unlimited forgiveness are uniformly upheld in the New Testament. On the other hand, the Bible does not seem to present only one picture of the role of women in the church.

4. Distinguish between principle and specific application. Most American Christians never face the question of eating meat that has been an offering to idols (1 Cor. 8). But the principle urged here asks mature Christians to avoid even acceptable behavior if it actually hinders another believer's faith.

5. With great care, determine the cultural options open to the biblical writers. "The degree to which a New Testament writer agrees with a cultural situation in which there is *only one option*, increases the possibility of the cultural relativity of such a position."[33] Attitudes toward slavery and the status of women in the New Testament world were singular; the degree to which they reflect the prevalent cultural attitudes of that day may be due to the fact that these were the only options.

6. Be alert to cultural differences between the biblical times and the present day that are not immediately obvious. Paul's charge, "Let every person be subject to the governing authorities" (Rom. 13:1), was used in England to support the divine rights of kings. But the government addressed by the apostle in the first century was not the participatory democracy desired by the early colonists, who revolted against King George.

7. Christians must exercise humility, love, and forgiveness toward one another. Sincere differences exist among Christians over the interpretation of passages that reflect cultural practices. To grow spiritually and intellectually, biblical exegetes must be willing to recognize honest disagreements and to discuss various possible interpretations.

Students sometimes say, "I just think it is safer always to accept the literal meaning of the Bible." Certainly, care should be exercised in the use of the cultural principle. The clearest and most obvious meaning may be the best interpretation. However (as we have noted before), no one applies the Bible literally at every point. The real challenge is to know when to accept the obvious teaching of the biblical text and when to understand the passage as a cultural norm.

A few rules of thumb may help solve this dilemma. Ordinarily, a cultural interpretation of a passage is justified if the literal meaning: (1) gives a teaching in conflict with a basic biblical doctrine, such as the practice of polygamy and concubinage; (2) justifies un-Christian behavior, like the wars of the Crusades; (3) denies acceptable behavior, such as wearing jewelry; (4) denies church practices that are practical without fault, as using musical instruments in worship; (5) and encourages a spirit or attitude that does not reflect the spirit of Jesus, such as hating **homosexuals.**[34]

To summarize, our approach in discerning the ethical teachings of the Scriptures will be to approach every subject on the basis of the entire canon, rather than isolated passages. With full confidence in the authority, inspiration, and relevance of the Scriptures, we will give careful attention to the rules and tools of biblical exegesis.

The obvious meaning of the text will be accepted unless there is some valid hermeneutical reason for a cultural one. Every passage will be exegeted on the basis of the meaning and message to the community that first received it. This means that an understanding of the historical, grammatical, literary, social, and theological contexts of the passage is indispensable. For ethics to be truly Christian, the Bible must be correctly understood and properly applied.

FOR THOUGHT AND DISCUSSION

1. Debate this proposition: "The Bible is the exclusive source of authority for Christian ethics."
2. Define the moral nature of God and explain the importance of this doctrine for Christian ethics.

3. Explain the relation of faith and ethics in the Bible, and give examples of this teaching in the Old and New Testaments.
4. Compare the authority of the Bible with the authority of Christ and the authority of the Holy Spirit for ethics.
5. Apply the cultural principle of interpretation to Paul's words in 1 Corinthians 8 concerning meat offered to idols.

CHAPTER THREE

THE ETHICS OF THE BIBLE

The last chapter affirmed the significant role the Bible has played in the formulation of **Christian ethics.** Biblical faith is relevant for **ethics** in every age because the God of the Bible is **moral**—Jehovah is revealed as a holy, righteous, just, merciful, and loving Redeemer. The Scriptures are a totally reliable revelation of God's will and, as such, constitute our primary objective authority for Christian ethics.

After affirming the Bible's central place, we next examined the challenging task of biblical interpretation. Our first concern was to establish sound **hermeneutical** principles for accurate biblical interpretation. An urgent aspect of the exegetical task is cultural interpretation, which is vital for translating biblical truths to contemporary society.

Now it is time to survey the Bible itself—to investigate the ethical teachings of the Old and New Testaments. This discipline is normally referred to as "Biblical Ethics," the study of the ethical teachings of the Bible in the day in which they were given. Strictly speaking, the application of these biblical insights to modern social issues is the discipline of "Christian Ethics," which we will deal with in part 2.

ETHICS OF THE OLD TESTAMENT

Christians have more difficulty using the Old Testament as a resource for ethics than they do the New Testament. The many meticulous laws, bewildering narratives, mysterious prophecies, and ancient wisdom passages seem to apply more to Israel than to Christianity. Yet there is no doubt that a continuity exists between the Old and New Covenants, and "an understanding of Hebrew ethics is essential to an adequate knowledge of the ethics of Jesus and the New Testament as a whole."[1]

Approaches to the Old Testament

How does the Old Testament reveal its ethical ideals? A common approach is to look into the first thirty-nine books of the Bible for *laws and rules*. Obeying these commandments constitutes ethical living. The problem with this method is more than interpretation, for there are enormous differences between life in ancient Israel and in our world. What should be done with commands that run counter to modern life, like the prohibition of interest (Deut. 23:19), or laws that seem irrelevant, like the leprosy codes (Lev. 13–14)? After the Reformation, many interpreters viewed the Old Testament as a book of laws followed only by those trying to earn salvation through works. For some Reformers, the New Testament proclaimed a gospel of grace and thus superceded the Old Covenant and made it irrelevant. Jesus Himself denied this view (Matt. 5:17).

One school of Christian thought, known as reconstructionism or theonomism, argues that Old Testament law applies today in "exhaustive" and "minutial" detail.[2] God's pattern for ancient Israel (other than ceremonial laws) is a blueprint for all nations today, a view most evangelicals consider extreme.

So approaching the Old Testament as a book of rules is an inadequate method. However, the role of the law in the life of God's people must not be overlooked.

Another approach is to view the Old Testament as a book of *principles*. In his approach to biblical ethics, T. B. Maston looked for the principle behind the laws and precepts, suggesting "that more important than the commandments are the principles or ideals that may be expressed through the commandments and may be the source of the commandments."[3] Evangelical scholar Walter Kaiser also argued for the relevance of the Old Testament, contending that universally applicable principles lie behind the specific laws and commandments in the Old Covenant. By observing the morality and theology that undergird or inform each law, we can discover moral and theological principles for life today.[4]

The **principlist** approach allows seemingly irrelevant laws to find application in contemporary life by uncovering the intent of

God both then and now. This approach has much to commend it, but if used exclusively the abstract principles gleaned from the Bible could promote **legalism** or **situationism,** especially if they are separated too far from their sociohistorical settings.[5]

A third approach to the Old Testament is to view it as a ***paradigm*** or *pattern* for life. In its stories of kings and commoners, patriarchs and prophets, Israelites and foreigners, the Old Testament reveals an overall view of life. Ethical standards are derived not from rules or principles but from the patterns of living revealed in these biblical models.

In a new study of Old Testament ethics, Waldemar Janzen uses five different stories as paradigms for correct ethical behavior. The five models he chooses are the holy life (priestly model), the wise life (wisdom model), the just life (royal model), the serving and suffering life (prophetic model), and the familial paradigm, which represents the comprehensive model.[6]

The paradigm approach often uses principles to construct an overall pattern of life as a framework for ethics. However, as with principles, the historical setting may be lost in the model, and the Bible may become only one of several authorities.

A fourth possibility is to approach the Bible as a book for *character building*. The main way the Old Testament affects ethics is in its impact on the moral agent—the decision maker. The real moral purpose of the Scriptures is to develop ethical **character**—a virtuous person—rather than instilling rules, principles, or paradigms. Certainly moral character is basic to ethical living—a just person acts justly in society. This viewpoint, however, usually suffers from a concentration on individual moral perfection (pietism) to the exclusion of social concerns.

A final proposal is to understand the Old Testament as *story*. One advantage of this approach is its focus on the essential nature of the Old Testament—"the story of God with ancient Israel . . . [which] bears witness to events in which God was revealed."[7] Narrative ethics asserts that the biblical story gives roots to persons and communities. As Hebrew families heard the stories of God's dealings with Abraham, Moses, and the Jewish people, this script became a Hebrew lens for viewing life. **Virtues** and **values** vital for Hebrew morality were formed by these narratives.

The proposers of the Old Testament as story have rightly reminded us of the importance of moral formation in the community of faith. Nevertheless, Christian ethics requires more than just becoming a good person in a biblical community. Life in society also requires the ability to make good moral choices.

Each approach to the Old Testament aids our understanding of biblical ethics. In chapter 5 a method will be proposed that incorporates many of these perspectives.

Characteristics of Hebrew Morality

To understand the unity of biblical ethics, we need to discover the basic themes that run throughout both testaments. A primary task, then, is to identify major characteristics of Hebrew morality.[8]

The first characteristic is that Hebrew moral thought is radically *theocentric,* or *God-centered.* In fact, Hebrew ethics and religion are so closely related, they are seldom distinguished. God is the highest good and the source of all moral requirements. The Ten Commandments began with, "I am the LORD your God, who brought you out of the land of Egypt, out of the house of slavery" (Exod. 20:1-2). The fundamental unifying element of Hebrew faith is the one living God of Israel, who is holy (Lev. 19:2), righteous (Isa. 45:21), and just (Amos 5:24).

Another major characteristic of Hebrew morality is its *imperative tone.* Obedience to God is a basic virtue; disobedience is the greatest sin. Ethically, the Old Testament is concerned with the question of duty—"What is right?"—rather than the question of ideals: "What is the chief good?" Micah's widely used summary of biblical morality, though written in the indicative mood, declares God's imperative: "What does the LORD require of you but to do justice, and to love kindness, and to walk humbly with your God?" (6:8).

A third outstanding feature of Old Testament ethics is its *relational* character. Hebrew ethics are concerned with right relationships to God, to persons, and to communities of persons. Personal fellowship with the living God is inseparable from the good life, and it is the basis of all goodness (Mic. 6:8). Unlike Greek **philosophy,** which focused on abstract values, the Old Testament stresses behavior, which affects neighbors and Israel.

Another quality that distinguishes Hebrew ethics from other types of ethics is its *equalitarian* attitude. Because Jehovah God has made all humanity, God loves all, cares for all, and seeks to redeem all. The Old Testament recognizes the fundamental equality of all persons, rather than their differences. Throughout the Scriptures, the children of God are admonished to care for the slave, the orphan, the widow, and the poor, for the God of Israel shows no partiality.

A fifth feature of Hebrew morality is its emphasis on *salvation from evil* rather than aspiration toward the good. Israel's hope is in God, not in human perfection. Jehovah is the healer of Israel (Exod. 15:26), the God of deliverance (Isa. 38:17), the coming "savior" (Isa. 19:20), and the Redeemer (Isa. 41:14) who saves with an "everlasting salvation" (Isa. 45:17).

Finally, Hebrew morality is *incomplete.* Though higher than the ethics of its ancient contemporaries, Israel's moral level reflects a people at an early stage of development, moving toward fulfillment in the ethics of Jesus and the New Testament. Paul declared, "The Jewish laws were our teacher and guide until Christ came" (Gal. 3:24, TLB).[9]

In some ways, the ethics of the Hebrews suffered from a dualism. Justice for the Israelite was different from justice for the foreigner (Deut. 23:19-20), and Hebrew slaves were treated better than foreign slaves (Exod. 21:2). Even among the Jews, women were denied many personal and religious rights.

Old Testament ethics also moved steadily toward legalism, especially after the Exile. Morality came to be defined in terms of obedience to external customs and codes, while concern for motives and attitudes disappeared. The Jewish Talmud and Midrash of Jesus' day reflected legalism at its most intensive level.

The most troubling evidence of the incompleteness of Hebrew morality is the practice of *cherem,* which seems contrary to the Christian ethic. *Cherem* was the total annihilation of an enemy city—men, women, children, animals, and property—as an act of devotion to Yahweh (Deut. 13:12-18; 1 Sam. 15:3; Josh. 11:20).

Why would God command such destruction? Four possible explanations have been proposed: (1) prevention of Israelite amalgamation with pagan cultures; (2) God's judgment of a wicked people; (3) an incomplete understanding of God's will; and (4) an accommodation of God's will to human limitations.[10]

As the chosen people grew in their knowledge of God, they also matured in their expression of faith and ethics. Let us be careful not to judge the ancient Hebrews by Christian ethical standards they neither possessed nor understood.

Ethics of the Law

The Jews considered the Law as the highest **authority** because it was given by God as an expression of God's will for His people.

The **Torah** ("to teach") originally referred to all teachings regarding a person's relation to God and others, but later Torah came to mean the five books of Law or the Pentateuch. The other major divisions of the Old Testament, the Prophets and Writings, were subordinate to the Law.

The earliest piece of Hebrew legislation in the Old Testment was the *Covenant Code* (Exod. 20-26). The Hebrew word *berith* (covenant) referred to many types of agreements but was most significantly used of God's covenant with Israel. Muilenburg observed that "the ethical terminology of the Old Testament is derived in large part from the covenant relationship."[11]

The Covenant Code is best summarized in the Ten Commandments (Exod. 20:1-17), which were "the cornerstone of Hebrew ethics, standing in the same relationship to the religion of Israel as the Sermon on the Mount does to Christianity."[12] The **Decalogue** is no mere collection of Hebrew **mores** and folkways, but it contains commands written by God Himself (Deut. 5:22). The Ten Words reinforce the morality of creation and thus constitute "eternal, universal values indispensable for the fulfillment of the individual and society."[13] Tertullian declared they were written on human hearts long before they were engraved in stone.[14]

The first four commandments sum up our duty to God and provide religious principles foundational for morality. The first law calls for singleness of worship ("no other gods before me," v. 3), followed by the second prohibition to "not make for yourself an idol" (v. 4), which ensured spirituality in worship. Commandments one and two establish ethical monotheism—Yahweh is the only God, and Yahweh is inherently moral.

Commandment three addresses sincerity in worship and reverence for God ("not make wrongful use of the name of the LORD," v. 7). To the Hebrews "name" meant personality; God's total person—words and deeds—is to be taken seriously. The prohibition applies to oaths, vows, profane language, and efforts to control God by manipulation of God's name. The fourth word, "Remember the sabbath day, and keep it holy" (v. 8), is a command for God's chosen people to turn aside regularly from work to remember their covenant (Ezek. 20:12), to be instructed in the Law, and to maintain the discipline of a life of righteousness.

The second section of the Decalogue covers duties to others and to self. Commandment five, "Honor your father and your mother" (v. 12), upholds parental authority and family solidarity, which cannot be lost without injuring religion and society. The sixth word, "You shall not murder" (v. 13), embodies the principle of the sacredness of human life, because to murder destroys the image of God in persons (Gen. 9:6). The sanctity of the marriage relationship is affirmed in the seventh command, "You shall not commit adultery" (v. 14), which calls for sexual purity before and after marriage and makes possible the relationship prescribed in the fifth command.

An ethical principle embraced in the eighth commandment, "You shall not steal" (v. 15), is the protection of the right to personal property because property is an entrustment from God. The ninth word in the Decalogue is an obligation to bear true testimony, "You shall not bear false witness against your neighbor" (v. 16).

The last commandment, "You shall not covet" (v. 17), is often listed as a separate duty to self. The tenth word forbids inordinate desire for your neighbor's possessions and is the first implied awareness that wrong ideas precede wrong actions. This last imperative explains the origin of wrongful actions prohibited in commandments one to nine.

The Ten Commandments, then, are not just legal codes for Israel. These simple but comprehensive principles are foundational standards for our relationship to God and to our fellow humans. In the uncertain moral climate of the twenty-first century, these Ten Words provide an ethical nucleus around which moral communities can grow.[15]

A second ethical component in the Law is the *Holiness Code* (Lev. 17–26). The primary example of this code appears in Leviticus 19, which opens with the classic imperative, "You shall be holy, for I the LORD your God am holy" (v. 2). The chapter is uniquely constructed, containing five pentads of five principles each, a total of twenty-five statements concerning ethical obligations (vv. 9–18). Each pentad concludes with, "I am the LORD your God."

The passage culminates with the monumental statement that summarizes all that has gone before: "You shall love your neighbor as yourself" (v. 18), an ethical ideal quoted by Jesus, Paul, and James (Matt. 22:39; Rom. 13:9; James 2:8). Many scholars view this statement as one of the highest expressions of ethical feeling and biblical morality. The close relation of these verses (19:1–18) to the Decalogue strengthens the argument for the ethical nature of the Holiness Code in the Old Testament.

A third ethical section of the Law is the *Deuteronomic Code* (Deut. 12–26), which relates closely to the Covenant Code but is distinct in its emphasis on "steadfast love" *(hesed)*. Jehovah's love is faithful and constant toward those who love Him and keep His laws (7:9).

Deuteronomy is profoundly ethical. The book contains a magnificent code of morals and is quoted often by New Testament writers and Jesus. A central passage is chapter 6, which opens with the charge given to Israel by Moses, calling for reverence toward God evidenced in obedience (vv. 1–3).

The next word is the Shema, Israel's confession of faith recited twice daily by devout Jews: "Hear, O Israel: the LORD is our God, the LORD alone" (v. 4). Then follows the most basic commandment: "You shall love the LORD your God with all your heart, and with all your soul, and with all your might" (v. 5).

This command simply means to love God supremely, with every part of your being—your total personality. Jesus called this the "greatest and first commandment" (Matt. 22:38), for such single-minded devotion results in obedient service to God and love for others. "Love of God is revealed as the basic motive for obedience to the commandments of God, which again points up the ethical nature of the central concepts of the books of the Law."[16]

As we have discovered, the Law is saturated with ethical content. In the Pentateuch, faith and ethics are one because Jehovah is a moral God. The ethical concepts of the covenant, holiness, and love evolve from God's moral nature and character. "God expects His people to be like Him. He is a covenant-keeping God; He expects them to keep His covenant with them. He is holy; they are to be holy. He loves them; they are to love Him and one another. This idea of likeness to God is more basic and more pervasive than any other moral concept in the Law and elsewhere in the Scriptures."[17]

Ethics of the Prophets

In the beginning, Israel was a simple agricultural society. By the time of the eighth-century prophets, life had become complex. Socially, Israel had moved from seminomadic tribal life to a more settled rural and urban culture. Politically, the nation moved from theocracy to monarchy, and at times survived as a vassal state under foreign rule. Within two centuries (587 B.C.) Jerusalem would be destroyed and the leading citizens exiled to Babylon.

Economically and morally, the greedy rich oppressed the poor, the courts were corrupt, judges were easily bribed, political leaders lived in luxury, and immorality reigned. These increasing social tensions were exacerbated by a declining morality and a growing ritualism in religion.

Religiously, Caananite practices had infiltrated the religion of Jehovah. Faith was more formal than personal and had little to do with righteousness. The religion of Abraham that had been "ethicised at Sinai had become materialised at Canaan, and mechanical relations had been substituted for relations that were originally personal."[18]

Like relentless termites, social injustices and spiritual infidelities ate away at the crumbling foundations of the house of Israel. Into that dark and decaying society came the prophets of Israel with their message of judgment and hope. The prophets were convinced that God Himself was involved in the struggle for spiritual awakening and social justice.

The term *prophet (nabi)* means one who spoke for God to God's people. Commonly misunderstood to be a predictor of future events, the prophet was primarily a messenger, a "forth" teller rather than a foreteller. A diverse group, the prophets had one thing in common—each testified of a calling from God to "prophesy to my people Israel" (Amos 7:15). The prophet's message usually began, "Thus says the LORD" (Amos 1:3).

With the possible exception of Ezekiel, none of the *nabi* were trained theologians, but the prophet's message was always based on theological principles: God is the sovereign creator of all (Jer. 27:5); God's covenant and election endures; sin is rebellion against God; the day of the Lord is judgment (Amos 5:18-20); a remnant will survive judgment; and the day of the Lord will bring a new covenant of the heart (Jer. 31:31-34) and an ideal kingdom through God's Messiah (Isa. 9:6-7).[19]

Few scholars would deny that "Hebrew morality reaches its high-water mark in the teachings of the prophets from about 800 to 400 B.C."[20] Though Amos, Hosea, Micah, and Isaiah are sometimes called "the ethical prophets of the eighth century," it would be wrong to suppose them mere social reformers. First and foremost, they were religious prophets for "their insistence upon right conduct was religious in its origin, and its root was never anything else than religious."[21]

Old Testament scholar James Muilenburg outlines five major areas addressed by the prophets: the political order, the economic order, the land, the administration of justice, and the world of nations.[22] Specific social sins condemned by God's messengers included:

- Marital infidelity (Hos. 2:9-10; Mal. 2:14-16)
- Dishonest business practices (Amos 8:4-6)
- Exploitation of laborers (Mal. 3:5; Hos. 5:10-11)
- Political corruption (Amos 5:7; Isa. 1:23; Mic. 3:9)
- Excessive personal indulgence (Amos 6:1-14)
- Corruption of priests and false prophets (Mic. 3:11)
- Refusal to accept personal responsibility (Jer. 31:30)

The herdsman Amos cried out, "Let justice roll down like waters, and righteousness like an everflowing stream" (5:24). Speaking to the rulers and the people, Isaiah called out, "Cease to do evil, learn to do good; seek justice, rescue the oppressed, defend the orphan, plead for the widow" (1:16-17).

Ethical emphases are also found in the early prophets Nathan, Samuel, and Elijah, as well as the later prophets Haggai and Malachi. However, it is God's eighth-century messengers who made a unique and lasting contribution in their unification of religion and ethics, their balance between judgment and hope, and their elevation of righteousness over ritual.

Ethics of the Writings

The third section of the Hebrew Bible is the Writings, a large body of wisdom literature developed after the return from Exile. H. Wheeler Robinson aptly defines Israel's wisdom as "the discipline whereby was taught the application of prophetic truth to the individual in the light of experience."[23]

Sometimes called "the philosophy of the Old Testament," the Writings are not speculative theory but realistic practical wisdom. Theologically grounded and God-centered, the teachings of the sages disclose insights into the meaning of existence, the mastery of life and its difficulties.

Proverbs, as its name implies, is almost entirely a book of practical morality emphasizing the worth of true wisdom (1:7). Through teaching sentences (proverbs), readers are reminded that the righteous life is found in practical obedience to God's will in every area of life.

Family life is given a prominent place in Proverbs, especially the ethical obligations of the father (1:8-9; 6:6-8, 32), parents (22:6), and children (13:1). King Lemuel's portrait of the ideal woman (31:10-31) is unexcelled in the Bible: "Many women have done excellently, but you surpass them all" (31:29).

Wisdom also applies to business practices (11:1; 22:16) and the uses of wealth (30:8-9), for "better is a little with righteousness than large income with injustice" (16:8). Little is said about political issues other than warnings to rulers (28:15), condemnation of bribes (17:23), and the discouragement of violence and revolution (24:21-22).

In one sense *Job* and *Ecclesiastes* complement Proverbs, for "they react to a simplistic understanding of Proverbs by asking: What about ethics when life falls apart?"[24] The Book of Job records the classic dialogue of a righteous man struggling with undeserved suffering. Contrary to the popular belief that the theme of Job is suffering, many scholars suggest the drama deals with the true motive of morality, as expressed in Satan's question: "Does Job fear God for nothing?" (1:9).[25] Stated positively, the genuinely moral person serves God from a heart of love, not for hope of reward.

The powerful dialogue between Job and his so-called "friends" (and ultimately with God) suggests that righteous living does not guarantee success and God's blessings. Job maintains his integrity throughout, discovering a new self-understanding and a more personal relationship to God (42:5-6).

One of the highest ethical standards in the Bible is found in Job 31, where Job defends his moral life as free from lust (vv. 1-4), deceit (vv. 5-6), adultery (vv. 9-12), and the unjust treatment of the weak (vv. 13-23). Job's conduct is open to public scrutiny without embarrassment (vv. 35-40).

The Teacher *(koheleth)* of Ecclesiastes is searching to know "what was good for mortals to do" (2:3)—the *summum bonum* of life. This royal philosopher experiments with four possibilities: philosophy and wisdom (1:12-18); pleasure (2:1-11); work and wealth (2:18-6:12); and fame (7:1-11:8). His conclusion: "all is vanity" (12:8). In the end the Teacher finally realizes that humans do not control life, for life is a gift from God; therefore, "Fear God, and keep his commandments; for that is the whole duty of everyone" (12:13).

As a hymnbook of the Hebrew people, the *Psalms* consist of 150 songs of Israel expressing every mood of their faith. Because the book centers on worship and the relationship between God and the worshiper, it is easy to overlook its ethical dimensions. The idea of justice is prominent, both in describing God (82; 89:14) and in declaring the responsibility of the Davidic king (72:1, 4) and the worshiping community (37:27-28). Of particular importance to the psalmist is the ethical life of the worshiper (24:3-6). Psalm 15 is a key passage, giving eleven qualifications for worship, all ethical: "O LORD, who may abide in your tent? Who may dwell on your holy hill? Those who walk blamelessly and do what is right" (15:1-2).

Often overlooked in the Old Testament is the *Song of Songs*, a book containing an "ethical gem" in its theme, the beauty of faithful sexual love in marriage (8:6-9).[26] The main purpose of this inspired poetry is to uphold the purity and strength of true love, opposing polygamy and exalting the exclusive devotion between marital partners.[27]

Like streams in the desert, ethical themes flow throughout the Old Testament. The Pentateuch first expresses God's concern for creation, for life, and for relationships in community. The Decalogue provides a moral foundation for persons and for society. God's concern for justice, especially for the powerless in society, is shouted from the lips of the prophets. According to the Old Testament, ethics is not peripheral or secondary but at the very heart of the faith of Abraham, Moses, and the prophets.

ETHICS OF THE NEW TESTAMENT

The Old Testament is the necessary foundation for the understanding of the New. From the beginning, Christians have realized the close relationship between the two Covenants. God's self-disclosure of His nature and will to Israel finds its completeness in the life, death, and resurrection of Jesus of Nazareth. The writer of Hebrews began his book by announcing that "Jesus Christ is the full-orbed revelation of God's will and way (Heb. 1:1-2)."[28]

The ethics of the New Testament centers around Jesus. In Christ the Law is fulfilled (Matt. 5:17-20) and to Him all the prophets bear witness (Acts 10:43). Jesus might well have discarded the whole moral tradition of the Jews in view of what the Pharisees did with it, but He did not. Christ explicitly stated, "Do not think that I have come to abolish the law or the prophets; I have come not to abolish but to fulfill" (Matt. 5:17). In a word, the moral teachings of the Old Testament find their meaning and intent in the fullness of the gospel of Jesus Christ.

Over the centuries, the ethical teachings of the New Testament have been interpreted in various ways. Many early Christians approached the New Testament allegorically, while some Jewish interpreters practiced excessive literalism. The Reformation brought a more reasonable exegesis of Scripture. In recent centuries a critical analysis of the Bible by more liberal theologians has caused them to question the supernatural in the Scriptures, as well as many traditional interpretations. Evangelicals have maintained a strong conviction about the inspiration and authority of the Bible, while also utilizing valid hermeneutical insights from biblical studies.[29]

The ways in which Christians approach the New Testament for ethics today are varied. Broadly speaking, four major methods of using the New Testament emerge: (1) as a book of laws or codes for human conduct; (2) as a book of universal principles; (3) as a book that leads the reader to an encounter with God through the Spirit; and (4) as a book that promotes an individual's loving response to the situation confronted.[30]

To these could also be added three closely related approaches that view the Bible as a paradigm for life, as a book that builds character, and as a story that forms communities. In chapter 5, all of these ethical methodologies will be evaluated in detail.

The Ethics of Jesus

Christians may be so absorbed in the work of Christ as Savior that they overlook His role as teacher. In fact, the Gospels speak more about Christ as teacher (*didaskalos*) than as preacher (Mark 4:38; 12:32; John 3:2). Christ came not only to announce how to be "saved," but also to teach the saved how they are to live.

Many call Jesus a "Master Teacher" of morality.[31] "Though from the Christian point of view, Jesus is *far more* than a mere ethical teacher, yet He certainly *is* that, and ethics is a prominent and distinctive feature of His message."[32]

A cursory reading of the Gospels reveals that Jesus deals with those perennial issues of right and wrong, as well as the age-old question of what the good life really is and how to attain it. Jesus Himself modeled the art of living. Even the cynical Bernard Shaw admitted, "We have always had a curious feeling that though we crucified Christ on a stick, he somehow managed to get hold of the right end of it, and that if we were better men, we might try his plan."[33]

Characteristics of Jesus' Ethics. Over the years, religious scholars have debated about the uniqueness of Jesus' ethics.[34] Partial parallels to practically all His teaching can be found in the writings of Greek philosophers, Jewish thinkers, and Buddha.[35] One Jewish writer contends that the Gospels contain not one item of ethical teaching that cannot be paralleled in the Old Testament and other Hebrew writings. Yet later he admits that "there is a new thing in the gospels . . . Jesus gathered together and, so to speak, condensed and concentrated ethical teachings in such a fashion as to make them more prominent. . . . A man like Jesus for whom the ethical ideal was everything, was something unheard of in the Judaism of the day."[36]

A primary characteristic of Jesus' ethics is its *religious* nature. As was true in Hebrew morality, the ethics of Christ are inseparable from Jesus' religion—"all the ethical teachings of Jesus are rooted in His religion, in God."[37] The moral ideals of Jesus are radically theocentric (Matt. 5:48).

The ethics of Jesus are also distinctive as a *disciples'* ethic, primarily intended for transformed persons who have received new spiritual life (John 3:3). "The ethical ideal of Jesus is an ideal only for the man who is in touch with . . . God."[38] The linking of morality with the radical regeneration of individual followers is unique in religious thought.

The *inwardness* of morality is another characteristic of Jesus' ethics. The good life (as well as the evil life) flowed outward from within. For the Master Teacher, motive is primary—murder begins with anger in the heart, and lust is the origin of adultery (Matt. 5:21–30). Dewar goes too far when he writes that Christ was "concerned with *thoughts* rather than deeds."[39] Jesus was concerned with both, but He emphasized that evil deeds spring from an evil heart (Matt. 15:19). This emphasis on inward morality also explains why Jesus condemned more sharply the sins of the spirit than the sins of the flesh.

The value of the *individual person* is a fourth distinctive in the ethics of Jesus. Because every human person is valuable to God (Matt. 12:12), Jesus healed, helped, and treated with respect people society had rejected—lepers (Matt. 8:2), adulterers (John 8:3), children (Mark 10:13), tax collectors (Luke 19:5), and "sinners" (Luke 15:2). This emphasis on the individual in no way diminishes the role of the Christian community as the shaper, bearer, and deliberator of Christian ethics.

Another trait found in Jesus' ethic is its *perfectionistic* or eschatological emphasis.[40] The ethics of the **kingdom of God** really belong to another world, yet these ideals are solidly a part of this world. Christ called His disciples toward perfection in ethical behavior—a love that extends to enemies (Matt. 5:44-46) and a forgiveness that is unlimited (Matt. 18:22). Reinhold Niebuhr termed Jesus' ideals of perfection as "impossible possibilities": although we never attain them, they constantly challenge us with their potentiality. This tension between the ideal and the actual stimulates us for higher ethical living.[41]

One "ideal of perfection" that is often considered a distinctive of Jesus' ethic is His new concept of love *(agape)*. In Jewish thought love was limited to fellow Israelites. In the parable of the good Samaritan, Jesus redefined neighborly love as a selfless, unqualified, and inclusive compassion that serves others (Luke 10:25-37). Christians are to love one another as Christ has loved us, a mark of discipleship (John 13:34-35).

Selfless service was another distinct application of Jesus' perfectionistic ethic. Jesus taught His ambitious disciples that greatness was found in service (Mark 9:35), a truth He modeled in the upper room as He washed the feet of the Twelve (John 13:5).

The teachings of Christ were also characterized by a *positiveness* not found in other ethical systems. In the mind of Jesus, negative goodness was inadequate. Morality is more than a list of "don'ts," which often lead to a legalistic self-righteousness like that of the scribes and Pharisees (Matt. 5:20). Jesus' positiveness is seen in teachings like the "Golden Rule" (Matt. 7:12) and the responsibility of the offended to initiate reconciliation (Matt. 5:24).

With rare exception, ethicists agree that the most distinctive element in the Christian ethic is Jesus Himself.[42] The ethic of Jesus is an *exemplified* ethic. Bishop H. H. Henson noted that no other religion exists in which the historic founder is recognized "as a **norm** of personal morality. . . . Jesus alone is able to offer himself as the sufficient illustration of his own doctrine."[43] Plato, Socrates, Kant, Mohammed, and Buddha spoke theoretically about the good life, but none of them were able to follow their own teachings. Only the life of Jesus Christ was an exposition of the ethic He taught. T. B. Maston exclaimed, "How glorious it is to have a teacher, yes, more than a teacher—a Saviour and Lord, who demonstrated fully in His own life the way He would have us to go!"[44]

Jesus and the Law. How did Jesus relate to the Torah in the Old Testament? Jesus knew the Law (Matt. 5:21, 27, 31), recognized the Law as God's revealed will (Matt. 8:4), but rejected most scribal interpretations of the Torah, saying, "You have a fine way of rejecting the commandments of God in order to keep your tradition!" (Mark 7:9).

Jesus clearly stated His attitude toward God's Law—He came not to destroy the Old Testament commands, but "to fill them up to the brim," (Matt. 5:17, Williams). Jesus "filled full" the Law by explaining the original purpose of the Lawgiver, the true moral principles underlying the Mosaic code.

In the Sermon on the Mount, Jesus used six examples, all in the ethical area, to compare His teachings with the Law (Matt. 5:21-48). Each one is introduced with the formula "You have heard that it was said, . . . But I say to you." In these comparisons, Jesus fulfilled the Law by showing the internal nature of the Law (vv. 21-29), by going beyond the Law's requirements (vv. 30-42), and by going beyond the common interpretations of the Law (vv. 43-47).[45]

Conflict with religious leaders over the Law was common (Mark 7:1-13), especially clashes over Jewish understandings of Sabbath laws and the practice of Jesus and His followers (Matt. 12:1-14; Mark 2:23-3:6; Luke 13:10-17). Jesus' response to controversy over the Sabbath was twofold: He reminded critics of God's intent in the Sabbath (Mark 2:27) and condemned both scribes and Pharisees for their hypocrisy and legalism (Matt. 23).

Jesus and the Kingdom of God. A popular understanding among Christians is that the kingdom of God is entirely future.[46] In Jesus' day, orthodox Jews expected the Messiah to restore the Davidic kingdom on earth. Jewish apocalyptic literature "envisioned a divine revolution that would create a society in union with its God and end oppression forever."[47]

When the Pharisees asked Jesus *when* God's kingdom was coming, Jesus replied, "The kingdom of God does not come with observation; . . . the kingdom of God is within *[entos]* you" (Luke 17:20-21, NKJV). In contrast to popular Jewish opinion, Jesus taught that the kingdom is spiritual, universal, and invisible (Matt. 8:11; Rom. 14:17; John 18:36).

Basically the kingdom of God is "the rule and reign of God within each person living under divine sovereignty; whenever a life surrenders to the Father, there the Kingdom has come."[48] It is both a present reality and a future hope, a gift of God which comes both by growth and in catastrophic ways, and it is never to be identified with human institutions, although it appears in the world as a society, the people of God.

For Jesus, the kingdom of God was central: it was the theme of His preaching (Luke 4:43), the objective of His ministry (Mark 1:15), the *summum bonum* of the Christian life (Matt. 6:33), the main theme of most parables (Matt. 13:44), and a major petition of the model prayer (Matt. 6:10).[49]

L. H. Marshall sums up the importance of the Kingdom for Christian ethics: "All the ethical teaching of Jesus is simply an exposition of the ethics of the Kingdom of God, of the way in which men inevitably behave when they actually come under the rule of God."[50] Jesus' ethics are ethics of the Reign. Because the Kingdom is present, inward, and ethical, God's rule must govern every area of the life of believers in society.[51]

The Sermon on the Mount. Considered the most significant passage in the New Testament for Christian ethics, Matthew 5–7 is widely regarded as the fullest and clearest description of the kind of people Jesus wanted His followers to be.[52] Though the Sermon on the Mount is brief (107 verses) and an incomplete statement of Jesus' ethics, it does capture the essence of His moral teaching.[53]

The Sermon was delivered near the beginning of Jesus' public ministry when He announced the good news that the kingdom of God was at hand (Matt. 4:17). The parallel passage in Luke (6:17–49) indicates that the occasion for the message was Jesus' choice of the twelve apostles (6:12–16)—thus He spoke directly to them. However, Matthew notes both "the crowds" and His disciples were in the listening audience (5:1). As Charles Gore put it, the Sermon "was spoken into the ear of the church, but overheard by the world."[54]

The accuracy of the title "sermon" has been widely questioned because of the notable differences between the two versions. Some conclude the passage is a collection of sayings; others contend the sermons reflect two different occasions, especially since Luke's version states Jesus taught from a "level place" (6:17). After all the facts are considered, it seems that we have either the epitome of all the sermons Jesus preached or two versions (or summaries) of His "Teaching on the Hill."[55]

Since this passage contains the heart of Jesus' teachings about the Christian life, a correct understanding is critical. Over the years Christians have proposed a wide variety of opinions.[56]

Leaders in the early church viewed the Sermon as an absolute code to be followed literally, an alternative to Jewish legalism. Monastics interpreted the words of Jesus as a way of life for a select few who lived "outside the world," an ethic for "super saints." Lutheran Reformers applied the Sermon to all Christians but limited the ethics to personal relationships. Some Protestants came to believe the teachings were unattainable ideals designed to drive believers to greater dependence on God.

Missionary physician Albert Schweitzer proposed the message was an interim ethic intended to prepare people in Jesus' day for the imminent advent of the Kingdom—since Jesus' plans were thwarted, the Sermon is now irrelevant. Some modern theologians consider the ethic of the Sermon irrelevant for other reasons. Reinhold Niebuhr developed a more realistic ethic because he felt Jesus' ideals were inadequate for modern moral questions. Classic dispensationalists taught the ethics of the Sermon were primarily for the future Kingdom when it would be established on earth.

One thing is certain. The Sermon on the Mount is Jesus' call to discipleship—a call for Christians to live distinctly different from the world (Matt. 6:8). We concur with Stott that the Sermon "depicts the behaviour which Jesus expected of each of his disciples, who is also thereby a citizen of God's kingdom."[57] The righteousness of the kingdom of God is the new righteousness of Christ, as contrasted with the old righteousness of the Law.

Jesus begins the Sermon on the Mount with the Beatitudes, which present the essential elements of Christian *character* (Matt. 5:3–12). To be truly righteous, the follower of Jesus must be transformed within. The truly "blessed" (*makarios*, inner joy) are disciples who possess a right relationship with God (vv. 3–5), a right attitude toward themselves (vv. 6, 8), and a right response to others (vv. 7, 9–12). The Beatitudes profile a mature Christian's personality. Citizens of the Kingdom know their spiritual poverty and God's comfort; they are Christ-controlled and they intensely desire to be and do right; out of a pure heart they cultivate the inner virtues of mercy, peace, and patience during persecution.

After establishing the character of the disciple, Jesus then stresses the importance of Christian *influence* in the world (5:13–16). Like salt and light, disciples of Jesus are to have a preserving and illuminating effect upon society. Christians are to penetrate the world and retard the moral decay, as well as reflect the pure light of Christ in a society darkened by sin.

The remainder of the Sermon addresses Christian *conduct.* Jesus first discusses the new quality of righteousness in Christian disciples through six comparisons between the old law and the new way (5:17-48). The Master Teacher then outlines the proper way for Kingdom citizens to practice their religion, including the example of the Model Prayer (6:1-18). A challenging word about life's priorities follows, especially the constant temptation to displace God with money (6:19-34). Relationships with other persons guided by the Golden Rule is the subject of the last section on Christian conduct (7:13-27). The Sermon concludes by calling upon each disciple to choose between the two ways—one that brings destruction and death, and the other which brings salvation and life (7:13-27).

The Ethics of Paul

Paul the apostle, missionary to the Gentiles, wrote thirteen letters to churches across the Roman Empire. The Epistles of Paul are rich in theological truth, but they also contain an abundance of ethical teachings. The recipients of Paul's counsel were recent converts from paganism, who had little knowledge of the Old Testament and lived in morally decadent societies. Paul's instructions to Gentile churches gave him many opportunities to apply the ethical ideals of Christ to concrete issues.

The interpreter of Christ often made explicit what was implicit in the Gospels, but as C. A. A. Scott stated, "Paul may supplement but he never contradicts his Master."[58] In many cases, particularly in Corinth, the specific moral questions addressed by Paul were closely tied to the culture. Paul's detailed advice about some first-century issues, such as the role of women, has led many to misunderstand and misinterpret him.[59]

Paul based his ethical teachings on the teachings of Jesus (1 Cor. 7:10; 9:14; 1 Thess. 4:15; Rom. 12-14), but he was more specific (1 Tim. 2:9-15), more negative (Col. 3:5-14), and more focused on "ethics in the life of community."[60] The reason for these differences in emphases can be found in the nature of Paul's audience—new Christian converts needing specific guidance on how to live in an immoral environment.

Theological Bases. Paul's main concern was not theology but his experience with Christ. Out of a heart set aflame by an encounter with the living Christ on the Damascus road (Acts 9:1-9), the missionary-apostle fused great theological concepts with ethical principles. C. H. Dodd suggests, "The twofold character of Christianity as ethical religion is reflected in the very structure of these documents."[61] Most of Paul's major epistles first build a theological foundation, which is followed by moral applications. The transition from doctrine to ethics is introduced by the bridge word "therefore" (Rom. 12:1; Eph. 4:1).

To understand Paul's ethical teachings, it is important to know the theological bases upon which they are built.[62] First and foremost, Christian ethics for Paul is *Christ-centered*. The apostle used the phrase "in Christ" 164 times to describe his intimate relationship with his Lord (Rom. 16:3, 9; Gal. 3:28). Paul was truly "A Man in Christ," as James Stewart titled him.[63]

The Christian life flows out of this mystical union between the believer and the Savior, who provides the pattern (Col. 3:1 ff) and the power (Phil. 4:13) for Christian living.

Another prominent theological base for Paul's ethic is the *ministry of the Holy Spirit*. In the apostle's understanding, the Spirit is Jesus Christ in the believer's life (2 Cor. 3:17), thus the historical Jesus becomes the Christ of personal experience. The Christian life is life in the Spirit (Rom. 8), for it is the Holy Spirit who creates new life in the believer (2 Cor. 5:17), who reveals the will of God (1 Cor. 2:12-16), who produces the ethical fruit of the Spirit (Gal. 5:22), and who provides the power for this new walk in Christ (Eph. 3:16).

Though Paul rarely used the term, no one seriously doubts Pauline ethics is grounded in *repentance*. "Renewing of the mind" (Rom. 12:2) is the term used by Paul to describe repentance *(metanoeo)*, which literally means "being of another mind." Barth holds repentance "is the 'primary' ethical action upon which all secondary ethical conduct depends."[64] For disciples to be directed to a new behavior, a change of mind must first occur.

Closely related to repentance is the necessity of *faith* for ethical living. Paul the theologian never describes faith as an intellectual assent to truth; it is an ethical commitment of life to Jesus Christ as Lord (Acts 16:31), the yielding of the total self to the will of God (Rom. 4). Paul did proclaim that salvation is by grace through faith, totally apart from works (Eph. 2:8-9), but he quickly added that the purpose of faith is to produce a life of good works (2:10).

A major theological principle in Paul's ethic is his teaching that the sphere of life in Christ is the *church*. The New Testament knows nothing of isolated discipleship. We do come to Christ individually, but we cannot live for Christ solitarily. To be "in Christ" is to be part of the body of Christ, for we are "members of one another" (Eph. 4:25). All Christians share in the fellowship of the gospel (Phil. 1:5), in corporate worship (1 Cor. 14:26), and in the gifts of the Spirit, which are given for the benefit of one another (Rom. 12:5 f.; 1 Cor. 12).

Ethical Principles. Like Jesus, Paul was no new Moses with a code of laws to follow. Paul's specific moral instruction flowed from basic ethical principles which undergirded his teachings.

Without a doubt *love* is the chief moral principle of Paul's ethics. *Agape* is the crowning virtue in the Christian life (1 Cor. 13) and the supreme all-embracing ethical force (Gal. 5:14). Paul's conviction about the priority of love most certainly came from his knowledge of Jesus. A. M. Hunter describes love as "the dominant principle of Paul's ethic" and "the master key" of his morals.[65] No wonder then that Paul told the Romans to owe no one anything but love (Rom. 13:8), encouraged the Corinthians to put love first (1 Cor. 14:1), called the Ephesians to "live in love" (Eph. 5:2), and prayed for the Philippians and Thessalonians that their love for one another might overflow (Phil. 1:9) and increase (1 Thess. 3:12).

For Paul the former Pharisee, the *law* was holy, just, and good (Rom. 7:12). But as a way of salvation, the law is a hopeless remedy, for no one can keep all of the law (Rom. 3:10, 23; Gal. 3:10). It is Christ who redeems us from the curse of the law (Gal. 3:13), for justification comes by faith apart from the works of the law (Rom. 3:28).

The problem, however, is not the law, for it is spiritual; the problem is human nature, "sold into slavery under sin" (Rom. 7:14). Does the law then have any purpose? It served as our "tutor" until Christ came, to teach us morality (Gal. 3:24). The law also convicts us of sin (Rom. 4:15). But ironically, it also provokes us to sin by stimulating a desire for the forbidden (Rom. 7:8). Thus the law may define sin, convict of sin, and even stimulate to sin, but it can never free us from sin.

Another important principle for Paul was Christian *freedom and responsibility.* The apostle plainly declared, "For freedom Christ has set us free" (Gal. 5:1). To be in Christ Jesus is to be free from sin's enslavement, free from the law's condemnation, and free from death and its destruction (Rom. 8).

The mark of Christian maturity is what a believer does with this freedom. Christian freedom always submits to the law of Christian love (Gal. 5:13). Freedom in Christ never becomes a hindrance to the weak (1 Cor. 8:9), it always seeks the good of others (1 Cor. 10:24),

and above all it glorifies God (1 Cor. 10:11). Paul often applied the
principle of the voluntary surrender of freedom to human relationships (Eph. 5:22–24; 6:5–8; 1 Cor. 14:34–35).

The Pauline concept of human responsibility views the person as
a basic unity, in contrast to the Greek body-soul dualism of that
day.[66] The body must not be the scapegoat for moral failure. For
Paul the "flesh" *(sarx)* was neither sex nor the body; it was the
arena of moral struggle. As James Stewart points out, "Though not
evil in itself, the flesh is that part of man's nature which gives evil
its opportunity."[67] The apostle never assumed moral perfection for
himself, yet he was always pressing toward that goal (Phil. 3:12).

Another ethical principle in Paul's thought is the *example of
Christ*. The *imitatio Christi* motif is one Paul used often to motivate
Christians to live ethically. The disciple of Christ is to follow Jesus'
example in humility (Phil. 2:5), generosity (2 Cor. 8:9), love
(Phil. 2:2), and forgiveness (Col. 3:13). Paul goes so far as to say,
"Be imitators of me, as I am of Christ" (1 Cor. 11:1). R. E. O. White
contends that the imitation of Christ is the "nearest principle in
Christianity to a moral **absolute**" and "remains the heart of the
Christian ethic."[68]

The Ethics of John

The five New Testament books penned by John differ from the
Synoptic Gospels and from Paul's letters, mainly due to the lateness
of John's writings (about A.D. 90). The author of the fourth Gospel
painted with broad strokes, describing the Christian life through
abstract terms like *life, love,* and *light.* Though John's style of writing is more general, his commentary amplifies many ethical principles taught by Jesus and Paul.

Johannine ethics have several distinguishing characteristics.[69]
Like Jesus and Paul, John's ethic is nonsystematic and nonlegalistic.
It is also a faith ethic, for faith has a moral quality—outer behavior
springs from an inner commitment. Another trait of John was to
make ethical statements through contrasts; he compared good and
evil, light and darkness, love and hate, life and death. Johannine ethics are also strongly theological and God-centered. For John, God is
light, love, and life—attributes that stress God's moral qualities. For
the apostle whom Jesus loved (John 13:23), *agape* love is the central characteristic of God and the supreme commandment and identifying trait of Christians (John 13:34-35).

The Gospel of John. One of the key phrases in Johannine writings is "eternal life" (3:36; 5:24). For John it was the *summum*

bonum of Christian ethics, a present possession as well as a future hope. In the fourth Gospel, the apostle emphasized that eternal life is primarily a quality of life in the present. To have eternal life is to allow the indwelling Christ to live in you and through you; ethical conduct is the inevitable result of union with the Eternal Christ.

John records a profound conversation Jesus had with His disciples about the fruitful life (15:1-16). Followers of Christ were reminded that they were chosen by God to bear fruit, the fruit of a good life like the one Jesus lived. However, there is one condition: a vital relationship with Christ is necessary, for "the branch cannot bear fruit by itself" (15:4).

On the night before His crucifixion, Jesus said, "I give you a new commandment, that you love one another. Just as I have loved you, you also should love one another" (13:34). The special word Jesus used for "new" *(kainos)* meant "fresh," as opposed to "worn out"; thus Jesus' command was for a new kind of love, by which "everyone will know that you are my disciples" (13:35).

The Epistles of John. John's first letter is a mother lode of ethical instruction, setting forth "the specific ethical demands of the Gospel's deeper religious principles."[70] The Book of 1 John proposes seventeen proofs or tests whereby Christians may "know" that they possess eternal life (5:13). These evidences of eternal life fall into four categories: the believer's relation (1) to sin and righteousness (1:8-9; 3:6-10); (2) to light and darkness (1:5-6; 2:9-11); (3) to love and hate (3:14; 4:8-11); and (4) to life and death (5:4-5, 11-12). Christian morality is a natural expression of a disciple's relation to his Master—Christians "ought to walk just as he walked" (2:6).

The Revelation. The ethics of John's Apocalypse, written for a time of crisis rather than as a teaching document, is often overlooked. A major political statement was made in Revelation 13, where John undoubtedly had the Roman totalitarian state in mind. In contrast to Paul's positive view of government in Romans 13, John in Revelation considered the Roman state under the authority of Satan (13:1-2). The hostile government also had exiled John (1:9), continued to persecute Christians (11:7), but would ultimately be defeated by Christ (11:15). The implied Christian response was rejection and withdrawal.

Other New Testament Writings

"To assume that after Paul 'no new ethical note is struck' in the New Testament is to dismiss nearly one-fifth in length and about one-third in time of the available material. . . . Moreover, in ethical matters the latest pages of the New Testament are in some respects those nearest to our own situation."[71] Although no unique note is sounded, the ethical teachings of Jesus are echoed in these writings.

The Book of Hebrews. Hebrews has been called "sub-apostolic doctrine" because it was written after the first Christian leaders had passed away (2:3) and the "later times" had begun. Evidently some Christians were contemplating returning to Judaism.[72] The author stressed the importance of loyalty and perseverance (10:22-24; 12:1), fidelity in marriage (13:4), the cultivation of Christian virtues (6:10, 12; 13:1), and the imitation of Christ (12:2).

The Book of James. One of the most practical books in the New Testament is James, written in the wisdom tradition by the brother of Jesus who was the leader of the Jerusalem church. As one of the first New Testament books, this ethical tract reflects the essence of early Christianity and echoes the Sermon on the Mount.[73] In this letter to Jewish Christians, James states that pure religion is both hearing and doing the Word of God (1:22-25), which includes controlling the tongue (1:26), caring for orphans and widows (1:27a), and keeping "unstained" from the world (1:27b). Class distinctions and social snobbery have no place in the church, for God is impartial (2:1-5), and partiality violates the royal law of love (2:8-10).

The heart of James' message is his discussion of faith and works (2:14-26). A "professed" faith devoid of works is useless, because it lacks compassion, helpful action, and life (vv. 14-17). Genuine faith is more than intellectual assent to truth (vv. 18-20); it is a faith that inevitably results in helpful service (vv. 21-26). James concludes with a word of caution about the use and abuse of the tongue (3:1-12), an appeal for practical wisdom (3:13-18), and a warning to rich oppressors of the poor (5:1-6).

The Epistles of Peter. The First Epistle of Peter refers both to Jesus' example (2:21-25) as well as His teachings (5:6; cf. Luke 14:11). Three principles of ethical behavior emerge. First, based on the example of Christ, Christians are to submit voluntarily to all social authorities: civil (2:13-17), domestic (2:18-3:7), and congregational (4:8-11). Second, Christian disciples are to follow the example of Christ (2:21). Third, believers are to be holy (1:15-16). Six times Peter commends Christians for "well-doing," which describes active kindness, usefulness, and a heart open to others' needs.[74]

Peter's brief second letter sought to combat antinomian heretics who claimed ethical living was unimportant for the Christian life (2:1-22). In both 2 Peter (1:5-9) and in the small letter of Jude (20), holy living was urged.

The Ethics of the Holy Spirit

Before we conclude our survey of ethics in the Bible, one neglected teaching central to our study is the role of the Holy Spirit. As Christ provides the pattern for Christian living, so the Spirit provides the enabling power. Sad to say, few books on Christian ethics recognize the work of the Spirit as a vital topic.[75] Barnette suggests the reasons for the neglect of the ethics of the Spirit are threefold: a misunderstanding of the doctrine, a reaction to "charismatic" excesses, and the experiential nature of the topic.[76]

The Synoptic Gospels. In the Old Testament, the Spirit is revealed more as a power than as a Divine Person (Gen. 1:1 ff.; 2:7). Not until the New Testament do we know the personal and ethical nature of the Holy Spirit. The synoptic Gospels relate the work of the Spirit with Jesus (Matt. 12:28; Mark 1:10), but in John's Gospel we first see the personality of the Spirit (14:26), who counsels, teaches, and guides Christians (16:12-15).

The Book of Acts. The Holy Spirit is the central character in Acts, which could be titled "The Acts of the Holy Spirit." The Spirit is the One who added members to the church (9:31), guided church decisions (15:28), and directed missionary expansion (6:10; 13:2 f.).

The Pauline Epistles. The letters of Paul, however, provide the fullest revelation of the Spirit as the indwelling moral guide and sustainer of the Christian life. At conversion, the Holy Spirit brings new spiritual life to believers (2 Cor. 5:17) and begins to live within each Christian (1 Cor. 6:19-20). Fellowship with God and with believers is a gift of the Spirit (Rom. 8:14-17), who also distributes to Christians abilities for the common good of the body of Christ (1 Cor. 12). The fruit of the Spirit as listed by Paul are all ethical: love, joy, peace, patience, kindness, goodness, faithfulness, gentleness, and self-control (Gal. 5:22).

The Spirit also indwells the church and acts in and through the body of Christ to develop an ethical community (1 Cor. 3:16). The Christian life, in simplest terms, is walking in the Spirit (Rom. 8:4). "Recovery of the Spirit as the central moral force in the church and the individual is imperative. This would place Christian ethics in its true perspective. Only then will Christian ethics recover its radical theocentricity."[77]

For the last two chapters we have surveyed the place of the Bible in Christian ethics. By now you should realize ethics is a major concern of the Scriptures; in fact, biblical faith and ethics are so intertwined that it is impossible to separate the two. Although E. F. Scott may have exaggerated his point, he did stress the centrality of ethics in biblical religion: "The unchanging element in our religion has been its ethical teaching. Its doctrines have been differently understood in each generation; its institutions and ritual have assumed many forms and have given rise to countless divisions. But the ethical demands have never varied. They were set forth two thousand years ago, and in the interval the whole framework of man's life has been remodeled; but they are still valid, in practically their whole extent, for all sections of the church."[78]

FOR THOUGHT AND DISCUSSION

1. Compare the four approaches to Old Testament ethics with the four ways Christians approach the New Testament for ethics.
2. Explain the statement: "Old Testament ethics are incomplete."
3. Debate this proposition: "The Ten Commandments provide foundational moral principles for any society."
4. Discuss what message the eighth-century prophets might deliver to modern American society.
6. Explain the relationship between Jesus' ethics, the Law, the kingdom of God, and the Sermon on the Mount.
7. Discuss the relationship between Paul's theology and ethics.

CHAPTER FOUR

THE CHRISTIAN, THE CHURCH, AND THE WORLD

Simeon Stylites lived on top of a pillar for thirty-six years. Like other "pillar saints," he was escaping from the world. At first he tried living in a cave, but that was not remote enough, so he buried himself with only his head above the ground. Finally, east of Antioch he erected a pillar six feet high on which he sat. His fame spread and multitudes, including high officials, came to see this "athlete of God." When he died in 459, his pillar was sixty feet above the immoral and evil earth, from which he sought separation.[1]

How does a Christian relate to the world? Every generation of believers has struggled with that question. On one hand, the Bible warns, "Do not love the world or the things in the world" (1 John 2:15). On the other hand, Jesus calls His disciples to be "salt" and "light" in a dark and decaying world (Matt. 5:13-16). Typically we respond by saying, "We are to be *in* the world but not *of* the world." But exactly what this means is widely debated.

The people of God in the Old Testament felt threatened by the idolatrous and immoral practices of surrounding nations, so they built religious and social walls to keep evil out of Israel. Christians in the New Testament likewise faced a hostile environment—the Graeco-Roman world was socially degenerate, morally depraved, and religiously decadent. The challenge for disciples of Jesus was not just to survive; they were called to transform society (Rom. 12:2), and, indeed, they were accused of "turning the world upside down" (Acts 17:6).

In the beginning God created the world "very good" (Gen. 1:31). Immediately, however, sin infected the human race, and the entire created order was contaminated (Gen. 3). However, a day is coming when "creation itself will be set free from its bondage to decay" (Rom. 8:21).

In the meantime, what are Christians to do? How does the community of faith live in a tainted world without being corrupted by it? And more importantly, how do God's people join the Creator in redeeming the world from its fallen state?

At the beginning of our study we explored the origins of **Christian ethics,** noting the impact of Greek **philosophy** and other social influences upon Christian thought and morality. In the last two chapters our attention was centered on the central **authority** for Christian ethics, the Word of God. Now we approach the study of Christian ethics from another perspective—through the trifocal lens of church history, theology, and culture.

First we will walk through centuries of Christian tradition, observing how each generation confronted the moral challenges of that period, evaluating the responses with basic theological questions. In our brief overview of the social teachings of the Christian church, one major truth will emerge: how each generation of Christians relates to the world is a key factor in its ethic.[2]

In this chapter we shall also attempt to answer what H. Richard Niebuhr called "The Enduring Problem"—how the Christian judges between loyalties to Christ and loyalties to culture.[3] Cultural **values** are easily confused with religious values, which may result in cultural Christianity. Niebuhr warns that to worship culture is to absolutize the finite, "an aberration of faith as well as of reason."[4]

So our basic question is this: how do we view the world—as good or evil? Is God working in culture, or is culture the enemy of Christian values? Should Christians withdraw from society or work to transform society? Our response to these questions will ultimately determine our belief about our own capacities, our attitudes toward other people, and our sense of social obligation.

THE CHURCH AND THE WORLD

The history of Christianity can be written by tracing the effects of the church upon the world or the world upon the church.[5]

T. B. Maston contended that the nature of the church, as a divine-human institution, is a key factor in determining the relation of the church to society. The history of the church "is a record of a 'divine-human process.' It has both a this-worldly and an other-worldly aspect. It was and is divine in its origin and in its mission, but it cannot escape its human and worldly environment. . . . The proper blending and balancing of the human and divine elements of the church create for it some of its most difficult problems, and yet give to it its greatest influence and power."[6]

The Church Separated from the World

During the first three hundred years of Christian history, the basic movement of the church was withdrawal from the world. The attitude of early Christians toward society was separation, one of "renunciation of the world, and not world reform."[7] The church's message was one of judgment against the world, rather than redemption for the world.[8]

The early church began well, placing a high premium on moral purity. Baptismal candidates had to undergo long periods of instruction, and church discipline was rigorously enforced. Even pagan observers were attracted to this new "Way" (Acts 9:2), noticing how the followers of Jesus cared deeply for each other and for the helpless and the outcasts of society.

About the year 140, Aristides wrote an impressive work named *Apology*. Aristides defended Christianity on the basis of the moral character of Christians, which he testified was marked by freedom from false witness, covetousness, adultery, and unchastity. Christian women and men were known to be pure, honest, kind, truthful, hospitable, and generous.[9]

If the early church was attracting large numbers and transforming society, why did it so quickly withdraw from the world? One main reason was the unfriendly attitude of the Graeco-Roman culture toward the Christian movement, especially the growing oppression of all Christians. Jesus had warned that hatred and persecution would come to His followers (Matt. 10:16–23), which began with the imprisonment of the apostles (Acts 5:18), followed by the stoning of Stephen (Acts 7:58) and a great persecution of the church at Jerusalem (Acts 8:1–3).

This unfriendly attitude of the world, particularly of the Roman state, continued throughout the first three Christian centuries. The periods of the most severe persecutions were those during the reigns of Nero (64), Domitian (95), Decius (249), and Diocletian (303). The last period of persecution continued until about 311.[10]

A second factor that influenced the early church to separate from the world was the moral condition of Graeco-Roman society. The world into which the church was born and nurtured through infancy was, by New Testament standards, very evil. The prevailing tone of Roman society was one of vicious immorality, characterized by the worship of wealth and luxury, the search for new pleasures, the cheapening of life involved in the public games and gladiatorial shows, the vanishing of purity and chastity, and the feeling of moral helplessness.[11] Symptomatic of the pervasive moral corruption of society were the common practices of infanticide, sexual perversion, religious prostitution, widespread suicide, and slavery. One authority estimated that in the Roman Empire of the first century were 60 million slaves, with 20 million in Italy alone and 650,000 in Rome.[12]

A third reason early Christians separated from the world was the conviction that Christ would soon return and judge the world and all worldly powers. This eschatological hope of Christ's imminent return diminished any concern for the world order—it was soon to be destroyed, so why try to improve it?

Another factor that influenced Christian withdrawal was the increasing numbers of converts from among the lower social and economic classes. Most early Christians were the disinherited of society, who had no stake in the existing order and no power to effect any change in the social structure.

Some evidence also exists that certain aspects of Greek philosophy, namely the influence of **gnostic asceticism** (which reached its apex in the second century), influenced early Christians to separate from the world.[13] Hellenistic heresies about the evil nature of physical existence were first confronted in the late New Testament writings of Paul (1 Tim. 1:3ff) and John (1 John 1:3ff.). Gnostic dualism and so-called "Christian Platonists" taught the way of salvation was escape from the evil material world. This influence explains many world-renouncing tendencies in Christianity, such as celibacy, social passivity, and mysticism.

As Christians sought escape from a social environment both corrupt and miserable, the church recoiled into an increasing authoritarianism. A firm discipline of moral instruction was required of all catechumens, to protect new believers from backsliding. A strict moral code developed alongside the creed, which included an elaborate penitential system and the threat of excommunication. The end result of this process was the growing tendency to moralize and legalize the gospel. Although the intent was sound, to fight the moral infection of pagan society and the gnostic ethical heresy, the ultimate consequence was the obscuring of the gospel of grace.[14]

This general rejection strategy does not mean the church had no influence on the world. Quite the contrary, for the spread of Christianity throughout the civilized world precipitated a widespread religious revival. Historians note a certain glow of ethical enthusiasm began to spread throughout the Empire during the second century. One consequence of this "spiritual awakening" was the infiltration of the higher ranks of society by the gospel. Increasing moral and social concern led to many converts among the wealthy and educated. Pliny reported that many "of all ranks" were being converted, and Tertullian warned the persecuting proconsul of Carthage that he would find "men of your own order, and noble ladies, and all the leading persons of the city" brought before him.[15] The historian C. J. Cadoux noted, "The achievements of the early Church can defy comparison with those of any other moral or religious movement known to history."[16]

The conflict between the church and the world continued with varying but generally diminishing intensity during the first three Christian centuries. As the church entered the last half of this period, Christians faced unprecedented ethical problems arising from diverse social pressures. The methods of ethical debate and ethical deliberation illuminate the attempts of the earliest Christians to utilize scriptural guidance, a limited Christian tradition, and inward impulses to discover the mind of Christ upon unexplored issues.[17]

Church historian R. E. O. White dedicates an entire chapter to the discussion of five major ethical issues confronting the early church: wealth, slavery, the state, military service, and **capital punishment.**[18] Property, wrote Troeltsch, was the first social problem with which the church had to deal.[19] The early church fathers were suspicious of wealth and warned against the danger of riches. Clement of Alexandria gave the fullest treatment of economics in his homily "The Rich Man's Salvation," which Beach claimed was an effort to calm the fears of well-to-do Christians.[20] Most agree with White that "all in all, the early church dealt realistically, but also generously, with the issue of wealth in Christian hands, when changed circumstances called for revised attitudes. . . . Subsequent generations have not added greatly to the insights then attained."[21]

Though the treatment of slaves varied widely, the institution of slavery was an important economic fact of life in the Roman world. As increasing numbers of slaves became believers, Christians were instructed to treat them as equals, brothers and sisters in spirit. Within her own community the church neutralized the slave relationship. Soon the manumission of slaves became a solemn act of thanksgiving to God by wealthy converts.[22] Compassion, New Testament appeals, and the principle of equality through Christ influenced the church's judgment against slavery, but the early church was unable to apply this ethic to the society at large.

Because of intermittent persecution, the church's attitude toward the state vascillated between Pauline support (Rom. 13) and Johannine resistance (Rev. 13). As Christians began to infiltrate the higher ranks of society, a new historical and political self-consciousness emerged. With enthusiastic loyalty toward government, Tertullian outdoes Paul in asking Christians to pray for the Roman emperor and respect him as chosen of the Lord,[23] a far cry from the attitude of the Apocalypse. The growing influence of the church within society opened the door of temptation for Christians with political ambition and a lust for power, as well as preparing the way for **Constantinianism**.

The **ethics** of military service has been a constant tension from the earliest years of Christianity. Along with exhortations for peaceableness, early writers gave no evidence that Christians served in the Roman army before the second century. Origen, for example, did not deny Celsus's rebuke of Christians being unwilling to serve.[24] By 172, the Twelfth Legion had Christians in its ranks, but Tertullian was certain no convert would voluntarily enlist in the Roman army, which Bainton contends "is a witness to the practice which he condemns."[25] The pacifist tone of the first two centuries can partly be accounted for by the potential conflict of loyalties military service would demand: paying homage to Caesar as a god, the coercive power of the state to enforce order, and the guilt of bloodshed. It seems unimaginable that an early ethical tradition so passionately argued would be adjusted by Ambrose in the fourth century to accept the need for war (if just), reserving **pacifism** for priests and the pious.[26]

The issue of capital punishment arose in connection with officership in the army, which Tertullian felt was another reason against military service. The early church opposed putting a person to death, even one justly convicted of a capital crime. After the state's recognition of the church, Ambrose was embarrassed by the appointment of Christian judges because of his aversion to capital punishment. In time, the church came to accept the death penalty as necessary for social order and even condoned the punishment for certain heretics.[27]

The World Accepted by the Church

The fourth century ushered a new era into Christian history, as the church gradually accepted the world. With the ascension of Constantine to the throne of Rome in 323, Christianity was legitimized as the state-subsidized religion. The power of the state was used to protect and promote the church. In return, the church supported the state and gave official approval to Roman culture.[28]

In addition to Constantine's patronage, a number of other factors influenced this change of attitude. As the church infiltrated society, persecution decreased, the moral climate of society improved, Christians moved upward socially, the church lost its hope of the early return of the Lord, and second and third generation believers lacked the devotion of their ancestors. These trends influenced the church to make peace with the world and accept its sponsorship.

However, some Christians refused to accept this compromise. They became the sectarians who opposed "worldliness" and maintained a separation from society that often resulted in persecution from both church and state. The sectarians believed they alone maintained original Christianity.

With recognition as the official religion of Rome, established Christianity believed faith had finally triumphed. Instead of executing Christians for not worshiping him, the emperor now used state funds to build churches and sponsor theological conferences. The state also appointed bishops and other church officials, promoting an ecclesiastical hierarchy that closely resembled the hierarchy of the Roman Empire. This conquest was not without cost to church and state.

How did this change impact Christian ethics? Philip Yancey laments, "Ever since Constantine, the church has faced the temptation of becoming the 'morals police' of society. The Catholic Church in the Middle Ages, Calvin's Geneva, Cromwell's England, Winthrop's New England, the Russian Orthodox Church—each of these has attempted to legitimize a form of Christian morality, and each has in its own way found it hard to communicate grace."[29]

As organized Christianity found itself identified with the state, the church moved toward becoming a worldly power. At first the state was in control, but the next one thousand years brought a mounting struggle for dominance between these two institutions. In order to conquer and control both the state and the world, the church adopted worldly methods. Enlisting civil power, the state-sponsored religion made Christian discipleship a matter of civil duty. The church's policy of extension led to wholesale "conversions" and the "promiscuous baptism of hundreds of thousands."[30] Swamped with new "converts" from the pagan world, the church deliberately made religious and moral compromises with pagan rites, ceremonies, and customs.[31]

The Church As a World Power

In the millennium between 400 and 1500, the church increasingly became a dominant world power, as the line between the church and the world was erased. "The Church made alliance with a World which became Christian in name, but only in name."[32] Most historians would agree that in becoming a worldly power, the church lost much of its spiritual power.[33]

Two movements significant for Christian ethics—monasticism and scholasticism—developed during the medieval period. Ascetic monasticism, with its twin sister mysticism, was basically world renouncing. "The *summum bonum* of the monk was spiritual perfection in the contemplation and love of God, to be achieved by the renunciation of the world and the uncompromising imitation of Christ."[34] The influence of monasticism lay not so much in this ideal as in the method of attaining this goal. For the monk, three worldly barriers prevented a vision of God: possessions, the flesh, and self-will. The remedy took form in the specific disciplines of poverty, chastity, and obedience. Although most Protestants would consider monasticism as an escapism falsely based on an unhealthy dualism, it must be admitted that the mystics rightly stressed that morality begins in the heart and the first ethical task is self-conquest. Though heroic in ideal, monastic ethics suffered two serious shortcomings: in reality the ideal was seldom practiced, and monasticism tended toward an idolatry that substituted the way to the vision of God for God.[35]

Scholasticism reached its zenith during the time of its greatest proponent, Thomas Aquinas (1225-74). The unique achievement of Aquinas was his synthesis of Aristotelian philosophy and Christian theology, revealed best in his voluminous work, *Summa*

Theologica.[36] Using human rationality to discover internal **principles** of morality and external constraints in the structure of law, Thomas (agreeing with Aristotle) identified the supreme end of humanity as *eudaimonia*, usually translated "happiness." For Aquinas, the chief constituent of happiness was neither within humans nor in the world, but found in God alone, in a "vision of the Divine Essence."[37]

Despite the significant place of Aquinas in Roman Catholic ethics, most scholars find his teaching too academic, too dependent on Aristotelian logic, and too incongruent with modern thought and social realities. Thomist teachings on the family, sex, and contraception, for example, were determined exclusively by **natural law**. Though his system seemed to be the final word for Christian ethical development, Christian understanding eventually "departed from the whole medieval world-view, and sought other theological bases for the concept of the good life."[38]

Twelve centuries of accommodation and adjustment also led to a dramatic development in theology and ethics. Gradually the very definition of "Christian" changed, as sacramentalism (salvation through baptism and the Lord's Supper), sacerdotalism (the bishop controlled the rites of salvation), and the idea of Christendom (the church as a political-geographic entity) became the **norm**. "The results of this particular combination of religion and ethics were disastrous for the Christian faith."[39]

Attempts at Reform

The unified cultural vision of late medieval Christianity was shattered by several turbulent events. The Crusades opened new worlds for explorers and traders, which in turn increased commercial activity and greater economic freedom. The intellectualism stimulated by Thomas supported the independence of reason, the recovery of classical culture, and the growth of humanism. Feudal principalities merged into larger nation-states, whose rulers were increasingly independent. By the sixteenth century, the unity of the Catholic Church fractured under the weight of moral corruption and an unwillingness to respond to reform movements.[40]

Like a volcanic earthquake, the Protestant Reformation broke the medieval world apart and forever changed the political and religious map of Europe. While the Reformation appeared to be a doctrinal and ecclesiastical revolution, it also reestablished and preserved vital moral themes of the early church. Asceticism and clerical celibacy were repudiated. The recovery of the view that every Christian's work was a calling, a "station" assigned by God, deeply impacted social ideas and institutions.

Three kinds of reforms appeared: Magisterial, Roman Catholic, and Radical.[41] Martin Luther and John Calvin represent **Magisterial Reform,** promoting changes that were largely theological. What they did not change was the way the church related to the world, for they continued to believe that the magistrate (power of the state) should defend and protect the church, and the church should keep certain citizenship records for the state (birth, marriage, and death records).

Luther's division of the world into "two kingdoms" along with his pessimistic view of human nature, led his followers to be socially passive. On the other hand, Calvin sent his disciples into the world to create a sanctified society to God's glory.

The Roman Catholic Church attempted its own counterreform. Although a few of its moral abuses were corrected, the main thrust seemed to be an attempt to consolidate its position, especially the power of the pope.

A third reform has been termed a Radical Reform movement by those in the "believers' church," mainly small groups of Anabaptists and Mennonites. The idea of Christendom was repugnant to these Christians, who preached personal faith, voluntary discipleship, and believer's baptism. True faith could not be coerced or legalized—church and state should be separate. **Radical Reformers** were often persecuted by the state church, which forced many to migrate westward to North and South America. English and American Baptists had strong ties with these nonconformist believers, and Baptists often were persecuted alongside of them.

Since the Reformation of the sixteenth century, other Christian groups have emerged. Mainline denominations, like the Methodist Church, generally forged some type of accommodation with the world. Many churches were involved in the Social Gospel Movement early in the twentieth century, which focused on solving social problems by establishing the reign of God over society.

In the early 1900s, various Holiness and Fundamentalist groups appeared in reaction to "**Modernism**" in the churches. For them "worldliness" was not so much a political force as a description of liberal theology and immoral activities. At the moment, television has spawned the "electronic church," which has closely aligned with culture, using mass marketing to solicit large sums of money and exert significant political influence.[42]

T. B. Maston concluded that "organized Christianity tends to go through a regular cycle in its relation to the world. There is a period of withdrawal for revival and renewal, followed by a gradual adaptation to the world, which means an infiltration by the world. The world so completely permeates and dominates the church that another period of withdrawal from the world for renewal is necessary."[43]

CHRIST AND CULTURE

The interaction of the church with the world has been the basis of much theological debate and the occasion for many historical movements. Perhaps no one has better portrayed the struggle of Christianity to relate to society than H. Richard Niebuhr in his classic work, *Christ and Culture*.[44] The Yale Divinity School professor proposed a question every generation of Christians must answer. In the midst of proximate loyalties in every society (family, state, church), how does the Christian judge between loyalty to Christ and the many loyalties of culture?

Utilizing Ernst Troeltsch's basic two-volume social history of Christianity as a springboard, Niebuhr portrayed five patterns of relationships between culture (civilization) and Christianity. The first two he called "radical answers," namely the stance of Christ *against* culture and the Christ *of* culture approach. Niebuhr rejected both of these extreme positions for basic theological reasons. The Yale professor preferred the strategies of the "Church of the Center," which he outlined in three categories: Christ *above* culture, Christ and culture in *paradox*, and Christ the *transformer* of culture. The first is a synthesist approach, the second a dualistic method, and the third a conversionist strategy.

Niebuhr intended that every Christian ask, "If Christ has captured my life, how do I adjudicate between my loyalty to Christ and my cultural loyalties?" The real debate over Christ and culture occurs within the church, where all believe in the same Christ, but all have different answers to the church-world question.

Every generation struggles with this "enduring problem." The Christian ideal is to sustain integrity (resist identification with culture) while also upholding intelligibility (remain relative to culture). Niebuhr's own proposal provides a way for each generation to maintain continuity within the Christian tradition.

Scholars of H. Richard Niebuhr have systematized five theological motifs that Niebuhr used as his method for evaluating the major church-world strategies.[45] Niebuhr also intended that the contemporary church use these motifs to analyze present approaches to the Christ and culture issue.

Five Theological Motifs for Church-World Patterns

Each category poses key theological questions. These questions help us evaluate the grounds upon which each church-world strategy stands.

Motif 1: Reason and Revelation. The question raised by the first motif is, "What are the sources of knowledge that are reliable for Christian ethics, and how are they related?" This concept focuses upon two sources of authority, the revelation of God and human reason.

Motif 2: Sin/Evil and Good. The next theological category inquires, "Where is sin/evil located, how extensive is it, and how does sin/evil relate to the powers of goodness?" This examination seeks to identify where sin resides, how powerful it is, and how the forces of good will triumph over evil.

Motif 3: Law and Gospel. Another basic question for the typical responses to the church-world tension is, "What is the relation of the 'Good News' of the gospel to the demands of life?" To put it another way, "Are the issues of life simply a matter of right and wrong, or do circumstances affect morality?"

Motif 4: Nature and Grace. A knotty problem is raised by this category, namely the essence of God's relationship to the material world. The question might be stated, "What is the relation of God—the Creator of nature, Governor of history, and Redeemer of the world—to nature and to culture?"

Motif 5: Church and World. The final theological motif poses this query: "How is the Christian community related to the people and the institutions in the world?"

Having defined the theological motifs, it is now time to review the typical ways the church has responded to the world. Niebuhr acknowledged considerable overlapping of these "types" and the difficulty of classification. Nevertheless, he catalogued five major stances. Although some strategies have predominated during certain periods of church history, each approach has existed in every generation, including our own. Relying on Niebuhr's seminal outline, let us therefore review the five main patterns and evaluate each one with the motifs.

Christ against Culture

One of the first responses of the Christian faith to society was a radical antagonism between the church and a corrupt world.[46] The natural tendency of sectarian groups that condemned culture was to reject the world by withdrawing from it. "This withdrawal has to be a matter of degree because they [sectarians] cannot avoid some contact with the world while they live in the world."[47]

Mainly due to persecution from an immoral and idolatrous society, early Christians separated themselves from Roman culture. Tertullian was "one of the foremost illustrations of the anticultural movement to be found in the history of the church."[48] The great North African theologian directed Christians to shun political life, avoid military service, trade only as necessary, abhor philosophy, and abstain from the corruption of the arts and the theatre.[49]

A modern representative of this position was Leo Tolstoy, who indicted every phase of culture. The Russian novelist believed he was interpreting the gospel faithfully when he taught that evil resided in human society: in the state, the church, economic systems, the arts, science, and philosophy. Ironically, Tolstoy condemned the writing of fiction, though many consider him the greatest modern novelist.

Religious groups were formed to adopt the anticultural strategy, beginning with the medieval monastics. Smaller sectarian bodies such as the Anabaptists, the Mennonites, the Quakers, and the Amish have rejected some forms of culture that they deem evil.

Though it may seem so, the "Against" position is not entirely negative in its emphasis. To their credit, the group normally displays a deep love for Jesus Christ and the community of faith. Adherents point out that only by withdrawal from an evil world can the church display the true Christian ideal. A contemporary ethicist, Stanley Hauerwas, has resurrected the Anabaptist vision of the "alien" status of Christians in the world. The narrative theologian contends the church is to be "a colony, an island of one culture in the middle of another."[50]

A fair appraisal of this method recognizes a valid place for some separation from sin and evil in the world, which both John and Paul taught (1 John 2:15; 2 Cor. 6:17). As was true in Jesus' life (Mark 6:45–47), withdrawal is often needed for personal renewal and deepened fellowship with God. In addition, Christian rejections of certain institutions of society "have maintained the distinction between Christ and Caesar, between revelation and reason, between God's will and man's."[51]

While the views of separationists must be respected, their isolationist attitude is not the spirit of original Christianity. Jesus challenged His disciples to be positive influences in a morally dark society (Matt. 5:13–14).

The sectarian rejection of culture is based on several faulty beliefs. For them, *revelation* is the sole source of knowledge; *reason* is worthless. Tertullian's famous observation was, "What has Jerusalem to do with Athens?"[52] For Tertullian, Tolstoy, and many Protestant sectarians, human reason is inadequate, erroneous, and deceptive.[53]

A second theological weakness of the "Against" position is the belief that *sin/evil* abounds in culture and the Christian community seems exempt from the effects of sin. Since Christians have passed out of darkness into light, they have separated themselves into a holy community free from corruption. Ascetic practices easily arose from this radical view that temptation to sin came from culture, not human nature. In addition, the view that *good* was reserved for the Christian colony stimulated a negative and passive view toward redeeming society.

Closely connected is the question about *law and gospel.* Opponents of the "Against" response often accuse its representatives of **legalism** and neglect of the gospel of grace. In emphasizing that Christianity is a new law for a select community, separatists often forget the gospel is for all humanity.[54] Leanings toward legalism are obvious in Tertullian, Tolstoy, monastics, and Protestant sectarians.

The most difficult problem raised by the Christ-against-culture position is that posed by *nature and grace.* If the dominant tendencies in culture do not reflect God's control but oppose God's redemptive activity, then how can God be Creator of the world and the Governor of history? The temptation of the radical approach is to convert their ethical dualism into a divided view of reality, separating the world into a material realm governed by evil and a spiritual realm guided by God.[55] If God's relation to the natural world is lost, the Jesus of history may also be abandoned for a spiritual principle.[56]

By now it is obvious that the "Against" group views itself as an alternative society; the *church* is counterculture, opposing the dominant tendencies of the *world.* From Tertullian to Tolstoy, from the Anabaptists to the Amish, the sectarian radicals rejected culture, withdrew from society, and established a community in which the new life of holiness could be lived. The loss of interaction with the world prevents this type from impacting and influencing society with the gospel of Christ.

Christ of Culture

A second type is at the opposite extreme, the Christ of culture strategy.[57] "It depicts Christian ethics as little more than an expression of the highest values generally shared in a world that is capable of goodness and reason in its common life."[58] Early Christian Gnostics and modern cultural Protestants selectively identified certain aspects of culture with Christ. For them culture interprets Christ; the best insights of civilization harmonize with God's revelation.

Liberal theologian Albrecht Ritschl is generally considered the best modern example of what Niebuhr called "Culture-Protestantism."[59] Other examples are the Eastern Orthodox churches, which tend toward a mystical identity of church and world, and the Social Gospel Movement, which associated the Christian ideal with particular political and economic changes.

Opponents of this position should not overlook certain values in the "acculturation of Jesus Christ."[60] Christianity attracted many followers when its proponents harmonized the gospel with the moral and religious philosophy of the leading teachers. As the Christian faith became intelligible to the world and identified with cultural loyalties, society was missionized.

In order to be relevant, a certain degree of identification with society by the church is inevitable. However, as a major Christian approach, the Christ-of-culture type is self-defeating. Proponents of this response to the world have usually so diluted the Christian ideal that they have lost the power to challenge and influence the world toward Christian values. In addition, the identity of Jesus is distorted. The Christ of culture becomes a chameleon, "a wise man, a philosopher, now a monk, now a reformer, now a democrat, and again a king."[61]

The application of the five theological motifs reveals other weaknesses. The "Of" approach enthrones *reason* over *revelation*. Cultural Christianity proposes that the best insights of culture, such as science and philosophy, harmonize with revelation. Through selective identification of certain aspects of culture, Christ is identified—for Hellenists Jesus is like Socrates, for Indians the deaths of Jesus and Ghandi are similar.

For this Christ-of-culture type, *sin* is located in an "ethically irrational" nature and in certain bad social institutions. However, the best of culture is exempt from the effects of sin; Christ is identified with what culture conceives to be its best ideals, its noblest aspirations, and its finest science and philosophy.

Like the radical Christians, the identification approach collapses the *gospel* into the *law,* but it is the law of culture. By obeying the laws of God and of reason, humans can achieve the **kingdom of God** in society—reliance upon grace is demeaning and discouraging.

What is the *nature* of God's relation to the world? The cultural Christians believe God's redemptive work in the world fulfills the best tendencies in culture. Scientific discoveries that eradicate disease and eliminate evil are evidences of God's governance. Therefore, the *church* cooperates with the institutions of the *world,* for the community of Christians has a common cause with the best tendencies of culture.

Niebuhr's conclusion is that both of these extreme positions should be rejected on theological grounds. The rejection strategy and the identification strategy both separate nature from culture, declaring God is totally absent or totally present in each. Both of these approaches view the gospel as a new law, leading to legalism in one and humanism in the other. The first type moves only toward Christ; the second group only toward culture.

Niebuhr makes clear that he prefers the position of the "Church of the Center," which works to change society by properly relating Christ and culture. Centrist movements maintain basic theological convictions that God is Creator, Governor, and Redeemer; that sin is radical and universal; that the law will not save; that grace takes precedence; and that reason, though affected by sin, is not opposed to revelation. Niebuhr discerns three distinguishable families among the accommodation strategies: the synthesists, who relate the natural to the supernatural world; the dualists, who divide the world into the secular and the sacred; and the conversionists, who transform the world to conform to the will of God.

Christ above Culture

The first accommodation strategy, one generally followed by the Roman Catholic Church, is a synthesist response that affirms both the world and faith.[62] Although it gives superior value to Christ over culture, the "Above" response does draw some information and revelation from culture. For the Roman church, the natural world and the supernatural world are closely related—the natural provides a foundation upon which the church builds a supernatural structure.

Clement of Alexandria, probably the first great representative of this type, sought to build a bridge between Christianity and philosophy, often equating Christian ethics with the **etiquette** taught in **Stoic** handbooks.[63] The scholastic Thomas Aquinas best illustrates the "Above" response. Thomas accepted the ethics of Aristotle (discovered through natural law) almost entirely. Upon this natural foundation of moral and intellectual **virtues,** Aquinas developed a superstructure of theological virtues—faith, hope, and love. Aquinas synthesized the ethics of culture with the ethics of the gospel, combining "into one system of divine demands and promises the requirements cultural reason discerned and those which Jesus uttered."[64]

Another aspect of this position obvious in Roman Catholicism is the twofold approach to the Christian life. Two levels of **morality** are upheld: one for average Christians in ordinary life, and a higher level maintained by the clergy, particularly those committed to the monastic life.[65]

The application of the five theological motifs to the "Christ above Culture" strategy may be summarized in this way. On the level of human wisdom, common sense and experience reveal what a person should do; *revelation* goes beyond and fulfills the valid insights of *reason*. Likewise, redeeming *grace* goes beyond and fulfills *nature* and the best contributions of culture. Although *sin* disorients nature and culture, it does not radically infect reason. *Law* is understood as a form of the *gospel*; divine law goes beyond and fulfills the best of human laws. The *church*, therefore, builds upon and completes society's best achievements.

The synthesist approach contains both strengths and weaknesses. On the positive side, most Christians agree with the "proclamation that the God who is to rule now rules and has ruled, that His rule is established in the nature of things, and that man must build on the established foundations."[66] This attitude promotes the cooperation of Christians with nonbelievers in society, since the Savior and the Creator are one. Another advantage of this type is the unswerving witness of the synthesist that the gospel requires more than rational knowledge alone and willing obedience to the laws of nature.

Acknowledging these contributions, it is important also to recognize inherent errors in this response. The effort to bring Christ and culture into one system of thought tends to absolutize the relative by equating a cultural view of God's law in creation with law itself. The resulting hierarchical view of the natural order is historical, identifying Christ with medieval culture.

Another criticism leveled against this approach is the problem of a dual ethic, which distinguishes grades of Christian perfection, dividing Christians into two groups who obey higher and lower laws. The major objection to the synthesists' response to culture is their failure to face up to the radical evil present in all human enterprise, including culture. This objection is effectively raised by the dualists, whom we now consider.

Christ and Culture in Paradox

Another accommodationist strategy is the dualistic conviction that the Christian is a citizen of two worlds.[67] Life is divided into the secular and the sacred, the temporal and the eternal, the kingdom of this world and the kingdom of God.

> [T]he fundamental issue in life is not the one which radical Christians face as they draw the line between Christian community and pagan world. Neither is it the issue which cultural Christianity discerns as it sees man everywhere in conflict with nature and locates Christ on the side of the spiritual forces of culture. Yet, like both of these and unlike the synthesist in his more irenic and developing world, the dualist lives in conflict, and in the presence of one great issue. That conflict is between God and man.[68]

The dualist idea of a twofold citizenship is applied specifically to church-state relations. The Christian lives in two kingdoms—the state has final authority in secular matters, the church in religious matters. The disciple of Jesus lives in paradoxical tension between two authorities who do not agree, yet both must be obeyed.

Martin Luther is considered the major historical example of this accommodation strategy. In defending his pamphlet written against the peasants, Luther wrote, "There are two kingdoms, one the kingdom of God, the other the kingdom of the world. . . . Now he who would confuse these two kingdoms—as our false fanatics do—would put wrath into God's kingdom and mercy into the world's kingdom; and that is the same as putting the devil in heaven and God in hell."[69] After noting Luther's "double attitude" toward all areas of life, Niebuhr suggested the German reformer had "divided life into compartments, or taught that the Christian right hand should not know what a man's worldly left hand was doing."[70]

Proponents of the dualistic motif point out the strategy mirrors the actual struggles of the Christian, who must act responsibly in a fallen world. Although sin is prevalent, the disciple of Christ cannot withdraw from the world but must mitigate its evil by creating space within which the power of Christ can work.

In addition, dualists are commended for upholding the dynamic nature of God, humanity, grace, and sin. Luther's own spiritual pilgrimage illustrates the conclusion of the "Paradox" position that Christ is both Lawgiver and Savior. As Lawgiver, Christ convicts all persons of their sinfulness; as Savior, Christ creates in those freed from self-love a faith in God that produces the love of neighbor.

Accompanying these virtues of dualism has been an equal number of **vices.** The two most frequently voiced charges are that dualism leads to antinomianism and cultural conservatism.[71] The antinomian tendency results from a relativization of all laws of society. The rules of civilized living are human attempts to maintain order and restrain evil—divine judgment has no place over human laws. Luther and other dualists would never encourage subcultural behavior, yet they must accept some responsibility for a rationale that tempts toward antinomianism.

Both Paul and Luther have been labeled cultural conservatives. Though deeply concerned about changing the religious institutions of their day, the two seemed content to let the state and economic life go unchallenged on issues like slavery and social stratification. If the laws of state are viewed "as restraining forces, dykes against sin, preventers of anarchy, rather than as positive agencies through which men in social union render positive service to neighbors,"[72] then dualists will have little reason to change a dying world.

An analysis of the "Paradox" strategy using the five theological motifs further illustrates the position's distinction between a corrupt, fallen world and the pure gospel. For the dualists, *revelation* is valid in the spiritual realm; *reason* is valid in the secular world. The Bible reveals the way of salvation but not how to build bridges or political systems. Also *sin* is very powerful, infecting both nature and culture. Society is unable to pursue the *good;* it can only restrain *evil.* For Lutherans, *law* and *gospel* are divided. In the temporal realm law reigns; forgiveness is the rule and end of the law in the spiritual realm. As Redeemer, the God of *grace* forgives sin in the spiritual kingdom; as Governor, the God of *nature* and nature's laws restrains evil in the world. Thus for the dualists, the *church* and *world* are dialectically related.

Christ the Transformer of Culture

The preferred approach discussed by Niebuhr is the conversionist answer to the problem of Christ and culture,[73] one which the author claims stands in "the great central tradition of the church."[74] The conversionist strategy would neither reject the world nor identify the Christian ethic with culture. The transformationist works to reconstruct the world into conformity to the will of God, from the conviction that the claims of Christ extend to all of life and society.

Like the synthesists and dualists, the conversionists see Christ as Redeemer more than lawgiver and rely on God more than human resources. What distinguishes conversionists from dualists is their more hopeful attitude toward culture, based on a positive view of creation, a realistic view of sin, and a promising view of God's work in history.

The conversionist motif appears in the New Testament in the fourth Gospel and in the first letter of John, where the apostle affirms the goodness of God, the perversity of humanity, and hope for the spiritual transformation of the world. Among Christian thinkers, Augustine is generally believed to be the theologian of cultural transformation by Christ.[75] Other representatives of this strategy are John Calvin and some leaders of the Great Awakenings (1726–1810) and the Social Gospel Movement.

To transform the world into the likeness of the Christian ideal is the goal of the conversionist, although the definition of that community may vary. The important thing, however, is the conviction that every phase of the world's life can be influenced and changed toward God's will. No part of culture is outside the sovereignty of God.

However, reality warns the conversionist that total transformation is impossible in history. Those who are optimistic about social change may surrender to disillusionment and despair when hopes go unrealized. Yet the failure to achieve Christian ideals in society must never be attributed to God or to the Christian faith—it is a failure due to human limitations.

Niebuhr provided little critique of this position. A fair evaluation of the "Transformation" strategy finds much to commend. For the conversionists, *revelation* transforms or reorients *reason*. Although *sin* has corrupted *nature* and culture, redeeming *grace* can transform both of these worlds, as well as reorient the human will toward *good*. The *gospel* of grace completely transforms *law*, so that law becomes a form of the gospel. The *church* may be the realm of the conscious acknowledgment of God's sovereignty, but the reality of God's rule should also be seen in the *world*.

T. B. Maston proposed an additional approach as a possible accommodation strategy, which he described as a refinement of H. Richard Niebuhr's "Transformationist" type.[76] John Bennett lists William Temple, Reinhold Niebuhr, and Emil Brunner as examples of this strategy, which seeks to balance "the relevance of Christian ethics to action and emphasis upon the transcendence of Christianity and upon the sin of man. . . . The doctrine of sin becomes a reason for supporting social policies based upon the radical criticism of the *status quo*, and the transcendence of Christianity provides a perspective from which these policies are kept under criticism."[77]

Reinhold Niebuhr, for example, makes a distinction between private and public morality.[78] His ethics of realism promotes the idea of choosing the "lesser of two evils," especially in social policy, where groups are less ethical than individuals. This approach asserts that the very best Christians can achieve in public policy are "middle axioms," provisional definitions of behavior required of Christians under given circumstances.[79]

Commenting on the constructive role of "tension" in this adaptation, Maston concluded:

> The tension between the church and the world should not become so great that the church would lose all opportunity to minister to the world. . . . The individual or the group, church or otherwise, that serves most effectively the world and the people of the world must progressively seek to move it and them toward the Christian ideal. This means that the Christian ideal for the individual and for the world is never static; it is always dynamic, always in movement. As we move toward it, it moves ahead of us.[80]

H. Richard Niebuhr believed that each of the five types represents a valid aspect of Christian understanding, though he clearly regarded the last three as most authentic and preferred the fifth type. These five historic types are also contemporary strategies, followed to some degree by various Christians today.

As disciples of Jesus, we continue to struggle with the basic church-world question, "How do I maintain my loyalty to Christ in relation to cultural loyalties?" The major answers proposed by Christian tradition, along with the tests of Christian theology, should assist us in resolving that dilemma. The Christian must guard against a negative withdrawal from the world and a utopian identification of the gospel with culture. The desire to live in the world without being corrupted by culture requires some measure of accommodation. To truly transform the world toward God's ideal will produce tension, but it is the constructive tension that moves the relevant toward the transcendant and the human toward the divine.

FOR THOUGHT AND DISCUSSION

1. Why did the early church renounce the world rather than attempt to reform it?
2. Evaluate the conclusions reached by the early Christian community concerning the "unprecedented ethical problems" they faced in the second and third centuries.
3. What effect did the legitimization of Christianity by the Roman state after 323 have upon Christian ethics?
4. Using the five major responses of the church to culture, determine which one(s) apply to your denomination today.
5. Give your personal answer to Niebuhr's basic question: "How do I relate Christ to culture?" Evaluate your answer by using the five theological motifs.

CHAPTER FIVE

MORAL DECISION MAKING

Martin Marty tells the story of a nineteenth-century American who tried to explain why he had been tarred and feathered in a small town. The hapless fellow related to interviewers that the community had put him to the test on the Monroe Doctrine: "I told them that I loved the Monroe Doctrine. I lived by the Monroe Doctrine. I said that I would die for the Monroe Doctrine. I just told them I did not know what the Monroe Doctrine was!"[1] Although at first he seemed to believe right and talk right, this unfortunate fellow did not convince his audience in the end that he would "do right."

The Christian faith is more than believing and talking; it involves right doing. To the earliest Christians the apostle James wrote, "But be doers of the word, and not merely hearers" (1:22). Jesus also stressed doing right in the Sermon on the Mount: "Everyone then who hears these words of mine and acts on them will be like a wise man who built his house on rock" (Matt. 7:24).

At the heart of "doing" **ethics** is moral decision making. Everyone makes decisions. Some are simple everyday choices, like what food to eat or what clothes to wear. Other decisions are more serious and may even put us in danger of being tarred and feathered. Among the most complex decisions we face are those moral dilemmas that involve life and death.

During the delivery of his second child, a friend of mine faced such a choice. The doctor came to tell him his baby was lodged in the birth canal. The obstetrician had two choices, neither of which was ideal. The doctor could save the baby, but the hemorrhaging caused by the operation would endanger the mother's life. Or the infant could be extracted in a way that protected the mother, but it probably would cause the death of the newborn child. "What do you want us to do?" asked the physician. After several anguishing minutes, the father replied, "I only have one wife, so please make sure she is safe."

To live in this world requires making decisions, often as difficult as the one my friend faced. No one can evade the responsibility. But often we wonder, *Did I do the right thing?* Sooner or later, most of us realize we have made some mistakes.

How do we know what is right and what is wrong? And once we know what is right, how do we have the courage to act? Is there a reliable method for Christian decision making? Most of us want a simple formula for discerning the ethical way, but doing the right thing usually requires more than that.

One of the primary goals of our study of **Christian ethics** is to develop a trustworthy style for making moral judgments. If (as we have stated before) we are concerned with both the discipline and the practice of ethics, then learning how to analyze our decisions and to make wise choices is central to our purpose.

In these opening chapters we have explored several foundational aspects of Christian ethics: philosophical and historical origins, the role of biblical **authority,** the ethical teachings of the Old and New Testaments, and the historical relation between the church and the world. Now our task is to use these insights as a basis for developing a Christian strategy of moral decision making.

We begin by analyzing some twentieth-century approaches to moral judgments in light of their historical and theological backgrounds. This appraisal has two purposes: first, to reveal the significance of contemporary Christian movements upon ethical methodologies; and second, to understand the influence of each person's spiritual heritage upon ethical decision making.

Morality is not a hit-or-miss game. Nor is there a tried-and-true formula that will work every time. The ultimate aim of this chapter is for you to develop a style of moral decision making that enables you to respond to the issues of life with moral consistency and ethical accountability.

TWENTIETH-CENTURY APPROACHES TO CHRISTIAN DECISION MAKING

Why do fundamentalist Christians tend toward **legalism,** secular theologians toward **situational ethics,** and neoorthodox thinkers toward relational approaches? In order to comprehend twentieth-century Christian approaches to decision making, it is necessary to understand an eighteenth-century movement called the **Enlightenment.**[2]

The two hundred years preceding the twentieth-century were times of turbulence and creativity. The 1800s climaxed a period of worldwide exploration and discovery, culminating in the expanding Industrial Revolution, which forced peasants to abandon the land for work in the industrialized cities. Working conditions helped create urban ghettos, where social problems associated with the exploited poor multiplied. New levels of dehumanization accompanied the growing African slave trade. Growing **racism** and struggles over slavery in America eventually erupted into an American Civil War.

In addition, revolutionary political movements swept across Europe and America. In France and the American colonies, new political and social theories precipitated revolutions that shook the foundations of both continents. Science made major strides in astronomy, physics, chemistry, biology, and psychiatry. The scientific method profoundly changed the way people viewed their world. "The new era, optimistically referred to as the Enlightenment, offered further challenges to the intellectual and spiritual dominance of Christian theology while also influencing the direction of Christian ethics. Thinkers as diverse as Hobbes, Locke, Hume, Kant, Rousseau, Hegel, Marx, and Nietzsche put a secular stamp on the moral thought of the eighteenth and nineteenth centuries and beyond."[3]

Liberalism and the Social Gospel Movement

Near the beginning of the twentieth century a movement emerged in Europe and America that broke away from the conservative theology of reformation orthodoxy. Liberalism sought to develop a reasonable account of Christianity that harmonized with modern science. Deeply tinged with humanism, rationalism, idealism, and Darwinian evolution, Protestant liberals felt compelled to dismiss biblical supernaturalism. Reason was pitted against faith; all beliefs had to pass the test of rationality and experience.[4]

In the effort to modernize Christianity, liberalism developed a new and distinctive theology. The acceptance of the scientific method led liberals to adopt the critical analysis of the biblical text. "The liberals welcomed the higher criticism of the Bible. Not only did the liberal believe that the Bible has no claim to preferential treatment among the books of man, but the liberal was happy to be freed from the need to apologize for the whole Bible as the infallible Word of God."[5]

Along with complete acceptance of higher criticism, liberal theology stressed God's imminent presence in the world. God was not a sovereign power that appeared in a few miraculous events in history, but God was in the world working through nature and all of life—evolution was God's handiwork.

A hallmark of liberalism was the movement's idealistic view of human nature. Most liberals denied original sin, believing human beings were innately good. Sin was viewed more in its social context, evident in corrupt institutions, greedy economic exploitation, racial discrimination, violence, and war.

Parallel with an optimistic view of humanity was liberalism's imminent view of the **kingdom of God.** Liberals worked toward the establishment of God's universal rule on earth. In a society of love and justice, human progress would usher in an age of cooperation and peace—a Christian century.[6]

As one might expect, ethics occupied a central place for liberal theologians. In fact, "Culture-Protestantism"[7] regarded ethics as the purpose of religion. Faith could be judged by its contribution to society. Liberalism championed the causes of peace, human rights, social justice, racial equality, and economic opportunity.

Liberalism strongly supported the Social Gospel Movement, a new emphasis among North American and European Christians around the turn of the century. The major thrust of the social gospel was to solve the social problems growing out of the Industrial Revolution, although some impetus came from earlier antislavery and temperance movements. The growing prosperity after the Civil War made some persons fabulously wealthy, but most working-class people remained poor. "For them, industrialization meant backbreaking toil, long working hours, child labor, exploitation of women, adulterated food, periods of unemployment, vulnerability to industrial accidents and disease, little educational opportunity, inadequate medical attention, and general impoverishment."[8]

The plight of the working poor, along with intellectual impetus from the social sciences, led many in mainline churches to apply the Christian faith to social relationships. Social gospel leaders insisted the new interpretation was actually a rediscovery of the original tenets of the Christian faith.

Historians identify three overlapping but distinct strategies in the Social Gospel Movement.[9] The more conservative strategy focused on meeting the needs of immigrants and the poor, such as Jane Addams's Hull House in Chicago. A second approach could be termed "radical" in the sense that it viewed the social problems in structural terms. Advocating sweeping social change, W. D. P. Bliss and other Christian socialists believed the teachings of Jesus "lead directly to some specific form or forms of Socialism."[10]

The final and dominant strategy was more reformist. Although socialist in their objectives, leaders like Congregational minister Washington Gladden were gradualist in style. While advocating the rights of workers and an equitable distribution of wealth, the strategy was to influence business leaders to assist in social reform, rather than incite workers to dismantle the system. A major leader in this phase of the social gospel was the German-American pietist Walter Rauschenbusch, whose writings brought the movement into the mainstream of American Protestant theology and church life.[11]

The Social Gospel Movement must be commended for its Christian concern for victims of economic and political injustices. Although flawed by a faulty view of human nature and social progress, the movement did initiate many changes that benefited society, such as child labor laws. However, because of its connection with liberal theology, the movement was rejected by most conservative Christians, who "generally assumed that the Social Gospel was an American theological aberration . . . the product of preachers who had strayed from the gospel of the grace of God."[12]

The reality of an economic depression and two world wars forced liberal theologians at midcentury to abandon earlier optimistic views of human nature and utopian progress. Leaders like John Bennett began to fashion neoliberalism,[13] which maintained liberalism's traditional belief in human goodness, rationality, freedom and responsibility, and the primacy of social relationships, but also recognized the perversity of sin and the illusory nature of utopian hopes. Neoliberals strengthened the role of the church, especially in the social arena, and also developed a new strategy of "middle-axioms," concrete **norms** that guide social policies.

To some degree, most major theological and ethical movements of the twentieth century developed in response to liberalism and the Social Gospel Movement. In one sense, the social gospel represents an adjustment ethic, emphasizing love and Christlike service to the new political and economic challenges of democratic **capitalism.** But there was also something new, a "breadth and strength of **conscience,** and eventually, a theology, of its own. . . . Christian ethics can never again forget the social implications of the gospel." [14]

Fundamentalism and Legalism

As increasing numbers of American theologians accepted German higher criticism, Darwinianism, and Protestant liberal theology in the early 1900s, a heated controversy developed. Opponents of liberalism sought to preserve orthodox Christianity by defending the "fundamentals" of the Christian faith—hence the name "fundamentalists."[15]

Amid cries of consternation and warning, conservatives united in a meeting in 1909 in Los Angeles, with plans to establish a Bible institute and publish materials. A series of twelve small pamphlets was produced by the group entitled *The Fundamentals: A Testimony of the Truth* (1910–15), which listed a variety of enemies— Romanism, socialism, **philosophy,** atheism, Eddyism, Mormonism, and above all, liberal theology.[16]

Immediately, however, the list of enemies narrowed and the fourteen-point "Niagara Creed" (1878)[17] was condensed to the five essential doctrines of fundamentalism: (1) the virgin birth of Christ; (2) the bodily resurrection of Christ; (3) the inerrancy (infallibility) of the Scriptures; (4) the substitutionary theory of the atonement; and (5) the imminent, physical second coming of Christ.[18]

Although the movement often was charged with being naive and simplistic, conservative scholar Carl F. H. Henry claims, "In its early stages, fundamentalism was neither anti-intellectual nor hostile to social ethics."[19] Little evidence can be found that fundamentalist apologists were inherently unthinking. Indeed, many were committed to a pattern of thought structure and logic that dominated nineteenth-century American theology, articulated best by J. Gresham Machen and Benjamin Warfield, both of Princeton Seminary.[20]

What actually divides the fundamentalist from the liberal higher critic is not doubts about the Mosaic authorship of the Pentateuch or that the Bible is reliable history. "The real difference lies in totally different world views. The liberal . . . assumes that the world is a self-contained unity that can be fully comprehended. . . . In short, he denies the reality of the supernatural; nature is all and explains all. The conservative accepts the reality of supernatural God and of God's supernatural intervention among men."[21]

Increasingly, however, fundamentalists found themselves on the defensive. Soon denominational seminaries were controlled by the "modernists," forcing many conservatives to withdraw from mainline churches and to form alternative denominations, seminaries, and Bible colleges. Unfortunately, what began as an attempt to uphold doctrinal purity hardened into a theologically rigid and socially isolated form of Christianity.[22]

An ultraconservative attitude soon dominated fundamentalism, especially evidenced in its suspicion of secular education, its resistance to change, its militant opposition to communism and socialism, and its authoritarian attitude. In the end, fundamentalist teaching became a "strange mixture of orthodox theology, on the one hand, and frantic efforts to rationalize and reinforce faith, on the other. . . . for the vital experience of personal faith in Jesus Christ, fundamentalism has often substituted intellectual acceptance of the doctrine of his deity, undergirded by a series of rational proofs."[23]

Before midcentury, fundamentalism became increasingly polemic in theology and legalistic in ethics. In support of the authority of the Scriptures, a literal approach to biblical interpretation became the norm (except in prophetic books). For ethical purposes, the Bible primarily became a book of moral rules, divine **absolutes** to be followed in obedience to God. For fundamentalists, God has spoken clearly and propositionally in the Bible. Humanity possesses no trustworthy norm for moral behavior apart from revelation, for "both the Old Testament and the New are very careful to define in great detail the content of Christian ethics."[24]

Legalism in fundamentalist ethics linked with ethical pietism, commanding Christians to abstain from worldly **vices** such as drinking, smoking, gambling, dancing, and attending movies. In *The Uneasy Conscience of Modern Fundamentalism*, Carl F. H. Henry warned that fundamentalists, in reaction to liberalism and the social gospel, had recoiled from sociocultural matters, linking social concerns with evangelism.[25] Henry chastised his fellow fundamentalists for their narrowness, otherworldliness, anti-intellectualism, and failure to apply their faith to culture and social concerns.[26]

Legalism in ethics was not the sole property of the fundamentalists, but a rules-approach did become the dominant pattern for the group. As an ethical method, legalism seeks to prescribe rules for every moral decision. Sometimes referred to as "absolutism" or "rules **deontology**," the pattern is especially prominent in Jewish, Roman Catholic, and sectarian ethics, as well as in early church leaders like Tertullian.

Although most ethicists reject legalism, the moral rules approach does possess certain strengths: biblical norms are seriously considered, decision making is simplified, and the method is less subject to manipulation for selfish purposes.

Let it also be noted that rules do have an important function. In response to the so-called "new morality," Joseph C. Hough Jr. proposed four functions of moral rules: (1) they always apply in the same way to every situation; (2) moral rules are the guidelines for ordinary behavior; (3) rules provide guidelines for what I want to be; and (4) rules form the public document by which others learn what to expect of us.[27]

However, as a predominant method, the legalistic approach to ethical choices has a number of weaknesses. First, every moral decision cannot be covered by a rule—the list of rules is never long enough. In addition, moral laws often conflict with each other—telling the truth may lead to the loss of innocent life (Exod. 1:15-20). Conflicting absolutes may create another problem: Which of the two rules should be obeyed?

Another weakness of legalism is the danger of observing the letter of the law, while missing altogether its spirit and intent. Jesus chastised Jewish legalists who violated the spirit and intent of the fifth commandment in their practice of a religious duty (Matt. 15:3-9). The meticulous keeping of the law can also lead to spiritual pride, like that of the proud Pharisee in Jesus' parable (Luke 18:11-12). The most crucial weakness of legalism is its normal failure to develop moral character; in code morality, the right choice is always predetermined by another authority that the legalist obeys.

Though moral rules have a positive function, as a major method of decision making rules deontology has a basic deficiency. Code morality tends to set some authority—the church, a religious leader, or some tradition—upon God's throne, substituting human authority for the will of God.

Evangelicalism and Principlism

Evangelicalism is difficult to define, both as a theological position and a historical movement. Evangelical beliefs coincide with the historic orthodox teachings of the Christian faith, especially the theological orientation of the Reformation. The distinguishing features of evangelical doctrine are its view of the Scriptures as the infallible revelation of God to humanity, and its emphasis on personal faith, missions, and evangelism. Evangelicals believe social service is a logical result of saving faith, but it is never a substitute for the proclamation of the gospel.[28]

During the German Reformation, the term *evangelical* was applied to Lutherans who sought to reform Christianity through Bible study and salvation by faith alone. In Great Britain, evangelicalism arose out of the eighteenth-century revivals led by the Wesleys and George Whitefield. John Wesley's view of salvation connected the personal and the social, as he opposed slavery, supported prison reform and education, and established many social agencies.[29]

Evangelicalism in the United States is associated with the revivalism of George Whitefield and Jonathan Edwards in the eighteenth century and of antebellum evangelist and social reformer Charles Finney. However, during the early part of the twentieth century, evangelicals withdrew from efforts aimed at social reform in reaction to **modernism** and the "social gospel."[30] By the mid-twentieth century, however, many conservatives had rejected the excesses of fundamentalism and began to reverse their reactionary withdrawal from the social arena. Refusing to abandon society to the liberals or shield themselves and the gospel from the world by withdrawing into "holy ghettos," a new American evangelicalism emerged.[31]

Although evangelical beliefs found a home among Christians in many denominations, the diverse movement most often is identified with the National Association of Evangelicals, the journal *Christianity Today*, schools such as Wheaton College and Fuller Theological Seminary, and initial leaders like Carl F. H. Henry and Edward Carnell. Ron Sider and Jim Wallis represent a group of counterculture evangelicals committed to social action, who oppose secularism, militarism, and materialism in American society.[32] Evangelicals like Richard Mouw and Lewis Smedes stress reforming culture by changing traditional social institutions.[33]

A major method used by evangelicals in moral decision making is **principlism.** Sometimes called "Conflicting Absolutism"[34] and

"Dynamic Equivalence Ethics,"[35] the approach defines a method of interpreting the ethical teachings of the Scriptures and a way of resolving moral conflicts. In his preface to *Biblical Ethics*, T. B. Maston defines principlists as those "who place the emphasis on the principles or ideals of the Bible instead of on laws or specific precepts. Those who take this approach do not necessarily turn to the Bible for specific answers for every question or as a solution for every problem. They suggest that more important than the commandments are the principles or ideals that may be expressed through the commandments and may be the source of the commandments. Also, some would say that more important than any specific principle or ideal is the spirit or attitude revealed by and through the ideal."[36]

Principlists hold a high view of the authority of the Bible. While fully appreciating biblical precepts, the method avoids the errors of literalism and of legalism by insisting the emphasis of the Bible is upon ethical principles. The context or situation posed by the ethical question is always important to principlists, but never is it determinative.

Most principlists agree that **agape**-love is "the crowning **virtue** and the guiding principle in every area of human relations,"[37] but translating love into social policy is problematic. Although justice never fulfills all of the demands of love, it is the closest expression of love in society.[38]

As a method for interpreting the ethical teachings of the Scriptures, the principlist procedure ordinarily follows this **hermeneutical** pattern:[39]

- Uncover the social, historical, cultural, theological, and situational facts of the passage;
- Determine the meaning of the facts;
- Identify the biblical norms involved;
- Discover the values and ideals expressed in the norms;
- Determine which values are cultural and which values are transcultural;
- Define the principles reflected in these values;
- Test the principles by comparing them to other values and principles revealed in the Scriptures;
- Apply the biblical principles to contemporary moral issues that are relevant.

The principlist contends that behind every biblical command or rule is a value that may be expressed as a principle. A value or principle is transcultural and abidingly relevant if it reflects some element of God's nature and character.[40] For example, Paul's prohibitions to Corinthian women who were discarding the "veil" and cutting their hair (1 Cor. 11:5–6) were not meant as permanent precepts. The real value expressed through each command was the good reputation of the early church, which was threatened by behavior that Graeco-Roman culture linked with immorality.[41] The transcultural principle might be stated: "Any behavior that disgraces the good name of the church is wrong."

Within the family of those ethicists who have developed a principlist approach, great variety exists. Philip Wogaman proposed certain principles for guidance in decision making that he termed "positive moral presumptions."[42] Others have utilized principles for determining proper goals in ethics.[43]

Principlists in the tradition of Paul Ramsey have stressed the importance of right conduct. The respected Princeton professor is best known for pioneering work in medical ethics and an almost singlehanded renewal of just-war theory. In his oft-quoted book, *Deeds and Rules in Christian Ethics*,[44] and in his *Basic Christian Ethics*,[45] Ramsey criticizes code morality, but he articulates the importance of a more normative ethic.

In a 1965 letter to Joseph Fletcher (the father of situation ethics), Ramsey responded to all who trivialized Augustine's maxim—"Love God and do as you will": "The candid issue between us is whether agape is expressed in acts only or in rules also, which question is generally begged; or else the structures in which human beings live are attributed to other than uniquely Christian sources of understanding (**natural law**, etc.) while Christians go about pretending to live in a world without principles. The latter was about my position in *Basic Christian Ethics*. I have come to see that agape can also be steadfast."[46]

Ramsey rejects Fletcher's "act-agapism," which assesses the facts of each case and decides on the most loving course of action. In contrast, he proposes "rule-agapism," which "asks which rules of action most embody the demands of love and seeks to analyze particular circumstances in light of guidance from prior and independently articulated norms."[47]

Many principlists also support the concept of choosing the lesser evil as a method of dealing with conflicting absolutes, an idea espoused by Martin Luther and developed by Helmut Thielicke and Reinhold Niebuhr.[48] In a fallen world, conflicts emerge between God's ideal will and human reality. Many moral decisions involve choices that are less than ideal, like Rahab's deception of the king of Jericho (Josh. 2:1–7). Christians sometimes must make a choice that involves unavoidable evil. In such cases the person is guilty of sin, but God's forgiveness is available.[49]

As an ethical system, principlism has many strengths. By discerning the intent behind biblical commands, the approach does make the Bible relevant for all times and cultures. In addition, principlism avoids the restrictions of legalism and the subjectivism of situationism, while maintaining the primacy of agape-love. By encouraging the proper understanding and application of biblical principles, the method develops moral maturity in Christians and a relational knowledge of God.

On the negative side, the approach often lacks detailed guidance for applying principles, especially when principles seem to conflict. In extreme cases, principlism could also become legalistic or even highly subjective. The greatest weakness of this method is probably its failure to incorporate the vital role of character and community into decision making.

Neoorthodoxy and Relational Ethics

The roar of the cannons in August 1914 sounded the death knell for the utopian dreams of the previous century and signaled the beginning of a mood of pessimism. Modernism had been fatally wounded.

Neoorthodoxy was a reaction against the theological optimism of liberalism and a protest against the nontheistic humanism that lingered for a decade after World War I. The financial depression and the deterioration of the international situation in the 1930s closed the coffin on the corpse of liberalism and its confidence in human ability and social progress. In response to the failure of modernism, neoorthodoxy reaffirmed the uniqueness of God's self-revelation as recorded in the Scriptures and culminated in Jesus Christ.[50]

The proponents of this new orthodoxy had a paradoxical relationship to liberalism. On the one hand, neoorthodox theologians, like their liberal forebears, accepted higher criticism of the Bible and the discoveries of Enlightenment science. On the other hand, the new thinkers rejected the cultural Christianity of liberalism, which "had been so intent on making the Christian faith palatable to the modern mindset that it had lost the gospel."[51]

The neoorthodox movement was foremost "an attempt of theologians to rediscover the significance for the modern world of certain of the doctrines that had been central to the older Christian orthodoxy."[52] Like other movements of this century, neoorthodoxy displayed marked variety. Major tributaries flowed in Europe, although the tide of influence quickly overflowed the continental dike and spread into American theology.

Neoorthodox theology called Christians back to the Word of God—the voice of the Transcendent One who speaks from beyond. Drawing inspiration from the nineteenth-century Danish philosopher Søren Kierkegaard, neoorthodoxy reasserted themes of human sin, divine grace, and personal decision.[53] God is "wholly other," known only through an existential "I-Thou" relationship. Rather than being self-sufficient, humans are so corrupted by sin that they can accomplish no good thing alone. Reason is inadequate; right knowledge comes only through revelation and obedient submission to God. The essence of sin is pride, which alienates from God.

The neoorthodox understanding of the Bible is one belief that troubles many. Although the Scripture is the indispensable witness to Jesus Christ, it is at the same time a human message colored by human frailties. The Bible contains the Word of God, but God's Word is different from the words of the Bible. Brunner steadfastly refused to identify revelation with the words of Scripture.[54] Only in the crisis moment of faith do these human words mediate and become the Word of God.

For neoorthodox thinkers, ethics are very important.[55] The neoorthodox methodology for moral decision making has often been termed **relational ethics,** which was central in the European repudiation of liberal Protestantism.[56] Important for relationalism is the basic conviction that the right act is never determined beforehand—only in the "crisis" moment of decision does God reveal the good.

For most relationalists, agape-love is the only absolute. To depend on biblical rules or principles for ethical guidance is legalism, which denies the freedom of the gospel.

The relation of Christians to the institutions of society is also an important aspect of ethics; though ordained by God, social institutions are corrupted by sin and thus are questionable resources for justice. A variety of approaches have developed under the general rubric of relational ethics. This response-type method is not so much concerned with what is good (end result) or what is right (obligation) as with what is fitting (responsibility).

A pivotal model in the European reaction to liberal Protestantism was Karl Barth's ethic of divine command. To the question, "What ought I to do?" Barth answered: "Listen to the personal command of God directed to you and respond in obedient faith."[57] Christian ethics must be theological, derived from the overall witness of the Scripture. If we know the grace of God, we will also experience the sovereignty of the Divine Commander, who always directs the believer toward the imitation of Christ.[58]

The obvious problem with Barth's approach is how to recognize God's call. Also, something seems to be missing—where is the moral self (character) between moments when God is commanding? The moral life is more than simply existential moments of decision. Though Barth restored normative and dispositional resources to Christian ethics, which his colleagues had banished, the command model remained a sporadic affair.[59]

Emil Brunner was unique among his European counterparts in presenting his ethical views in a separate and systematic work— *The Divine Imperative*. Like Barth, Brunner set forth a divine command ethic, one motivated by love and illuminated by the Spirit in the moment of decision. However, the command can never be understood apart from the "ordinances of creation," those institutions of human organization normally found within the communal life of humanity (family, economic order, state).[60]

Another relationalist was Rudolf Bultmann who, like Barth, wrote ethics only as an aspect of writing theology. His main contribution was to explicate his existential philosophy for the Christian faith. Ethics is "radical obedience" and must never rely on rules, ideals, or principles.[61] "If men are standing in the crisis of decision," wrote Bultmann, "and if precisely this crisis is the essential characteristic of their humanity, then every hour is the last hour."[62]

A younger theologian who studied under Barth and Bultmann was Dietrich Bonhoeffer, whose writings gained credibility because of the remarkable life behind them. His *Letters and Papers from Prison* were written during the final months of his imprisonment for opposing the Nazi regime. Bonhoeffer's classic work, *The Cost of Discipleship*, was a call for a radical discipleship that withstands secular culture: "When Christ calls a man, He bids him come and die."[63] The Cross is the true measure of discipleship and ethics, for to hear the call of Jesus is to hear the command to follow the crucified and risen Christ in suffering, rejection, and death.[64]

Relationalism has been presented not only in the **paradigm** of divine command but also in the version of responsibility. H. Richard Niebuhr's articulation of this category has been widely influential since its appearance in 1963 in *The Responsible Self.*[65] Niebuhr's ethic of responsibility proposes that God is present and acting in all actions upon a person, as Creator, Governor, and Redeemer. This model turns the moral question around and asks, "What is God doing in my life?"[66] The responsible person is the one who responds to God, valuing all things as they are valued by God.[67]

It seems inequitable in this summary of formative ethicists to include two from the same family. But Reinhold Niebuhr, brother of H. Richard, was a prolific writer who made a singular contribution in applying the Christian faith to the social world. Niebuhr never saw himself as a theologian. In his wife's eyes, he was a preacher and pastor; others saw him as an apologist, social ethicist, and a "circuit rider" among the nation's colleges and universities.[68]

Similar to Rauschenbusch's experience in New York's "Hell's Kitchen," Reinhold Niebuhr's pastorate in Detroit profoundly influenced his theology and social outlook. The simple idealism of his traditional faith was irrelevant for the complex social issues confronting exploited assembly-line workers in Detroit.

Best known for his emphasis on original sin and realism about power politics, Niebuhr was deeply influential in the United States from the late 1930s through the 1960s.

Along with other realists, Reinhold Niebuhr stressed the impossibility of realizing social ideals because sin (mainly self-interest and the desire to dominate and control others) is present in every person and in every act. The thesis of his first major work, *Moral Man and Immoral Society,*[69] was that "individuals in face-to-face settings can manifest a high level of morality that is belied by the immorality of the larger groups and institutions in which they participate."[70]

On the basis of this distinction, Niebuhr also contrasted love and justice. As selfless regard for the other, love is the purest form of the Christian ethic. But love cannot be translated into social policy. Though humans have enormous potential to become like God, because of sin and human finitude love is an "impossible possibility." The best to be hoped for in society is proximate justice, the tolerable but imperfect accommodation of fairness and equity in life, characterized by balances of power.[71] "Man's capacity for justice makes democracy possible, but man's inclination to injustice makes democracy necessary."[72]

Relational ethics has influenced many who do not adopt it fully, for it has much to commend it. Being in a right relationship with God and with others is the biblical formula for a morally responsible life (Matt. 22:37–40). Relationalists seek to avoid a calculated legalism by determining the responsible action God wills in the moment of decision. However, relationalism fails to give concrete guidance, especially in the face of competing values and choices. Greatest of its inherent flaws is its relativistic bent. To derive norms exclusively from the circumstances of the decision inevitably leads to subjectivism.

Secular Theology and Contextual Ethics

Secular theology was a short but influential movement in the 1960s, based on a renewed interest in Bonhoeffer's writings and certain themes in Barth's theology. Common features found among these radical thinkers include: (1) Bonhoeffer's call for "religionless Christianity"; (2) christocentric theology; (3) removal of the emphasis on the "otherworldly" in Christianity; and (4) the language of "belief."[73]

The first stream of thought was the death-of-God movement, virtually a two-man show by William Hamilton and Thomas J. J. Altizer,[74] which never gained a wide following. Responses to the movement in the popular media created an uproar.[75] Surprised by the reaction, Hamilton attempted to explain their intent was not to declare "God is dead": it was to deny belief in the traditional God of Christian theism.[76]

Another short-lived expression of this radical theology was known as the "secular Christianity" movement. Theologians celebrated the rise of secularism, believing the church should see secularity as the work of God and join in building a new secular city of humanity. John A. T. Robinson, bishop in the Church of England, wrote a controversial book titled *Honest to God*, which was instantly popular and influential. In his words, "there is a growing gulf between the traditional orthodox supernaturalism in which our Faith has been framed and the categories which the 'lay' world . . . finds meaning today."[77]

For secular theologians, social action and involvement in world events are at the heart of "religionless Christianity." **Prescriptive ethics** are rejected. For moral guidance, only one absolute exists— the norm of love. Secular theologians stressed two ethical methodologies: contextualism (act-*koinonia*) and situationism (act-agapism). Although the methods are different, many used the two terms interchangeably.

Paul Lehmann was the best known proponent of contextual ethics, a motif that focused on ethics emanating from within the Christian *koinonia*. The moral question was, "What am I as a believer in Jesus Christ and as a member of His church to do?"[78] In a 1967 article Lehmann sharply distinguishes contextualism from **ethical relativism,** stating: "The point of departure for Christian thinking about ethics is the concrete reality in the world of a community, a *koinonia*, called into being and action by Jesus of Nazareth. In this community, what God is doing in the world is clearly discerned as exposing the human meaning of behaviour by giving human shape to action. God is doing in the world what it takes to make and keep human life human."[79]

The popularizer of the phrase "situation ethics," Joseph Fletcher, proposed a "new morality," a third way between legalism and antinomianism.[80] A moral decision is made by analyzing the situation, calculating the consequences of each option, then choosing the most loving response. In situation ethics, the primary principle is love.[81] Other principles and rules may illuminate, but they are only advisers, not deciders. Professor Fletcher often said, "Christian obligation calls for lies and adultery and fornication and theft and promise breaking and killing—sometimes, depending on the situation."[82]

For many persons struggling with the complexity of modern moral decisions, Lehmann and Fletcher offered an alternative to the rigid legalism that viewed the moral universe in two colors—black and white! To its credit, contextual ethics recognized the significance of the situation, the primacy of love, and the importance of persons.

Numerous critics have noted, however, that contextualism and situationism are flawed at several common points. To begin, contextualism holds a very unrealistic view of sin and human nature, assuming the individual has the capacity to rightly discern the context and determine the response of love. Believing ethical decisions must be uncoerced, the situationist overlooks the value of the Bible, moral rules, principles, and other resources for guidance.

In his critique of Fletcher, R. E. O. White notes that Fletcher's "love" is individualistic, subjective, and not too clearly defined, concluding, "Love needs to know how persons *ought* to be treated, how they *desire* to be, how they *need* to be. . . . [and love needs] at least something like the Golden Rule, to give good intentions safe direction."[83] In a devastating critique, Paul Ramsey charged that situation ethics has no clear word that the Christian moral life has any definable course, which meant for him that situation ethics is no different from antinomianism or existentialism.[84]

A major weakness of contextualism is one you would not expect to find. Both Lehmann and Fletcher seem to ignore social morality—the emphasis of situation ethics is upon personal moral choices, with little or no discussion of social issues.[85] In contrast to other relationalists, Fletcher's method "involves the rational calculation of consequences rather than free choice, intuition, conscience, or God's command and action."[86]

Neofundamentalism, Civil Religion, and Hierarchicalism

By the end of the 1920s, reactive fundamentalism had been expelled from the circles of influence and would not be heard from for more than forty years. In exile, those who retreated from modernity licked their wounds and began building an alternate "righteous empire."[87]

The first fundamentalists to return from exile were called "neo-evangelicals" by many until some of the more intolerant types emerged and were named "neofundamentalists." After the acclaimed "Year of the Evangelical" in 1976, a noisy and aggressive group surfaced in 1979, announcing themselves the Moral Majority and calling themselves fundamentalists. Led by Jerry Falwell, the group acknowledged that social withdrawal was a mistake, which aroused the ire of many ultraconservatives.

At first the presuppositions of the Moral Majority were vague, except for energetic support of the political right. In 1981 Falwell wrote "An Agenda for the Eighties" in which he called for biblical morality, stressed that the organization was not theologically based, and outlined key positions: separation of church and state, prolife, protraditional family, antidrugs, antipornography, pro-Israel, pronational defense, and proequal rights for women but anti-Equal Rights Amendment.[88]

The Religious Right (as the movement was named) became nationally prominent during the 1980 presidential campaign of Ronald Reagan, offering an answer to the social, economic, moral, and religious crisis in America. The real enemy was secular humanism, which neofundamentalists believed was responsible for the erosion of families, schools, churches, and the government.

Leading the attack was a new generation of television and print fundamentalists: Falwell, James Kennedy, Charles Stanley, Tim LaHaye (American Coalition for Traditional Values), and Pat Robertson (Christian Coalition). Their basic support was Baptist and southern, but the Religious Right reached into all denominations and into all parts of the nation, blurring the distinction between fundamentalist and evangelical. They claimed one-fourth of the American population was in their camp, though not all conservative Christians accepted these new leaders.[89]

The gravest error of neofundamentalism is its penchant for **civil religion,** the confusion of God and government so that national values and religious values blend together.[90] In opposing the Panama Canal Treaty and SALT II, in supporting military buildup and nuclear arms, and in regarding foreign aid as "welfare," the Religious Right revealed its tendency toward a narrow nationalism. The kingdom of God was confused with the American way of life.[91]

Another trend of civil religionists is to give complete Christian sanction to the economic policies of the secular right. Falwell claimed "the free enterprise system is clearly outlined in the Book of Proverbs," and that "ownership of property is biblical," yet he ignored the passion of the prophets for social justice and the identification of Jesus with the poor and the victims of society.[92]

Richard John Neuhaus concludes that the majority of Americans probably agree with Falwell on prolife, promorality, profamily, and pro-American; however, the New Religious Right "has been shrewd, and sometimes ruthless, in exploiting the Left's default."[93] When the church confuses spiritual and political convictions, it ordinarily succumbs to the temptation to use political power to promote its "spiritual" agenda.

In 1971 a new ethical method termed **hierarchicalism** (or graded absolutism) was proposed by Norman Geisler.[94] Though some would call Geisler an evangelical, in his training, vocational service, and theological perspective, the seminary professor seems better to fit the category of neofundamentalist.[95]

Geisler advocates a deontological emphasis on norms and underscores the duty to do what is inherently right without regard to consequences.[96] Building upon the theology of Charles Hodge, Geisler attempts to resolve conflicting absolutes without compromising the moral nature of God. He asserts the existence of higher and lower laws in the character of God, which allow the choice of a **greater good** (e.g., the Hebrew midwives' actions in Exod. 1:16-20) or even justifiable deception (e.g., Rahab's lie in Josh. 2:4). When moral values conflict, a person is exempt from keeping the lower norm by virtue of acting in accord with the higher norm. Geisler admits the difficulty of determining the pyramid of values, though he gives his own list of principles.[97] The apologist insists there are no exceptions to absolute commands—only omissions in view of a higher priority. How does one know the difference? The knowledge of these principles may be intuitively grasped, as well as known through revelation. For Geisler, the choice is always a greater good—the moral agent has done no wrong and thus needs not repent of the act.

To its credit, hierarchicalism recognizes the complexity of competing values and the priority of some values over others. This alternative method also has a positive focus, establishing a greater good while not eliminating the lesser good which is only temporarily suspended.

Nevertheless, at the heart of ethical hierarchicalism is a major difficulty—who determines the scale of values? If that choice is left up to each person, the danger is ethical subjectivity. If some external authority sets up the scale, an incipient legalism is probable. The choice of the greater good creates another difficulty: the risk of minimizing the "absoluteness" of the lower command. And most importantly, to justify the decision as a greater *good*, needing no repentance, seems unrealistic—the midwives did lie and Rahab did deceive!

No one denies that the neofundamentalists of the 1980s were different from their predecessors in many ways and that they faced very different issues. Yet they continued to exhibit traits common to fundamentalists since the 1920s, "certain that they possessed true knowledge of the fundamentals of the faith and that they therefore represented true Christianity based on the authority of a literally interpreted Bible."[98]

Liberation Theology and Ethics

Although liberation theologies often include feminist and African-American expressions, our focus will be on the Latin American form first popularized by Gustavo Gutierrez in the 1970s.[99] A theology of praxis (practice rather than theory), the movement focuses on liberating the oppressed, especially in Two-Thirds World nations. Christians are called upon first to act in their geopolitical situation, then to develop a theory that critiques action.

In a 1988 speech given in New Orleans at Loyola University, Gutierrez described liberation theology as a way to follow Jesus. The poor have always been present in the world, but now for the first time they are politically and socially significant. All poor persons have a right to live—poverty means injustice, destruction of families, loss of personhood, and early death. One way to be a Christian in Latin America is to choose life.[100]

In light of the domination and oppression of the poor (often by colonial powers), liberation theologians declare God is working in history on the side of the oppressed, not because the oppressed are superior but because God is compassionate. The biblical paradigm is the deliverance of the Hebrews from slavery in Egypt (Exod. 7-14). For liberationists, sin is primarily social. Christians must be involved at all three levels of liberation: the sociopolitical transformation of society, the anthropological creation of new persons, and the theological liberation from sin.

The ethical motif of liberation theology is clear: actions that join God's work in liberating the persecuted are moral; actions that hinder liberation are immoral. Because powerful nations have exploited weaker nations and created dependency, liberated societies must break radically from First-World domination. Even violence and revolution are justified to achieve social and political change. However, in the revision of his classic text, Gutierrez questions some of the Marxist theories of social change he earlier accepted.[101]

On the positive side, liberation theologians have challenged academic theology to unite theory and practice through critical reflection on the concrete experiences of Christians. Moreover, this movement has probably done as much as any group to keep the plight of the oppressed and the poor before the public.[102]

Nevertheless, in substance and methodology, liberation theology has serious weaknesses. In method, liberationists place a critical social theory in a constitutive position, which predetermines the theological approach. For example, liberation models in the Bible are lauded; redemptive suffering paradigms are usually ignored. Also, if the pivotal social theory (Marxist or otherwise) is revised, how does this impact the theology?[103]

While liberationists have reawakened the biblical demand for social justice and peace, their theologians "have been content to reduce the ethical task to ideological criticism of a variety of oppressive **ethoses.**"[104]

Narrative Theology and Ethics of Community and Character

In the 1970s a new approach to theology and ethics appeared, which has gained a widespread following. Narrative theology incorporates the importance of story for human understanding, utilizing the story and the storyteller as the central motif for theological reflection. "The genius of narrative theology lies in its assertion that faith entails the joining of our personal stories with the transcendent/immanent story of a religious community and ultimately with the grand narrative of the divine action in the world."[105]

An early voice in the exploration of narrative ethics was that of theologian James McClendon, who wrote *Biography as Theology* in the early 1970s.[106] A decade later he began his three-volume systematic theology with the publication of *Systematic Theology: Ethics*, in which he declared ethics to be the logical starting point in theology.[107] Writing out of the Anabaptist tradition, McClendon stressed the importance of character, virtues, and corporate life in ethics, and the corollary necessity of narrative to shape all three.

Rather than focus on formal theological categories related to the story, narrative thinkers usually draw out the ethic expressed in the story and its implications for life. In the opinion of Stanley Hauerwas, modern ethical systems are excessively concerned with dilemmas and quandaries.[108] As the most articulate proponent of narrative ethics, Hauerwas maintains that there is a question prior to "What shall I do?" That question deals with character and asks, "What shall I be?"

This emphasis does not mean Christian ethics is unconcerned with decisions or with principles that guide in decision making. What it does mean is that decisions grow out of a history, a narrative "which is more about what kind of people we are than about particular acts."[109] Christians are people with a distinctive history—a story-formed community. "We are not called on to be 'moral' but faithful to the true story, the story that we are creatures under the Lordship of God."[110]

Narrative ethics is often identified as ethics of community and character because moral choices are never made from a neutral position.[111] Each person brings to a decision the dispositions, experiences, traditions, heritage, and virtues embodied in his or her character.[112] Because character is shaped by a community, the church must be a faithful community, a colony of "resident aliens"[113] that forms and informs the people of God. "The first task of Christian social ethics, therefore, is not to make the 'world' better or more just, but to help Christian people form their community consistent with their conviction that the story of Christ is a truthful account of our existence."[114]

In sum, narrative ethics is based on three central affirmations: (1) the knowledge of God in Jesus Christ provides us with a vision of God in narrative form, (2) which forms and informs the Christian community and its agents by giving them identity in the form of character and virtue, (3) thereby equipping them to confront without illusion the deceitful and false narratives of the world and respond to them in faithful witness.[115]

The major value of character ethics lies in the formation of the moral self in the community. Character gives unity, definition, direction, and dominant convictions to the moral life. Moreover, the lifelong cultivation of virtues develops continuity and consistency in both being and doing—what we are determines what we do. Finally, ethics of character creates moral vision—a Christian perspective on the world and the disciple's place in it.

However, acting ethically usually involves more than just having a sterling moral character or being a good person. Character may be basic to ethics, but some consistent method of discerning the right choice is also needed, especially for modern ethical dilemmas. A major weakness of character ethics lies in its individual nature: social and institutional moral questions involve not so much the inner lives of people as they do inherently evil social structures. Justice is more than a virtuous attitude; it must be defined and applied to society.

A MODEL FOR MORAL DECISION MAKING

In 1804 a Kentucky Baptist congregation was divided because they could not decide the right thing to do. The moral question was raised whether a man, when captured by the Indians, was justified in lying to protect his family concealed nearby.

Some believed the man had a duty to lie in those circumstances, while others maintained he should tell the truth even if it meant the sacrifice of his family. The argument was so vehement that the church split into two congregations known as the Lying Baptists and the Truthful Baptists.[116]

Moral decisions are never easy. One writer lists ten obstacles to overcome before good decisions can be made.[117] How does a Christian determine what is right or wrong? Is there a tried-and-tested formula for analyzing an ethical issue and making moral judgments?

In our overview of various approaches to Christian ethics, several methodologies have been explored. Our final task in this chapter is to utilize the insights gained from these approaches in order to construct a basic outline for moral deliberation. Our goal is to construct a model that is biblically and theologically sound, ethically credible, and logically consistent.

The model suggested here claims no uniqueness, for many ethicists employ one or more of these steps in their systems.[118] Nevertheless, each one of the five procedures suggested here is important to the total task. To omit any of these considerations is to risk a serious flaw in ethical analysis. Although the order of the steps has a logical basis, the process of decision making is always dialogical in nature. Ideally the moral agent moves back and forth between each of the suggested procedures, listening and responding, before reaching a final conclusion.

Be True to Your Character

A beginning point in decision making is to develop a mature Christian character. Character is basic to ethical decision making—being affects doing. In the Sermon on the Mount (Matt. 5–7), Jesus emphasized that character precedes conduct and morality is a matter of the heart.

Character is the inner moral orientation that fashions our lives into predictable patterns. The question posed by character is, "What values do you wish to express through your life and practice?" No person approaches a moral choice objectively; who you are determines what you do. Character ethics encourages the cultivation of virtues—moral excellencies essential to the good life. In Lewis Smedes's words, to become a "pretty good person" requires living with common qualities like "gratitude, guts, simple integrity, self-control, discernment, and fair love."[119]

Probably no one more than Stanley Hauerwas has emphasized the role of community in shaping character; "habits of the heart" are shaped by our family, our church, our schools, and our society. Participation in a moral community is the main way we develop ethical character.

Character ethics supports moral choices in two important ways: first, "a certain sense of calmness in doing the right thing and courage in resisting the wrong," and second, "a measure of discretion" leaving "final judgment up to the individual."[120]

Ethics based on Christian character also gives a certain completeness or wholeness to persons—a spiritual unity at the core of personality. Because what I am affects what I do, nothing is more basic to moral decision making than character. As Jesus put it, "Every good tree bears good fruit, but the bad tree bears bad fruit" (Matt. 7:17).

As important as is character, the ability to analyze ethical issues and make prudent choices is also vital. Both "being good" and "doing good" are essential in ethics. Like the bow and the violin, the two elements work together to produce the music of a life of moral integrity.

Face the Facts

Moral discernment requires an accurate analysis of the pertinent facts. Only some facts are relevant, but all facts are interpreted facts, "felt" facts, and evaluated facts.[121] In addition, significant facts are always filtered through our own beliefs, feelings, fears, desires, and values; only then can we identify them as "the facts of the case."[122]

An elementary rule in responsible moral decision making is to know the facts in the case. How do we gain accurate information? Four main procedures are necessary:[123]

1. Collect data. Asking the right questions is essential—who, what, where, when, why, and how? Determine the circumstances surrounding the issue.

2. Examine the persons involved. Find out who the players in the situation are and understand each one's point of view and apparent motives.

3. Evaluate the information. Incorrect understanding of the facts can lead you to make a wrong decision. Be aware of personal biases.

4. Explore all possible options. Identify the obvious alternatives, search for other possibilities, and deliberate about the different choices available.

For example, a current dilemma questions carrying a concealed weapon (handgun) for protection against criminals. To analyze this moral issue, a person should first gather facts—the biblical, theological, and social data about crime and the Christian response to it. What ethical norms apply? Why are crimes against persons committed? What could be done to prevent crime and to protect victims? If a Christian were confronted by a criminal, what are the possible responses? Which one is best?

Follow the Guidelines

Once we understand the issue, the persons involved, and the options available, we are then ready to consider the values that will guide our decision. First we must heed the moral rules that guide us toward good decisions: "Moral rules are not fetters to bind us into moral straitjackets and steal our freedom. Nor do they take all of the risks out of making choices or relieve us of the agony of making decisions when we are not sure which one is right. Rules help us to use our freedom wisely."[124]

Behind every rule there is a reason, a value which can be stated as a principle. Ethical principles act like a compass to direct us toward the good. For Christians, ethical norms and principles primarily come from the revelation of God in the Bible. Chief among numerous ethical guidelines in the Scriptures are the Ten Commandments (Exod. 20:1-17), the Sermon on the Mount (Matt. 5-7), and the principles of love for God and humanity (Matt. 22:36-40) and justice (Amos 5:24). Other resources that guide us toward the moral will of God include the Holy Spirit, Christian tradition, experience, reason, conscience, and prayer.

The mature Christian will evaluate the obligations and duties that apply to the issue faced. Sometimes competing values will require a person to prioritize the moral goods, selecting an option that is the greater good or the lesser evil. A Christian should be able to state the norms, values, principles, and other resources that confirm that a right decision has been made.

Consider the Consequences

An important test of right choices is to consider what happens afterward—the results. Anyone interested in doing the right thing must consider consequences, for bringing good to people's lives is a major part of what morality is about.

In one sense, consequences conform God's ethical ideals. "The rules of justice and love are God's own absolutes, which are never up for grabs in anybody's world. . . . goodness and decency will eventually break down when these rules are ignored. I need a faith that assures me that respect for human life, for truth, and for property produces better results for the most people in the long run."[125]

Consequentialism is present in both the Old and New Testaments.[126] Wisdom literature seldom takes the imperative form, but usually gives practical advice about how to achieve the good life (Prov. 9:10). Hebrew midwives who "feared God" made their decision to deceive Pharoah on the basis of consequences: to save the male babies (Exod. 1:15-20).

If what we choose to do brings good results, then we assume we have made a good choice. But how do we know which results are good? Before we depend on results to justify our actions, we need criteria for knowing what is good, better, or best, or maybe what is bad and what is worse.[127] The weakness of **teleological** ethics is that you never know for sure what the consequences will be.

Another way to consider the consequences of a decision is to ask a series of questions: Which consequences are beneficial and which are harmful? Which are immediate and which will occur in the future? Which will only last a short time and which will last a long time? Will the consequences help me achieve an ideal or will they involve compromise?[128]

The question of consequences is usually raised when two values seem to conflict. As Nazis came knocking on Corrie ten Boom's door during World War II, the heroine of *The Hiding Place* faced a dilemma. Would she reveal that Jews were hiding in the house, or would she lie to the Gestapo? Her decision involved conflicting values and potential results: to tell the truth probably meant Auschwitz and the furnaces. With much courage and some anguish, she chose a "lesser evil" to achieve a higher good; she lied to the soldiers. Her decision was like Rahab's misleading of the king of Jericho (Josh. 2) and Elisha's deception of the Syrian soldiers (2 Kings 6).

Although results matter and we cannot live by moral rules alone, we must also remember we cannot live by results alone either. The "lesser evil" is an evil, not a good. The decision maker should express repentance over the necessity of such a choice and work toward the day when such decisions are unnecessary. The focus on results can also deceive us into believing "our loving lies" are gallant when they actually are meant to save us from trouble.

Act Responsibly

Making moral decisions is a lot like driving on a crowded freeway. Certain rules of the road must be followed—speed limits, lane changes, and not driving while drinking. However, on any given trip there are hundreds of decisions not covered by the rules. Some situations require you to make your own rules or even change the rules in order to prevent a catastrophe, such as avoiding a reckless driver cutting in front of you. The catch-all rule for driving on a freeway that covers all situations is this one—drive responsibly.[129]

H. Richard Niebuhr taught that responsible people have three qualities: (1) they are able to initiate action; (2) they are able to respond to any situation; and (3) they are accountable.[130] The chances are that you acted responsibly if you:

- used discernment,
- interpreted the question before you answered it,
- considered whether the act was appropriate,
- used your imagination,
- acted in congruence with your commitments and your roles,
- were willing to let your acts be seen in public, and
- accepted accountability for your actions.[131]

To summarize, then, making moral decisions requires a mix of types of ethics. No single method of moral reasoning covers the entire range of moral experience or fits every moral question.

In day-to-day situations you may operate by a set of norms and principles. In the face of unique, nonrepetitive decisions you may bring calculation of consequences into operation. If really pushed to the wall by a situation in which you cannot compromise, you may act according to convictions drawn from your character. "As people mature in decision making they achieve an artful ability to make appropriate ethical responses by drawing selectively from their repertoire of ethical knowledge."[132]

The "artful ability" referred to above is similar to the skills of a baseball pitcher. In Little League play, a youngster with a terrific fastball can win many games, but if that is his only pitch, he will never play baseball in the major leagues. A skilled baseball pitcher not only has a "repertoire" of pitches, from slider to change-up, he also has a knowledge of the game—what pitch to deliver to which batter at what target around the plate. Likewise, the mature Christian develops the skill to deliver the right "pitch" for each situation to the right target.

The ability to make good moral decisions is not genetically inbred at birth or miraculously infused at conversion or baptism. Christian discipleship is a lifelong process. The believer identifies with Jesus Christ in a community of faith shaped by the biblical story. Character is formed, conduct is informed, and moral vision is developed—a life of ethical integrity unfolds.

The most encouraging words for decision makers are the closing words in Smedes's classic text: "Nothing you do wrong can get God to love you less than he did when you did things right. Nothing need ever separate you from the love of God. After all is said and done, being right is not the most important thing in the world. Being forgiven is."[133]

FOR THOUGHT AND DISCUSSION

1. Imagine you were living in 1910—discuss which theological and ethical movement(s) might have influenced you the most.
2. Answer the same question for the years 1940, 1970, and 1990.
3. Compare and contrast the relational ethics of Barth, Brunner, Bultmann, Bonhoeffer, H. R. Niebuhr, and Reinhold Niebuhr.
4. Define your own method of moral decision making; then evaluate it by using the "Five Theological Motifs" in chapter 4.

PART TWO
ISSUES IN CHRISTIAN ETHICS

CHAPTER SIX

THE CHRISTIAN AND PERSONAL ETHICS

Eric Liddell was Scotland's Olympic champion in the games of 1924 in Paris. The story of his athletic skills and his Christian faith was dramatized in the award-winning film *Chariots of Fire*. A scene from the movie illustrates Liddell's deep religious convictions. When he was assigned to run the one-hundred-yard dash on Sunday, his faith told him he could not. All efforts to persuade him failed. A British dignitary finally said in frustration, "What a pity we couldn't have persuaded him to run." After a moment's pause, his coach responded, "It would have been a pity if we had, because we would have separated him from the source of his speed." Later he entered the four-hundred-meter race and won in the world record time of 47.6 seconds.[1]

Whether you agree with Liddell's moral conclusions or not, you cannot help but admire the Scotchman's refusal to compromise his ethics for personal gain. Sooner or later, every believer will face such a test.

By now you should understand the influence of **philosophy** on **ethics,** the meaning of **Christian ethics,** the role of the Bible and other sources in Christian ethics, and the main categories of ethical deliberation. Through an overview of Christian history you have discovered the difficulty facing every generation of believers—how to relate to the world without being corrupted by it. Finally, you have explored the process of moral decision making. By comparing and analyzing major theological and ethical movements, you have prepared yourself to construct a personal method of moral judgment.

Now we have arrived at the second half of our text in which we address contemporary ethical issues. Our aim is not to give you answers to every moral question, but rather to introduce the major categories of applied ethics and the key moral problems of the emerging century. In each chapter we will develop a Christian response to particular issues, one which also illustrates the model proposed at the close of chapter 5. We shall begin by introducing present social and moral trends to prepare you for the practical side of Christian ethics.

SOCIAL AND MORAL TRENDS

The 1900s began with optimism and hope; this was to be a "Christian century." After numerous moral catastrophes, the twentieth century now winds down in apocalyptic despair and pessimism. Theologians are already describing the present as **"postmodern"** and "post-Christian," believing that Western society is secularized and that traditional Christian faith has been eclipsed by materialism, relativism, and pluralism.

Social and moral trends in the 1990s point toward key issues awaiting persons living at the beginning of the Third Millennium. By 1995 most people in the U.S. believed their nation was in trouble. For twenty-four years the Fordham University Institute for Innovation in Social Policy has been grading the U.S. in sixteen key social areas. In the first year (1970), the nation's score was almost 74 out of a utopian 100. In 1994 it was a record low of 35.[2]

No one doubts that Americans are beset with a host of problems at the close of this century. Social changes during the last fifty years have created new moral dilemmas, as well as exacerbated old ones. Chief among the trends may be the ones altering the nature of the American family.[3]

- The traditional family of a working father, a wife at home, and children is almost extinct—less than 10 percent.[4]
- Single-parent families are growing, numbering about 27 percent in 1994, double the total in 1970. Of children born in 1995, one of four will never have a father in the home.

- Single adults have increased to about 23 percent of all U.S. households and about 40 percent of all adults, including over 3.5 million unmarried couples who are living together.
- Singlets (single-child households) will increase from 15 percent of homes with children in 1989 to 25 percent by 2000.
- The American population is aging, the median age rising from thirty in 1983 to thirty-six by the year 2000. Persons over sixty-five will increase from 31 million in 1995 to 64 million by 2025.

The aging of America has helped create another social problem. Increasing generational distinctions will probably heighten tensions between the major groups of adults: the "can-doers" of the G.I. generation (b. 1901–1925); the process-oriented negotiators of the silent generation (b. 1926–1944); the committed and creative seventy-seven million boomer generation (b. 1945–1962); the Xers generation (b. 1963–1981), who are hard-edged pragmatists; and the millennials (b. 1982–2000), who could be overprotected.[5]

Culture analyst Tom Sine identifies five trends in the 1990s: (1) the erosion of the middle class; (2) an epidemic of autonomy; (3) the polarization of young and old; (4) a cross-cultural future; and (5) the preservation of our earth home.[6]

Contemporary American society, therefore, presents numerous challenges. The social trends of the last half-century have led futurists to identify the most pressing moral questions in the Third Millennium. One center for the study of ethics published these major issues facing the churches of tomorrow:

- Resisting the attempt to define faith in terms of political views
- Determining the proper role of faith in public life
- Reconciling divisions among Christians over abortion
- Translating Christian principles into "traditional values"
- Redesigning church programs to minister to older adults
- Developing creative ways to minister to blended, extended, single, and single-parent families
- Developing greater openness and ministry to homosexuals
- Eliminating racism and ethnocentrism in churches
- Facilitating a true spirituality in churches, rather than a success mentality based on materialistic values
- Leading churches to have a vision of a global community in need of peace, justice, hunger relief, environmental protection, and a just economy[7]

In 1993 an exhaustive study of Southern Baptists was conducted to prepare the denomination for the next century. A random sample of more than 1,200 responded to the first questionnaire, followed by 1,400 replying to the second one. In addition, a target group of 2,150 received both questionnaires. One question asked each respondent to rank a long list of critical social issues. The survey revealed this order of importance:

1. The family
2. AIDS
3. Abortion
4. The economy
5. Health care
6. Homosexuality
7. Aging
8. Race relations
9. Drug and alcohol use
10. Crime
11. Homelessness[8]

To summarize, these trends and moral concerns indicate that ethical deliberation in the first part of the twenty-first century will focus on family concerns, **biomedical** issues, economic and political questions, and human relationships. Another revelation from these surveys is no surprise: the prevailing American culture has significantly impacted both the beliefs and the behavior of contemporary Christians. In addition, the values and views of the "Religious Right" seem to have impacted a sizable number of evangelical Protestants.[9]

PERSONAL ETHICAL ISSUES

A distinction is often made between personal and social ethics. Personal ethics focuses primarily on issues related to the individual, while social ethics looks at moral questions involving groups, institutions, and society. Conservative Christians have tended to emphasize personal ethics, while neglecting many social concerns.[10] Conversely, the focus of liberal Protestants leans heavily toward social ethics.

Decisions about personal ethical questions rely heavily on moral **character.** The Bible itself recognizes the importance of the inner moral life, listing **vices** to shun and **virtues** to attain (Gal. 5;

Col. 3).[11] Certainly Christian **morality** is more than acquiring the right virtues, but, as Aristotle suggested, virtues are a "kind of second nature" that direct us to do the right thing rightly.[12]

Every day Christians face numerous ethical decisions in their personal lives. Many are ordinary choices, such as paying our debts, which do not require a great deal of deliberation. Some ethical questions, however, are more difficult and complex, not only in terms of our personal moral evaluation, but also in terms of our responsibility for social action and ministry.

For the purpose of our study, we will explore three personal issues of major concern for twenty-first-century disciples: alcohol and drugs, gambling, and **AIDS.** Three other issues of personal ethics—the environment, media morality, and **professional ethics**—will be briefly summarized. Our examination of these concerns will focus on interpreting the facts, applying biblical and theological insights, and developing a Christian response. The analysis will use the model suggested in chapter 5, but the procedure is by no means a step-by-step process. Moral discernment is always a dynamic interaction between the moral agent and all of the relevant resources. As disciples of Jesus Christ and members of the community of believers, our ultimate goal is to act responsibly in doing the will of God at every level of life: personal, family, community, and global.

Alcohol and Drug Use and Abuse

America is an addictive society. By definition, an addiction is whatever controls your life in such a way that more important matters are ignored or rejected. Alcohol and drug abuse usually involve chemical or physical addictions, and often psychological dependence.[13] Occasional use of drugs is not without problems.

Interpreting the Facts. Destructive addictions to alcohol and drugs are costly. In 1995, the U.S. Department of Health and Human Services estimated that alcoholism cost $150 billion in lost productivity and medical bills, or $606 for every man, woman, and child. According to the National Clearing House for Drug and Alcohol Information, alcohol use is a contributing factor in 68 percent of manslaughters, 54 percent of murders, 48 percent of robberies, and 30 percent of suicides. One out of every three state prison inmates admits drinking heavily before committing the crimes of rape, burglary, and assault.[14]

In recent years the number of adult Americans who drink has averaged 65 to 69 percent, although one current survey claims abstinence in the U.S. has now reached 44 percent, a 10 percent increase of non-drinkers in the past decade.[15] More than eighteen million adults in the U.S. are problem drinkers, at least eleven million (5 percent of the population) suffer from alcoholism, and seventy-six million are affected by alcohol abuse at some time.

A major concern is increased drinking among teenagers and children. The surgeon general of the U.S. reported that 87 percent of high school seniors have used alcohol, 700,000 tenth graders are "binge" drinkers, and 7 percent of eighth graders have been drunk during the last month. The report noted 35 percent of fourth graders say they have been pressured to drink; by the sixth grade, 49 percent have drunk alcohol.[16]

The so-called "hard drugs"[17] cost another $150 billion annually, due to economic loss, treatment cost, and criminal justice expense. In the U.S. 20-25 million persons have tried cocaine and at least five million regularly use the drug. In addition, an estimated 500,000 are addicted to heroin.[18] A 1993 University of Michigan study revealed illicit drug use among America's teens is rising after an eleven-year decline—more young people are using LSD, marijuana, inhalants and stimulants, and alcohol, the most abused drug by teenagers.[19] In 1996 The Partnership for a Drug-Free America reported marijuana use by young people (ages twelve to seventeen) is continuing to rise after three years of decline earlier in the decade. "A profound reversal in adolescent drug trends is continuing," the national survey notes.[20] Among college freshmen, support for legalizing marijuana has risen to nearly 34 percent—double the 17 percent held in 1989.[21]

Addiction is not the only problem related to alcohol and drug abuse. So-called "moderate" drinkers and "recreational" drug users are a very significant part of the 100,000 deaths resulting from alcohol misuse, including about one-half of all highway accident fatalities. The estimated $60 to $117 billion annual economic loss due to drug use involves many occasional users and drinkers. Judges and law enforcement officials have consistently named alcohol and other drugs as causative factors in child abuse, delinquency, divorce, and other family-related problems.

Drinking and drug problems begin early. A recent two-year survey of 58,000 students on seventy-eight college campuses reported 85 percent of students drank alcohol in the past year, each averaging five drinks per week. A dean of students said, "Alcohol is the drug of choice and is an epidemic in this country. If an institution tells you it doesn't have a problem, it is lying."[22]

This statistical overview of the multifaceted social problems resulting from alcohol and drug use illustrates the enormity of the issue. Although human societies have never succeeded in eliminating the use of drugs and alcohol, Christians should not be deterred from working to solve drug-related problems.

Applying Biblical Insights. A beginning point for action is a clear understanding of biblical teachings and Christian principles that apply to alcohol and drug use. In both Old and New Testaments, the Scriptures uniformly condemn drunkenness (Prov. 31:4-5; Lam. 4:21-22; Eph. 5:18; Gal. 5:21). Intoxication is denounced as socially disruptive (Isa. 28:7-8), physically damaging (Prov. 23:29-30), morally corrupting (Gen. 19:32), spiritually deadening (Isa. 5:11-12), and ecclesiastically disqualifying (1 Tim. 3:3).

Biblical teachings about the moderate use of "wine" are not as clear. The Hebrew word for wine is *yayin*, which is equivalent to the Greek word *oinos*,[23] both of which refer to the "fermented juice of the grape."[24] *Yayin* was given as a gift by Abraham to Melchizedek (Gen. 14:18-20); it was designated as a daily offering to God (Exod. 29:40); and it was the functional equivalent of "the fruit of the vine" (Matt. 26:29) drunk at the Last Supper.[25] Although Jesus spoke against drunkenness (Matt. 24:49; Luke 12:45), He miraculously produced high-quality wine *(oinos)* at the wedding in Cana (John 2:1-11) and Himself drank *oinos* (Luke 7:33-35).[26]

At the same time the Bible contains several prohibitions against alcohol use. Members of the Aaronic priesthood were not to drink alcoholic beverages before they entered the tabernacle to prevent accidental profanation of the service (Lev. 10:8-11). Nazaritic legislation forbade those who took this special vow to use wine (Num. 6:2-3), but the prohibition was temporary (6:20).[27] An oft-quoted verse in Proverbs cautions, "Do not look at wine when it is red, when it sparkles in the cup" (23:31); some interpret this as an "absolute prohibition," but most exegetes believe the words warn about the attraction of wine to the eyes.[28] A New Testament prohibition is found in an angel's revelation to John the Baptist's father that the prophet was not to drink "wine" *(oinos)* or "strong drink" *(sikera),* for John was to be full of the Holy Spirit (Luke 1:15).

How do we correlate these prohibitionary passages with the common biblical practice of drinking wine? A starting point is to understand the way wine was used in biblical times.[29] After the grape harvest, wine was normally stored in jars covered by a layer of oil. This *yayin (oinos)* was used as a table beverage, either straight from the jar or diluted with water. Over a period of time natural fermentation usually produced a 3 to 4 percent alcoholic level, or even higher. Due to impure and inadequate water supplies, wine was safer and preferred to water.[30] *Oinos* was often used on festive occasions as a part of joyful celebration. Obviously, in Hebrew society the social risks of drinking this slightly fermented wine were substantially less than today.

What conclusions can we reach from these biblical teachings?

1. Drunkenness is strongly condemned throughout the Bible.
2. Naturally fermented wine was commonly used in biblical times.
3. An ideal of abstinence was required of Nazarites (Num. 6:1), Rechabites (Jer. 35:1-11), and John the Baptist (Luke 1:13-15).
4. Certain New Testament principles apply to this issue:
   - Care of the body as the temple of God (1 Cor. 6:19)
   - Concern for the weaker brother (Rom. 14:21)
   - Necessity for Christians to be a positive moral influence upon society (Matt. 5:13-16)
   - Challenge to exhibit a Christian lifestyle that needs no alcohol or drug stimulation, but only the inner joy and peace of the Holy Spirit (Eph. 5:18)

Developing a Christian Response. In light of the biblical and social data concerning the dangers of drug and alcohol use and abuse, how should Christians respond? Social action by believers should center on protecting potential victims, especially through alcohol and drug education. Very few persons understand exactly what alcohol and drugs do to the human body, how serious are the social problems related to drug use, and the real possibility of addiction for anyone who drinks or takes drugs. Churches should regularly provide for their members (especially the young) credible and creative programs of drug and alcohol education.[31]

Another important preventive action for churches and Christian citizens is to work for greater legal controls. Every state struggles to enact laws that limit and discourage alcohol misuse and illegal drug use. In the state where I live, a miswriting of legislation prohibiting the sale of alcohol to minors did not prohibit minors from possessing or drinking alcohol. Recently the law was clarified, which probably will result in the saving of many lives in Louisiana, as drivers age fifteen to twenty-four account for about 41 percent of all alcohol-related fatal and injury collisions.[32]

In terms of ministry to victims of drug misuse, an effective approach is to help addicts gain freedom from drug dependence. Churches need to be aware of specific rehabilitation programs in their areas that treat the addicted. Resources are now available that train Christians to minister to persons with drug-related problems.[33] Some churches support halfway houses for people who are seeking to rid themselves of drug dependence. Often the most valuable ministry is to family members of abusers.

Christians must remember that alcohol and drug misusers are morally responsible persons who need help—physical treatment, psychological counseling, and spiritual guidance. Regardless of their present condition or past behavior, every abuser is a person of infinite worth whose life can be transformed by the grace and power of God (Rom. 12:1-2).

As far as your personal moral decision about this issue is concerned, let us review the relevant facts:

- Alcohol and drug use and abuse can damage your mind and body, endanger your family life, and diminish your ability to work.
- About one of nine persons who drink becomes an alcoholic—to date science has no way to predict who will become addicted.
- Alcohol and drug misuse are major contributors to some of our most serious personal, family, and social problems.
- Due to the complex nature of modern society, even "moderate drinking" poses some risks, including the danger of influencing others to drink (Hab. 2:15).

Many Christians have reached the conclusion that the safest, sanest, and most responsible position in America's "addictive society" is total abstinence. Certainly the follower of Jesus does not need the inebriating effects of drugs, nor does a believer want to be a contributor to the evil results of alcohol and drugs upon our society. In this culture and in these times, abstinence seems to be the best option for those who expect to deal successfully and effectively with the drug problem.

Gambling

In 1970, Nevada was the only state with legalized gambling. On November 3, 1992, Utah turned back a referendum that would have made it the 49th state to adopt some form of gambling. The decision left only Utah and Hawaii as states without legalized gambling. The extent of gambling in its various forms reveals that a broad range of gambling is available throughout the United States, with lottery as the most common form.

Senator Richard Lugar, campaigning for the 1996 Republican presidential nomination, raised the moral issue of state-sponsored gambling: "The spread of gambling is a measure of the moral erosion taking place in our country. . . . It says that if you play enough, you can hit the jackpot and be freed from the discipline of self-support through a job or the long commitment to ongoing education." After quoting Lugar, columnist William Safire added that state-sponsored gambling is a $40 billion-a-year cancer ravaging society, corrupting public officials, and fast becoming the number one teen-age addiction.[34]

Interpreting the Facts. Predicted to be the fastest-growing industry in America in the 1990s, the proliferation and acceptance of gambling has been phenomenal. The amount of money Americans wager has grown from $17.3 billion in 1976 to $329.9 billion in 1992, according to the National Council on Problem Gambling.[35] In New York, a form of keno introduces casino-style gambling to youth at candy stores. In Mississippi, the money spent on gambling in 1994 exceeded all the taxable retail sales in the state. In Las Vegas, organized gambling offers "family-oriented" entertainment—MGM Grand advertises thirty-three acres of rides, shows, themed streets, restaurants, shops, and casinos.

Casino gambling currently is allowed in twenty-seven states, and other states have legislation pending. At $16.5 billion, casino revenues doubled in the first half of the nineties, outgrossing spending on movies, sports, and music concerts combined. In just two years (1993-95), casino visits are up 36 percent, people who say casino gambling is acceptable for everyone is up 16 percent to a total of 59 percent, and the average household casino spending is up 10 percent from $139 to $153.[36]

The dramatic growth of gambling in the 1990s is not the result of a popular movement. Rather it is driven by the greed of the gambling industry with its high-priced lobbyists and pie-in-the-sky promises. In a recent study, Robert Goodman explained, "Initiatives have come from a gambling industry attempting to increase business and public officials attempting to create jobs and raise revenues. . . . New ventures have grown in an ad hoc manner as legislators, state gambling officials and private companies respond to the financial and political opportunities of the moment—often by simply copying the gambling operations of other states."[37]

According to some, the spread of commercial gambling is inevitable. *Time* called it the "great American obsession." David Johnston, author of a book about casinos, claims that "by the end of this century almost every place in America where it has not already arrived will join the trend."[38]

Others disagree. The National Coalition Against Legalized Gambling reported that the November 1995 election scorecard recorded seventeen gambling defeats in seven states and only four approvals in four states.[39] In addition, legislation has been introduced in Congress to establish a blue-ribbon commission to study gambling in the United States and make recommendations for public policy actions.[40]

Aside from the economic promises of more jobs and increased tax revenues, what liabilities does gambling bring to a community? A study on "Legalized Gambling as a Strategy for Economic Development" notes the promise and reality of gambling are not congruent. Professor Goodman concludes, "The gambling industry has indeed created many jobs in gambling enterprises as well as those in related businesses like hotels. But by diverting consumer dollars into gambling, it has also been responsible for the decline of jobs and revenues in other businesses. In addition, the expansion of legalized gambling is increasing the public and private costs of dealing with the social and economic problems among the rising numbers of people who gamble."[41]

One real danger is cannibalization—diverting money from existing businesses to gambling. The Atlantic City experience supports this contention. In the decade after gambling was introduced, the number of restaurants declined from 243 to 146; in four years retail businesses were reduced by one-third, property values fell by millions of dollars, and the city went from fiftieth in the nation in per capita crime to first.[42] Thirty-three million people visit Atlantic City each year, but the population has shrunk 20 percent since 1976. In this gambling mecca there are eighteen-thousand slot machines, but no car washes, no movie theaters, and only one supermarket. The police department budget has tripled, but the crime rate is the highest in the state.

Earl Grinols, former research economist for the Department of the Treasury and senior economist for the Council of Economic Advisors in the Reagan administration, informed Texas lawmakers that gambling costs at least $100 to $300 per adult each year in an area where gambling has been prevalent for three to five years, mainly from the social price of regulation, lost productivity, and crime. Citing estimates by the American Insurance Institute, Grinols said 40 percent of all white collar crime has its roots in gambling, and $1.3 billion annually in insurance fraud is due directly to gambling.[43]

A major liability of legalized gambling is the increasing numbers of problem gamblers. In 1975, fewer than 1 percent of all Americans were considered compulsive gamblers; today it is between 5 percent and 11 percent.[44] Authorities estimate that 9.3 million adults and 1.3 million teenagers have gambling problems. The Texas Council on Problem and Compulsive Gambling reports 59 percent of compulsive gamblers have financial problems, 29 percent are addicted to alcohol, and 25 percent are jobless.[45] Another major concern is the impact of gambling upon youth. Since the mid-1980s, juvenile gambling has increased steadily. A study of high school youth and gambling by Durand F. Jacobs found one-third of gamblers started wagering before the age of eleven, 80 percent wagered before the age of fifteen, and about one of every twenty-five Americans may be the child of a problem gambler.[46]

An independent researcher discovered that electronic games, such as poker and blackjack, were being marketed by the casino industry to train and attract a new generation of gamblers.[47] The *Wall Street Journal* expressed concern that a visit to Las Vegas revealed large numbers of children and teenagers wandering in the casinos unsupervised, many of them admitting to gambling there regularly.[48] Although statistics are scarce, psychologists who work with young people talk of an epidemic of compulsive gambling among youth, which soon may overshadow drug usage as the primary destructive addiction among adolescents.[49]

Researchers who have done an objective study of the economic and social costs of gambling to society reach one common conclusion—gambling is a bad bet for any community. John Kindt of the University of Illinois concluded: "Legalized gambling is inherently parasitic on any economy . . . it always hurts the economy, it always creates large socioeconomic problems. And that intensifies the needs for tax dollars to address the new problems that they are creating by legalizing gambling."[50]

Applying Biblical Insights. A letter written to the editor of a Gulf Coast newspaper began, "Using a concordance and a Bible, I cannot find one verse which says gambling is a sin." The writer then noted examples of the "casting of lots" in the Bible by Aaron

(Lev. 16), Moses (Num. 26), and the disciples (Acts 1:26), implying that biblical heroes gambled.[51]

The writer is correct if he is looking for a direct command, "Thou shall not gamble." However, many moral ideals in Scripture clearly oppose gambling. The first clear and direct reference is found in Isaiah. Apparently the Hebrews in Exile had been influenced by the Babylonians, who widely engaged in games of chance. The prophet protests against those who "forsake the LORD, who forget my holy mountain, who set a table for Fortune and fill cups of mixed wine for Destiny" (Isa. 65:11). The two deities mentioned here, Fortune *(Gad)* and Destiny *(Meni)*, were the gods of fate and were symbols of good and bad luck. Israelites were trusting in chance rather than God. Isaiah denounced their trust in the cult of luck rather than Jehovah.[52]

What about the biblical practice of casting lots? In the Old Testament, land was assigned by "lot" (Num. 26:52–56); leaders were sometimes chosen by this procedure (1 Sam. 10:20–21), as were sacrificial animals (Lev. 16:7–10); and the "sacred dice" were sometimes used to identify a guilty culprit (Josh. 7:26).

Biblical scholars note two facts. First, the purpose of the practice was to find God's will, not to practice witchcraft, magical arts, or necromancy, for Israel's religion prohibited idolatrous worship. Second, the practice of "casting lots" was eventually discarded by Israel, although it did reappear at the disciples' selection of Matthias (Acts 1:26). The Christian church never again used this method, but depended on the Spirit of truth to guide them in their decisions.

A third possibility should be added. In the Old Testament are many practices that are less than God's ideal, such as polygamy, concubinage, divorce, and wars of extermination. Although "casting lots" was not God's ideal method for determining His will, is it possible God "allowed" (cf. Matt. 19:8) this method until the fuller revelation came?

Thus the "casting of lots" in the Bible is not justification for modern gambling. Nor does the fact that the Bible never specifically condemns gambling make it allowable or amoral. The Bible builds moral character and guides ethical conduct in many ways in addition to direct commands.

One way the Bible shapes our ethics is by forming a redeemed community. Christians are members of a "colony of heaven" (Phil. 3:20, Moffatt)—"resident aliens" whose values stand in sharp contrast to a morally dwarfed society. The mentality of gambling is

the very opposite of the attitude of Christians, which is characterized by hope and trust in God's care (Matt. 6:25-34).

The Bible also contains numerous principles that serve as guide-
posts for Christians developing a response to gambling:

1. Gambling questions the sovereign rule and providential care
   of God over our lives, encouraging greed, materialism, and
   idolatrous worry about wealth (Matt. 6:25-34).

2. Gambling violates the central moral imperative of the Bible—
   the law of love—"You shall love the Lord your God. . . . You
   shall love your neighbor as yourself" (Matt. 22:37, 39). Love
   meets needs; gambling exploits. Love entreats; gambling mis-
   treats. Love strengthens; gambling weakens. Love builds up;
   gambling tears down. Love never fails; gambling ever fails.[53]

3. Gambling encourages the sin of covetousness and stealing.
   Two of the Ten Commandments speak to gambling. The sixth
   Word reads, "You shall not steal" (Exod. 20:15). In one sense,
   gambling is robbery by mutual consent. The tenth Word
   states, "You shall not covet" (20:17). The insatiable desire for
   money you do not have and for wealth you did not earn is a
   vice to shun (Luke 12:15).

4. Gambling violates the biblical principle of stewardship of possessions. Christians are to be responsible managers by using
   whatever possessions we have for God's glory and human
   good (Matt. 25:14-46). Gambling is wrong because it encourages pleasure and profit at the loss and pain of other people.

5. Gambling depreciates the value of honest work. As God's creative purpose for humanity (Gen. 2:15), honest labor honors
   the worker and the product of his or her work.

6. Gambling destroys Christian influence. Paul emphasized that
   freedom must always be exercised responsibly, especially
   when an action may injure a weaker or more immature person
   (1 Cor. 8). Disciples of Christ should exert a positive moral
   influence upon society, one that builds up community life
   (Matt. 5:13-16).

7. Gambling corrupts the God-ordained purpose of the state. The
   role of government is to be "God's servant for your good"
   (Rom. 13:4).

Could the apostle Paul imagine God approving any state that used
a basic human weakness as a means for taxation?

Seen in the light of Christian values and biblical principles, gambling must be described as personally selfish, morally irresponsible,

and socially destructive. In precept, principle, and narrative revelation, the Bible calls Christians to a life incompatible with gambling and its social results.

Developing a Christian Response. In light of the growth of gambling in the 1990s, almost every Christian will be faced with a personal moral choice about wagering, as well as with questions about Christian response. Though churches may broadly agree that gambling is harmful to individuals and society, the Christian community "cannot keep yielding moral ground and expect to be any force for good in society."[54] In order to develop a Christian strategy, let us summarize the case against legalized gambling:

- Gambling depresses legitimate business and redistributes wealth on an inequitable basis.
- Gambling victimizes the poor.
- Gambling increases crime and social problems.
- Gambling corrupts government.
- Gambling destroys the work ethic.
- Gambling contradicts social responsibility.
- Gambling revenue is regressive, irresponsible, erratic, and violates sound theories of taxation.
- Gambling helps create compulsive addiction to gambling.
- Gambling is socially disintegrating.

A person does not have to be a Christian to find a basis for opposing gambling. When biblical principles and Christian values are added to the equation, the disciple of Christ has little trouble rejecting the false promises and saying "No" to the question of legalized gambling.

The responsibility of the church for ministry and action in this arena is similar to the Christian community's role in confronting alcohol and drug misuse. Education about the nature of gambling and its many attendant evils is vital. For example, most who play the lottery do not realize the odds of getting struck by lightning (about one in two million) are better than the one-in-three or four million odds of winning most lottery jackpots.[55] Educational programs expose the dangers of gambling and motivate people to remove it from their communities.

Effective legislation by state and federal government is needed to control and eliminate gambling. Antigambling laws will be effective only if they are backed by legal enforcement. A responsible public, led by Christian citizens, holds the key to just laws, strict enforcement, and appropriate sanctions.

Rehabilitation treatment for those addicted to gambling is preferable to jail sentences, for compulsive gamblers need spiritual and
psychological help. Participation in groups like Gamblers Anonymous proves beneficial for many. The church needs to work with
the community in providing rehabilitation for addicted gamblers
and ministry to their families.

A unique but needful area of ministry is helping churches and
communities adjust to legalized gambling after it has come. After
studying several municipalities where gambling came suddenly,
John Allen identified "Eight Phases Which Most Churches Pass
Through When Gaming Is Introduced into Their Community"—
apathy, alarm, anger, ambivalence, assessment, analysis, decision,
and assimilation.[56] For the first time many churches have had to
face very divisive congregational questions related to members and
gambling.[57] Given present trends, most churches will need to
accept the reality of gambling in their community and develop a
holistic response through evangelism, education, discipleship, and
ministry.

AIDS

In 1981 the disease had no name, only symptoms and victims. Fifteen years later most Americans not only knew the word, but they
also knew someone who had died from AIDS. In 1981 only 153
cases were reported in three cities. The present U.S. estimates
(1995) are that 1 to 1.5 million people carry the AIDS virus, 476,899
more are actual cases, and 291,815 have died from diseases caused
by AIDS.[58] Eight to 14 million worldwide are infected by the HIV
virus and more than 600,000 have AIDS—by the year 2000 the number of AIDS cases could grow tenfold to 6 million.[59] The malady has
become the number one killer of men aged twenty-five to forty-four
in the U.S.[60]

Several reasons make AIDS an important ethical concern beyond
its being a major health crisis and a life-and-death issue. To consider
AIDS seriously requires considering homosexuality and drug abuse,
for the primary high-risk groups in our country have been from
these two populations.[61] The church has not done well in responding to AIDS, partly because of the association of the disease with
immoral lifestyles. Although the risk groups are changing, to understand and respond to AIDS requires addressing some tough biblical
and moral questions.

Another reason for studying AIDS is a practical one. The illness is
not only prevalent in our society; AIDS also has come to church. As

the virus has spread among all social groups, congregations have had to decide how they will respond to afflicted persons and their families.

The widely publicized story of the Scott Allen family vividly portrays the crises AIDS brings to families and churches.[62] In 1985 Scott Allen told his father, a prominent minister and former president of the Southern Baptist Convention, that his wife Lydia and both of their children had AIDS. During her first pregnancy in 1982, Lydia was infected through a blood transfusion, while Scott was attending a seminary in California. Soon Matthew was born, followed by his brother Bryan.

When the church in Colorado where Scott served in 1985 learned that Lydia and the boys had AIDS, the young minister was fired. The Allens moved back to Texas and sought a church for refuge, but every door slammed shut. After Bryan and Lydia died, the Allens went public in 1992. With his father beside him, twelve-year-old Matt stood before 699 sixth graders at his school and explained his disease. Just before his death in 1995, the students honored Matt with a "Circle of Life" celebration.[63]

Interpreting the Facts. Where did AIDS come from?[64] The complete answer remains a mystery. In the early 1980s it appeared primarily in the homosexual community and was first termed GRID (Gay Related Immune Deficiency). After it was also linked to blood transfusions and drug abuse (contaminated needles), the condition was renamed AIDS—Acquired (premature loss of immune function) Immunodeficiency (loss of part or all of the function of the immune system) Syndrome (a collection of abnormalities).

In 1984 researchers identified the cause of the malady and Congress budgeted $81 million for research: known AIDS cases exceeded seven thousand persons (72 percent homosexuals, 17 percent drug abusers, 1 percent receivers of transfusions, and 9 percent other). By 1985 cases were doubling every ten months. Religious leaders debated about AIDS—many called the virus God's judgment against homosexuality. Others claimed such statements ridiculous, comparing the malady to leprosy and calling for compassion. Surgeon General Koop and others emphasized the need for prevention education.

In 1987 the Federal Drug Administration approved the chemical AZT for treatment of AIDS-related diseases. By 1993 the group ratios of AIDS cases had changed to 47 percent homosexuals,

28 percent intravenous drug users, 9 percent heterosexual transmissions, and 16 percent other.

Exactly what is AIDS? The cause of the debilitating disease is a retrovirus that reproduces itself in human cells. The virus destroys a cell's CD4 receptor and the ability to control, neutralize, and eliminate infectious agents that invade the body or cancer cells within the body. Strictly speaking, the virus causes an infection that can result in AIDS, a loss of the body's ability to fight infections and diseases.

The HIV (Human Immunodeficiency Virus) is very weak and cannot survive in food, insects, animals, or outside the body. Infection requires direct access to the bloodstream, large amounts of the virus, and host cells that permit survival.[65] The known modes of transmission of the AIDS virus are (1) sexual contact between an infected partner and a noninfected partner (heterosexual or homosexual); (2) intravenous drug abuse (sharing of needles); (3) blood transfusions with contaminated blood;[66] and (4) children born to infected mothers (about one of four).[67] HIV carriers may not experience any symptoms of AIDS for as long as ten years, during which time they can transmit the disease to others.

Applying Biblical Insights. Does the Bible teach that AIDS is the punishment of God? The answer is no. In the U.S., AIDS is more prevalent among homosexuals and drug abusers. Certainly the Bible condemns immoral behavior and warns of the tragic results of sexual promiscuity and drug abuse. However, to confuse the disease itself with the mode of transmission is wrong. Would God punish with AIDS an innocent baby born of an HIV-positive mother or the wife who is infected with AIDS by an unfaithful husband?

Jesus never explained why diseases like leprosy or afflictions like blindness exist. When confronted with the question about the cause of blindness from birth in one man, Jesus spoke about the works of God and our responsibility to do God's work—then Jesus healed the man (John 9:1-12).

Jesus always responded to human need, regardless of the moral condition of the needy. Once His disciples were asked, "Why does your teacher eat with tax collectors and sinners?" Jesus overheard them and replied, "Those who are well have no need of a physician, but those who are sick. Go and learn what this means, 'I desire mercy and not sacrifice.' For I have come to call not the righteous but sinners" (Matt. 9:11-13).

In the face of ignorance, hunger, sickness, sin, and death, Jesus' "heart went out" (Luke 7:13)—He was moved with compassion. The compassion of Christ always expressed itself in ministry. To those grieving, He gave comfort (John 11:1-44); to the sick, He brought healing (Matt. 4:23; 9:35); to the wayward, Christ gave guidance (Mark 6:34); and to the sinful, the Lord spoke words of hope and love, saying, "Neither do I condemn you. Go your way, and from now on do not sin again" (John 8:11).

As followers of Jesus, can we overcome our **prejudices** and learn to love beyond our limited understandings to help meet the needs of dying people? If we love people as Christ did, we will not allow anyone's behavior to prevent us from ministering in Jesus' name.

Developing a Christian Response. How should Christians and churches respond to the AIDS epidemic? Again, education is an important starting point. Excellent resources are available for the church to instruct its members.[68] Congregations that make major mistakes usually lack correct information.

As we understand how AIDS is spread, it becomes obvious that the best way to prevent infection is to avoid the two main behavioral risks—sexual transmission and intravenous drug usage. The teaching of moral values and sexual discipline is primarily the responsibility of the family and the church. An encouraging trend is the widespread acceptance of programs that exalt sexual purity before marriage and fidelity within marriage.[69]

Every church also should develop infectious disease policies and child-care procedures before a particular case appears.[70] Christians can take active positions regarding public policy that affects schools, health care, and the rights of individuals and society.

In terms of ministering to people with AIDS, at least three factors must be considered: (1) AIDS is a fatal disease; (2) people with the malady experience alienation and struggle with guilt; (3) once persons get AIDS, the issue is not how they contracted it, but how they and their families can be supported.[71] Church ministries for HIV-positive persons include support groups, foster homes, and caregivers.

The church's real problem may be AFRAIDS—an acronym coined in 1985 for Acute Fear Regarding AIDS. For many Christians, AFRAIDS is more contagious than AIDS.

Lewis Smedes insists that God's own answer to suffering is to join it, feel it, and hurt with it.[72] To follow the example of Christ, we must learn to take another's pain into us.

Other Personal Issues

The twenty-first century poses many personal ethical concerns beyond AIDS, gambling, and drug and alcohol abuse. Chief among these are environmental ethics, media morality, and professional ethics.

Earthkeeping has been a God-given responsibility from the beginning when God made the first couple stewards of the earth (Gen. 1:26) and commanded them "to till it and to keep it" (Gen. 2:15). The present misuse of creation threatens the ecology in ways it never has before. The Christian community must become better informed about how the earth is endangered,[73] as well as develop sensible and long-range environmental protection plans.[74]

Not all evangelicals believe an ecological crisis exists. An ethics professor laments that reactions by evangelical leaders to the environmental movement range from mocking it, portraying environmentalists as deceived by lying spirits, or preaching that economic development should be free of environmental constraints.

Addressing evangelicals on their response to the ecological crisis, ethicist Jonathan Wilson urged that the doctrines of creation and redemption be kept in proper balance. Evangelical environmentalists assume the earth is basically in good shape and needs only tending; evangelical antienvironmentalists overlook the role of Christians as instruments of redemption on earth.[76]

In the foreword to a basic Christian text on protecting the earth, Vice President Al Gore wrote, "The solutions we seek will be found in a new faith in the future of life on earth after our own; a faith in the future which justifies action in the present; a new moral courage to choose higher values in the conduct of human affairs; a new reverence for absolute principles that can serve as guiding stars for the future course of our species and our place within creation."[77]

Concern about the impact of the *media* on **morals** is another hot topic. In his 1996 "State of the Union" address, President Clinton called attention to the negative impact of television upon children. Various surveys in the nineties indicate the average American adult views over four hours of television daily, the average child over three hours, and by age eighteen teenagers have spent more time watching TV than they have in school.[78] During an average of

2,300 hours of television a year, a child views 11,000 acts of violence, 1,900 murders, and 23,000 sexual situations.

With many experts linking the glorification of violence and the degradation of sexuality to the influence of television, movies, popular music, and other forms of media, it is imperative that the church respond. Reliable resources that promote greater awareness and responsible action are available.[79]

A final key area of concern in personal moralilty is *professional ethics*. Dennis Campbell contends the contemporary crisis in the professions is due mainly to the absence of shared values in a society increasingly secular and pluralistic.[80] Professionals today face a crucial question: Will I be an enabler or exploiter?[81] Not only lawyers and doctors, but also ministers are vulnerable to unethical behavior in their vocation.

Ministerial ethics can no longer be assumed, if they ever were. In this decade seminary courses in spiritual formation and ethics in ministry have multiplied, as well as numerous texts on the subjects.[82] Christian ministers, and other professionals, have a unique moral role to fulfill in our society.

The most respected Christian minister of our century surely must be Billy Graham. Early in his evangelistic ministry, Graham met with the members of his team to discuss how they could avoid any unethical conduct. Out of that discussion in 1948 came the "Modesto Manifesto," a set of practical guidelines for maintaining moral purity and avoiding even the appearance of evil.[83] Close observers believe a major reason for Graham's successful ministry and worldwide respect was this personal moral commitment.

FOR THOUGHT AND DISCUSSION

1. Debate this topic: "Personal ethics are more important than social ethics in the Christian life."
2. Discuss the pros and cons of the following statements:
   "The Bible allows the moderate drinking of alcohol."
   "Gambling is immoral only if it is excessive or addictive."
   "AIDS is God's judgment on homosexuals and drug abusers."
3. Develop and discuss a church program of prevention for:
   (1) alcohol use and abuse by youth;
   (2) legalized gambling in your community.

4. Develop and discuss a church program of ministry for:
   (1) alcoholic women in your community;
   (2) the families of compulsive gamblers;
   (3) persons dying with AIDS.
5. Write an "Infectious Disease Policy" for your church.

CHAPTER SEVEN

SEXUALITY AND MARRIAGE

A decade ago popular youth speaker and author Josh McDowell became concerned about teenage sexual activity. The Barna Research Group of California was commissioned to survey churched youth (regular attenders) in eight evangelical denominations.[1] The study revealed that 65 percent of these youth had some type of sexual contact by age eighteen, 43 percent had experienced sexual intercourse by that age, and more than 20 percent of them had participated in sexual experimentation by age thirteen.

McDowell was shocked that the sexual standards of religious youth in these conservative churches were only 10 to 15 percent ahead of the general youth population. In response, McDowell developed a series of studies in sexual **ethics** to provide resources for teens, parents, and pastors.[2]

Since that survey, sexual **morality** in America has continued to decline, not only among youth, but in all age groups. Recent surveys confirm that more than half the nation's high school students (54 percent) have had sex relations. Among ninth-graders, 40 percent have had sex; by the tenth grade it's 48 percent; by the eleventh grade it's 57 percent; and by the twelfth grade 72 percent have engaged in sex.[3] Another study found that by age twenty, three of four girls and five of six boys will have had sexual intercourse. To summarize, in a given year 10 million teenagers will engage in 126 million acts of sexual intercourse resulting in more than 1 million pregnancies, 406,000 **abortions**, 134,000 miscarriages, and 490,000 births, about 313,000 of which are illegitimate.[4]

Among adults one evidence of sexual looseness includes a rising number of unmarried couples living together: from 523,000 couples in 1970 to 1.9 million in 1986, 2.2 million in 1987, 2.6 million in 1990, and 3.5 million in 1993.[5] Another result of irresponsible sexual behavior is unwanted pregnancies, a major factor behind the 1.5 million abortions annually. Since 1960 births to unmarried women have risen from 5 percent to more than 20 percent. Rape, domestic violence, sexual abuse, incest, adultery, and marital conflict are other ethical concerns directly related to our failures in sexual matters.

Cultural forces also contribute to our growing sexual problems. Every day the entertainment and advertising medias bombard us with sexual messages. To the casual observer, Western society seems obsessed with sensuality. At the close of the twentieth century, Christians find themselves in a sex-oriented (or *disoriented*) culture similar to the sexually promiscuous world faced by the earliest Christians.

Another symptom of our moral disease is a widespread confusion about human sexuality. Any sidewalk survey of the public's definition of sex would undoubtedly include these misunderstandings:

- "Sex is love"—the romanticizing of sex;
- "Sex is life"—the deifying of sex;
- "Sex is evil"—the demonizing of sex;
- "Sex sells"—the commercializing of sex;
- "Sex is fun"—the hedonizing of sex; and
- "Sex is natural"—the biologizing of sex.

Our present problems spring in part from a distorted view of sexuality inherited from the past. The ancient Greek philosophers divided human beings into two parts: soul and body. Plato, for example, taught the soul was separate from and superior to the body.[6] This "soul-body" dualism led to a negative view of the physical side of life, since the "spiritual soul" was defined as the good element in humans. Hellenistic **Gnostics** believed the material body was the prison-house of the soul. Since procreation merely perpetuated imprisonment, sexuality was an evil to be suppressed, if not altogether avoided.

Asceticism, the belief that the physical and material are innately evil, became the basis for the disciplined life of the **Stoics,** Jewish ascetics, and Christian monastics.[7] For the monastics, the road to God was a *via negativa:* the elimination of all temporal distractions, including detachment from all things material, especially sexual desires. Christianity was deeply influenced by these views, in time elevating celibacy as an ideal state, exalting virginity, and viewing sexual activity as a necessary evil for ordinary Christians.

The influential patristic leader Augustine set the parameters of Christian sexual ethics for many centuries when he defined the purpose of sexual union as procreation. Marriage, the context of legitimate sex, has three purposes: children (proles), fidelity and the avoidance of fornication (fides), and the indissoluble and sacramental bond of Christian partners (sacramentum).[8]

Although the Protestant Reformation challenged many medieval sexual traditions and grounded the meaning of sexuality in biblical teachings, the belief that procreation was the purpose of sexual intercourse continued, along with a certain ambivalence regarding sexual desire. Contemporary **Christian ethics** has given more emphasis to the **norm** of love, and less to procreation, although marriage continues to be the normal context for sex. Today Christian thinkers view sexuality more in relation to personality and identity, seeing sexual desire as a positive good and an avenue for love and commitment.[9]

In the modern era, an effort has been made to redeem sex from its early bondage to sin. However, this liberation with its emphasis on "quality" sex has not been without negative effects—heightened expectations, performance-focused practice of sex, and a general secularization of sexuality.[10] As religion was relegated to the fringe of life, sex became a private matter devoid of religious meaning. By the second half of the twentieth century, technology paved the way for a sexual revolution. The triple fears of "infection, conception, and detection" were eliminated by the advent of penicillin, the birth-control pill, and the privacy afforded by separate rooms, motels, and the automobile. In the 1960s a "new sexual morality" was proclaimed—the double standard was overturned, women were liberated to join men in promiscuity, all sexual restraints were discarded, and a new era of enjoyment of sex was ordained.[11]

In the last two decades, however, a different mood seems to be evolving. Time magazine declared, "The Revolution Is Over."[12] The cries for "free love" and "recreational sex" have been replaced by calls for "responsibility," "caution," and "commitment." The Playboy experiment failed for most people, not because of sexually transmitted diseases but because of loneliness and the need for a caring relationship. In its place a new ethic emerged.

This new "Ethic of Intimacy" (as one author termed it),[13] though mildly positive about marriage and sex, is actually not about love. Proponents of this new attitude describe a feeling of openness and caring between two "partners" or "lovers." They use words like *compatibility, freedom, privacy*, and *maturity* to describe their relationship. However, the "Ethic of Intimacy" is inherently weak and vague—too weak to deal with the powerful human urges that make up our sexuality and too vague to distinguish between the sway of emotions and true intimacy that is created through persistent self-sacrifice.

So, how far have we come in our understanding of sexuality? Though we no longer worship at the shrines of fertility cults, modern Americans do seek salvation at the feet of a new Aphrodite. Today's secular version of sexuality attempts to create a new Eden in which intimacy is heaven and sensual fulfillment is God. In such a time as this, how can disciples of Jesus reclaim and proclaim a Christian understanding of sexuality?

A CHRISTIAN INTERPRETATION OF SEXUALITY

Sexuality is certainly more than sex; it is the whole way we live in our world as male and female body-persons. Likewise, our personhood is much more than our sexual nature. Nevertheless, sexuality and personal identity are so closely linked that it is impossible to separate the two.

The identity of your sex is the first statement about you after your birth. The first thing we usually notice about others is their sex. Many times we want to minimize or negate our sexuality, but our femaleness or maleness is a reflection of who we are. We are created sexual in God's image; sexuality is a good gift of God and an integral part of human personality (Gen. 1:27, 31; 2:25).

Ordinarily, sexuality is a more comprehensive term than sex. Although sexuality involves sex, it goes beyond sex acts, for it is a basic dimension of our personhood. "Sexuality includes our attitudes and understanding as male and female and affectional orientation toward those of the opposite or same sex. Sexuality is a sign, a symbol, and a means to communion and to communication."[14]

Thus sexuality is much more than anatomy or even sex-role attitudes. Sexuality expresses our authentic humanness in relationship; it is also intrinsic to our relationship to God. More than anything else, sexuality involves our capacity for companionship, the ability to open our hearts and minds to another and to God. As sexuality deals with the essence of who we are, a biblical understanding of personhood is vital.

Biblical Teachings about Sexuality

Eden: Perfect Sex. The biblical description of sex begins in the opening chapters of Genesis with an image of perfection in the Garden of Eden.[15] In the beginning "God created humankind in his image, in the image of God he created them; male and female he created them" (Gen. 1:27). In Eden's atmosphere of perfect freedom and unhindered intimacy, both sexes are formed by the Creator. This profound statement that *both* are created "in God's image" implies equality between the sexes and relates sexuality directly to the nature of God.

The second chapter of Genesis provides more details. The only "not good" (2:18) of creation is the isolation of *adam*,[16] who finds no suitable companion among all the other living creatures (2:20). To correct this, God creates Eve as a perfect complement for Adam (2:21-22). Note, however, that the woman is not formed out of "nothing" like the universe (1:1-2), nor out of "dust" like *adam* (2:7), but out of a "rib" from *adam* (2:21). Thus when the Lord God brought Eve to Adam, like a father bringing a bride, Adam exclaimed: "This at last is bone of my bones and flesh of my flesh; this one shall be called Woman *[ishshah]*, for out of Man *[ish]* this one was taken" (2:23).

The final verses of Genesis 2 provide a basic understanding of God's original intent for the relationship between male and female. Adam's cry of joy emphasizes the similarity of man and woman— they are called together because they are alike. Clearly there are some differences, but the overarching emphasis of the story is that the two are akin, right to the bone. This alikeness is profoundly good because God intended it so.

Next comes a comment on marriage, which emphasizes the couple's unique oneness: "Therefore a man leaves his father and his mother and clings to his wife and they become one flesh" (2:24). As Adam and Eve had no family to leave, this verse confirms the basis of marriage—a call to communion between husband and wife, which requires a separation from all other family ties.

This foundational statement of perfect sexuality closes with an eloquent description of the original intimacy: "And the man and his wife were both naked, and were not ashamed" (2:25). In the complete freedom of Eden, God meant for male and female to live together in shameless nakedness. "Without the aid of legal or social props, they were intimate, naked, and 'one flesh.'"[17]

God gave three major commands to the first couple: to oversee (1:26) and care for the earth (2:15), to procreate (1:28), and to develop oneness in marriage (2:25). Some interpret these directives to mean the primary purpose of sex and marriage is to raise children and thereby form the traditional family economic unit. A closer look at the creation story reveals four main reasons God designed sexuality: (1) companionship, the integrative purpose of marriage (2:18); (2) **reproduction,** the procreative purpose of marriage (1:28); (3) intimacy, the bonding purpose of marriage (2:25); and (4) pleasure, the recreative purpose of marriage (Gen. 4:1a; Prov. 5:15–21).

Why did God create humanity as male and female? In a word, to obliterate aloneness. As two persons become "one flesh" in marriage, their sexual relationship builds a life of companionship, intense intimacy, and fidelity. With such a union no human love can compete, and nothing short of death can part.

Sinai: Negative Protections. The Bible soon leaves Eden and goes to Sinai: "You shall not commit adultery" (Exod. 20:14). Why this stern negative prohibition? The perfect intimacy of Eden was disrupted by rebellion. Genesis 3 describes how Adam and Eve's natural union was shattered by sin. Together they revolted against God and became "one" in their sinning. Blaming each other, they shamefully put on clothes and hid from God (3:7–8). From that moment it was no longer natural to be "naked and not ashamed"; the normal response, due to sin, is to violate our sexuality, break our intimacy, and hide.

The need for Sinai's prohibitions is also revealed in the way sin distorted God's original commands to the first couple. The command to "multiply" (1:28) was made more difficult, for childbirth would now become painful (3:16a). Because of sin, the responsibility to "till and keep the earth" (2:15) became disagreeable labor, for the land would resist cultivation (3:17b–19). God's intent that Adam and Eve be united through intimate companionship was suddenly strained by male domination (3:16).

Though Eden was lost, the hope remained that some of the intimacy of the Garden might be regained by Adam and Eve's descendants. Sexual abnormalities such as rape, incest, bestiality, **homosexuality,** fornication, and transvestitism are clearly condemned.[18] Old Testament sexual ethics were meant to protect marriage, so that Eden's "unashamed nakedness" might be recovered. Two of the "Ten Words" brought down from Sinai by Moses commanded fidelity in marriage, in desire and deed, which made communion possible (Exod. 20:14, 17).

Nevertheless, a patriarchal and polygamous culture lost sight of Eden. Though glimpses of the ideal occasionally appeared (Song of Sol.; Job 31; Prov. 31), sexual misconduct and the mistreatment of women became the rule. Hebrew males justified divorce, allowed concubinage, and practiced the double standard.

Sermon on the Mount: Right Desire. To re-create the intimacy of Eden, it is important not only to do right but also to desire the right things. In the Sermon on the Mount, Christ emphasized the importance of inner thoughts in His warning about "adultery of the heart" (Matt. 5:28). The idea that adulterous thoughts as well as adulterous actions are wrong first appeared in the Tenth Commandment: "You shall not covet your neighbor's wife" (Exod. 20:17). This Old Testament concern for right desire involved more than property rights, for lusting after another person harms no one's property, but "it harms the one who lusts by confusing and diffusing the shape of his chief desire."[19]

In Matthew 5, Jesus "filled full" this **Decalogue** command about coveting by linking sexual thoughts and sexual actions together. If desire has gone astray, the deed is not far away. To foster "shameless nakedness" in sexuality, men and women must not only act right; they must also desire right.

Christians sometimes confuse lust with normal sexual feelings. Drawing the line between sexual excitement and sinful desire is not easy. On one hand, all personal interactions have appropriate sexual dimensions—every erotic feeling in response to a physically attractive person is not "looking with lust." At the same time (especially in a culture such as ours), normal sexual response to an attractive person easily may slip into wrong desires.

What then is "adultery of the heart"? Some define *lust* as a "second look," or in the words of a student, "When 'wow' becomes 'how'!" More precisely, in the words of Bishop Charles Gore, a person must "have the deliberate intention to sin; he looks on the woman *in order to* excite his lust; he is only restrained from action (if it be so) by lack of opportunity or fear of consequences; in his will and intention he has already committed the act."[20]

This word of Jesus about adultery of the heart is a reminder that we are fallen creatures in a fallen world. Wrong desire is intrinsic to who we are, but right desire is possible for the newborn in the **kingdom of God.** Our first need is to ask God to strengthen us within that we may develop control over our desire and train our passion toward our beloved. In addition we must not despair when we fail, but rather learn to thank God for forgiveness.

Corinth: Casual Sex. To Christians living in the sexually immoral city of Corinth, Paul the apostle warned against *porneia* (1 Cor. 6:9-20). Although the word originally meant "prostitute" or "premarital unchastity," by the time of Jesus it had become a blanket word that included every kind of unlawful sexual intercourse.[21] For Paul the word certainly described casual sex—in this case sex with a prostitute (1 Cor. 6:16-20).[22]

Why is *porneia* outside the boundaries of Eden? Recreational sex, some say, is strictly impersonal and therefore harmless. What could be wrong with meeting sexual needs before marriage? Premarital sex may even aid sexual awareness—after marriage a person can be faithful.

Paul's answer is profound. Even casual coupling makes two people who come together sexually "one flesh" (6:16). Lewis Smedes explains: "Sexual intercourse involves two people in a life union; it is a life-uniting act. . . . It does not matter what the two people have in mind. The whore sells her body with an unwritten understanding that nothing personal will be involved in the deal. . . . The buyer gets his sexual needs satisfied without having anything personally difficult to deal with afterwards. . . . But none of this affects Paul's point. The reality of the act, unfelt and unnoticed by them, is this: it unites them—body and soul—to each other."[23]

Some argue that extramarital sex is wrong only because it violates a marital covenant, but Paul insists it is wrong even when no covenant exists. Sexual expression is so powerful that only within the marriage bond is it suitable. Anywhere else it is out of place for a very practical reason: "Someone who has given himself sexually has less of himself to give to the love of his life. . . . he has memories, expectations, lessons from his experience; and these lessons go to the root of his **character.** We might put it another way: He is no longer a virgin. . . . virginity is of value primarily because it leaves the way open to the right kind of sexual formation: within marriage. Virgins have a greater openness to communion."[24]

Paul adds one final thought. In light of Eschaton and severe persecution facing Corinthian Christians, the missionary apostle raises the advisability of singleness (1 Cor. 7:1-9). However, celibacy was not presented as a higher or more spiritual state. Paul's conviction is that sex is good (7:2-5), celibacy is a gift (7:7), marriage is the norm (7:36-37), and sex relations in marriage are the mutual responsibilities of husband and wife (7:3-5).[25]

Sexuality and Love

In his book *Agape and Eros*, Anders Nygren argues that *agape* and *eros* are two distinct theories of love in theological ethics.[26] *Agape* is God-centered, while *eros* is anthropocentric. *Agape* is sacrificial, self-giving love, while *eros* is egocentric, possessive love. *Eros* is selective love, dependent on the lovable qualities it sees in its object; *agape* is universal love, creating value in its object out of the character of the lover.[27]

Nygren claims the writers of the New Testament deliberately rejected the *eros* motif (dominant in Greek **philosophy**) in favor of *agape*. While it is true that *eros* is absent from the New Testament and *storge* (family love) appears rarely, the exception is the verb *phileo* (friendly affection) and its derivatives, which are common. Nygren's critics believe his basic thesis is overplayed. Paul Tillich contended the two are really the same thing, while Aquinas said they complement each other—God's love made human love better.[28]

Nygren is certainly correct about *agape's* rich significance for Christian ethics and that love is multidimensional. Ethicists long have utilized four classic distinctions in the Greek words to explain different levels of love.[29] In relating sexuality to love, the four varieties of affection complement each other in a progressive and inclusive way.

This relationship can be pictured by four concentric circles. In the inner circle is *eros*, which represents "physical attraction." The basic aspect of our sexuality is the normal biological attraction created by God *(eros),* which leads to the "one flesh" union of males and females in sexual intercourse.

The second circle, which encloses the first, is *storge*, a term meaning "personal affection" and "mutual caring." This level of love moves beyond basic attraction toward emotional intimacy.

The ability to express love and affection *(storge)* is a step beyond *eros*, which enriches the physical union of marriage.

Philia is the third concentric circle of affection and describes "intimate communication." In both testaments the verb "know" means knowledge gained through experience, and it is used only for human sexual relations—"Now the man knew his wife Eve, and she conceived" (Gen. 4:1). In sexual intercourse, two persons reveal themselves to one another. *Philia* love is the basis for intimate communication; sexual intercourse "provides husband and wife with a language which cannot be matched by words or by any other act whatsoever. Love needs language for its adequate expression and sex has its own syntax."[30]

The final circle that surrounds the other three is *agape*—the unselfish love of the will that is neither dependant nor reciprocal. For sexuality, *agape* love means "total commitment." Sex relations for humans always express personal values. Properly expressed, sexual union represents the most complete commitment between two marital partners. "Coitus of its own nature means something like, 'I am yours utterly and completely. Because I can never do anything more intimate than this with anyone, I am yours in the most intimate possible union.' . . . To do it and not mean this is vainly to betray two personalities."[31]

Sexuality is a precious gift and a serious responsibility. Like other capacities, it may be rightly used or wrongly abused. Sexual failure is forgiveable, but sexual sins are serious and always result in the loss of Eden. For human fulfillment, God intended our sexuality to create and enrich the "one flesh" union of marriage—a physical, emotional, and spiritual bonding. The unashamed intimacy of Eden can happen only in an exclusive, lifelong, loving covenant. "Christian sexual ethics is inherently idealistic. We hold up an ideal of communion that is far from convenient. Few will experience it fully. Most will suffer trying to attain it. Yet it is worth the pain, because it is what God made us for in the garden."[32]

Homosexuality

In a "Dear Abby" letter, a twenty-five-year-old **lesbian** appealed to "all **homophobic** individuals" to correct their misunderstandings: "A person's sexual orientation is a natural part of a person that can't be changed. It is God-given. Since it is what nature intended, it should be celebrated. It can't possibly be immoral." Abigail Van Buren added, "I have always believed that one's sexual orientation is genetically predetermined before birth. Homosexuals are born—not made."[33]

A contrasting view is written by Chaplain Ray in his International Prison Ministry newsletter: "Homosexuals are not a third sex. They are not accidents of either creation or procreation. They are ordinary people, who, in the early years of life, responded to their emotional and mental stresses and strains with wrong attitudes and wrong actions which developed into serious neuroses."[34]

Twenty years ago, most homosexuals concealed their sexuality as a shameful secret. In today's postcloset era, gay men and women have emerged from the shadows, not as deviants, but as coworkers, family members, and political lobbyists. Unwilling any longer to remain hidden, homosexuals claim to be ordinary people who should not be denied civil rights—the right to teach school, adopt children, serve in the military, or pastor a church. To be despised for an attribute as accidental as **race**, so they say, is unwarranted **prejudice.**

Christians who think seriously about homosexuality have found these questions hard to answer. To begin with, biblical scholars have vigorously debated the Bible's message about homosexuality. Some declare the condemnation of homosexuality is conclusive; others contend the Scripture prohibits perverse behavior, but says nothing about homosexual orientation. In addition, is homosexuality set before birth, or is it determined by environment? Finally, it is one matter to censure sinful behavior, but quite another to offer Christian compassion and redemptive hope for persons with fierce homosexual longings.

Nature and History. A homosexual is one who is motivated by "a definite preferential erotic attraction to members of the same sex and who usually (but not necessarily) engages in overt sexual relations with them."[35] Researchers are divided over the nature of the condition. One school of thought believes homosexuality is a static state—it is unchanging, fixed, a third sex. Another group contends homosexuality is dynamic—it is a flexible condition that may move back and forth between a heterosexual and a homosexual identity.[36]

The number of homosexuals in the general population is another controversial point. Present estimates range from 1 percent to 10 percent. In the late 1940s, the Kinsey Institute surveyed American sexual behavior and reported about 9 percent of males and 2 percent of females were predominantly homosexual or bisexual.[37] A number of surveys in the 1970s cited incidences of 2 to 4 percent for males and 1 to 4 percent for females,[38] although one study by Judd Marmor quoted figures of 5 to 10 percent for men and 3 to 5 percent for women.[39]

The bold certainty of *10 Percent* (the name given a national magazine for gays and lesbians) is no longer an established statistic. Researchers at the University of Chicago and the State University of New York have recently reported much lower numbers for the homosexual population: 2.8 percent of men and 1.4 percent of women identify themselves as gay, lesbian, or bisexual.[40] Psychologist Stanton Jones concludes that the best estimates today suggest 1 to 3 percent of the population are practicing homosexuals, not 10 percent.[41]

Homosexuality is not a recent phenomenon. In the ancient world it was evident in prehistoric art, pictographs, and the legal codes of Assyrians, Egyptians, and Hebrews. From the sixth century B.C. onward, references to homosexual practices appeared in the art and literature of Greece and Rome, although their presence did not imply social approval. The Christianization of the Western world did not eradicate homosexual behavior; church theologians struggled with the issue from the patristic period to the present.[42]

In recent American history, the homosexual subculture has become more visible and vocal. During the 1960s many states eliminated sodomy laws from their statutes. Troy Perry (a Pentecostal minister) founded the Metropolitan Community Church for homosexuals, as gay clergy formed support groups like Dignity (Roman Catholic) and Integrity (Episcopal). Gay caucuses in many mainline Protestant denominations have worked to gain acceptance and ordination for homosexuals. In 1973 the American Psychiatric Association, by a vote of 5,854 to 3,810 (of 17,910 members), removed "homosexuality" from its list of mental disorders, replacing it with the terminology "sexual orientation disturbance."[43]

For years evangelicals believed the Scriptures so explicitly condemned homosexuality that no one but the most liberal Christians (who denied biblical **authority**) could defend the practice. Two events changed that attitude. First, at least three books written by competent Christian scholars called for a reassessment, claiming the Scriptures condemned perverse behavior but not constitutional homosexuality.[44] In the evangelical camp, two respected authors asked, *Is the Homosexual My Neighbor?* in a text that reexamined certain forms of homosexual expression.[45] Other evangelical writers proposed that a homosexual orientation may be a legitimate, alternative lifestyle.[46]

Biblical Teachings. When we turn to the Bible, we discover that homosexuality is not a major concern in the Scriptures. Victor Paul Furnish has pointed out that no words existed in Hebrew or Greek equivalent to our English words *homosexual* or *homosexuality.*[47] Eight or nine biblical texts do address the subject of homosexual behavior, however.

In the Old Testament, four passages condemn homosexuality by illustration (Gen. 19 and Judg. 19) and by legislation (Lev. 18:22; 20:13). The Holiness Code clearly labeled male homosexual practice as an "abomination" (Lev. 18:22) and prescribed the death penalty for offenders (Lev. 20:13). A primary reason for God's judgment upon Sodom and Gomorrah was the crime of homosexual rape (Gen. 19:1-25; cf. 2 Pet. 2:6-10 and Jude 7), a depravity also denounced among the inhabitants of Gibeah (Judg. 19:22-38).

In the New Testament, Paul censured homosexual behavior (including lesbianism) as unnatural (Rom. 1:18-27), incompatible with life in the kingdom of God (1 Cor. 6:9-10), and a violation of God's law and the gospel (1 Tim. 1:8-11). In his correspondence to the Christians in Rome, Paul justifies God's wrath upon the Gentile world by recounting their sordid record of idolatry, naming male and female homosexuality as proof of their rebellion (1:26-28).

Paul's comments to the Corinthians and to Timothy about homosexual acts reveal two important terms. *Malakoi* (1 Cor. 6:9) literally means "soft," but it was used to describe male prostitutes who offered their bodies for pay to older males. The compound word, *arsenokoitai* (1 Cor. 6:9; 1 Tim. 1:10), literally means "one who goes to bed with males," or "sodomites."[48] Here Paul classifies both passive and active homosexuals as persons in rebellion against God, but he also offers hope for the homosexual: "This is what some of you used to be. But you were washed, you were sanctified, you were justified in the name of the Lord Jesus Christ and in the spirit of our God" (1 Cor. 6:11).

Scholars with a more sympathetic view toward homosexuality have tried to soften these condemnatory passages. The sin of Sodom and of the inhabitants of Gibeah was not homosexual rape, say Derrick Bailey, John Boswell, and Robin Scroggs.[49] These biblical interpreters argue that the word *know* (*yadah*, Gen. 19:5; Judg. 19:22) referred to a serious breach of the rules of hospitality.[50] The prohibitions found in the Mosaic code, they contend, refer to idolatrous sexual relations. The Pauline injunctions either continue the Levitical condemnation of idolatrous acts or refer to ancient Greek practices of pederasty or homosexual prostitution. The scholars conclude that homosexual orientation was unknown to biblical authors, and therefore neither homosexual preference nor its behavioral expression is addressed in the Bible.

However, these exegetes (and many conservative Bible interpreters) make a major mistake by examining only the passages where homosexuality is explicitly addressed. The foundational text for the issue is Genesis 1-3. "To examine the specific texts on homosexuality without understanding the biblical revelation on human sexuality is like trying to account for a tree without reference to its trunk or roots."[51] The opening chapters of Genesis reveal that the "primal form" of humanity is the fellowship of man and woman (1:26-28). To be human is to share humanity with the opposite sex. The order of creation established by the Creator is that male and female are made for each other. A complementary heterosexual relationship is the biblically normative way for male and female to discover community (2:23-25). "Something more essential is at stake here: the reflection of the image of God through Man as male and female together. This unity of the sexes is then extended to their sexual relationship in the special command to be fruitful and multiply. Needless to say, a homosexual relationship is unable to fulfill that command. . . . Man is designed to live together as male and female, nothing else fulfills God's will."[52]

Origin and Causes. In *The Theory and Practice of Homosexuality*, Diane Richardson emphasizes that important distinctions must be made between homosexual identity (orientation), homosexual acts (behavior), and homosexual lifestyle. A person who has a homosexual orientation may not have engaged in homosexual acts or adopted a gay or lesbian lifestyle. Likewise, some who participate in homosexual behavior do so out of curiosity or perversity, not because of inner compulsion.

Richardson observed that common among those who do research is the conclusion that "sexual orientation is a relatively enduring characteristic, largely determined early in life."[53] The question of the origin and causes of homosexuality largely centers around two options: biological determinants or social learning theories.[54] Many researchers argue that such a rigid dichotomy is meaningless because the causes of homosexuality are not so simple, but seem rather to be a complex interactive process between the two.

A number of researchers have proposed **genetic,** hormonal, and chromosomal explanations for a homosexual identity.[55] In 1940 Lang hypothesized that chromosomal error was the significant factor in the origination of homosexuality, but when chromosomal analysis became possible, the theory was discredited. Studies of homosexual men and their twin brothers influenced several genetic theories, including genetic imbalances, gene-controlled variants, and the interaction between **genetic predispositions** and environmental factors. Another biological theory poses numerous endocrinological explanations (hormonal influences) of homosexuality.

The importance of early childhood experiences in psychosexual development, especially gender role development, is often proposed as a major factor in homosexual identity. Psychoanalytic models (heavily dependent on Freud) stress early parent-child relationships. A Christian psychiatrist, Dr. Elizabeth Moberly, treats homosexuals as persons who have a developmental deficiency in their relation with the same-sex parent. Psychological needs normally met through the child's attachment to the parent are left unfulfilled, a repression that prompts homosexual urges, claims Moberly.[56] Another theory is the social interactionist model, which emphasizes the social context in which the homosexual acts occur and identities develop.

A growing number of experts in the field agree with Dr. Evelyn Hooker, who sees multifactorial causation at work in the etiology of homosexuality. The diverse forms of homosexuality, she concludes, "are produced by many combinations of variables, including biological, cultural, psychodynamic, structural, and situational."[57]

What does this research mean? First, the evidence seems clear that few people choose to have homosexual inclinations. Research suggests that genetic factors may give some push in the direction of homosexual preference. At the same time, disordered family relationships that confuse children at a deep level about their sexual identity seem to play a major role. Early experiences of homosexual seduction or sexual abuse often appear in the history of homosexuals.

What about the assertions that homosexuality is biologically influenced and therefore normal, and those who are gay cannot change and did not choose their behavior? Medical ethicist Arthur Caplan calls such thinking "pure malarky" and "dumb," because "every human behavior has some basis in biology, but that does not mean we are not responsible for who we are and what we do. Morality does not follow from biology."[58] Most social scientists believe the presence of genetic and family variables do influence behavior, such as the propensity toward alcoholism and violence. However, do not persons so inclined have a responsiblity to practice sobriety, moderation, and self-control?

A Christian Response. In light of biblical teachings and our present understanding, what should be our Christian response to homosexuality? In the Christian community today are three basic attitudes: (1) homosexuality is the most degrading type of sin and homosexual orientation and behavior must be strongly condemned; (2) homosexuality is a biological condition that should be accepted as normal, as should faithful and loving homosexual unions; (3) homosexual orientation is a treatable abnormality influenced by genetic and social factors, but homosexual behavior is outside the will of God and is an illegitimate expression of human sexuality.

Many Christian bodies take a position on the issue of homosexuality that is analogous to the posture many churches have toward alcoholism. Certain people have a genetic predisposition toward alcohol addiction. Persons with an alcoholic propensity should refrain from drinking alcoholic beverages because the practice is destructive to the alcoholic, to others, and is not in accord with God's will for humanity. While the alcoholic orientation is in and of itself tragic but not sinful, practicing alcoholic behavior is sinful.[59]

To respond to the contemporary challenge, Christians and churches must move in two main directions: prevention and ministry.[60] First, we must speak the truth about homosexuality. We must not shrink from declaring God's view of homosexual behavior, nor do we need to fear facing scientific understandings of the causes behind homosexual inclinations. Christians are often accused of being unloving when they define homosexual conduct as immoral. Always we must be loving and fair when we voice opposition, but never does compassion require acceptance of a homosexual lifestyle. Even Derrick Sherwin Bailey in the conclusion of his pivotal study of homosexuality pled for even-handed treatment of all sexual sins and the strengthening of home life: "The only solution is to attack the problem at its root—to deal with the social and sexual evils in which the condition of inversion frequently originates. Promotion of good marriages and happy homes will achieve a result immeasurably greater and more valuable than punitive legislation aimed at the private practices of adult homosexuals, while the adulterer and adulteress are allowed to pursue their anti-social designs unchecked."[61]

The second response needed from Christians and churches is a ministry to homosexuals that exhibits the love and compassion of Jesus. Stanton Jones observes that Christians have a certain degree of natural revulsion to homosexual acts; but revulsion to an act is not the same as revulsion to a person. "If you cannot empathize with a homosexual person because of fear or revulsion, then you are failing our Lord. You are guilty of pride, fear, or arrogance."[62] The church has a unique opportunity to demonstrate the very love, respect, acceptance, and forgiveness that most homosexuals are looking for. We must deal with our own emotional responses, we must reject all negative and demeaning insults toward homosexuals, we must repudiate violence and mistreatment of homosexuals, and above all, we must make the church a place where those who feel homosexual urges can be welcomed.[63]

Many homosexual persons have discovered a better way and are now following Jesus in costly discipleship. Numerous ex-gay ministries, such as Exodus, include men and women eager to share their stories of how they are overcoming homosexuality.[64] Instant change through a quick repentance is not the norm. Yet, as Paul affirmed, Christ offers hope for healing (1 Cor. 6:11). In our permissive society, Christians of either sexual orientation must live out our maleness and femaleness in ways that honor God and build human community.

A CHRISTIAN INTERPRETATION OF MARRIAGE

Around the world, in all countries, the structure of marriage and family life is undergoing profound changes. In 1995 the Population Council released the report "Families in Focus," which concluded: "The idea that the family is a stable and cohesive unit in which father serves as an economic provider and mother serves as emotional care giver is a myth. The reality is that trends like unwed motherhood, rising divorce rates, smaller households and the

feminization of poverty are not unique to America, but are occurring worldwide."[65]

What will the twenty-first century family look like? Is the traditional view of marriage as a mutual, exclusive, lifelong union between husband and wife in jeopardy? How should Christian churches prepare to meet the needs they will inevitably face? A statistical look at the American family at the close of the twentieth century reveals the major areas of concern:[66]

- In 1960 there were four marriages for every divorce; in 1995 there was one divorce for every two marriages.
- A couple marrying today has a 60 percent chance of divorce or separation.
- Fifty percent of the persons marrying this year believe they will end up divorced.
- The number of unmarried couples cohabitating has increased from 1.9 million in 1986 to 3.5 million couples in 1993.
- A majority of people who marry this year will have cohabitated with someone before marriage, and 45 percent of them will divorce within ten years.
- Births to unmarried women rose from 665,747 (18 percent) in 1980 to 1,224,876 (30 percent) in 1992.
- By 1994 one of five never-married women had at least one child.
- About 40 percent of America's 67 million children live without their fathers.
- An estimated 4 million women will be battered this year by their husbands or boyfriends, and more than 3 million children will be abused.
- Twenty-five percent of all girls and 10 percent of all boys will be sexually abused by age eighteen.
- Each day in America, twenty-seven children die from poverty and twelve die from guns.

While these social trends threaten the stability of the home, other changes offer some hope. Although dual-income families still outnumber single-income families three to one, the number of working women, ages twenty-five to forty-four, declined in 1994 for the first time in twenty-five years. Some view this change as a new trend among younger moms to spend more time with family and less time at work.[67]

Recent reliable studies reveal that faithful monogamy is widely endorsed as the moral ideal and practiced by the vast majority.

Sexual behavior polls by *Playboy* magazine, researcher Shere Hite, and *Redbook* magazine created the image of extramarital affairs, casual sex, and rampant experimentation. However, major surveys by sociologist John Gagnon,[68] the University of Chicago,[69] and the University of Washington[70] have debunked the myth that everybody out there is having sex of all kinds. These national investigations reported 96 to 98 percent of married people have been faithful to their spouses in the last twelve months, and overall, 80 to 85 percent of women and 65 to 85 percent of men have had no other partners but their spouses while married.

Another positive sign is the Promise Keepers men's movement, which has grown from a gathering of seventy-two men in 1990 to 826,000 who came together in 1995. The movement calls men to total commitment to Jesus Christ and integrity in every area of life, especially in building strong marriages and better relationships with the women and the children in their lives.[71]

An encouraging movement is True Love Waits, a program that encourages youth to pledge to be sexually abstinent until marriage. At a 1995 rally in Atlanta 18,000 teenagers watched 350,000 True Love Waits commitment cards from fifty states and seventy-six countries reach the roof of the Georgia Dome. Supported by forty-two denominations and student organizations, the group's goal for 1997 is to display True Love Waits cards on every school campus in America.[72]

Nevertheless, the majority of trends in American domestic life challenge the Christian understanding of marriage and family. In such a time as this, the followers of Jesus have a unique opportunity to exemplify the Christian ethic. The teachings of the Scriptures are a basic resource for this task.

Biblical Teachings about Marriage and the Family

God's Plan. Although every society recognizes and regulates marriage, it is not a human invention—marriage is God's idea. From the beginning God ordained the home to be the most important social institution, the matrix of personality and the microcosm of society.

The opening chapters of the Bible record God's original plan. The family is grounded on the nature of the man and woman whom God created. "So God created humankind in his image, in the image of God he created them; male and female he created them. . . . Therefore a man leaves his father and his mother and clings to his wife and they become one flesh" (Gen. 1:27; 2:24). God gave the first couple three major responsiblities: reproduction (Gen. 1:28), supervision of the earth (Gen. 1:26; 2:15), and marital intimacy (Gen. 2:24–25).

The creation story focuses on *companionship* as the primary purpose of marriage: "It is not good that man should be alone; I will make him a helper as his partner" (2:18). The word *helper* is the Hebrew word *ezer*, here combined with *neged* ("partner") to mean "suitable companion."[73] God immediately remedied the only "not good" of creation by making woman as man's "supportive strength."

The major reason for marriage, therefore, is intimate union. The way God created humanity as male and female emphasizes relational compatibility. As theologians have noted, both *ish* (male) and *ishshah* (female) originated in the undifferentiated humanity of *adam*.[74] Marriage, therefore, is not only a union, it is also a reunion of two who were originally one. Only as we follow the original intent of marriage—a mutual, one-flesh union characterized by faithful love—is the "unashamed intimacy" of Eden possible.

A related purpose of marriage is *constructive sexual fulfillment*. God also instituted marriage as a physical ("one flesh") union. Although the marital covenant includes emotional, psychological, and spiritual oneness, at its base marriage is a sexual union. God planned for the physical union of husband and wife to allow "a continuous form of association for man and woman in which the powerful sex urge is sublimated so that it may serve to meet human needs and to avoid disrupting personality and society."[75]

A corollary purpose of marriage is *procreation* and the propagation of the human race: "Be fruitful and multiply, and fill the earth and subdue it" (Gen. 1:28). Implied in this command are the blessing of children (Ps. 127:3–5) and the opportunity to teach and train offspring in the way of God (Eph. 6:4).

These purposes support God's intent that marriage be an *exclusive commitment*, a faithful monogamous union. The original description of marriage dictates "leaving" and "cleaving," words that denote the replacement of one relationship (parent) by another (partner). Marital oneness requires a new family unit, one free from interference by parents or the inclusion of other partners.

Both Jesus and Paul made many comments about marriage and family beyond the declarations found in Genesis 1–2, but never did the teachings of either contradict God's original plan. John Stott asserts that Genesis 2:24 contains the most complete biblical definition of marriage: "An exclusive heterosexual covenant between one man and one woman, ordained and sealed by God, preceded by a public leaving of parents, consummated in sexual union, issuing in a permanent mutually supportive partnership, and normally crowned by the gift of children."[76]

Human Failure. Early in the creation story sin entered human history, and every part of creation was corrupted, including family life (Gen. 3). God's plan for marriage and the home was perverted by polygamy (Gen. 4:19), adultery (Lev. 20:10), concubinage (Gen. 25:6), prostitution (Lev. 19:29), incest (Lev. 18:6), mistreatment of women (Exod. 21:1-11), and divorce (Lev. 21:14).

One interesting response to human failure in marriage was the Mosaic "law of divorce" found in Deuteronomy 24:1-4. Strictly speaking, it was not a law establishing the practice, for "divorce was known in Israel from the earliest days. The . . . passage from Deuteronomy merely formulated as a definite law what had previously existed as a very old custom."[77]

By the time of Moses, divorce was common, women were treated like property, and husbands could "put away" their wives for almost any reason. The Mosaic code attempted to regulate divorce by placing requirements on the husband that gave the wife a degree of protection she had not formerly had. The law required the husband to give his wife a legal document, a certificate of divorce (Isa. 50:1), and then to dismiss her with the words, "You are free to marry any man."[78]

The whole procedure was a formal legal act giving the woman evidence that she was no longer married. Without the certificate, another man who took her as his wife could be accused of stealing the first husband's property. The main purpose of the law, however, is found in verse 4: "Her first husband, who sent her away, is not permitted to take her again to be his wife after she has been defiled." The law underscored the seriousness of divorce by diminishing the possibility of remarriage for capricious husbands, as well as protecting wives from cruel husbands.

Although Moses' law did not encourage divorce, the stated ground for ending the marriage was that the husband finds "something objectionable" about his wife (Deut. 24:1). The Hebrew phrase for the offense is *ervath dabar,* variously translated as "shameful" (NEB) or "indecent" (RSV, NIV). This could not refer to adultery or unchastity, for that transgression was punishable by death (Lev. 20:10). Some commentators have suggested the flaw was a physical deficiency, such as inability to bear children, but this view is doubtful.[79]

The exact phrase occurs only in one other place in the Bible, where it refers to human excrement (Deut. 23:13-14). Various scholars conclude the term means some indecent or improper behavior, such as the wife exposing herself voluntarily or involuntarily (2 Sam. 6:12-20).[80]

During the first century before Christ, rival Pharisaic parties led by Rabbi Hillel and Rabbi Shammai debated the issue. Neither group denied the right to divorce, but they differed as to justifiable reasons for divorce. The stricter school of Shammai taught "indecency" referred only to unchastity, a sexual offense. The lax school of Hillel, however, focused on the statement that the wife "becomes displeasing" to her husband (Deut. 24:1). This could include even the most trivial reasons, such as the wife spoiling food she was cooking, or quarreling, or even if the husband found another more beautiful woman.[81]

God's intent for marriage was not entirely lost in the Old Testament. Glimpses of God's ideal did appear in three Old Testament prohibitions of divorce (Deut. 22:13-21; 22:28-29; Lev. 21:7, 14) and in the proclamation of Malachi, "I hate divorce, says the LORD" (2:16). However, the prevailing trend in Judaism was not toward the ideal. The Mosaic law was remedial at best, anticipating the need for a Prophet who would reaffirm God's original plan.

Jesus' Ideal. Jesus was born into a Jewish family and nation that held a high view of marriage. For Hebrews in the first century, marriage was a sacred duty, not to be entered carelessly or lightly. To remain unmarried after the age of twenty was to violate God's commands to "be fruitful and multiply" (Gen. 1:22). Ideally, Jewish laws of marriage and sexual purity aimed very high, and it was said that "the very altar wept tears when a man divorced his wife."[82]

But ideal and actuality were far apart. Divorce was allowed, as was remarriage. Women continued to be mistreated. Though rabbis debated the justifiable reasons for divorce, by the time of Jesus the permissive view was predominant. In fact, this long-standing debate about "justifiable causes" for divorce was the occasion for the classical statement of Christ about marriage.

Jesus' instructions on marriage and divorce are found in four passages. The first passage (Matt. 5:31-32) is found in the section of the Sermon on the Mount where Jesus compares the law with His own teachings. Here Christ charges with sin the husband who divorced his innocent wife, thus exploiting her and "stigmatizing [passive verb] her as adulterous."[83] Christ added that he who marries her is also "stigmatized" as adulterous (5:32). Luke 16:18 also records this statement of Christ, which condemns actions common in that day.

The comprehensive statement of Christ on the subject is found in Matthew 19:3-12, recorded also in Mark 10:2-12 (although Mark's account includes some important differences).[84] Certain Pharisees came to test Jesus with a question, "Is it lawful for a man to divorce his wife for any cause?" (19:3). The inquirers believed they had Jesus on the horns of a dilemma. Would He side with the strict Shammai school and be rejected by the crowds as too narrow, or would He side with liberal Hillel and be accused of violating Moses' law?

Jesus indicated the Mosaic legislation was not the ideal, but an accommodation to the people's hardness of hearts (19:7-8). The law of Moses was meant to mitigate an existing problem. The scribes, however, did nothing to restrain the caprice of husbands, but busied themselves solely with a proper document of separation to prove the woman was free to remarry. "They probably flattered themselves they were defending the rights of women. Brave men! Jesus . . . asserted a more radical right of women—*not to be put away*, except when she put herself away by unfaithfulness."[85] Pointing back to the original intent of the Lawgiver, Christ noted that God created one man for one woman; He then restated the ideal of "leaving" and "cleaving" whereby "the two shall become one flesh" (19:4-6).

At this point, Jesus added a most difficult word: "Whoever divorces his wife, except for unchastity, and marries another commits adultery" (19:9). The phrase, "except for unchastity *[porneia]*" was omitted by Mark (10:11), Luke (16:18), and Paul (1 Cor. 7:10), causing a number of scholars to question its validity.[86] This "**exception clause**" seems to be a statement of fact, affirming the "one flesh" relationship of marriage. Any act of "unlawful sexual intercourse" *(porneia),* therefore, fractures the marriage at its base, rupturing the physical and spiritual "oneness" of the marriage covenant.

The phrase "commits adultery" (19:9) needs closer scrutiny. Many assume the statement means that all remarried couples are "living in sin" (a phrase neither biblical nor theological). Language scholars point out that the verb *moichatai* ("commits") is a present indicative verb, an example of a "gnomic present"—in this context a characteristic part of the event, but not necessarily continuous action.[87] Thus the verb *commits* indicates that divorce and remarriage constitute an act of adultery, but not necessarily a continuous state of immorality. This grammatical point is supported theologically by the example and teaching of Jesus concerning failure and forgiveness (John 21:15-22).

So what does this key passage teach? In a day when divorce was not questioned, Jesus declared the practice violated God's original plan for marriage. To Jews who were concerned about never breaking the Law, especially one of the Ten Commandments, Jesus issued a startling word. To "put away" your spouse was the same as breaking the Seventh Commandment prohibiting adultery; both were equally wrong because they destroyed the sanctity of marriage. Thus, one who divorced and remarried did sin against God's plan for marriage, was "stigmatized" as adulterous, and needed forgiveness. However, nothing Jesus said here indicates divorce is an "unpardonable sin," a continuous state of adultery, or a failure that forever disables or disqualifies from Christian service.

Paul's Counsel. In his advice to Christians living in Corinth, Paul responded to questions previously raised in a letter we do not have (1 Cor. 7:1). The apostle's initial counsel was to couples who were both Christians. Quoting the teachings of Jesus, the apostle to the Gentiles directed "that the wife should not separate from her husband (but if she does separate, let her remain unmarried or else be reconciled to her husband), and that the husband should not divorce his wife" (7:10-11). Since the rule of Augustus, women in the Roman Empire had the legal right to initiate a divorce proceeding.[88]

The unknown questions prompting this response may have referred to a specific case of separation based on ascetic motives, or perhaps to wives in the church who believed singleness is preferable to marriage (advice Paul himself recommends in this passage, v. 6). However, the verb *separate* (*chorizo*, v. 10) is clearly used in the Greek papyri as a technical term for divorce.[89]

Thus Paul's instruction addresses divorce. In marriages where both are Christians, neither husband nor wife should initiate separation or divorce. If separation occurs between Christian spouses, they should remain unmarried or be reconciled. The absence of the exception clause of Jesus (Matt. 19:9) is puzzling; it may mean either Paul did not know of the clause or that the phrase is a textual addition.

Paul next addressed marriages in which only one of the partners was a confessing Christian, probably a situation in which husbands and wives became Christians after marrying nonbelievers. Even in cases like this, Paul opposed the dissolution of the marriage by the Christian mate for two reasons. First, because divorce is wrong; in addition, the unbelieving spouse is somehow "made holy" through the influence of the faith of the Christian partner (7:12-14).

Nevertheless, Paul recognized that the unbelieving mate may object to the new faith his or her spouse has embraced. If the non-Christian initiates separation, then the Christian mate "is not bound" (7:15). Does this mean the Christian is free to remarry? Some contend the right to remarriage is not included. Others argue that this **Pauline privilege** allows a second marriage, due to the "death" of the marriage relationship (cf. Rom. 7:2-3).[90] A few even broadly interpret desertion by the unbeliever to include abandoning the marriage covenant by such behavior as physical abuse, drunkenness, lack of financial support, or denial of conjugal rights.[91]

Since we do not know for sure the questions raised by the Corinthians, our interpretation of Paul's words is difficult. We do know one of the chief complaints against Christianity by unbelievers was that it disrupted domestic relationships (1 Pet. 2:12-15). In a day of marital instability, Paul's counsel to Christians affirmed marriage (7:9), prohibited divorce (7:10-11), and encouraged believers to sustain a mixed marriage, allowing the influence of the Christian to purify and evangelize the unbelieving mate (7:12-16).

In the last years of his life, the aging apostle wrote a letter to Timothy (who was ministering in Ephesus), in which he described the spiritual maturity required of pastors and deacons (1 Tim. 3:1-14). This summary was not a checklist for a job description, but a faceless portrait of the exemplary life required of a church leader to serve in ministry.

One stated expectation, "married only once" (vv. 2, 12), has been understood in a variety of ways. The phrase literally reads, *mias gunaikos andra*, or "one-woman man." Across the centuries five possible meanings have emerged: (1) necessarily married; (2) never divorced; (3) never remarried (even after a mate's death); (4) monogamous; and (5) faithful to one wife.

Few churces have espoused the first view, that a church leader must be married before ministerial service is allowed. Many churches adopt the second view, establishing qualifications that state "never divorced" as one requirement for deacons or pastors. However, Paul could have clearly barred divorced persons from church leadership by writing *me apoleluemenon* ("not divorced"), which he did not. The practice of the church in the fourth century favored the third view, mainly due to ascetic tendencies that viewed marriage as a necessary evil at best.[92]

The last two views have gained the most acceptance. In the New Testament world, polygamy and unfaithfulness were common, almost a pagan habit. The Graeco-Roman wife had one major responsibility: to bear a male heir. Husbands normally sought sexual pleasure and social companionship from prostitutes, concubines, and slaves. Furthermore, slaves were not allowed to marry legally and ordinarily mated with many partners.

In such a society, Paul stressed that a Christian leader must be a "one-woman man." The emphasis here seems to be on faithfulness and stability in the present marriage, rather than on marital history.[93] In fact, the apostle's expectation for deacons and ministers is much more demanding than just "never divorced." A person married only once may have had many partners in the past and developed a pattern that continues in the present. From his prison cell Paul insisted that church leaders must be faithful to one marital partner.

What then may we conclude the Bible teaches about marriage?

1. God's plan for marriage is one man and one woman joined for life (Gen. 2:24).

2. The Mosaic law of divorce was an accommodation to human failure (Deut. 24:1).

3. Jesus upheld God's ideal for marriage, though He recognized marital unfaithfulness fractured the "one flesh" relationship (Matt. 19:3–9).

4. Though not commanded, divorce seems permissible in cases of marital unfaithfulness (Matt. 19:9) and desertion (1 Cor. 7:15); remarriage is not so clear, but it seems to be allowed by implication.

5. Divorce violates the Seventh Commandment, but like any sin it is forgiveable and does not permanently disqualify one from service (John 8:3–11; 21:15–19).

6. Through forgiveness and God's grace, divorced Christians can find new beginnings, including remarriage to a Christian person.

7. Pauline qualifications for deacons and pastors emphasize present faithfulness in marriage, primarily prohibiting polygamy and infidelity (1 Tim. 3:2, 12).

8. The example of Jesus and the practice of the New Testament church supports the inclusion of divorced Christians into the life of the church, including Christian service and leadership roles (1 Cor. 6:11).

In marriage and family life, a number of ethical issues confront contemporary Christians: divorce and remarriage, alternate marriage styles, single adulthood, domestic abuse, one-parent families, and child rearing, to name a few. One serious question to which we now turn is basic to building a Christian home: "Who is the head of the house?"

Authority and Submission in Marriage

Marital roles and relationships is a major heading in any book on marriage and the family. A topic widely discussed and hotly debated is authority and submission in marriage, or "Who has the final word?" [94]

The wife of a close friend told me of a women's conference that she attended. The annual gathering of hundreds of Christian females focuses on teaching "The Joy of Submission."[95] The leaders claim this "biblical **principle**" of the wife's submission to the husband's authority is the key factor determining the success or failure of any marriage. A list of "Characteristics of a Submissive Wife" included her willingness to "submit *totally* and give up all her *rights* . . . obey her husband, even when she doesn't understand his decision . . . *live to love and please her husband* . . . become *identified with him* as an extension of him . . . allow him to take over his responsibilities *as head of the home.*"[96]

On the other hand, John and Letha Scanzoni contend that marriage should be equalitarian. These Christian authors decry role identifications: "The whole idea of labeling characteristics 'masculine' or 'feminine' is patently unscriptural."[97] The couple stoutly deny that male headship and female submission is prescribed in the Bible, declaring that Christian marriage must include role interchangeability.[98] For the Scanzonis, the best pattern for marriage is equality and partnership.

On the subject of husband-wife roles, most experts on Christian marriage fall into one of two groups: the authority-submission pattern or the equality-partnership pattern. The former insists the submission of the wife and the authority of the husband is *the* biblical model for the Christian home. The latter group is equally convinced that mutuality and partnership is the ideal model for family relationships. Within each group is widespread disagreement about what constitutes a "submissive wife" or an "equal partner"; even more amazing is the fact that both positions quote the same Scriptures to defend their point of view (Gen. 1:26–27, 2:18–24, 3:15; 1 Tim. 2:9, 11–15; 1 Pet. 3:3–7; Eph. 5:21–33).[99]

The key passage for both groups is Ephesians 5:22–23: "Wives, [be subject] to your husbands as you are to the Lord. For the husband is the head *[kephale]* of the wife as Christ is the head of the church." The larger context of this verse is Ephesians 5:21–6:9, a *Hausentafel* (a code of household duties) and a central Pauline statement on the Christian home.[100] My contention is that the passage supports a model of mutual submission under the lordship of Christ.

A Foreign World. To interpret correctly Paul's domestic teachings, an understanding of family roles and relationships in the first-century world is absolutely essential.[101] The apostle's instructions about the home may have arisen because of the breakdown of the family in the New Testament world.

In Jewish families, the wife had few rights and was regarded more as a possession than a person. Although a Hebrew woman held a position of esteem in the home, in social life she was little more than an appendage to her husband.

The woman's position in the Greek world was worse, for the respectable wife lived a secluded life; confined to her quarters; she did not appear even for meals. As Xenophon put it, females were to "see as little as possible, hear as little as possible, and ask as little as possible."[102] The Greek way of life made companionship in marriage almost impossible.

Roman marriages were no better. For the first five hundred years, the Roman republic recorded not one divorce. By the time of Paul, adultery was common, chastity was rare, and family life was crumbling. Seneca wrote that women were married to be divorced and divorced to be married; Jerome told of a woman in Rome who was married to her twenty-third husband, and she was his twenty-first wife.[103]

In contrast to the common denigration of women, Jesus treated females in a way that was revolutionary—He related to them as persons, never once regarding them as inferior. The Christian faith that Paul proclaimed liberated the oppressed from centuries of prejudice and mistreatment (Gal. 3:28).

This was Paul's world—a society of vicious immorality in which women, children, and slaves in the home suffered injustice, cruelty, and death. Against this stark background, Paul gave challenging advice to wives and husbands, children and parents, and slaves and masters: "Be subject to one another out of reverence for Christ" (Eph. 5:21).

Three Foreign Words. Paul's inspired counsel to Christian households in the region of Ephesus contains three key words: "subject" or "submit" *(hupotasso);* "head" *(kephale);* and "love" *(agapao).* Not only are the words written in a foreign language; they are "foreign" to us in their contextual meaning.

One scholar notes that the way the Greek text has been paragraphed in English versions has compounded the exegetical problem. Modern translations of Ephesians 5:21-22 vary: three versions make each verse a separate paragraph, four versions mark verse 22 as a new paragraph, while five versions do not.[104]

The paragraphing relates to the first key word: Does "be subject" refer to the previous paragraph, or the passage at hand? Again, the fact that Paul used no verb in verse 22 ("wives to your husbands . . .") or in verse 24 ("wives ought to be, in everything . . ."), supports the view that "be subject" is the implied verb in both cases. Thus, the submission of the wife in verses 22 and 24 is directly linked to the concept of voluntary, mutual submission in verse 21 (a participial form of *hupotasso).*[105]

Paul's statement in verse 21 is an outflow of Ephesians 5:18: "Be filled with the Spirit." Spirit-filled behavior transforms the Christian home. To illustrate the principle of mutual submission, Paul applies it in three areas: husband-wife (5:22-23), parent-child (6:1-4), and master-slave (6:5-9). Addressing the less powerful person in each dyad, the apostle offers to wives, children, and slaves the possibility of transformation. How? Believers are called to be radically counterculture, servants ("slaves") to one another without distinctions of status or gender (Gal. 5:13).

The second important but very difficult word is "head" *(kephale):* "For the husband is the *head* of the wife just as Christ is *head* of the church, the body of which he is Savior" (5:23, italics added). Significant exegetical studies on the meaning of this word in the Greek language have raised questions about the uncritical equation of *head* with "authority."[106] After examining the claim that *kephale* was used in ancient Greek texts to mean "ruler or person of superior authority or rank," several scholars have concluded, "There is no instance in profane Greek literature where a ruler or a hierarch is referred to as *head* such as 'Alexander was the head of the Greek armies.'"[107] Lexicographers also give no evidence of such a meaning.[108]

The best illustration of the reluctance of the Greek language to render "head" as "authority" is in the Septuagint (LXX). In the 180 instances where the Hebrew word *ro'sh* ("leader," "chief," "authority") appears, the normal Greek word used is *archon* ("ruler," "commander"). In only seventeen places did the translators use *kephale*—five of those have variant readings, and another four involve a head-tail metaphor, which leaves only eight instances out of 180 times the LXX translators chose *kephale* for *ro'sh*.[109]

If "head" *(kephale)* did not normally mean "authority over" in Greek, what did it mean? The common Greek definition of the word is "source, source of life, source of origin, exalted originator and completer."[110] In English we sometimes use "head" in this way when we refer to the head (source) of a river.

In the seven passages in the New Testament where Paul uses *kephale* in some figurative sense, the contexts of five of them indicate they mean "exalted originator" (Col. 1:18), "life-source" (Col. 2:10, 19; Eph. 4:15), and "top or crown" (Eph. 1:20–23).[111] The concept that "head" connotes a hierarchy with men in a role of authority over women rests largely on the two remaining passages: 1 Corinthians 11:3 and Ephesians 5:23. When we recognize the main Greek meaning of *kephale* is "source," it becomes clear that Paul is not establishing a chain of command—he is establishing origins. Rather than a "ruler" over the wife, the husband is the "source" or "beginning" of woman (made from the side of Adam), even as God is the "origin" of Christ (1 Cor. 11:3). "If you think 'head' means 'chief' or 'boss,'" declared Chrysostom, "you skew the godhead!"[112]

In Ephesians 5:23 "head" is used in a head-body metaphor to show the unity of husband and wife and of Christ and the church, a common Pauline analogy. Further, where "head" is used metaphorically to represent Christ's relation to the church, it never means authority but always emphasizes Christ's servant roles as Savior, provider, and fountainhead of life.[113]

The third word, *agapao,* is more familiar to most of us. Paul wrote, "Husbands love your wives, just as Christ loved the church and gave himself up for her" (Eph. 5:25). He repeats this admonition three more times, urging husbands to love their wives as they do their own bodies (5:28) and their own selves (5:28, 35). The word for love is *agape,* a distinctive type of love. The example of Christ defines the nature of *agape* love as it applies to marriage: it is a sacrificial love (5:25), a purifying love (5:26–27), a caring love (5:28–29), and an unbreakable love (5:31).

Agape love places high expectations on Christian husbands: "They are not to be brutish, crude, and rude; but they are to be understanding and considerate of their wives as being persons with feelings and rights. The wife is a *person* to be loved and respected, not a *thing* to be used."[114] As the love of Christ for the church is historic and pragmatic (paid with no less price than His death), so this *agape* love is the basis and model for the concrete and pragmatic love of the husband to the wife.

In Ephesians Paul challenges the Christian family to live by the principle of mutual yieldedness in love based upon the family's acceptance of Christ as Lord of the home. The apostle's counsel is radically countercultural. The first-century world required a woman to accept the authority of her husband, but Paul gave a new interpretation to authority and a new attitude about the marriage relationship.

Christian marriage involves a mutual submission of husband and wife to each other (5:21), based on *agape* love (5:25). Husbands and wives are to be "one flesh" (5:31). Just as Christ loved His body (the church), so the husband in loving his wife loves himself, for she is his body (5:28). The unity of husband and wife is so complete that they no longer exist as separate selves, but as one (5:28–31). Through love on the one hand, and honor and respect on the other, husband and wife are to mirror the great mystery itself, the union between Christ and His church (5:32–33).

Although Paul did not visualize an imminent change in cultural structures, the ethical principles he applied to the Christian home transformed existing social relationships. In any era, the most constructive way to build a Christian home is for each member of the family to work at surpassing the other in love and voluntary submission.

Some ask, "But when differences arise, who is the head of the house?" The answer is simple. The head of the Christian home is Christ. Christian marriage is not a struggle over power: it is a covenant commitment in which "two become one" through mutual love and consideration.

So what does all of this mean for the people of God today? In such a time as this, Christians must teach and exemplify the Christian ethic of sexuality, marriage, and the family. Likewise, the church of the twenty-first century must take a more active role in ministering to the needs of families.[115]

FOR THOUGHT AND DISCUSSION

1. Determine the impact of Greek philosophy and our secular culture upon present understandings of sexuality.
2. Discuss Genesis 1–3 as a key for a Christian interpretation of sexuality.
3. Discuss the difference between homosexual orientation and behavior.
4. Debate this proposition: If homosexual orientation is genetically predisposed, homosexuality should be accepted as normal and God ordained.
5. Debate this proposition: God's original plan for marriage is too idealistic for modern American society.
6. Compare Jesus' teachings on marriage (Matt. 19:3–10) with Moses' "Law of Divorce" (Deut. 24:1–4).
7. Answer this question: "Who is the head in the Christian home?"

CHAPTER EIGHT

HUMAN EQUALITY— GENDER AND RACE

In the early 1800s, Texas was a frontier territory. One historian noted that settlers believed "Indians were to be killed, African Americans were to be enslaved, and Hispanics were to be avoided." In the 1830s these "Texicans" built a Baptist church at Independence that had two doors: one for white males and the other for "women and other creatures."[1]

How people different from ourselves should be treated is a question faced by every culture. The battle between the sexes did not begin with Gloria Steinem, nor the conflict between the races with Martin Luther King Jr. From the earliest chapters of Genesis, the devaluation of human beings has been a constant story in human history. Patriarchy, male domination, racial **prejudice**, discrimination, and **sexism** have characterized almost every civilization.

The Greek myth of Amazon female warriors who ruled a society in Scythia is pure fantasy. Also idealistic was Plato's just state composed of three social classes of equal people. The reality is that in every society, including Plato's Greek state, women have been treated as second-class citizens, and slaves and ethnic groups have been deemed inferior and unworthy of equality.

Although human beings are unequal in intelligence, skills, physique, and beauty, in one ultimate sense they are equal—from creation all are made in "the image of God" (Gen. 1:27). Because all

189

have sinned and fallen short of what they ought to be (Rom. 3:23),
Christ died for all to reconcile them to God (Rom. 5:10).

Though equality will never be realized fully in society, Christians
affirm that every person, regardless of gender, **race**, or social
group, has inherent worth bestowed by God and deserves dignity
and respect. Human equality also means all social and economic
inequalities that are not necessary or justifiable should be eliminated.[2]

GENDER EQUALITY

Only in this century has complete equality for women become a
realization. Eighty years ago women could not vote. Today they are
elected as mayors, governors, senators, and Supreme Court justices.
Fifty years ago women were called into the workforce to aid their
country during World War II. Today career women work in almost
every vocation. Four decades ago, women in America had no guarantee of equal access to employment, housing, education, or credit.
Today these rights are established by law.

Also in this century a dramatic reversal has occurred in society's
attitude toward the abuse of females. In language and in law, in
business and in family life, the mistreatment of women and sexual
harassment have become major concerns.

In light of the many voices calling for liberation and justice for
women, what is the Christian church to do? Have Christian beliefs
and practices sometimes perpetuated female subordination? Is it
possible that the church of Jesus Christ has for centuries instituted
social customs rather than upholding God's ideal in gender relationships?

As we enter the Third Millenium, perhaps no issue is of greater
importance for the Christian community than male and female roles
and relationships. No one denies that women have always been
involved in the life of the church. At the same time, traditional
understandings of female roles, usually supported by biblical passages, have often deprived women from full involvement. Today, as
never before, Christians are deliberating over these matters.

A few years ago the Evangelical Theological Society (ETS) held
their annual meeting on the seminary campus where I teach. The
members of this group are known to be conservative evangelicals
who hold a high view of the Scriptures. As I browsed in their

display area, I was surprised to discover two groups promoting opposing viewpoints on the role of women and men in church and society. Leaders in both circles were well-known evangelicals who based their views on the biblical revelation and who were able to discuss their convictions with candor and mutual respect.

At one table marked "Christians for Biblical Equality" sat Dr. Catherine Kroeger, an expert in the ancient Greek language, classical Greek literature, and the Graeco-Roman culture of the first century. Her doctoral work at the University of Minnesota convinced her that many traditional Christian understandings of gender were based on faulty **hermeneutics.**

Through research, writing, and speaking, Dr. Kroeger has expanded our knowledge of the New Testament world and of biblical teachings on gender issues. In 1987 she founded Christians for Biblical Equality (CBE), "an organization of Christians who believe the Bible, properly interpreted, teaches the fundamental equality of men and women of all racial and ethnic groups, all economic classes, and all age groups."[3] The organization's statement of belief, "Men, Women and Biblical Equality," also lists endorsements by more than one hundred notable evangelicals.

At a second table at the ETS meeting was a representative of the Council on Biblical Manhood and Womanhood (CBMW), established for the purpose of "studying and setting forth biblical teachings on the relationship between men and women, especially in the home and the church." The council was formed in 1987 (in response to CBE) to clear up the "confusion about male and female roles in the Christian world today" and to affirm that "God made men and women to be equal in personhood and in value, but different in roles."[4]

At the first CBMW meeting, leaders in the group developed "The Danvers Statement," a declaration of the organization's rationale, purposes, and affirmations, published in final form in November 1988.[5] In 1991 this traditionalist group published a 566-page book of twenty-six essays, *Recovering Biblical Manhood and Womanhood,* significantly subtitled *A Response to Evangelical-Feminism.*[6]

As evangelicals debated the meaning of biblical teachings on gender relations, the World Council of Churches was calling mainline denominations to a decade-long (1988–98) focus on women. A central element in the feminist emphasis was the need for God, the community, and the church to be "re-imagined."

A RE-Imagining conference in the fall of 1993 brought together two thousand participants representing thirty-two denominations and twenty-seven countries. The content of the event was almost exclusively from the "gender feminists" perspective, rallying around key themes of women's suffrage, male patriarchy, sexism by the traditional Christian church, and the need to reinterpret the Bible and its teachings.[7]

The largest group attending the conference was the Presbyterian Church USA, which also financially supported the meeting. Reports from the gathering alleged the group "worshiped" Sophia as an Old Testament goddess of wisdom. This created an uproar. After hundreds of congregations withheld millions of dollars from the denomination, the PCUSA General Assembly at its 1994 meeting officially issued a ten-page statement that the controversial event went "beyond the boundaries" of Reformation theology.[8]

Few would deny that feminism has played a major role in bringing full equality to twentieth-century women. "The founding mothers of feminism, who wrote from the 1840s to 1940, generally portrayed the typical woman as a capable, intelligent human being who knows her own interests. All she needed to make a contribution . . . was an even break—the equal rights and opportunities to which she was entitled."[9]

Today there is pluralism within feminism. Some feminist bestsellers of the 1960s and 1970s projected a new and radically different image.[10] A radical feminist ethic emerged that taught that the only way to alleviate women's plight was to achieve total autonomy for women—political, economic, sexual, and reproductive freedom, either through separation or seizing power from men.[11] This radicalism divided the feminist movement.

Many contemporary theologians have noted a split in the Christian feminist movement, not unlike the way secular feminism in America has separated. The more radical "gender feminist" theologians emphasize the meaning of femaleness and the need to "re-imagine" traditional beliefs,[12] while "equity feminism" affirms orthodox Christianity is essentially correct but needs structural reform to achieve equality, civil rights, and to end discrimination.

Most Christians agree that men and women have equal value and worth because "God created humankind in his image, in the image of God he created them; male and female he created them" (Gen. 1:27). Yet even conservative theologians are divided over the interpretation of biblical teachings that speak to male and female roles. Some churches and denominations perpetuate a belief in the subordination of women, based on a conviction that females are in some ways inferior.

In light of intense concern about gender issues, coupled with widespread confusion, what is the appropriate Christian response? Let us begin with the biblical revelation.

A Biblical View of Women and Men

What does the Bible really say about women and men?[13] Did God ordain a hierarchy with specific roles for males and females? Or is the Bible a liberating resource for the oppressed of both sexes? Does Scripture command women to be under the **authority** of men, silent in worship, and excluded from leadership? Or does the Bible reveal examples of women assuming leadership roles, often in contrast to cultural **norms?** Do Paul and Jesus have different views about maleness and femaleness?

To track the questions Christians are asking about male and female relationships is like tracking the eye of a hurricane. Gender issues are storm centers, particularly in biblical interpretation. Scholars who are divided on the subject often quote the same Scriptures in support of their deeply held convictions.

When President Jimmy Carter was speaking in favor of the Equal Rights Amendment at a town meeting in Elk City, Oklahoma, he appealed to Christ, not Paul, for support. "I think if one reads different parts of the Bible you can find a good argument either way. . . . I know that Paul felt very strongly that there ought to be a sharp distinction between men and women and women's role ought to be minimal. But I have a feeling that Christ meant for all of us to be treated equally, and he demonstrated this in many ways."[14]

Is the problem really resolved as easily as choosing between Jesus and Paul? Didn't Jesus appoint only male apostles? Conversely, wasn't it Paul who wrote that in Christ "there is no longer male and female" (Gal. 3:28)? Like the issues of slavery, the Sabbath, and war, the role of women in relation to men has been hotly debated by commentators who use the Bible negatively and positively to uphold their positions.[15] We know what the Bible says. The real question is: What does the Bible mean?

In the Beginning. The Creation story in the first two chapters of Genesis reveals God's original intention in making humanity male and female. The first puzzle in these chapters is the appearance of two different Creation stories. On the surface, the first narrative seems to present woman equal with man (1:24-30); the second seems to subordinate woman to man (2:7-25). Traditionalists favor the second account, while feminists obviously favor the first one. But does a person have to choose between these two accounts? A closer look is needed.

The opening chapter of Genesis stresses that both sexes were created simultaneously in the very image of God. "Let us make humankind in our image, according to our likeness; . . . So God created humankind in his image, in the image of God he created them; male and female he created them" (Gen. 1:26-27).

Some argue with Augustine that the woman *with* her husband is the image of God, but she alone is not.[16] However, this passage clearly affirms that both male and female equally share God's image.

In addition, the first man and woman are equally responsible to God as stewards of the created order: "Let them have dominion" (1:26b). This **principle** is reemphasized in Genesis 2:15 when *adam* is put in the garden of Eden "to till it and keep it."

In the second account of Creation (2:4-24), God first formed "man *[ha adam]* from the dust of the ground, and breathed into his nostrils the breath of life; and the man *[ha adam]* became a living being" (2:7). Hebrew language authorities point out that the use of the definite article *ha* before *adam* usually indicates the more inclusive idea of "humanity" (as in Gen. 2:24), which the New Revised Standard Version translation reflects.[17]

Phyllis Tribble challenges the idea that male was created before female. This biblical scholar argues that the Hebrew *adam* (related to *adamah*, "earth") could be more accurately translated "earth creature," a human being originally without gender.[18]

This point is further supported by Paul Jewett, who built upon earlier theological formations of Karl Barth.[19] In *Man as Male and Female*, the Fuller Seminary theologian contends, "Not only do men and women alike participate in the divine image, but their fellowship as male and female is what it means to be in the image of God. . . . To be Man is to be male or female, male and female, and consequently the discussion of this mysterious duality cannot be postponed until one has said what is to be said about Man as such. To talk about Man as such is precisely to talk about Man as man and woman."[20]

In this second story of creation, the "earth creature" (*adam*) was separated into male *(ish)* and female *(ishshah)* in Genesis 2:22. Out of the undifferentiated humanity of *adam*, male and female emerged, and Adam cried, "This is bone of my bones and flesh of my flesh" (2:23). Adam awoke from his sleep to see a reflection of himself, a complement to himself, indeed a very part of himself.

John R. W. Stott claims this biblical truth affirms that marriage is even more than a union. Marriage is a kind of reunion of two persons who originally were one and then separated, and now able to become "one flesh" (2:24) again through heterosexual intimacy.[21]

Another verse in this second chapter often quoted to support some form of female differentiation is the depiction of the wife as a "helper" ("help meet," v. 18 KJV). Reflecting on this verse, one traditionalist wrote, "So, was Eve Adam's equal? Yes and No. She was his spiritual equal, and, unlike the animals, 'suitable for him,' but she was not his equal in that she was his 'helper.' . . . A man, just by virtue of his manhood, is called to lead for God. A woman, just by virtue of her womanhood, is called to help for God. . . . It is the word 'helper' that suggests the woman's supportive role."[22]

Does this term connote a secondary position? The word rendered "helper" (ezer) is the Hebrew word used fourteen of twenty-one times to refer to God as a superior helper (Exod. 18:4). Along with the next word in the verse, "alongside" (neged), the two words are sometimes translated, "a power equal to him." To argue that the word "helper" connotes an inferior or subordinate role is neither biblical nor consistent with the usage of these Hebrew terms.[23]

Thus the two Creation narratives are not contradictory, but rather present a consistent view of maleness and femaleness. From the beginning both sexes were created in God's image and, as such, were equally responsible to God.

However, something happened. In the third chapter of Genesis, sin entered the human race. The results for women and men were disastrous. Some think the statement found there, "Yet your desire shall be for your husband, and he shall rule over you" (3:16), is a biblical command. Conservative biblical scholars agree, almost without exception, that this was not intended as a prescriptive command from God, but rather a description of how relationships between men and women would be damaged by the work of sin.[24] Male domination became the order of the day, and women were quickly relegated to a secondary role in society, often treated more like property than as persons.

The Old Testament World. Given the male-oriented society prevalent in the Israelite community, it is indeed amazing to find any evidence of women occupying leadership positions in the Old

Testament. Yet we cannot ignore the stories of women leaders like the prophetess Miriam (Exod. 15:20-21), who was uniquely lauded by Micah as a spiritual leader (Mic. 6:4). Less familiar are we with Zipporah, Moses' wife, who assumed the role of a priest in a moment of crisis (Exod. 4).

A woman we know better is Deborah, a judge of early Israel (Judg. 4). Handpicked by God to administer justice in the land, Deborah was specifically chosen to deliver Israel from the oppressive regime of the Canaanites and the army of Sisera. At the Israelite commander Barak's request, she led the Hebrew army to victory. The song of Deborah (Judg. 5) lauds the woman who was judge, general, prophet, and poet of Israel.

One of the most interesting examples in the Old Testament is the prophetess Huldah. Hidden in the history recorded in 2 Kings (22:14-20) and 2 Chronicles (34:22-28) is her story, prompted by the rediscovery of the book of the Law during Josiah's reign. Hilkiah the priest is commanded by the king to "inquire of the LORD" about this discovered book. Although two major prophets were alive at the time (Zephaniah and Jeremiah), the priest "went to the prophetess Huldah, the wife of Shallum" (2 Kings 22:14).

Like other true prophets, Huldah delivered a message of judgment against Israel's idolatry and lifestyle, as well as a word of hope for the penitent. Huldah's message from God, coupled with her identification of the book brought to her as God's Law, triggered the great revival under King Josiah (2 Kings 23) and began the process of canonization.

Admittedly, these examples are not the rule but the exception. However, given the strong male orientation of the Hebrew culture before Christ, it is amazing that these models of female leadership existed in Hebrew society.

The New Testament World. One biblical scholar has observed that there are more than one hundred places in Scripture where women are affirmed as leaders, yet we tend to focus our attention on those few passages that are difficult to interpret and seem to propose a subordinate role for women. Both types are found in the New Testament. Although our purpose does not allow a treatment of all passages, a representative number will be addressed.

To correctly interpret the New Testament, an understanding of the first-century world, particularly in relation to male and female roles, is absolutely essential. From the Jewish perspective, the world was composed of two groups: Jews and Gentiles. However, to believe the twain were separated is a mistake: "Jew and non-Jew constantly met, interacted, resisted each other, and inevitably influenced each other."[25]

Although Jewish women occupied a position of dignity and responsibility in the home, in social life they continued to be little more than an appendage of their husbands. After describing a woman's official position as very low, William Barclay commented: "In Jewish law she was not a person but a thing; she was entirely at the disposal of her father or of her husband. She was forbidden to learn the law; to instruct a woman in the law was to cast pearls before swine."[26] Barclay added that Jewish women had no part in the synagogue service, could not teach in school, were not obligated to attend sacred feasts, and their testimony was not credible evidence in the courts.

Talking to women in public was strictly forbidden. A rabbi would never greet a woman on the street, not even his own wife or daughter. In the traditional Jewish morning prayer, a man offered thanks that God had not made him "a Gentile, a slave or a woman."[27]

In the Graeco-Roman world of the first century, the situation was no better. In fact, in many ways it was worse. The respectable Greek woman lived a secluded life, confined to her quarters. Normally the wife appeared in public only once or twice each year, usually during religious festivals or at a relative's funeral.

The reason for her seclusion is related to the role of the Greek wife. Demosthenes explained the accepted rule of life: "We have courtesans for the sake of pleasure; we have concubines for the sake of daily cohabitation; we have wives for the purpose of having children legitimately, and of having a faithful guardian for all our household affairs."[28] The wife's primary function was to bear a male heir for her husband. Companionship between the Greek man and wife was next to impossible.

The role of women in Greek religions was also inferior. The apostle Paul alluded to the thousand sacred prostitutes in the Corinthian temple of Aphrodite. The temple of Diana in Ephesus had its hundreds of priestesses whose function was the same.[29]

In Roman society a woman had greater practical freedom than in Greek society. A Roman wife could appear in public with her husband and was allowed by law to initiate divorce, but beyond that her rights were limited. At the same time, the Roman pantheon and the Roman theatre thoroughly degraded women by depicting in them the worst **vices** of the day.[30]

In stark contrast to this universal denigration of females in the first-century world, Jesus' attitude toward women was totally countercultural. Sweeping aside centuries of tradition and prejudice, Jesus' treatment of women was revolutionary. What did He do? Christ simply related to women in the same way He related to men, never regarding females as inferior in any way.

Four biblical examples illustrate the contrast:

EXAMPLE 1: THE WOMAN AT THE WELL. Jesus always recognized women as persons capable of responding to God. The first person to whom Jesus revealed Himself as God's Messiah was a woman (John 4:26). In fact, she had three strikes against her, for she was a sinful Samaritan woman. No rabbi would have spoken to any woman, especially this one. But Jesus did, inviting this thirsty seeker at Jacob's well to drink from the well of eternal life (John 4:14).

EXAMPLE 2: THE WOMAN TAKEN IN ADULTERY. In Jesus' day, the double standard prevailed.[31] Men could commit adultery with little consequence, but guilty women were often stoned. To the group about to execute a woman caught "in the very act of committing adultery" (John 8:4), Jesus wrote something in the sand. Did He ask, "Where is the man?" We do not know, but Christ did say, "Let anyone among you who is without sin be the first to throw a stone at her" (John 8:7). To men who would judge a woman but overlook a man's sin, Jesus clearly condemned this censorious spirit and double standard.

EXAMPLE 3: MARY AND MARTHA. Another episode occurred in the home of Martha and her sister Mary, where Jesus confronted **stereotyped** female roles (Luke 10:38–42). Martha was upset with Mary, not just because she was shirking her duties, but also because she was "out of her place." Mary had dared to relate to Jesus as only men were allowed, listening and learning about God. Jesus not only defended her right to do so, but also seemed to invite Martha to join her.

As Jesus and the Twelve traveled from village to village, many women accompanied the group and "provided for them out of their resources" (Luke 8:1–3). By allowing these healed and transformed women to join this missionary band, Jesus was challenging the idea that women were not to be involved in God's work or associated with men in this mission.

EXAMPLE 4: MARY MAGDALENE. A final example occurred on the first Easter morning. In ancient Judaism, only the witness of two or more men was admissible evidence in court. Yet all four Gospels record that the first witnesses to the empty tomb were women. Jesus' first resurrection appearance was to a woman named Mary Magdalene (John 20:1–18). By announcing the resurrection through the testimony of women, God affirmed their role in sharing the Good News.

What do these biblical examples mean? Simply this. Jesus refused to reinforce the cultural misunderstandings of His day about the status of women. Jesus intentionally treated women as persons of worth and value. "He does not suggest that the woman is weak and easily deceived. He does not forbid her to study theology or teach his word. He does not blame her for the first sin or remind her that men will rule over her because of it. Rather he treats all daughters of Eve as persons created and recreatable in his image and likeness."[32]

The New Testament church followed Jesus' example. The Book of Acts records the first thirty years of Christianity after the ascension of Christ. On the day of Pentecost, the Holy Spirit descended on all believers, just as the prophet Joel had promised (Acts 2:1–18). For females, Pentecost was Emancipation Day, for God's Spirit was equally poured out upon men and women, and both sons and daughters were gifted to prophesy (2:17–18).

As the Christian faith spread northward from Jerusalem to Antioch, and then westward to every corner of the Roman Empire, the strategic role of women became evident. Many churches first formed in homes of women like John Mark's mother (Acts 12:12) and Lydia of Phillipi (Acts 16:14–15). Women emerged as church leaders in Thessalonica (Acts 17:4), Berea (Acts 17:12), Athens (Acts 17:34), and Corinth (Acts 18:18). Priscilla, along with her husband Aquila, taught Apollos "the Way of God . . . more accurately" (Acts 18:26) in Ephesus. The Holy Spirit continued to distribute spiritual gifts upon all of God's people, both men and women (1 Cor. 12:1–31; Rom. 12:3–8; Eph. 4:11–16).

Paul's final personal greetings to the Christians in Rome began by commending the ministry of Phoebe (Rom. 16:1–2). Two words were used to describe Phoebe's ministry in the church at Cenchreae: *diakonon* and *prostatis*. The first term, *diakonon*, is translated "deacon" or "minister" in the twenty-one other places it is found in the New Testament. The word *prostatis* can be translated "ruler," or "one who leads out of caring," or a "servant-leader."[33] Whatever her role in the early church, Phoebe was undoubtedly a church leader.[34] In fact, this last chapter in Romans is a virtual roll call of women leaders in the church at Rome, as Paul names eleven of the most prominent ones.

Though women played an important role in the first-century church, traditionalists have noted that they did not play a leading role in missionary work, in writing the New Testament, or in directing the early church. Granted that be true, is it not remarkable that in a day when women were so severely restricted from participation, their involvement in the life of the early church was extraordinary? In fact, this change of women's roles in the New Testament churches was the main reason behind those "hard sayings of Paul"[35] concerning women.

For example, why did Paul command Corinthian women to cover their heads when praying (1 Cor. 11:5), to never cut their hair (1 Cor. 11:6), and to be silent in the churches (1 Cor. 14:34), basing his teachings on male "headship" (1 Cor. 11:3)? The apostle also instructed Ephesian women to "learn in silence with full submission," for they were not permitted "to teach or have authority over a man" (1 Tim. 2:11–12).

Space does not permit a complete exegesis of these troubling passages, which commentators agree are among the most difficult to interpret.[36] However, one hermeneutical principle is vital—the reader must always distinguish between cultural accommodations and permanent principles.[37] One way to accomplish this is to view the chronological development of women's roles in the New Testament church.

The sequence of events may have occurred something like this: (1) Jesus revealed a vision of human equality that was radically counter to culture; (2) Paul was converted to this Christian way; (3) Paul preached Jesus' vision of human equality (Gal. 3:28); (4) Christian women responded by discarding many cultural restrictions; (5) society misinterpreted these changes, often confusing Christianity with female fertility cults; (6) churches were divided over the discarding of cultural norms by Christian women; (7) Paul counsels the women to submit to some cultural norms in order to uphold vital Christian principles.

Although this historical overview does not answer every question, it does help explain the background for many difficult passages. The apostle was not a male chauvinist, nor was he contradicting Jesus or his own previous counsel. Indeed, Paul seemed to be writing that larger **values** were at stake.

Was not this same principle utilized when the Jerusalem Council agreed that believers should honor Jewish dietary laws (Acts 15:29), when Paul had Timothy circumcised (Acts 16:3), and when Corinthian Christians refused to eat meat that had been offered in idol worship (1 Cor. 8)? It seems so.

Let us then try to draw some conclusions from the teachings of the Bible concerning gender relations and human equality.

1. In the beginning both male and female were created in the image of God and were complementary to each other.
2. The Old Testament reveals the effects of sin on gender relationships: a male-dominated culture relegated women to a secondary role in religion and society.
3. Jesus was radically counterculture in His treatment of women, as He reversed the curse experienced by males and females.
4. As God's ultimate revelation, Jesus' treatment of women is determinative—all other passages about women must be interpreted in light of the life and teachings of Jesus.
5. Males and females enjoy full equality in Christ and are joint heirs of the spiritual gifts given to God's people.
6. The emerging church rejected both the traditional subordinate model and the extreme egalitarian model, affirming the servant model in all human relationships.[38]
7. The early church accepted some accommodation to Jewish and gentile culture in order to uphold vital Christian values.
8. Faithful biblical interpretation requires the Christian to distinguish between culturally time-bound practices and timeless Christian principles.

Women and Men in Christian History

How did the Christian church incorporate this biblical model during the ensuing centuries? In every generation there were forces working to include women, as well as powers working to exclude them. Following the New Testament period, women's names did not appear as prominently as men's in church history. As time removed the church from the revelation of Jesus, women were pushed further into the background.

Early Views. Some Christian leaders revived the ancient view that women are innately inferior. John of Damascus collected in his Parallels such patristic expressions as these: "A woman is an evil," "A rich woman is a double evil," "A beautiful woman is a whited sepulchre," and "Better is a man's wickedness than a woman's goodness."[39]

Although early church mosaics and inscriptions showed women as bishops and celebrating the Eucharist, later hands painted beards and male clothing over the women figures.[40] Church fathers looked upon women as the originators of sin and agreed with Tertullian that females are the "gateway to the devil."[41]

The influx of Greek ideas into the church by the fourth century increased the devaluation of women in the eyes of many early theologians, although the rise of monasticism gave women some alternatives to their social roles. The most highly acclaimed theologian of the medieval Roman Catholic Church, Thomas Aquinas, wrote that women are controlled by their sexual appetites, while men are controlled by reason. Because of their inferiority as a sex, Aquinas added, women are incapable of filling important roles in the church or in society.[42]

Reformation Adjustments. The Reformation led Protestants to dissolve women's religious orders, but it offered nuns little in exchange. All the reformers could ask these devoted women to do was to return to their families. However, because reformers allowed the marriage of clergy, a new role emerged for the wives of ministers. Tucker notes that the "hallmarks of the Reformation had great potential for eradicating gender distinctions in ministry, but somehow their full meaning was lost in a male-dominated world."[43]

Evangelical and lay movements in recent centuries have brought women into roles of leadership, especially among those Christians who look to the inspiration of the Spirit for authority rather than to institutions. Prominent examples are the Swiss Anabaptists in the sixteenth century, the Quakers in the seventeenth century, the Methodists in the eighteenth century, and the Holiness movement in the nineteenth century, from which sprang groups like the Church of the Nazarene, the Pentecostal churches, and the Salvation Army.

In the words of General William Booth, founder of the Salvation Army, "Some of my best men are women." One of the prime examples was his own daughter Evangeline, who was given major responsibilities in the Salvation Army, culminating in her service as general from 1934–39.[44]

Recent Trends. The emancipation of women began making its greatest headway in the last century. Influenced by Quakerism and

Methodism, Christian women began to analyze society and address social problems. For them the most significant issues were slavery and alcohol abuse, leading to the founding of the Women's Christian Temperance Movement. Intending to protect their homes and improve people's lives, women moved into every aspect of public life, including education, labor reform, and social work.[45]

Once women entered the political arena, they realized they could not be successful unless they could vote. Thus in Britain and North America the suffrage movement began. The right to vote for females came to Canada in 1918, to the United States in 1920, and to Britain in 1928. Strong opposition to women's suffrage in the United States came from the distilleries, and indeed in 1917 Prohibition became U.S. law in response to temperance movements.

The twentieth century has ushered into American life many dramatic social changes. To hear a grandparent tell about life in the early 1900s is like listening to a fairy tale—it seems unbelievable. Among the most drastic changes has been our understanding of male and female roles in the home and in society. The Christian community has not been immune to these social shock waves.

Church women of this century have assumed greater responsibilities. Almost every Christian denomination has a strong network of concerned women who are deeply involved in Bible study, mission activities, teaching and training, benevolent work, and financial support. Church and denominational leadership positions are open to women as never before, although many denominations continue to struggle over the issue of female leadership, especially women serving as deacons and pastors.

One thing is certain. With women serving as heads of state, governors, mayors, and chief executives in corporations, it will be difficult to refuse them leadership roles in the church. As T. B. Maston prophetically stated two decades ago,

> Some men as well as an increasing number of women have become conscious of the inequities suffered by women in most if not all of our churches. In churches where women frequently considerably outnumber the men, they have little voice in determining the church's programs and policies. They seldom hold a place of significant leadership responsibility in the work of the church. Even if they are represented on committees they are usually on a committee of minor importance, such as the Flower Committee, or as a minority member of a major committee. As teachers they are restricted to the teaching of children and women. There are

comparable limitations for women in the work of the denomination.[46]

Issues in Gender Relationships

One major social trend this century has been increasing diversity and cultural pluralism. Political correctness has become the "law of the Medes and Persians" in the nineties, as society denounces patriarchy, sexism, and gender exclusiveness. While not dancing to the tune of every cultural "Pied Piper," contemporary Christians cannot ignore the cries of females demanding equal treatment and the end to discrimination.

This new awareness of female mistreatment has also highlighted certain key issues: violence (rape, prostitution, sexual harrassment, domestic abuse), equality of economic treatment, political empowerment, exploitation of women in the Third World, **abortion**, child abuse, and poverty. The **"feminization of poverty"** is a recently coined phrase based on the new discovery that three-fourths of the very poorest people in the world are women and their dependent children.

Indeed, few issues are more crucial for twenty-first-century **Christian ethics** than the meaning of our maleness and femaleness. One female seminary student stated her concern this way:

> What is my role as a woman who is a Christian? On one hand I hear, in order to be a woman of God you are to be quiet in church, never assume a leadership position where you might be an authority over a man, etc. On the other hand I feel, what if I am the best qualified person to do the job? So what if there will be a man working under me! Should I be denied a position of leadership solely based on my gender? What if God gives me a message to share (that is assuming God does speak to women, of course)? Should I keep a word from the Lord to myself or tell my husband (if I am married) and let him speak for me? God gave me a voice and an agile mind—why can't I use them to serve Him? These attitudes make me feel like I am a second class citizen. . . . How can I reconcile what I believe I should be as a woman, with what I hear from Christian circles as to what I should be?[47]

For the purpose of this introductory study, we will focus on a few issues of major concern in gender relationships. One important issue, authority and submission in marriage, has been thoroughly discussed at the close of chapter 7.

Homemaker versus Wage Earner. Another family issue, one that extends into the marketplace, is the decision many women face concerning working outside the home. Traditionally in our society, the working husband and the homemaker/housewife seemed the ideal family arrangement.

A commonly accepted myth about the division of labor in the home is the belief that throughout history, women were mainly housekeepers and homemakers. The reality is that before the Industrial Revolution of the eighteenth and ninteenth centuries men, women, and children all worked together in their holdings. Even the biblical picture of the ideal woman in Proverbs 31 depicted a wife who "considers a field and buys it" (v. 16a), "plants a vineyard" (v. 16b), sells "merchandise [that] is profitable" (v. 18), "makes linen garments and sells them" (v. 24a), and "supplies the merchants with sashes" (v. 24b).

As time passed during this century, family members working together slowly disappeared; the husband was then designated as the "breadwinner." Some Christians came to believe this recent pattern was God's plan for every family.

A student shared a recent church conflict over this issue. A new pastor led the congregation through a Bible study in Titus, produced by a popular Christian writer. The author's exegesis of Titus 2:5 included the interpretation that the admonition for young women to be "managers of the household" meant that they should never work outside the home. The writer based his conclusion on the Greek word in the text, which he translated "home-worker."

The pastor convinced the church to follow this teaching and change their constitution. Henceforth, any woman who worked outside the home was automatically disqualified from serving in any church office. The result was disastrous. A divided church eventually split, the pastor left, and shell-shocked members nursed their wounds.

The key ethical question, therefore, is not the etymology of a Greek word or whether women should work outside the home— they have throughout most of history. The crucial issue is: What motivates a woman to return to the workplace?

In recent years, more and more women have felt the necessity to enter the workplace. While only 24 percent of women were in the labor force in 1940, their number increased to 49 percent by 1970, and 68 percent by 1990.[48] In 1960 only 19 percent of women with children under six were in the workforce; by 1985 half of them were,[49] and some predict the number will reach 70 percent by the end of the century. When children reach school age, the number of married women in the labor force jumps beyond 70 percent.[50]

Some working females see traditional sex roles as limiting. Other women claim housework is not what it used to be and decide to work because of boredom at home. More and more women have become career-oriented, finding personal fulfillment in a vocation. A large number of wives who work outside the home do so from economic pressures; one income is just not enough, especially if there are children.

Certainly a woman's decision about outside employment is a very serious one. Benefits and liabilities will need to be considered, as well as the added burdens facing a working wife and mother. Families will have to judge their motives very carefully, guarding against the materialistic attitude of simply wishing to buy more things. Jesus warned His disciples about undue concern over eating, drinking, and what to wear (Matt. 6:25).

A primary question comes to mind: "What effect does a wife's employment have on the marital relationship?" Studies indicate the answer is uncertain: some working wives seem more satisfied with their lives than some housewives. At the same time, Gallup surveys found that more than half of the adult women in America prefer the traditional role of mother and wife.[51]

In a day when the majority of women are wage earners, the church must not overlook the worth of being a wife and mother. The wife's role as homemaker and housekeeper has too often been depreciated or overlooked. Society seems to be rediscovering the importance of family values, a stable home life, and loving and caring parents. Beyond issues in the family, a heated debate continues in the church concerning female roles and leadership.

Church Leadership and Authority. A close relative of mine belongs to a denomination that attempts to reduplicate the New Testament church through literal obedience to every biblical pattern, regardless of cultural setting. As you might anticipate, the role of women in this church body is very limited. Men preach, men teach, and men alone serve as church leaders. What do women do? They attend services to listen and learn in silence, just as Paul commanded (1 Tim. 2:11).

To what degree should women serve in church leadership roles? My own denomination struggles over this question. Because Southern Baptist churches are autonomous, a variety of opinions guide local congregations. Some allow women to teach classes of males and females, while others restrict women teachers to children and female classes. Most elect females to serve on church committees, but few women are chosen to serve on certain powerful committees, and rarely are they chairpersons.

Denominational appointments of women are less representative than those in the local church. Most convention committees are heavily male dominated. Trustees of major institutions have some female members, but these women are often only token appointees, commonly the spouse of a well-known preacher.

Did Paul's words to Timothy, "I permit no woman to teach or to have authority over men" (1 Tim. 2:12), forever prohibit females from teaching men, speaking to a mixed congregation, or chairing a committee with mixed membership? A thorough study of the books of 1 and 2 Timothy and the situation in Ephesus that Paul addressed sheds much light on the meaning of this difficult passage. Errors plagued the congregation, and women had no small part in the problems (1 Tim. 1:3; 2:9-10; 5:11-15; 2 Tim. 3:6-7). Female apostates were spreading false doctrines, especially certain **Gnostic** myths (1 Tim. 1:4; 4:1-5; 5:13; 6:20; 2 Tim. 3:6-7).

Out of years of research in the Graeco-Roman culture and religions, Richard and Catherine Kroeger have suggested Paul was not laying down a transcultural truth, but rather opposing a local false teaching. The authors present a compelling case that the apostle was refuting a Gnostic religion ("Eve of Ephesus") that claimed Eve pre-existed Adam, infused Adam with life, and had a superior revelation of God.[52]

If their thesis is correct, Paul's statement was meant to warn Christians in Ephesus about creation heresies threatening the Ephesian church. The Genesis accounts had been embellished to give Eve a prior existence, even crediting her with being the one who gave Adam life.[53] Thus, Paul's counsel was a denial of the Gnostic teaching, rather than a permanent principle for the role of women in the life of the church.

The New Testament pattern, especially the examples of women like Priscilla (Acts 18:26) and Phoebe (Rom. 16:1-2), seems to support the role of women as church leaders. The fact that the gifts of the Spirit were distributed equally to males and females (Acts 2:17; 1 Cor. 12) indicates that leadership positions should be based on how people are gifted and called by God rather than on maleness or femaleness.

Why then are so many congregations reluctant to allow female laypersons full participation? The exclusion is usually not intentional but may be the subconscious influence of a male-oriented culture, reflected in everything from our language to our daily customs. Our church practice in the involvement of women in roles of leadership and positions of authority should be grounded in Christian principles, not cultural conditions. A reexamination of many restrictions is in order.

Ministerial Service and Ordination. Perhaps the most controversial gender issue is the ordination of women as deacons and ministers. Activists believe the admission of women to the ordained ministry is a second Reformation in Christendom. "The last time there was such a ground swell that was not heeded was the Protestant Reformation," claims feminist Sandra Schneiders.[54]

In 1992, by a margin of two votes, Anglican bishops swept away a 458-year rule that only men may serve as priests. In the angry aftermath of the vote, rumblings of schism erupted all across the seventy million Anglican Communion. Central players in the decision were 1,300 women deacons, who were now eligible for the priesthood.

The Vatican looked on this decision with alarm, having vowed that Roman Catholicism would never accept women for ordination. "The problem of the admission of women to the ministerial priesthood," declared a Vatican spokesman, "touches the very nature of the sacrament of priestly orders . . . [and] constitutes a new and grave obstacle to the entire process of reconciliation."[55]

This "woman's reformation" stirs up Protestants as well. The more progressive mainline denominations began struggling with the issue four decades ago. Women's ordination and female clergy were approved in the Methodist and Presbyterian denominations in 1956, in U.S. Lutheranism in 1970, and the U.S. Episcopal Church in 1976. Yet leaders in these communions worry about an implicit "patriarchy" that often excludes women from the better pulpits and assigns them to small parishes or as associate ministers.

Among evangelicals, a variety of opinions exists. The most conservative groups prohibit any type of ministerial service by females. Others allow women to serve as lay or associate ministers, as long as they are not ordained. Some evangelicals make a sharp distinction between deacon service and pastoral ministry, believing the role of pastor involves a position of authority not intended for females. Although many evangelicals are taking a new look at this entire issue, the majority of evangelical congregations resist ordaining a woman, unless it is required for military or other chaplaincy.

An exception to this norm are churches in the Wesleyan tradition who have always included female ministers: the Assemblies of God, the Church of the Nazarene, and denominations known as the Church of God. However, clergywomen in these churches usually serve as copastors with their husbands, or as evangelists. In 1993, the Christian Reformed Church delegates voted 95 to 88 to approve the ordination of women as ministers, elders, and evangelists.

The controversy that has divided the sixteen-million-member Southern Baptist Convention (SBC) since the 1980s has often focused on scriptural inerrancy, particularly as it relates to biblical teachings concerning the role of women. The more conservative segments of the SBC generally support the traditionalist position, whereas the moderate segment more commonly accepts women as deacons and pastors.

The number of women serving as SBC pastors or deacons among 90,000 ministers and more than 38,000 autonomous churches is only a sprinkling. Nevertheless, the number is rising faster among Southern Baptists than any other American religious body. Currently about nine hundred women are ordained for professional ministry roles by SBC churches, but only about eighteen serve as pastors. The largest number, more than two hundred, serve as chaplains.[56]

The way ordination is practiced today receives mixed reviews among evangelicals. The New Testament churches certainly did not view ordination as we do. According to the biblical record, every believer was a minister. "The Great Commission is the only apostolic succession ordained by Christ, and it applies universally to all believers, including women, who were also called disciples (Acts 9:1-2, 36)," writes Wheaton College professor Gilbert Bilezikian.[57]

Under the Old Covenant, a limited group of male priests ministered, but now every believer is gifted by God for ministry (1 Cor. 12:7, 11). The first-century Christian church required that all teachers demonstrate spiritual gifting. The only restriction for ministry was competency. No incompetent person—male or female—was permitted to teach (James 3:1; Titus 1:11) or minister (1 Tim. 2:11-12; 3:5-6). Only properly qualified persons should do ministry—that is the focus of Paul's instruction to Timothy for the Ephesian church.[58]

Many would argue that there is no scriptural basis for ordination—it is more a product of church tradition than biblical precedent. "The earliest record of an ordination rite is found in the *Apostolic Tradition of Hippolytus* (A.D. 200-220). By the fourth century there are many references to such a ceremony, particularly in the *Apostolic Constitutions*."[59]

What the Scriptures do reveal about ordination is this: the church community recognized that a person possessed certain gifts that were necessary for a needed job. The church, by the laying on of hands (Acts 13:1-3), signified an affirmation of that person for a task and the commissioning of that person to do that work for God. Lifelong credentials with accompanying authority and tax breaks were not part of the biblical practice.

My growing conviction is that the church today needs to restudy the entire process of ordination. Have we over the years moved away from the biblical example of "setting apart" for service toward an ecclesiastical credentialing that displaces the call of the Spirit of God? When the church at Antioch "laid their hands on them [Paul and Barnabas] and sent them off" (Acts 13:3), this was not a formal ecclesiastical ceremony, but a simple act of commissioning the two for missionary service.

Men and women in the Scriptures who were called by God to preach and to minister were not examined by a committee or called by a local congregation. Some, like Simon Peter and the woman at the well in Samaria, were called by Jesus Himself. Others like Priscilla and Aquila, Paul, and the four daughters of Philip were called by the Holy Spirit. Two of the greatest modern preachers, Charles H. Spurgeon and Dwight L. Moody, were never ordained. The only biblical requirement is the call of God.

Why then do we ordain today? For recognition. A church body needs to officially recognize a person to perform certain functions of ministry. But the main reason most ministers seek ordination is this: they must be ordained in order to qualify for certain church positions and to be eligible for the benefits and tax breaks allowed by the government.

What then should a church do? Ordination for women will be refused by some churches on the basis that the Scriptures forbid a female to serve in a ministerial position. Other churches will decide that the New Testament allows women to serve as deacons and be ordained. Though they be few, a growing number of churches will accept males or females in pastoral roles. Whatever the present practice, each church should make a serious attempt to study the biblical materials and the history of the early church concerning ordination and ministerial service. Neither past cultural tradition nor present social pressures should determine church practice. Our goal should always be to do God's will.

Women have always been vital to the life and ministry of the church. They will continue to be so. The world desperately needs the witness and service of women. Only as women and men work together in the **kingdom of God** will the job of sharing the love of Christ be faithfully accomplished in the twenty-first century.

RACIAL EQUALITY

Billy Graham recently was interviewed by television journalist Diane Sawyer, who asked the evangelist, "If you could wave your hand and make one problem in this world go away, what would that be?" Without hesitation, Graham replied, "Racial division and strife."[60] Writing about "**Racism** and the Evangelical Church" in *Christianity Today*, Graham added, "Racial and ethnic hostility is the foremost social problem facing our world today. . . . Racism— in the world and in the church—is one of the greatest barriers to world evangelization."[61]

Racial hostility exists worldwide. At the close of this century we have witnessed "ethnic cleansing" in Bosnia, racial riots in South Africa, and violence between racial groups in our inner cities. In Germany skinheads preach a new gospel of **anti-Semitism,** while Islamic terrorists in the Middle East wage holy wars against their enemies. National bookstores in the U.S. market a manual written by the leader of the American neo-Nazi party that explains how to kill Jews and blacks.[62] A tidal wave of ethnic tensions engulfs our globe.

Racism is not only a social concern, but it is also a **moral** and spiritual issue. Legal efforts may curb injustice and social efforts may diminish prejudice, but the heart of the racial problem is spiritual— only a transformation of the inner person will replace hatred with love, indifference with compassion, and oppression with justice.

Race and Racism

Our misunderstanding of race may contribute to an attitude of racism. Fifty years ago Swedish sociologist Gunnar Myrdal described the race problem in the U.S. as "an American dilemma."[63] By that description Myrdal meant a discrepancy exists between America's professed ideals of "liberty, equality and justice for all" and our actual treatment of large segments of people. Unfortunately, churches have contributed to the dilemma. While preaching that all persons have equality and dignity before God, many churches have refuted these truths by their actions.

The Concept of Race. The theory of "race" is a myth, for no pure race exists. Doctrines of race arose in the nineteenth century after biology and zoology developed categories in the animal and plant kingdom to differentiate between species. Similar attempts were made to classify humans according to physical criteria. A quasi-scientific effort subdivided the human species into Mongoloid, Negroid, and Caucasian. Darwinian evolution reinforced the idea of a hierarchy of human types.[64]

The truth is that cultural anthropologists cannot agree on the number of racial types—classifications range from nine to thirty-four major groups.[65] While taxonomies are useful for simple identification purposes, the attempt to determine "races" provided little more than sweeping generalizations. As modern **genetics** have shown, the basic human genotype suggests that human differences are less striking than the similarities.[66] Thirty years ago anthropologist Ashley Montagu first advocated the elimination of the term *race* in scientific discussions because it has been employed to refer to "fixed clear-cut differences."[67]

Most scientists have concluded what the Bible has always declared—in reality there is only one race, the human race. "From one ancestor he made all nations to inhabit the whole earth" (Acts 17:26). A vivid illustration of this human unity confronts the visitor to Yad Veshem in Jerusalem. Upon entering the museum, the tourist is surrounded with multimedia snapshots of Jews around the world. The stereotyped image of a "typical Jew" is quickly overshadowed by a panoply of faces on the walls—black, brown, red, and white images, some with thin blonde hair, others with thick auburn curls. In short, Jews come in a variety of shapes, sizes, and hues, as do most ethnic groups.

The Nature of Racism. Racism has existed among all peoples. Greeks believed all non-Greek-speaking humans were "barbarians." Jews felt superior to Gentiles, Spanish explorers subdued native Indians, and English traders made slaves of Africans.

Racism embraces the belief that certain groups or races are inherently superior and others are innately inferior—the belief "that hereditary biology determines the differences between groups, that cultural differences are predetermined and immutable, and that the distinguishing social and cultural features of the subordinate group are inferior."[68] This assumption fosters the mistreatment of minorities.

Prejudice and Discrimination. At the root of racism are prejudice and discrimination. As the word implies, prejudice means "prejudging"—a judgment before all the facts are known, often including hostile feelings. Prejudice thrives on inadequate knowledge, usually categorizing a whole group of people by characteristics that may fit only a few. Over time these stereotypes assume the role of facts—all Indians are drunkards, all Hispanics are lazy, and all blacks are musical.

What causes prejudice? Social scientists claim ignorance, economic competition, fear of amalgamation, and desire for personal advantage are major factors.[69] Racial prejudice is not inborn, but it is acquired or learned in a social environment.

Whereas prejudice is an attitude, discrimination is an action. Discrimination is "the differential treatment of individuals considered to belong to a particular social group."[70] Ordinarily, discrimination is the overt expression of prejudice; it is the categorical treatment of a member of a group simply because the person is a member of that group. In one sense, prejudice may be a result of discrimination, as a way of rationalizing and justifying the unfair treatment of persons.[71]

The American Racial Problem

Throughout the United States, several minority groups have been victims of racial prejudice and discrimination. In the West, Asians; along the Mexican border, Hispanics; in the Southwest, Native Americans; and throughout the land, Jewish persons. The major racial problem in America, however, has always been in relation to African Americans.

History of Slavery. Race relations in the U.S. cannot be understood apart from slavery and the slave trade from which it sprung. According to John Smith in *The Generall Historie of Virginia*, black slaves were brought to Jamestown in 1619, ahead of the Pilgrims.[72] Over the next two centuries, slaves from Africa were brought in increasing numbers to provide labor for the new world. Over the centuries nearly ten million African slaves were transported across the Atlantic, approximately four million of them arriving between 1700 and 1850.[73] The general understanding was that "the slave has three defining characteristics: his person is the property of another man, his will is subject to his owner's authority, and his labour or services are obtained through coercion."[74]

The Civil War erupted because people in the South believed slave labor was an economic necessity and "states rights" allowed them to continue the practice. Northerners held that slavery was based on economic exploitation and racism, and it violated the basic human rights provided by the U.S. Constitution.[75] The Thirteenth Amendment abolished slavery in 1865, precipitating the Civil War. The cruelty and degradation of slave life on the plantations led to the war between the states, but racial hostilities did not end after the surrender at Appomattox.

Segregation and Desegregation. After the war, provisional governments were set up in the South. White southerners were disfranchised, freed blacks were elected to public office, and tensions between the two groups increased. After 1872, southern whites regained the control of government and African Americans were disfranchised, segregated, and discriminated against in all areas of social life.

By the twentieth century, segregation was firmly in place. In 1896 the Supreme Court (*Plessy v. Ferguson*) had ruled "separate but equal" segregation was constitutional in all public institutions and facilities. For the next half-century black persons in the South experienced almost complete segregation. This influenced a mass migration of blacks to the cities of the North and West, which in turn motivated "White Flight" from these urban areas, leading to "Ghettoization." The result was "institutional racism," restricting African Americans to certain areas and certain roles, resulting in inferior education, housing, and employment.

On May 17, 1954, in the historic *Brown v. Board of Education* case, the Supreme Court ruled that in public education the "separate but equal" doctrine was unconstitutional. Within a year the Court applied the ruling to all public places. This action opened old wounds and stimulated the revival of "states rights" movements, prosegregation forces, and the rallying of racist organizations like the Ku Klux Klan and the White Citizens' Council.

At the same time organizations promoting racial integration, such as the National Urban League and the National Association for the Advancement of Colored People, worked through the legal system to eliminate discrimination and segregation in every corner of the land. The movement for racial equality reached a high point on August 28, 1963, when 250,000 people (75 percent black and 25 percent white) marched in Washington, D.C., and heard their dream articulated by Martin Luther King Jr.:

> I have a dream that one day on the red hills of Georgia the sons of former slaves and sons of former slave-owners will be able to sit down together at the table of brotherhood.
>
> I have a dream that my four little children will one day live in a nation where they will not be judged by the color of their skin but by the content of their character. . . .
>
> With this faith we will be able to work together, to stand up for freedom together, knowing that we will be free one day.[76]

Response to the Civil Rights Movement, along with the assassination of Martin Luther King Jr. and President John F. Kennedy, influenced the appointment of a National Advisory Commission on Civil Disorders by President Johnson in 1968. The Commission's report warned, "Our nation is moving toward two societies, one black, one white—separate and unequal."[77]

Clearly, the state of race relations in the nineties differs greatly from the sixties. Black scholar James Cone has researched one difference—a perennial dispute within the black American tradition. Cone sees this conflict personified in two major African American leaders: Martin Luther King Jr. and Malcolm X, the "two main resistance traditions in African American history and culture—integrationism and nationalism."[78] The ascension of Black Muslim protagonist Louis Farrakhan (who rallied 400,000 black men in Washington in 1995) as a leader in the black community is a signal to many that racial divisions may deepen.

Today's focus has also shifted from civil rights to economic justice,[79] education, and severe problems affecting African Americans. A recent study reported: about 43 percent of black families live in poverty; infant mortality rates are high (17.7 per 1000); black children are three times more likely to live in single-parent homes; homicide is the leading cause of death for black males aged 15-34; about 23 percent of all black males aged 20-29 are in prison or serving parole; and a majority of African Americans state the quality of life for blacks has gotten worse in the last ten years.[80]

Racial grievances continue to simmer in the cities and sometimes boil over into violence, as in Los Angeles in 1992 after the acquittal of the officers who beat Rodney King.[81] Deep-seated racial feelings also erupted throughout the country in 1995 after the acquittal of

African American celebrity O. J. Simpson, who was accused of murdering two white people—one being his former wife. In his book, *Man's Most Dangerous Myth: The Fallacy of Race*, Ashley Montagu wrote, "Racism is American society's most exposed weakness. It is America's greatest domestic failure, and the worst of its international handicaps."[82]

Biblical and Theological Insights

Is there a more disturbing example of Christians misusing the Scriptures and ignoring the spirit of Jesus than the attempt of white churches in America to justify slavery and segregation? Is there a clearer illustration of churches allowing cultural values to overshadow Christian values than the pattern of many congregations to exclude blacks? Since the Bible has been used both to defend segregation and to uphold integration, an analysis of these positions and of key passages is necessary to interpret God's will and Christian responsibility in race relations.

In Support of Slavery and Segregation. Although using the Bible to support racial separation and discrimination is rare today, it was not uncommon as late as midcentury. When I moved to a pastorate in Virginia in 1984, a deacon gave me a printed copy of his favorite pastor's final sermon—"Fusion of the Races: A Mongrel America Tomorrow." Preached in 1965, the sermon warned that racial amalgamation would lead to the intermarriage of the races and the downfall of America!

The most common passage used to support slavery and the segregation of blacks from whites is Genesis 9:24–27, the so-called "curse of Ham."[83] Segregationists contend that God cursed Ham (one of Noah's three sons), consigning him to be "the lowest of slaves . . . to his brothers" (v. 25). This interpretation assumes Ham is the founder of the "black race" (a theory having no basis whatsoever), destined by God to fill permanently a subservient position in society, never an equal to whites.

A number of obvious truths in the passage rebut this interpretation. First, God cursed no one. Noah declared the curse, and he uttered it while drunk. Again, Canaan was the one cursed, not Ham. Finally, no reference is made in this passage to racial or color identification of anyone. The descendants of Canaan were Canaanites (Gen. 10:15–19), not Africans.

Another misused passage is the one describing the "confusion of tongues" at the Tower of Babel (Gen. 11:1–9). The racial separatist argues that God opposed the "integration" of humanity, permanently segregating all people on the earth. The different languages served God's purpose to keep the racial groups apart.

However, linguistic differences have no clear relation to racial differences—some people groups have scores of dialects. The sin of the people at Babel was their intent to build their own center of security by their own power, with no dependence upon God.

Numerous biblical warnings against intermarriage (Deut. 7:3; Ezra 9–10) are used by supporters of separation to oppose racial mixing and inevitable intermarriage. Ezra, they say, took steps after the Exile to maintain racial purity; intermarriage with non-Jews was strictly prohibited. Again, contextual examinations of the passages make clear that the prohibitions prevented assimilation with pagan peoples, for intermarriage with idolaters would pollute the true faith of Israel.

In the New Testament, some have pointed to Paul's statement that God has "allotted the times of their existence and the boundaries of the places where they would live" (Acts 17:26b) as proof that God has determined racial boundaries. The passage actually refers to nations, not races, and in the first half of the verse God affirms that all persons come "from one ancestor," therefore all belong to the same human family.

During the nineteenth century, many supporting the status quo pointed to numerous passages in the New Testament that acknowledged slavery and encouraged slaves to obey their masters (Eph. 6:5). Slavery was commonly practiced in the Graeco-Roman world, and neither Jesus nor Paul specifically condemned slavery. Nevertheless, the life and teachings of Jesus, often explicated in Paul's epistles, affirmed principles that led to the eventual eradication of human slavery (cf. Philem. 16).[84]

In Support of Racial Equality. Neither Scripture nor Christian theology acknowledges a hierarchy of races. The weight of biblical evidence sustains the unity of the human race and the solidarity of individuals and groups. Numerous biblical passages support racial equality, such as Paul's classic statement, "There is no longer Jew or Greek, there is no longer slave or free, there is no longer male and female; for all of you are one in Christ Jesus" (Gal. 3:28). The heart of the biblical revelation concerning human equality is found in the example of Jesus, which we will review after we survey five major biblical themes.

Although theologians have debated the precise meaning of the *imago Dei* (Gen. 1:26-27), none question that all humanity was *created in the image of God.* Even the Fall of humanity does not destroy this image, though our likeness to God was damaged by sin (Gen. 9:6). "The fact that . . . this image is the possession of all men, regardless of condition, class or color, and the companion fact that Christ died for all men give to man his worth, value, and dignity."[85] If all persons are created in God's image and Jesus died for all, then we must consider every person our equal and treat each person with dignity and respect.

The *oneness of humanity* is another biblical theme supporting racial equality. In his sermon to the Athenians on Mars Hill, Paul was speaking to proud Greeks who considered themselves superior to all other people, whom they called barbarians. The apostle declared that Jews, Greeks, and all persons originated in one common source: "From one ancestor he [God] made all nations to inhabit the whole earth" (Acts 17:26a). Most biblical scholars believe the words "from one" refer to one human source for all the people of the world.[86] Paul's message stressed the oneness of God and the unity of humanity—we are all the creation of one "Father" and all are members of one "family."

Five times the Bible states that "God shows *no partiality*," or is "no respecter of persons" (Rom. 2:11; Acts 10:34; Eph. 6:9; James 2:1-9; Col. 3:25; italics added). This biblical theme is Simon Peter's revelation on the rooftop, when God convinced the Jewish leader that his prejudice against Gentiles was wrong. After the vision of "unclean" food declared "clean" by God, Peter testified in Cornelius's house, "I truly understand that God shows no partiality" (Acts 10:34). Some contend that the no-partiality principle applies only to the spiritual realm, but can anyone imagine Peter saying, "I now perceive that Gentiles are my spiritual equal, but I will not socialize with them"? If we are truly children of God, we cannot show favoritism at any level.

A basic biblical imperative found in both testaments is the command to *love your neighbor* (Lev. 19:18; Rom. 13:9). An expert in the law once came to Jesus with a question: "Teacher, which commandment in the law is the greatest?" (Matt. 22:36). The answer of Christ was twofold: "You shall love the Lord your God. . . . You shall love your neighbor" (Matt. 22:37, 39). Love for God was first (Deut. 6:5), but Jesus reminded the lawyer that a second imperative is necessary (Lev. 19:18).

In declaring love for God and neighbor as *the* Great Commandment, Jesus was correcting an error that still persists today. Love for

God and neighbor cannot be separated—they belong together, for it is impossible to love God and hate persons. In parables and by His example (Luke 10:25–37; 15:1–2), Jesus showed that neighbor love sets no limits; it is based on God's *agape,* which is inclusive. Christian love is more than superficial sentiment—it includes all persons, even enemies (Matt. 5:43-44).

A final major theme of the Bible that supports human equality is the *Great Commission*: "Go therefore and make disciples of all nations" (Matt. 28:19). The last command of Christ is a call to carry the gospel to "all nations," suggesting the disciples of Jesus are not to exclude anyone. The gospel of Jesus Christ is geographically, nationally, and racially inclusive. To the degree that we "go" to all persons with the good news of the gospel, we have the promise of Christ's presence: "Remember, I am with you always, to the end of the age" (Matt. 28:20). At home and on foreign mission fields, Christian churches must exclude no one from the body of Christ (1 Cor. 12:12).

As important as these five major scriptural themes may be, the clearest evidence for the practice of racial equality is found in the *example of Christ.* In His relation to the Samaritans (who were the hated race of His day), Jesus demonstrated the way Christians should respond toward any racial minority.[87]

When Israel was a divided nation, Samaria was the capital city of the Northern Kingdom (2 Kings 17:29), whose inhabitants were often called "Samaritans." After the Assyrians conquered the Northern Kingdom and exiled 27,290 Israelites in 721 B.C., they left behind a remnant of poorer people to tend the land. The Assyrians also sent colonists to the territory from various places (2 Kings 17:24), who brought with them their customs, traditions, and religion. During the Exile these foreigners intermingled and intermarried with the remnant Samaritans. The inhabitants soon became a heterogeneous population who neglected the temple, forgot the covenant, and disregarded the Law.

When the temple was rebuilt during the days of Zerubbabel, the Samaritans (claiming to be good Jews) offered assistance, but their help was refused (Ezra 4:1–3). Manasseh (an expelled priest) obtained permission from Persia to erect a temple on Mount Gerazim. The Jewish inhabitants of Samaria identified this temple as the only center of worship, limited their scriptures to the Pentateuch, and declared Moses to be the only prophet and intercessor in the final judgment.[88]

These acts of defiance and rivalry incensed the Jews in Jerusalem. Vigorous reforms under Ezra and Nehemiah only widened the breach. For orthodox Jews, the Samaritan was socially, culturally, and religiously an enemy. By the time of Jesus the word *Samaritan* became a term of abuse, and Jews avoided all contacts with these northern outcasts (John 4:9). Indeed the Jews had a worse hatred of the Samaritans than of the heathen.[89]

The Jewish-Samaritan prejudice was not one-sided; the Samaritans held no fondness for Jews either. This was probably the reason a Samaritan village refused to receive Jesus and His disciples (Luke 9:51-56). When James and John, the "sons of thunder," asked Jesus, "Lord, do you want us to command fire to come down from heaven and consume them?" (v. 54), Jesus rebuked them. Christ refused to reinforce their narrow nationalism and rabid racism. John must have caught the spirit of Jesus, for later he went on a mission of love to Samaria (Acts 8:14-25).

The animosity between the two groups was so great that the Jews bypassed Samaria as they traveled between Galilee and Judea. Jesus once insisted He had to go through Samaria. At Jacob's well He conversed with a most unlikely candidate for discipleship—a sinful Samaritan woman (John 4:17-30), which astonished Jesus' disciples.[90] Jesus reached across the barriers of race, sex, and moral condition to offer this Samaritan living water, revealing to her that He was God's Messiah. The woman returned to tell her city the news, and many Samaritans believed in Christ (4:39-42).

Jesus' ministry often focused on Samaritans. Once Jesus healed a Samaritan leper and stressed that he was the only one of ten cleansed lepers who returned to give thanks (Luke 17:11-19). In His most famous parable, Jesus made a "good Samaritan" the hero of the story (Luke 10:30-37). The last words of Christ before His ascension challenged His followers to be witnesses "in Jerusalem, in all Judea and Samaria" (Acts 1:8). Shortly after this command, Philip the deacon began mission work in Samaria (Acts 8:5).

What do all of these references connecting Jesus and Samaritans mean? The point is obvious: Jesus confronted the racial hostilities of His day by intentionally treating Samaritans as persons, worthy of ministry, compassion, and grace.

Once when Jesus spoke of the spiritual nature of His work and kingdom, certain Jews who trusted in their nationality for salvation became upset saying, "You are a Samaritan and have a demon" (John 8:48). A. T. Robertson observed, "In their rage and fury they can think of no meaner thing to say."[91]

Jesus did not respond to the critical remark of the Jews who called Him "a Samaritan," because for Him it was not an insult. He knew that Samaritans were equal to Jews, and in some ways might excel them. Jesus' example is our best revelation for Christian race relations. We are to relate to those whom the world despises in the same way Jesus related to the Samaritans.

A Christian Response

On Sunday morning, September 15, 1963, a terrorist bomb exploded in the Sixteenth Street Baptist Church in Birmingham, Alabama. Four young girls attending Sunday school were killed; a church was demolished; a city was shocked; and a nation mourned.

The response of my denomination during the week following the bombing typified the attitude of too many. The Executive Committee of the Southern Baptist Convention (SBC) heard a resolution proposed by one of its members, which joined the church in "mourning your dead and lamenting the tragedy," pledging both prayers and "energetic efforts in healing the rift between the races," closing with a promise to encourage contributions for the "restoration of your building." The resolution failed. A substitute statement was approved, which spoke in vague language about the "tragedy" of racial strife.[92]

Response of Churches. In contrast to years of foot dragging, church groups during this decade have made monumental statements of confession, repentance, and hope for racial reconciliation. In 1990 and 1992, two Baptist groups adopted statements of "confession of complicity with racism," pledging through repentance "to commit ourselves to be agents of Christ's reconciling peace."[93] Also in 1992, Pope John Paul II apologized in Africa for church complicity in the slave trade and in Latin America for Catholic exploitation of Native Americans.[94]

Acknowledging that their repentance came thirty years too late, leaders of twenty-one white Pentecostal groups gathered in Memphis in 1994 to close the racial rift with their African American brethren. Both whites and blacks met for three days to embrace, wash each other's feet, and join forces in a new ministerial organization without color barriers.[95]

At the annual convention in June of 1995, the SBC apologized for its past to black Americans, acknowledging it still suffers from the bitter harvest of racism. The nation's largest Protestant denomination passed a historic resolution, "On Racial Reconciliation on the 150th

Anniversary of the Southern Baptist Convention," which stated, "We apologize to all African Americans for condoning and/or perpetuating individual and systematic racism in our lifetime; and we genuinely repent of racism of which we have been guilty, whether consciously or unconsciously."[96]

Positive denominational pronouncements are an important first step for church groups. However, the Christian community also must develop other strategies for improving race relations. A joint meeting of several denominations called churches to:

- take concrete action that demonstrates the authenticity of repentence, such as an open-membership policy;
- disavow race-based economic and political exploitation, calling upon business and political leaders to embrace and implement a biblical vision of justice;
- engage the church in open and frank discussion about the sins of racism and seek racial healing;
- call America to prayer and repentance for the sins of racism and offer spiritual healing.[97]

In addition, churches should utilize a number of programs and activities that strengthen efforts to foster racial harmony: distribution of helpful literature, education in the cultural history of minorities, participation in "Race Relations Day," provision of church facilities, development of an interracial task force, involvement of members in multiethnic ministries, and interracial activities, such as exchanging worship services.

Response of Individual Christians. As vital as church and denominational actions may be, the ultimate solution of the race problem is a person-by-person process. Racist attitudes and discriminatory practices long have been part of the life and experience of most Americans. Racial barriers are difficult to dismantle; like the Berlin wall they come down one piece at a time. The temple in Jerusalem also had walls that divided—Jew from Gentile, male from female, and laity from priest. Paul may have had these dividers in mind when he appealed to the Ephesian Christians, "For he is our peace; in his flesh he has made both groups into one and has broken down the dividing wall, that is, the hostility between us" (Eph. 2:14).

In recognition of this need for personal healing, the popular Promise Keepers movement has made racial reconciliation one of seven commitments each member must live by.[98] For all Christians, a conscious personal effort is necessary to "break down the walls" that divide the human family. Some positive actions each person can take include:

- Establish personal friendships with people of different color; this simple step will remove many stereotypes.
- Eliminate racist language—racial jokes, slurs, derogatory names, and ethnic put-downs demean God's most precious artwork.
- Be sensitive to various forms of anti-Semitism.
- Reject and oppose all forms of institutional racism, such as segregated private schools and clubs.
- Defend public policies that improve ethnic relations, especially those related to segregated neighborhoods.
- Encourage your church and denomination to include minority persons at all levels of responsibility.
- Support ministers who work for racial harmony—they are key persons for change in the church and the community.
- Model Christian race relations in your life and home.

At six years of age Ruby Bridges became the first African-American child to attend William Frantz Public School in New Orleans in 1960. Each day federal marshals escorted her through a threatening mob of angry hecklers that assembled to intimidate her. Child psychologist Robert Coles interviewed Ruby to discover how she endured the daily insults and screaming mobs. Ruby replied, "Before and after school I prayed: 'Please, God, try to forgive those people. Because even if they say those bad things, they don't know what they're doing. So You could forgive them just like You did those folks a long time ago when they said terrible things about You.'"[99]

Progress in race and gender relations seems to move slowly, inch by inch. Nevertheless, transformation does occur—the gospel of Christ changes people, changes churches, and changes communities. In a speech in Montgomery, Alabama, at the close of the march from Selma, Martin Luther King Jr. called upon justice seekers to conquer despair and keep hope alive: "However difficult the moment, however frustrating the hour, it will not be long, because truth pressed to earth will rise again. How long? Not long, because no lie can live forever. How long? Not long, because you will reap what you sow. How long? Not long, because the arc of the moral universe is long but it bends toward justice."[100]

FOR THOUGHT AND DISCUSSION

1. Interpret the account of the creation of man and woman in Genesis 1–2 in relation to the equality of the sexes.
2. Explain the status of women in the Graeco-Roman world.
3. Debate this question: If Jesus' treatment of women was counter to the culture of His day, why did Jesus choose only men for His twelve disciples?
4. Debate this proposition: "Paul was a male chauvinist."
5. Develop a Christian response to the gender relations issue you consider to be the most critical today.
6. Read Martin Luther King's "Letter from Birmingham Jail,"[101] then discuss or debate the validity of King's response to the charges that his activities were "unwise and untimely."
7. What did Billy Graham mean by the statement that racism is one of the greatest barriers to world evangelization?
8. Answer this question: "Does the Bible prohibit racial integration and racial intermarriage?"
9. Write a report on the subject: "What my church can do to improve race relations in our church and community."

CHAPTER NINE

BIOMEDICAL ETHICS

Two calls interrupted the writing of this chapter. The first came from a former student now a pastor in Houston, who requested my advice on an ethical dilemma. A never-married adult woman in his church raised this question: "I am almost forty. Though I pray for a husband and a family, it appears I will never marry. I still would like to raise a child of my own. My first choice is **artificial insemination,** but this procedure would require using the sperm of a donor. Is this wrong for a Christian?"

A second call came from an old friend whose husband was comatose after a serious illness. The doctors gave no hope for his recovery, suggesting it would be best to take him off life-support systems and allow him to die. "I don't feel right about their advice," she said. "Would God hold me guilty of murder if I agreed to remove the machines that keep my husband alive?"

Biomedical **ethics** have suddenly taken center stage in pastoral counseling and in personal decision making. Advances in science and technology have improved health and lengthened life, but also they have created new dilemmas, "with **abortion** and **euthanasia** leading a long list of policy and professional questions on which passions run high and the likelihood of resolution runs low."[1]

The term *bioethics* is of recent origin, one of the earliest uses being by V. R. Potter. In 1971 Potter defined bioethics as "the science for survival," and he focused on using the biological sciences to improve the quality of life.[2] A more common definition labels bioethics "the application of ethics to the biological sciences, medicine, health care, and related areas as well as the public policies directed toward them."[3]

Since the prefix *bios* ("life") is much too broad for what is treated under "bioethics," and since bioethics may suggest an independent discipline rather than the application of ethics to certain arenas, the phrase **"biomedical ethics"** is gaining in preference. However, "bioethics" is still handier for most.

In an early article on "The Nature of Medical Ethics," Paul Ramsey called for medical education and the profession in general to become more literate in "the application of evaluative **norms** of some sort in appraisal of practices in medicine."[4] Ramsey elaborated by noting that medical ethics is not the same as *law,* nor is it a matter of deciding the *procedures*—normative ethics is always more than simply obeying the laws of the state, and medical ethics is not a matter of settling the procedures for deciding difficult medico-moral issues. In our relativistic and pluralistic culture, the temptation is to abandon the belief in universal warrants or **principles** for medical ethics.[5]

Accurately defining bioethics is not the only problem. Because of the continuing advances in medical and scientific technology, the questions raised by biomedical ethics come faster than the solutions. Although the urgency of the problems demands immediate resolution, even clear statements of the issues are difficult. The field of bioethics is further complicated by the interdisciplinary nature of the problems—no other area of ethics requires such a wide range of disciplines.[6]

Consensus on issues in biomedical ethics is rare for many reasons. Every dilemma has both personal and social dimensions, which normally spells conflict. In addition, the ethical, philosophical, and religious frameworks applied to bioethics bring a diversity of interpretations to each issue.

In spite of these inherent problems, the seriousness of the subject and the gravity of its influence upon the future has given rise to major institutes, the introduction of bioethical courses in colleges and medical schools, and a veritable flood of publications. Although the medical ethics community displays a wide variety of approaches to the subject, it also holds a common agreement about certain basic issues that are important for all problems in biomedical ethics: "The constitutive elements of personhood, the rights of a person, the rights of society, personal integrity, consent and distributive justice."[7]

Ever since medical researchers Watson and Crick discovered the structure of DNA in 1953, scientific pioneers have been exploring the wilderness of human biology with new zeal. The U.S. government, through the National Institutes of Health and the Department of Energy, has launched the **Human Genome Project**,[8] the $200-million-per-year gene blueprinting venture. "The objective of the entire initiative is to create an encyclopedia of the human genome—a complete map and sequence. Indeed, the sequence will be the ultimate map, a tool useful for all time and a source book for biology and medicine."[9]

What does this project mean for nonbiologists who have religious and ethical concerns? Martin Marty identifies both a "gee-whiz" camp ("God has put into our hands the possibility demanded by the world religions—to change what was defective in humanity") and a "greed and gloom" camp ("Playing God and interfering with nature threatens our sense of identity, uniqueness, and primacy among the creatures of the earth").[10]

Too often evangelicals ignore biomedical issues because the subject seems too complicated or because the Bible does not speak directly to bioethical concerns. David Neff has suggested five reasons Christians must pay attention to biotechnology:

1. Bioethics reflects how we view the human race;
2. Bioethics reflects how we view individuals;
3. Decisions about bioethics must proceed from the biblical teaching to love our neighbor;
4. Decisions about bioethics are colored by how clearly we perceive the nature of power;
5. Our understanding of bioethics is colored by our understanding of pain, suffering, and death.[11]

In the broadest sense, biomedical ethics is about life and death issues. Though the questions baffle and frighten us, though the concerns are many and complex, though medical advances create new problems faster than present ones can be solved, the life and death arena cannot be avoided. A beginning point, contends ethicist Daniel McGee, is to ask four fundamental questions: Shall we play God? How do we define human life? What is our attitude toward technology? Who should decide?[12]

Concerning the first inquiry about "playing God," how far should humans go in managing reproduction or the dying process? This bioethical question juxtaposes two paradoxical truths: God's sovereignty and human responsibility. In common parlance, the cautious say, "God will provide," while the adventurous assert, "God helps those who help themselves."

A conservative approach, called "God of the gaps theology," contends human wisdom is appropriate except in spheres beyond human control. Within these "gaps" of human knowledge, God operates. Humans should not invade God's realm of controlling life and death—this is haughty and an affront to God.[13]

An alternative view promotes human creativity and initiative, believing God ordained humanity to join Jehovah as a partner—discovering, creating, and acting in history (Gen. 1:26-28; 2:19). This approach focuses on the responsibility to use our talents and skills to reduce suffering and to bring healing.

In response to the possibility of "playing God," Martin Marty observes, "In a way, all biology applied to humans—all medicine—is 'playing God' and 'interfering with nature'; so the question is how to do this intelligently. Slopes can go up and down. Scientific findings may be ethically neutral, but scientific activity is not."[14]

The second question fundamental to bioethics asks how we define human life. The answer will determine what **values** guide our bioethical choices. In contrast to Greek dualism, which divided persons into body and soul, the biblical perspective is holistic—the human being as a mysterious body/soul unity (Gen. 2:7). Because we are created in the very image of God to live in relationship with others, human autonomy and human sociality are essential to our existence (Gen. 1:27; 2:21-25). This biblical view of humanity is axiomatic for life and death decisions.[15]

How do you view science and technology—as a blessing or a curse? This third question recognizes that a person's attitude toward science will determine his view of medical advances. In our technocratic society, the dominant attitude toward scientific inquiry is positive. Technology is the savior of our modern world, conquering disease, famine, and pestilence. The information explosion since the advent of computers has further increased the human options and integrated the human community.

However, science is not God. An increasing number warn that technology is a Frankenstein monster that can destroy us. High-tech machines in the medical arena may become the master rather than the servant. Critics also claim technology destroys orderly community, blurs traditional values, endangers human freedom and diversity, and rejects historic definitions of life and death.

Finally, one of the most persistent puzzles in biomedical ethics is: Who should decide? When contemplating abortion, **in vitro fertilization**, or "pulling the plug" on a comatose patient, what **authority** is final? Options include the patient, the family, the physician, the nurse, the hospital administrator, the minister, the law, and the insurance provider.

In our interdependent society, each of these interest groups has a valuable contribution to make. At the same time, each group has a limited perspective. Since we are all sinful, no one group should have absolute power. Ideally, health care decisions should include the wisdom of all through a decision-making process that is communal and guided by Christian principles.

Like the Houston pastor who called me with his dilemma, when we are confronted with a bioethical question we search for assistance—facts about the issue, biblical principles, Christian traditions, personal experience—any and every source of help is needed. In this chapter we shall attempt to provide help by studying the recent history of biomedical ethics, establishing guiding principles from biblical and theological sources, and surveying four relevant areas: abortion, euthanasia, **genetic engineering**, and reproductive technologies.

A BRIEF HISTORY OF BIOMEDICAL ETHICS

Reflection on the ethical practice of medicine predates Christianity. Certainly it began as early as Hippocrates (460–377 B.C.), who gave his name to the **Hippocratic Oath**.[16] Edmund Pelegrino contends the history of bioethics displayed such a fixity that his own periodization would include everything from the Hippocratic physicians until 1960 in a single sweep.[17]

The biblical emphasis on health and healing influenced the early church to establish medical institutions that flourished from the fourth century onward. The church soon found itself forced to reflect on the ethics of medicine, especially life-and-death issues.

Abortion was common in the Graeco-Roman world, as was the practice of infanticide by exposure. The church fathers were united in condemning both. However, they failed to agree on the status of the fetus. Two divergent views emerged, which still exist today. One group insisted on the full personhood of the unborn child from the time of conception, while the other group made a distinction between the "formed" and "unformed" fetus.[18] The Christians who took the latter view did not justify early abortions, but believed they warranted less severe punishment. Both groups agreed life at all stages was sacred.[19]

Daniel Callahan—a widely respected authority in **moral philosophy**—has written a short history of modern medical ethics.[20] Callahan's brief survey traces the beginnings of bioethics as a field of inquiry to the 1954 book by Joseph Fletcher, *Morals and Medicine*,[21] although he acknowledges that the explosion of interest came a decade later.

In the 1960s public attention was drawn to a series of hard moral questions about medicine—questions about human experimentation, organ transplants, **genetic counseling**, allocation of health care resources, and the definition of death. Out of these inquiries bioethics was born.[22] At that time most of the resources for bioethics were found in religious traditions; thus, theologians played a major role in what one scholar termed "the renaissance of medical ethics."[23]

One of the earliest Christian voices to explore medical ethics was Paul Ramsey, whose *The Patient as Person* in 1970 established the Princeton professor as the most influential American Protestant writer of his generation.[24] Other compelling theological voices of this era were Protestant James Gustafson,[25] Roman Catholic Richard McCormick, and Immanuel Jacobovits, who had written *Jewish Medical Ethics* a decade earlier.[26] Over the last quarter century a growing number of religious ethicists have entered the discussion and debate.[27]

As Callahan's "short history" made clear, after the initial "renaissance" of medical ethics came the **"enlightenment"** period. In the next decade, the scholarly attention to medical ethics moved religious traditions from the center to the circumference. Callahan identified many reasons, but the chief cause was the conviction within the field that public debate about medical ethics in a pluralistic society would be best served by the application of "an ethic of universal principles—especially autonomy, beneficence, and justice."[28]

Although some theologians of this period accepted this model, many others raised their voices in protest against the "secularization" of medical ethics. Nevertheless, there was and continues to be "an enlightenment suspicion of particular traditions and an enlightenment celebration of individual autonomy over against the authority of priest or magistrate and that new figure of arbitrary dominance, the physician."[29]

At the end of his "short history," Callahan called attention to "the discontents of secularization," acknowledging the muting of religious voices has been costly to the field and to public discourse.[30] The contemporary effort to speak a universal moral language, what Jeffrey Stout terms "moral esperanto,"[31] reduces morality to a set of minimal expectations.

Perhaps, as Alasdair MacIntyre claimed, the enlightenment project has failed.[32] On the other hand, a person "need not deny that there are some minimal moral standards which can be defended rationally to a universal audience to recognize that such standards do and can provide only a minimal account of what is morally at stake in medical decisions. . . . More candidly, theological talk about medicine and **morals** may at least remind a pluralistic culture of the minimal **character** of the standards it presumes are universal, rational, and sufficient."[33]

Too often, however, the impact of Christian ethical thought upon the history of medicine has been that of opposing new developments. With the advent of techniques like anesthesia, medicinal use of narcotics, and vaccination, misguided and uninformed Christians have resisted and condemned such procedures. Nevertheless, the Christian community has occupied an important role: "Bioethics may have a 'short history,' but the religious traditions of reflection about the ordinary human events of giving birth and suffering and dying are long and worthy ones."[34]

BIBLICAL PRINCIPLES AND THEOLOGICAL INSIGHTS

Bioethics is more than a list of questions that have their focus in medical practice. Many Christians wrongly conclude that biomedical ethics is "an esoteric academic discipline discussed by myopic professors in ivory towers."[35] As such, it seems to have little to do with the actual practice of medicine or ministry, and even less to do with our personal lives. However, as Paul Ramsey observed, the problems of medical ethics "are by no means technical problems on which only the expert can have an opinion. . . . They are rather the problems of human beings in situations in which medical care is needed. Birth and death, illness and injury are not simply events the doctor attends. They are moments in every human life."[36]

Since God is the author of human life and is concerned about the whole person, these "medical moments" in every person's life are religious events. The Christian faith is intrinsically involved in moral judgments about life and death issues. Indeed, biblical and theological values about human life form the basis for a biomedical ethic. "Although seemingly disparate, the many issues in 'bioethics' are united in the perspective of the Christian tradition in this: they all address the question of how we treat human beings, in the specific context of the frailties of human life in the aftermath of the Fall."[37]

In light of the modern collapse of a Judeo-Christian anthropology and the attempt to replace it with a humane medical tradition, "a case could be made for seeing bioethics as the cockpit of the struggle with post-Christian concepts of our nature, the test-bed for new understandings of what it means to be human in the twilight of the Christian Era."[38]

For example, the debate about end-of-life issues revolves around the meaning of suffering. Questions of human dignity inevitably lead to the meaning of human life. Discussions about the beginning of life and abortion cannot be separated from the meaning of sexuality, **reproduction**, marriage, and whether or not the fetus is part of the human community.

The point to note is this: our bioethical choices must lie in our understanding of humanity. "Ultimately," wrote Gustafson, "a biblically-informed theology provides the basis for the final test of the validity of particular judgments."[39] As we face a list of new issues and at the same time revisit old ones, the true shape of the debate for Christians and post-Christians must find its grounding in a biblical theology that provides a Christian vision for bioethics.

The Use of the Bible

The Bible is an indispensable and reliable source of ethical wisdom for Christians. In the fascinating but disturbing area of biomedical ethics, the way in which the Bible is authoritative is by no means obvious. Some medical ethicists discount the biblical witness as irrelevant and turn to **philosophy**, **natural law**, or the empirical sciences for guidance.[40] Because of a dearth of ethical teaching in medical institutions, many decisions are made on purely pragmatic grounds: mainly technical (what can we do?) and financial (how can we pay for it?).[41]

Relating the Bible to biomedical decisions poses several obvious problems. The major difficulty is the lack of material in the Bible dealing with biomedical issues. Although in biblical times medical remedies for illnesses were used (Jer. 8:22; Luke 10:34) and physicians practiced healing (Luke 8:43), medicine as a science emerged only in the last three centuries.

Because of the scarcity of biblical materials dealing with bioethical issues, another related problem has developed. Out of a desire for a straightforward word from God on the matter, evangelical Christians in particular are tempted to wrench a verse out of context to prove a point. Present discussions of the issue of abortion aptly illustrate the need to use the Bible carefully, accurately, and sensitively.[42]

Another problem in relating the Bible to bioethics is the Christian interpretation of healing—what is God's business and what is the responsibility of humans? If you believe life and health are entirely a matter of divine action (Christians need only to have faith in God's power), then bioethics is off-limits to believers.

Most Christians, however, walk the tightrope between trust in God's care and cooperating with God in redeeming fallen creation. The Bible affirms the healing ministry of Jesus and of His disciples (Matt. 9:35; Luke 10:1-8), as well as the medical practice of Luke the physician (Col. 4:14). God heals the sick, and physicians heal. The Bible makes clear that humans are called to share in God's work in the world by acting as responsible stewards, harnessing earth's resources, improving social conditions, and reducing human suffering. To trust in God's sovereign will without abdicating human responsibility is the ideal.

Biblical Principles for Bioethics

How does the Bible assist us in the ambiguous arena of biomedicine? English ethicist Richard Higginson offers this answer: "It is in the development and careful application of theological themes present in the Bible that Christians can contribute most helpfully to the ethics of medical care."[43]

Many Protestant writers focus on **virtue** and character as the basis for bioethical decisions, especially the principles of veracity, benevolence (including nonmalevolence), respect for persons (particularly their autonomy), and justice.[44] Though textbooks and articles on medical ethics pursue convoluted discussions about these principles, they seldom reach a conclusion about the rightness or wrongness of an action or offer convincing arguments about how to act in an ethical manner. Without denying these ethical standards are helpful (especially for hospital ethics committees), it must be noted that most patrons of these relative principles use them mainly to build a rationale and foundation for medical ethics.[45]

Like the cardinal virtues of ancient Greek philosophy, these medico-moral principles are good as far as they go—but for most Christians, they do not go far enough. Beyond our best reasoning about bioethics is revelation—truth from God that guides our thinking and acting. One basic proposal by Christian ethicists is to identify biblical principles that can be applied within the contextual dimension of any biomedical situation, upholding *agape*-love as the highest ethical imperative.[46] A basic list (though not exhaustive) of biblical principles for biomedical ethics might include these ideals:

- Every human being has been created in the image of God (Gen. 1:26-27; 2:7-25).
- Human life is sacred, and each person has equal worth and dignity (Ps. 8:4-6; John 1:14; Gal. 3:28).
- Life is a gift from God for which each person is a responsible steward (Exod. 20:13; Matt. 25:14-30).
- Each person is a unity of body and spirit, thus both body and soul have worth and dignity (1 Cor. 6:19-20).
- God is aware of and relates to prenatal life (Ps. 139:13-16; Jer. 1:4-5).
- Physical health is a positive value (Lev. 13; Matt. 8:1-17).
- Life and death are serious matters to God (Pss. 72:12-14; 116:15; John 11).
- Salvation involves the total well-being of persons, including their physical health (Mark 5:1-43).
- The physical body of the Christian is meant for moral purity and service to God (1 Cor. 6:13-19; Rom. 12:1).
- God requires the just treatment of persons (Amos 5:24).
- The universal ethical guideline in bioethics is the Golden Principle:[47] "Do unto others as you would have them do unto you (Matt. 7:12).

Theological Insights for Bioethics

The identification of biblical principles is an important step for bioethical decision making, but not the final one. For example, the application of the principle that human life is sacred may raise as many questions as it answers. In the modern context of complex and fast-changing medical technology, Christian thinkers have had to develop theological principles that maintain biblical presumptions while addressing problematic situations.

Double Effect. Roman Catholic moral theology has been at the forefront in developing sophisticated concepts for enigmatic biomedical questions. One such is the principle of double effect, which allows the *indirect* killing of human beings. It attempts to chart a moral course that is neither rigidly **absolutist** nor completely utilitarian. The principle states that "one is justified in permitting incidental evil effects from one's good actions if there is a proportionate reason for doing so."[48]

In the case of a pregnant woman who has cancer of the uterus, are doctors justified in removing the womb, knowing the surgery will kill the fetus? Catholic moralists would answer yes, because the act meets the principle's fourfold conditions:[49]

1. The procedure (removing the womb) is morally neutral;
2. The intent of the act (saving the mother) is good;
3. The good effect (saving the mother) occurs at the same time as the evil effect (death of the fetus);
4. The life or death situation is grave enough to justify the criterion of proportion.

Roman Catholic moralists also apply the double effect principle to the care of terminally ill patients.[50] When the battle to cure a fatal illness is lost and imminent death seems certain, patients should be allowed to die. Large doses of pain relievers may be administered, even if a side effect is the shortening of the patient's life.

Ordinary and Extraordinary Means. Another theological conclusion from Catholic tradition is the distinction between ordinary and extraordinary means. According to this principle, the patient and those who care for the ill person must employ all available means to preserve life and to restore health. "Ordinary means are all treatments which offer a reasonable hope of benefit and can be obtained and used without undue expense, pain or other inconvenience."[51] But a patient need not feel obliged to submit to treatment that would cause great expense or distress, if the benefits are negligible. A person dying with cancer may decide against chemotherapy, which at best would extend life only a few months.

The distinction between ordinary and extraordinary means can be defended on theological grounds as a positive Christian attitude toward life and death.[52] For Christians, life is a gift of God (Ps. 90:9-12), suffering can be purposeful (2 Cor. 12:9), and death is meant to be a positive experience (Phil. 1:21).

However, this distinction has its limitations. In some cases, patients are unable to communicate their wishes about prolonging their lives through extraordinary means. For the comatose or the mentally retarded person, who decides the therapy? In addition, the line between ordinary and extraordinary means keeps moving—procedures that once were considered extraordinary (organ transplants) are now standard methods. Finally, the fact that death is diagnosed as imminent may pose a paradox in treatment. Antibiotics that are now considered ordinary means may actually prolong dying for the elderly ill.[53]

Consent and Confidentiality. Consent is an area where two principles coexist in a state of tension.[54] In medical matters, the patient's permission is crucial. The principle of "informed consent" is based on the conviction that patients should be informed about and agree to medical treatment. Consent is justified in the theological concept of human dignity and freedom, and it serves as a protection against a person's being used unknowingly for medical experimentation.

The tension occurs when the urgent medical needs of a person render his or her consent as secondary. The doctor's best judgment may contradict the patient's wishes, as in the case of the refusal of a Jehovah's Witness to receive a life-saving blood transfusion. Normally we presume the doctor's professional competence and ethical commitment will lead to better medical decisions than the patient's.[55]

Like consent, confidentiality is a revered principle in medical practice. Crucial to the medical task of gathering all relevant information and making a correct diagnosis is the promise of confidentiality. A relationship of trust between physician and patient is crucial. However, this **prima facie duty** may be overridden if keeping information a secret endangers the well-being of the patient or others (such as evidence of physical abuse or an **AIDS** patient who is infecting partners).

Confidentiality has limits.[56] Promise keeping is normally honored in the name of honesty, truth, and love of neighbor, but in exceptional circumstances when injustice would result, breaking promises is justified (Exod. 1:15–21).

Care for the Dying. American Protestant ethicist Paul Ramsey has developed one of the most helpful theological principles for medical ethics: a policy of *only* caring for the dying. Before a patient begins to die, medical personnel use their skills to cure his or her diseases. When a person enters the final stages of a terminal illness, the requirements of care enter a new stage: medical objectives switch from saving life to providing the best quality of care. Now the most serious problems are discomfort and loneliness: medical care for the dying requires providing comfort.[57]

This principle also applies to handicapped newborn babies. When death can be predicted for an infant, futile operations and procedures should be discarded. "But the fact that a baby is handicapped should not be used as an excuse for neglecting routine operations and feeding procedures without which a child born with, e.g., Downs Syndrome or spina bifida will starve and die. . . . Christians should be in the vanguard of those affirming the value of children born with severe handicap."[58]

To identify exactly when a patient is dying is probably more difficult than Ramsey concedes. Nevertheless, he stands in sharp contrast with another Protestant ethicist, Joseph Fletcher, who proposes a utilitarian solution that severely disabled children would be better off dead. Ramsey concludes his discussion of care for the dying by specifying the only circumstances in which mercy killing might be permissible: deeply comatose patients and those whose pain cannot be relieved. If the patient can no longer be ministered to by another person, then the issue of care is removed from human hands.[59]

Commission and Omission. The work of Paul Ramsey in medical ethics has upheld the traditional view that in some situations allowing a patient to die may be right, but killing of the patient is always wrong. In recent years this view has come under attack by secular philosophers and medical practitioners.

The point of contention is the moral distinction made between acts of commission and omission. Critics of the distinction contend that deciding not to pursue a course of action (such as surgery to save a life) makes one just as responsible for the result (death), as if one caused it. Though free of evil motives, a doctor should accept responsibility for her decision to withdraw support or withhold treatment that brings an earlier death for her patient. Moreover, to allow some to die without hastening death may increase suffering (an argument used for voluntary euthanasia).[60]

However, most Christian thinkers and the majority of experts in medical ethics stand by the distinction between acts of commission and omission. A doctor who withholds treatment does bear responsibility for what occurs, but he does not know for sure the patient will die. In this case his motive was not to hasten death; it was to refuse to prolong life.

Love and Justice. The primacy of love and justice for **Christian ethics** is clearly taught in the Scriptures, but both principles have unique theological applications in bioethics. *Agape*-love in medical matters not only influences relationships; it also means "a commitment to seek what is best for another, even when he or she makes that difficult."[61] The love imperative is a constant challenge to improve health services and maintain the priority of patient welfare in treatment.

The imperative "to do justice" (Mic. 6:8) is the call to fairness and the demand to give others what is due them. Of the different models for justice,[62] which one should be applied to the difficult issue of the allocation of medical resources? Individuals and groups often compete for limited resources, such as kidney dialysis and organ transplants. Most Christian ethicists argue against the consideration of wealth, status, occupation, and family situation as decisive factors, but they also argue in favor of extremity of need and a random method of selection as valid criteria.

By now you realize that issues in biomedical ethics are extremely complicated. The explosive growth of medical technology in the last three decades has raised ethical questions before unimagined: fetal tissue transplantation, abortifacient pills and vaccines, gene repair, cloning, artificial insemination, behavior control, and surrogate motherhood, to name a few.

ISSUES IN BIOMEDICAL ETHICS

To introduce the reader to issues in biomedical ethics, four major areas will be considered: abortion, euthanasia, genetic engineering, and **reproductive technologies**. Numerous books and countless articles have been written on each of these subjects. Obviously, it will be impossible to deal adequately with any of these concerns. Our purpose, rather, is to give you a basic understanding of each topic by presenting the most pertinent biblical, historical, and scientific data for developing a basic Christian response. For an in-depth study of each issue, a number of helpful resources will be listed.

Abortion

Abortion is difficult to define. Generally it is described as "the expulsion from the womb of an embryo or a fetus, not yet able to sustain life."[63] At least six methods are used to terminate the life of the unborn child.[64] Spontaneous abortions (miscarriages), which may make up 12 to 20 percent of conceptions, should be distinguished from human intervention.

Abortion is the second most common surgical procedure in the U.S., exceeded only by circumcision. Since 1980 abortions in this country have numbered around 1.5 million annually, although in 1994 the total dropped to 1.2 million, down 5 percent from 1993 and the fourth straight annual decline.[65] More than 90 percent of abortions occur during the first twelve weeks of pregnancy; the remaining 10 percent include numerous late-term abortions.[66]

Controversy over abortion did not begin with the Supreme Court's *Roe v. Wade* decision. In ancient history, the practice of abortion was fairly common—even Hippocrates instructed a young lady how to end her pregnancy.[67] In Jewish thought, life tended to be identified with breathing (Gen. 2:7), but at the same time the Talmud and Jewish tradition upheld a strong commitment to procreation and the sanctity of human life from conception onward.[68]

In the early church, abortion was strongly condemned and forbidden for Christians.[69] From the time of Constantine until the Reformation, the official Roman Catholic position vigorously opposed abortion, although moral theologians debated ensoulment—the time when the soul entered the body.[70] After the Reformation, the declaration of the Immaculate Conception of Mary (along with newer medical facts) led Pope Pius IX in 1869 to support immediate ensoulment at conception. Though many modern Catholic theologians disagree, the normative position of the Roman Church became opposition to all abortions.[71]

In Protestant history, reformers Luther and Calvin both opposed abortion. For two centuries after the Reformation, most major branches of Protestantism held views about the subject not very different from the Roman Church. In this century, however, many Protestants have moved away from the Catholic position on this issue, due to theological and cultural reasons.[72]

The recent emergence of the New Religious Right, and its alignment with political conservatism, has made abortion a major political issue. In the 1996 presidential election, pro-life and pro-choice lobbies threatened to divide both political parties, but the conflict especially endangered Republican solidarity.

The contemporary debate in American society juxtaposes two antithetical views. At one extreme are those who argue that the fetus is essentially "tissue" belonging to the woman, having no independent humanity of its own. On the opposite side are those who contend that the fetus is an innocent human being, totally dependent upon society for his or her right to life. The first position absolutizes the rights of the woman; the second does the same for the fetus.[73]

The question of when life begins has become a pivotal one. Medical science supports the genetic and biological completeness of the fetus from the time of conception, but researchers differ about when a "true" person is in the womb.[74] For some it begins at *fertilization*, when egg and sperm unite, but the possibility of twinning[75] and the more than 40 percent loss of fertilized eggs in the monthly cycle without indications of pregnancy weaken this view.[76] *Implantation*, when the fertilized egg attaches to the womb, is another option suggested.

A Christian family-planning physician has proposed that individual life begins when the first primitive *blood cells* form (four weeks after conception),[77] while another theory is that the beginning of *brain activity* (third month) signifies personhood (since the absence of brain waves denotes death).

Quickening (when the child moves in the womb) is the sign for some. Most medical practitioners favor *viability* (when technology can preserve life outside the womb) as the point—a time line that medicine has reduced to twenty-one to twenty-four weeks. At the time of *birth* is a view that emphasize individual existence is necessary before full personhood is achieved. Christians and Jews who hold this opinion stress that the Genesis account links life with the breath of God (Gen. 2:7).

The legal, psychological, and theological definitions of "personhood" are even more varied. In the 1973 *Roe v. Wade* decision, the Supreme Court said it did not need to decide when life begins and that the unborn have never been recognized in the law as persons. In 1993 the Court refused to hear a case that would determine if an unborn child was a legally protected person from conception. However, legal decision about inheritance *in utero*, and the awarding of damages for injuries *in utero*, seem to suggest the fetus does have some legal rights.[78]

Pro-choice theologians maintain that the biblical portrait of a person involves capacities that a fetus does not have—spiritual, relational, moral, and intellectual powers. A person, they say, must have the God-like ability to make choices.[79]

Most pro-life Christians believe the Bible teaches that person-hood begins at conception.[80] Five kinds of texts are often cited: personal language applied to the unborn (Ps. 139:13-16; Luke 1:44), texts relating God to the unborn (Job 10:8-12; Ps. 51:5), Mosaic law provisions (Exod. 21:22-25), unity of human nature (Rom. 12:1), and the incarnation of Christ (Luke 1:26-56).

The first two types are inspired poetry that focus on God, "someone looking backward to see God at the very beginning of his existence, creating him, knowing him, caring for him."[81] The last two types are valid theological conclusions: human beings are body-soul persons and the history of Christ's incarnation began with conception. But how do these apply to personhood?

The one passage in the Bible that refers to an unborn child is Exodus 21:22-25. The Mosaic law describes a pregnant woman injured by two men who are fighting. The fetus "goes forth" (*yalad*), but if "no harm" follows, the penalty is a fine. But if "harm" follows, "then you shall give life for life" (v. 23).

Even versions of the Bible differ on the meaning, some calling this a miscarriage (NASB, RSV, LBT), and others translating it a premature birth (NIV, NKJV).[82] The "miscarriage" interpretation would assume the fetus does not have equal value with the mother, since the penalty differs for the death ("harm") of each. The "premature birth" view would hold that mother and child are of equal value, since the greater penalty is levied only if the infant dies.

Honest exegesis of the passage reveals "goes forth" (*yalad*) can mean either miscarriage or premature birth, "harm" can mean serious injury or death, and "life for life" often denotes a legal "fair compensation."[83] The conclusion: the passage may be interpreted either way. Jewish rabbis opted for the second view, not considering this murder or applying the rule of *lex talionis* in the case of abortion (Niddah 44b).[84]

What then can we say about the personhood of the fetus? "Even if we could agree about when life begins," wrote E. D. Cook, "that would not in itself solve the dilemma of the value implicit in or attached to human life at its various stages."[85]

Whatever we conclude, the fetus is on its way to becoming a person. As Bonhoeffer argued, we know God's intention: "The simple fact is that God certainly intended to create a human being and that [if aborted] this nascent human being has been defrauded of his life."[86]

What conclusions can we reach on the subject of abortion?

1. Abortion involves many competing values. We must never be so involved in theoretical discussions about abortion that we overlook the human factors. Of prime importance are the life of the mother, fetal life, and the genetic wholeness of the fetus. The crucial problems created by rape, incest, and fetal deformities must never be trivialized. Social reasons for an abortion may be suspect, but not the social problems of abused children, unwanted pregnancies, and overpopulation.

2. The sanctity of human life principle directs a powerful bias against killing fetal life. Since life is a gift from God and abortion is the termination of life, human life must be respected at all stages of development. The question is not when life begins, but whether life should ever be taken.

3. The burden of proof always rests on those aborting. Two questions must be asked by anyone considering abortion: Would continuation of the pregnancy destroy more than it would preserve? Is God's creative and redemptive will best served by abortion? Some Christians justify warfare and the death penalty, but not aborting innocent life; others contend for a consistent "seamless garment" ethic that is "pro-life" on all issues.[87]

4. In our society the law should restrict but not entirely prohibit abortion. In a pluralistic nation, all citizens have to tolerate the religious and moral beliefs of persons with whom they disagree. Some women believe in certain circumstances it is right to terminate a pregnancy. Should not the law allow abortion in rare situations when termination seems fitting?

5. Abortion on demand should be opposed as an abdication of moral responsibility. About 97 percent of all abortions are for social reasons and convenience, the so-called "abortion on demand." Abortion as a form of birth control or as an easy solution to a sexual mistake is morally reprehensible. To terminate the life of an unborn child simply because of financial, vocational, or other personal reasons is to devalue life.

6. Abortion may be excusable in those rare instances when moral values conflict. In our fallen world, sometimes every choice is a bad one. Is abortion allowable when the mother has an ectopic (tubal) pregnancy? Cancer of the uterus? When a teenager is pregnant due to rape or incest? When extreme fetal deformity is diagnosed? The taking of life to prevent a greater evil may sometimes be necessary, but only in those special cases when it is a "lesser of evils," and then always with profound sorrow.

7. Christians should seek to influence society with values that uphold the sanctity of human life. Christians must live as an alternate community, resident aliens whose counterculture ethic is a witness to a world living by false values.

The above conclusions and many of the judgments concerning abortion also apply to other biomedical issues. To avoid repetition, the presentation of the three remaining issues will focus on relevant facts, additional resources, and the specific way each ethical question impacts our lives.

Euthanasia

A recent *ABC News* report stated that more than one-half of the people who die, die the way they dreaded—in the hospital or in pain.[88] In recent years our society has witnessed a growing campaign in favor of a person's right to "death with dignity." The inference is that "people who are terminally ill should have the right to choose death rather than have their lives prolonged at great expense and often with considerable suffering."[89]

Though in this sense the idea is of recent origin, the practice of intentional killing was widespread in the ancient world and endemic in many early cultures. Only lately has euthanasia been added to serious ethical discussion in Western law and medicine.[90]

The term *euthanasia* is a combination of two Greek words that mean "good death." Normally it has been applied to persons who are hopelessly incurable, whose bodies are so wracked by pain and disease that they choose death, or if they are in a "vegetative" state, it may be chosen for them by others.

Often called "mercy-killing," proponents argue for euthanasia on the basis of compassion and autonomy. Advocates claim that in the majority of cases euthanasia prevents the prolongation of suffering in hopeless situations.

Medical technology has created a new dilemma. Patients who would otherwise die can be kept "alive" through machinery that maintains their vital functions. Supporters of euthanasia contend that the medical profession's attempt to maintain life, often in the interest of extended medical payments, drug experimentation, or threat of lawsuits, imposes "life" upon someone.[91] Doctors and ethicists generally agree that there comes a time when further treatment is not called for—in such a case, "letting a person die" is appropriate.

Traditionally Christians have opposed actively terminating the life of any person, whatever the circumstances, because life is a gift of God and is not to be taken by any human decision. Many ethicists are concerned that if our society lifts this prohibition—even in the limited environs of hospitals and terminally ill patients—the door would be open to a "slippery slope" that inevitably cheapens life.[92]

The issue of euthanasia is complex. There are many ethical and practical variations. Ordinarily, distinctions are made between euthanasia that is *active* (inducing death through the positive action of an attendant), and *passive* (allowing death by omitting or discontinuing life-sustaining treatment). Recent legal decisions have debated the definition of "treatment," as plantiffs sought the court's permission to "withdraw treatment" and thereby cause death by denial of nutrition and hydration.[93]

A more fundamental distinction contrasts *voluntary* (requested by the patient) and *involuntary* (determined by someone else, usually a relative, a physician, or the state) euthanasia. *Compulsory* (against the will) euthanasia in Nazi Germany led to the death of thousands of German civilians and millions of Jews.

Advocates of legalized euthanasia emphasize the autonomous character of their goal.[94] But "voluntary" euthanasia also has its problems: the decision may be made at a time of great distress or too far in advance to be accurate, during clinical depression, or when one is unduly influenced by relatives, doctors, or circumstances. In addition, the request for euthanasia is often difficult to distinguish from suicide.

A further complication may be raised by the advanced directive, the so-called "living will." Most states have legalized the preparation of a document that directs future medical treatment for a terminally ill patient who becomes incompetent. On the positive side, the "will" offers patients a choice about the kind of care they will receive when they can no longer express their will. A major difficulty is the fact that the directive may be so couched in general terms, the ill are vulnerable to abuse by others. Concerned ethicists see the document as evidence of the loss of shared medical values.[95]

The Christian understanding of human life created in God's image (Gen. 1:27) is the ground for belief in the supreme value of life. The Sixth Commandment (Exod. 20:13) prohibits murder and clearly supports the sanctity of human life.

In an article on assisted suicide, Richard Doerflinger musters strong disapproval on both **deontological** and **teleological** grounds. Maintaining that life is a fundamental good, he questions the assumption of euthanasia advocates that "happiness" is the ultimate value. While not glorifying suffering, the moral theologian insists there is an element of living and dying that we must face rather than evade. Turning to consequences, the Catholic writer raises suspicions about society's ability to set clear boundaries, a risk he calls a "loose cannon."[96]

Most Christians flinch at the thought of a loved one enduring prolonged suffering from a terminal disease or languishing for years in a coma. Medical practitioners point out two common misconceptions: that death is normally preceded by serious pain, and medical technology intends to prolong the dying process. In fact, modern drug therapies free most terminal patients from serious discomfort and good medicine rejects futile treatment that draws out the time of dying.[97]

Two competing values influence us on this issue: the freedom of individuals and the value of life. A person's right of self-control is a precious gift—human freedom is a basic theological doctrine. The Bible also teaches that our life is not our own (1 Cor. 6:19-20)— God owns us and has a purpose for every life. Although physical life is not the ultimate value, "a life is to be preserved no matter what qualities may have been lost and no matter what the individual may personally desire."[98]

Is it ever right to let someone die? Lewis Smedes answers "yes," when four conditions are met:[99]

1. When dying might be better for a patient than living.

2. When the alternative is forcing them to live.

3. When we indicate the sorts of situations in which it is appropriate to make such a decision.

4. When no one has exclusive or absolute authority to make the decision.

The apostle Paul wrote, "We do not live to ourselves, and we do not die to ourselves. If we live, we live to the Lord, and if we die, we die to the Lord; so then whether we live or whether we die, we are the Lord's" (Rom. 14:7-8). This is a challenge to faith and to understanding. As we struggle with complexity and ambiguity, as we clarify the Christian vision of human existence, as we face the dilemmas of modern medical technology, "the more difficult task is to take those answers and embody them in our living and in our dying. For that, much grace is required."[100]

Genetic Engineering and Reproductive Technologies

All of us are products of a genetic stream that originates in Adam and Eve. From the beginning of human history, genes have carried the genetic code that determines our physical makeup. The idea of genetic engineering raises fears regarding futuristic abuses of science in manipulating human nature. For some, it is "playing God" in the most objectionable sense.

Modern human **genetics** is far less monolithic than the term implies—genetic screening, DNA probes, genetic counseling, selective abortion, gene therapy, the human genome project, cloning, and **eugenics** are all involved.[101] This range of inquiry is possible because molecular genetics allows for the manipulation of the genetic content of human cells. The field holds great promise for new medical therapies—diseases such as cystic fibrosis and muscular dystrophy are being unravelled, and the genetic nature of cancer is being clarified.[102]

The field can be divided into two distinct areas: genetic manipulation and reproductive technologies. The first includes the traditional practices of breeding plants and animals as well as newer techniques of gene splicing, recombinant DNA research, and cloning. The second field embraces such practices as artificial insemination and *in vitro* fertilization.

Genetic Engineering. The substance of which genes are a part is DNA (deoxyribonucleic acid), a long chainlike molecule. DNA is the chemical record in which hereditary information is encoded. Human genes become defective by mutation and by chromosome aberration (each person carries three to ten potentially harmful genes).[103] The term *eugenics* means "well born through the judicious matching of superior genes," and it may be categorized as *negative* (altering genetic endowment by removing or correcting harmful genes) or *positive* (creating new beings).

Genetic counseling aims at preventing the conception of individuals with serious hereditary disorders. Genetic data is gathered, the counselor presents the facts, and risks are stated, but the counselee must make the ultimate decision.

Genetic screening is the testing of an individual or group of persons to determine whether they are carriers of defective genes. Prenatal screening is done by amniocentesis, a process opposed by pro-life advocates since it often encourages abortion. Ethical questions include who is to be tested, what those with positive results are to be told, and whether privacy and confidentiality can be maintained.

Somatic cell gene therapy, first tested in humans in 1989, entails the correction of gene defects in a person's own body cells. "The strategy involves gene replacement, gene correction or gene augmentation, the genes being introduced via retroviral vectors."[104] The purpose is to modify a particular cell population and so correct a definite disease in a patient. Technical difficulties probably mean the therapy will be limited to correcting single gene defects. Since its aim is to alleviate disease rather than improve the human species, most Christian bioethicists believe it fits as a health care procedure.

Germ line gene therapy consists of inserting the gene into the germ line (sperm, eggs, and embryos), so that when the modified offspring reproduces, all children will have the inserted gene instead of the defective one. Animal experiments have shown this method to be risky; it also requires obtaining embryos via *in vitro* fertilization, determining which ones need treatment, and carrying out therapy. A simpler method includes the disposal of defective embryos, which many consider unethical.

Enhancement genetic engineering concerns the insertion of a gene in an attempt to alter a particular trait of an individual, such as a growth hormone to improve sports skills. Since the extra gene alters a healthy person in a permanent manner and may have adverse consequences, the approach raises ethical questions. However, if the goal is the alleviation of disease, then as preventive medicine it may be justified.[105]

Recombinant genetics is a method for mixing genes from any two organisms to produce an entirely new creature. Called *gene splicing* or *recombinant DNA,* the result is a "hybrid plasmid" bearing some characteristics of both original organisms. Recent benefits of gene splicing are progress against genetic diseases (human insulin), new and improved forms of plant life (superwheat), and combating pollution (organisms that eat oil). Dangers do exist: the production of disease-causing bacterium, the development of creatures that can reproduce, the disruption of the ecology, and new diseases in humans and plants.[106]

In 1997, embryologists at the Roslin Institute in Edinburgh, Scotland, announced the [cloning] of lambs using DNA from mammary cells from an adult sheep. In theory, the same techniques could be used to take a cell from an adult human and create a genetically identical twin. This long anticipated and dreaded event has raised the thorniest of ethical and philosophical questions. President Clinton immediately asked the National Bioethics Advisory Commission to consider whether federal policies relating to human embryo research should be reconsidered in light of this procedure. Many ethicists believe this first cloning of an adult mammal suggests a host of quandaries about the future of our society, the nature of self, the role of sex, and the question about whether our ethics can keep pace with our technology.[107]

A bundle of ethical issues arises from genetic engineering, ranging from personal privacy issues to that of government control and the many inherent dangers of manipulating the human gene pool. The Bible does not speak directly about genetics; however, the God of biblical revelation desires the health and wholeness of His children. When genetic engineering is used to improve human life physically, socially, and culturally, certainly it is fulfilling God's will for His creation.

Reproductive Technologies. Aldous Huxley's *Brave New World* appeared in 1932. A half-century later many of his prophecies seemed to be coming true. Techniques developed to deal with male and female infertility have opened Pandora's box to a host of procedures.

On the positive side, thousands of married couples who have been unable to bear a child (about one in seven) now have hope through artificial reproduction. While adoption is an option for some, available healthy children are fewer than the demand.[108]

The least controversial **reproduction technologies** are *surgical repair* of Fallopian tubes and *medical treatment* of endometriosis. Drugs are also used to stimulate ovulation.

Artificial insemination (AI) is a common and inexpensive means of assisting reproduction. Concentrated sperm is injected into the female reproductive system artificially in the clinic. Other than the methods of obtaining and delivering the semen, nothing is biologically unusual. When the sperm of the husband is used (**AIH**), the conception of the couple's own child results.

More controversial and more common is artificial insemination by donor (**AID**). Usually because the husband is infertile or carries a genetic disorder he might pass on to his offspring, sperm from an anonymous donor is used—sometimes this is frozen sperm that has been screened for disease and matched by physical characteristics of the donor and couple. Thus the conceived child is genetically linked only to the mother.

Surrogate parenting utilizes artificial insemination to deal with female infertility. In partial surrogacy, the sperm of the husband is used to fertilize a surrogate mother who will carry the child and give it up at birth, usually for a fee.[109] Full surrogacy defines a woman becoming pregnant with another woman's egg, fertilized by the woman's husband.

Artificial *sex selection*, previously used in animals, is now available to humans. The technique (separation of the X-sperm from the Y-sperm) is not perfect, but it seems to increase the probabilities of predetermining a child's sex.[110]

In vitro ("in glass") *fertilization* (IVF) is the procedure whereby the women's egg (removed by laparoscopy) is fertilized with sperm in a laboratory Petri dish—the so-called "test tube" baby.[111] "Typically, the ovaries are stimulated by a fertility drug, and then a few ova are removed and fertilized. The most promising zygote is then placed into the uterus, and hopefully it develops into a pregnancy and birth."[112]

IVF technology has made possible many questionable techniques: the production of human embryos for research, the possibility of genetic manipulation of embryos, the use of eggs from a miscarried or aborted female fetus, and *embryo transfer*—"the surrogate mother merely carries the embryo for a few days and then the embryo is flushed out of the surrogate and transferred to the infertile wife."[113]

Gamete intra-Fallopian transfer *(GIFT)* is the process of collecting eggs (stimulated to ripen by fertility drugs) from follicles, and then introducing them, along with sperm, into the Fallopian tubes. Less difficult than IVF, this method is more acceptable to some Catholic theologians because it simulates the natural process of conception.

New reproductive technologies raise numerous social, legal, theological, and ethical questions. J. K. Anderson is convinced that two major ethical concerns surface with nearly every technique. The first is the issue of the sanctity of life—large numbers of fertilized embryos are destroyed or used in research, which forces us to ask if embryos and fetuses share our humanity. The second ethical concern is the moral integrity of the family. Many techniques involve third parties, which violate God's intent for marriage and family, including the purpose of sexual union, bonding, and the role of relationships in the family.[114]

A professor of bioethics asks these probing questions: "Is it ethical to reproduce in a way that is not 'natural'? Does the use of a stranger's sperm, egg or uterus violate the integrity of marital child-begetting? Should children be told that they were conceived by means of donor sperm or *in vitro*? Is it ethical to perform research on human embryos, and if so, up to what point? What is to be done with embryos that are discarded in fertility treatment? What are the moral and social limits on possible genetic manipulation of human beings in embryo?"[115]

The inability to have children is a painful ordeal. Many Christian couples will investigate reproductive technologies to help them overcome infertility, which is understandable.

At the same time, investigation of the causes for childlessness may take months or years, consuming financial and emotional resources, and the success rate is not high. However, if couples choose drug or surgical therapy, or if they use their own gametes in AIH, GIFT, or IVF techniques, or even if they must use a surrogate motivated by love (usually a mother or sister) to carry the couple's own child, few would find moral fault.

To introduce third parties into the reproductive process, however, does seem to violate the "one-flesh" nature of marriage (Gen. 2:22–24), as well as exposing the child to unknown emotional risks. The question of Christian stewardship is another concern when large sums of money are expended.[116]

In the area of bioethics, Christians must guard against the cultural temptation to succumb to whatever is useful, marketable, convenient, self-serving, possible, and lawful, rather than what is right. We must not become like Eustace, the nasty little boy in C. S. Lewis's *The Voyage of the Dawn Treader*, who realized to his horror that he had "turned into a dragon while he was asleep. . . . Sleeping on a dragon's hoard with greedy dragonish thoughts in his heart, he had become a dragon himself."[117]

Nigel Cameron writes a profound assertion in the opening essay of *Bioethics and the Future of Medicine: A Christian Appraisal*: "The cultural significance of the changes which are taking place in medical values—and, behind the specifics, in the disjoining of any distinctive ethical commitments and medical practice—can hardly be overstated, in the unravelling of the Western cultural tradition."[118]

This theologian and bioethicist contends the interlocking of Christian and Hippocratic values in the public square of medical tradition is in danger of collapse, not so much from secularism as a neopaganism. Cameron calls upon Christians to engage "the new barbarians" (as he termed them) in two ways: first, by energetic exploration of both the biblical-theological distinctives and the tradition of Christian-Hippocratic medicine that have grounded medical anthropology; and second, by building and nurturing institutions that will keep alive the Christian vision of bioethics.[119] If Cameron is correct, the future of bioethics may be central to the task of the church in a post-Christian generation.

FOR THOUGHT AND DISCUSSION

1. If the Bible does not speak directly to biomedical ethics, why should Christians pay attention to biotechnology?
2. Debate this proposition: Despite its benefits, biotechnology is a curse upon humanity.
3. Does the recent history of bioethics reflect a Christian or a post-Christian culture?
4. How should the Bible be used in making bioethical decisions?
5. Evaluate the validity of these theological principles for bioethics: Double Effect, Ordinary and Extraordinary Means, Consent and Confidentiality, Care for the Dying, Commission and Omission, and Love and Justice.
6. Debate one of the following propositions:
a. A completely pro-life position is the only option for Christians.
b. Voluntary passive euthanasia is acceptable for Christians.
c. Genetic engineering is "playing God."
d. GIFT is the only ethical reproductive technology.

ECONOMICS AND POLITICS

Anglican evangelical John Stott has left an enduring legacy through his thirty-four books and his role as a premier preacher, teacher, and Christian leader. In a recent interview, the theologian explained his dual commitment to social concerns and evangelism, noting that "God is not just interested in religion but in the whole of life—in justice as well as justification."[1] When asked about the chief Christian blind spot of the last quarter of the twentieth century, Stott mentioned three: the immorality of nuclear arms, the environment, and poverty—particularly the economic oppression of the Third World.[2]

Most Roman Catholic and Protestant ethicists would agree with Stott that the world's most serious problems are economic and political. Ethical issues in these two social arenas are closely related. While mutual influence binds the two powers together, economics and politics are not the same. Notable differences distinguish the two, and there is always tension between them. "To be sure, one is severely damaged when the other fails, and the health of one bodes well for the well-being of the other. Even more, the interests of one inevitably shape the actions of the other. But the little gap between the two terms . . . symbolizes the fact that the two are not the same and that one of the greatest questions of **modernity** is how large that gap should be."[3]

Economy normally refers to the processes by which the material means for the satisfaction of human needs are produced, distributed, and consumed. The term also includes the social institutions that cut the channels through which the economy navigates. Indispensable to modern economies are complex laws, corporations, management technologies, and sophisticated systems of communication.

Politics, on the other hand, stands for the role of the constituted **authority**, particularly the state's authority to maintain law and order.[4] At its core, politics is about power. Governments exercise the power to give commands and enforce those edicts. The commands may be laws, orders, or policies, and they may be formulated by rulers, military elites, charismatic leaders, revolutionary parties, or representative bodies. When political power is gained, authorities implement and enforce the commands of the governors.[5]

Sixty years ago Reinhold Niebuhr criticized the naive optimism of the liberal church in its attempt to apply the law of love to politics and economics. In his "realistic" approach, Niebuhr observed, "In modern society the basic mechanisms of justice are becoming more and more economic rather than political, in the sense that economic power is the most basic power. Political power is derived from it to such a degree that a just political order is not possible without the reconstruction of the economic order."[6]

In our study of economic and political **ethics,** it is important to recognize that politics and economics involve actions that may be profoundly sinful. Economic policies often promote oppression and poverty in the name of free enterprise. Politics sometimes uses violence and war to achieve national interests, as well as to establish peace and justice. At best, believers feel ambivalent about the two. Politics and economics may establish order and encourage economic stability. However, the two powers are easily corrupted by human greed and the insatiable desire to dominate.

During the twentieth century, mainline denominations and ecumenically oriented churches have spoken out vigorously on political and economic issues. In contrast, evangelical churches have seemed reticent to address concerns like wealth and poverty, liberation and oppression, war and peace, or crime and punishment.

The retreat of evangelicals from the ethical arena of economics and politics is ironic, for evangelical revivals in nineteenth-century England and America were grounded in social reform.[7] Charles G. Finney, the American lawyer-turned-evangelist, was convinced the gospel "releases a mighty impulse toward social reform," and "the great business of the Church is to reform the world."[8] Finney's evangelism raised an army of young converts who became the troops for economic and political reform, in particular the antislavery movement.

But something happened during the first thirty years of this century. American historian Timothy L. Smith termed it "The Great Reversal," an evangelical neglect of social responsibility, which David O. Moberg investigates in his book of that title. Although Moberg does not attempt a thorough analysis of origins, the main causes for the reversal seem to include: (1) the fight against theological liberalism, (2) reaction to the so-called "social gospel," (3) widespread disillusion and pessimism following World War I, (4) the spread of premillennialism, and (5) the identification of Christianity with culture by believers.[9]

During the 1960s the evangelical mainstream began to "Reverse the Great Reversal." Christian scholar and founding editor of *Christianity Today*, Carl F. H. Henry, was among the first to call evangelicals to reconsider their social responsibilities.[10] In 1974 an international meeting on world evangelization in Lausanne, Switzerland, challenged Christians to accept "social responsibility," declaring "evangelism and sociopolitical involvement are both part of our Christian duty."[11] Church groups in the United States who once looked upon social involvement as a sign of liberal compromise now joined the "Moral Majority" and organized to address issues like separation of church and state, pro-life, pro-family, illegal drugs, pornography, military defense, and women's rights.[12]

Today most branches of Christendom recognize the importance of Christian involvement in the social order, especially in economic and political areas. These two realms are among the most powerful forces in shaping modern society. Economic and political systems stamp their image upon persons as well as products, upon individuals as well as institutions. The Christian faith has the responsibility, in the name of love and justice, to challenge every economic and political program that is detrimental to human life and to social betterment.

This chapter will survey the basic ethical challenges in American economic and political life. Our approach will begin by examining biblical teachings and theological insights on each subject, as well as the historical attitudes of the church about possessions and politics. We will conclude each section by utilizing our decision-making model to construct a Christian response to major issues in economics and politics.

ECONOMIC ETHICS

Emil Brunner claimed **Christian ethics** is distinguished from natural ethics by the fact that in it God's action is always regarded as the basis for human action.[13] To ground human action in God's action in the economic sphere is to recognize that all resources are divinely provided and are to be used for divinely ordained purposes. The Christian word for this conviction is *stewardship*.

Economic ethics is primarily concerned with property and wealth: owning and using, buying and selling, growing and making, borrowing and lending, and spending and giving.[14] In a series of books on "Ethics and Economic Life," ethicist John Bennett wrote, "Economic activity is an important part of human experience. It fills most of our waking hours, and to it we devote much energy and talent. . . . It involves us in many of our most rewarding (and most difficult) human relationships. . . . It places heavy responsibilities on us."[15] For most people, economic **values** have become the chief values of life. Disciples of Jesus need a clear understanding of the Bible's message on property and wealth.

Biblical Teachings and Theological Insights

In his book *The Challenge of the Disciplined Life*, Richard Foster explores three ethical themes crucial to people of faith—money, sex, and power.[16] Foster affirms the Scriptures contain an overall clarity of witness about economic matters, but the Bible also presents two divergent streams, always paradoxical and sometimes downright contradictory. The prolific writer describes the two ways as the "dark side" and the "light side" of money.[17]

The Dark Side of Money. One stream of teaching in the Bible about possessions is the warning that money is not completely neutral, a mere medium of exchange—materialities are always a threat to our relationship to God!

The Eighth Commandment, "You shall not steal" (Exod. 20:15), specifically demanded of Israel respect for the possessions of others. The Old Testament prophets regularly condemned the people of power whose greed led them to steal the houses and land of the weak (Isa. 5:8; Amos 5:11–12; Mic. 2:2; Jer. 22:13).

Jesus spoke about money more frequently than any subject other than the **kingdom of God.** In Jesus' teachings are numerous radical criticisms of wealth: "Woe to you who are rich" (Luke 6:24); "You cannot serve God and wealth" (Luke 16:13); "Be on your guard against all kinds of greed" (Luke 12:15).[18] Paul reflected Jesus' words when he taught that the inordinate desire for riches can lead to a host of other evil desires (1 Tim. 6:9–10, 17).

Wealth has many inherent dangers and deceptions: it can choke the Word of God (Matt. 13:22), promote spiritual apathy (Matt. 13:22), and create a false sense of security (Luke 12:16–21). In addition, the prosperous often have divided priorities that may hinder them from entering the kingdom of God (Matt. 6:24; 19:23).

Throughout His ministry Jesus warned about the "dark side" of possessions: Christ condemned theft (Mark 7:21), attacked scribes who "devour widow's houses" (Mark 12:40), denounced Pharisees who were "full of greed" (Matt. 23:25), and led Zaccheus to repent of his extortion by restoring his gain (Luke 19:2–10).

In the Sermon on the Mount, Jesus cautioned against undue concern over money. Whether one is rich or poor, anxiety over possessions is an indication of a lack of trust in God's care (Matt. 6:25–34).

Although Jesus never condemned the acquisition of wealth, absolute property rights were denied by the Lord. Christians are stewards of all possessions and must always subordinate property rights to human need (Matt. 25:40, 45).

The overall biblical witness, especially the words of Jesus, is disturbing to our affluent age. "For Christ money is an idolatry we must be converted *from* in order to be converted *to* him. The rejection of the god mammon is a necessary precondition to becoming a disciple of Jesus."[19] When Jesus used the Aramaic term *mammon* to refer to wealth (Matt. 6:24), Christ was describing the spiritual character of money to become a rival god. The best way to conquer this "dark side" of money, therefore, is to embrace the "light side."

The Light Side of Money. To focus only on the negative warnings about wealth and property is to distort the biblical revelation. The "light side" of money is the positive revelation of the Scriptures that possessions are a blessing from God—property and possessions can be used to enhance our relationship with God and to enable us to serve humanity.[20]

The Bible clearly teaches that everything God created was "very good" (Gen. 1:31) and belongs to God the Creator of all (Isa. 66:2; Ps. 24:1). God's absolute right as owner and humanity's relative rights as stewards are unmistakenly clear. Possessions are a gift from the Creator to be held in trust—we are accountable to God for our use of material possessions (Lev. 19:9 ff.; Job 31:16–33; Isa. 58:7–8).

One responsibility of God's covenant people is to have compassion for the poor and use our possessions to eliminate hunger and poverty (Exod. 22:25; 23:11; Deut. 15:1-11; 18:8; Jer. 22:13-17; Ps. 72). The Old Testament laws of the Sabbatical Year and the Year of Jubilee (Lev. 25) established requirements that freed slaves, dissolved loans and debts, returned the land to its original owner, and helped the poor. Though seldom observed, the seventh and fiftieth years in Israel were intended to minimize economic differences, discourage excessive wealth or excessive want, and give everyone a chance for a new start.

Although Jesus Himself had few possessions (Matt. 8:20; John 19:23), He recognized the rightfulness of personal property (Matt. 21:33-41; Mark 1:29; John 20:10). Joseph of Arimathea was lauded as a disciple of Jesus though he was wealthy (Matt. 27:57), and Nicodemus used his wealth and high position for the good of the Christian community (John 7:50; 19:39).

In the parable of the talents, Jesus emphasized good stewardship and the management of money (Matt. 25:14-30). Christ approved the use of money to meet family needs (Matt. 7:11), to support religious institutions (Matt. 17:24; Mark 12:14), to aid the poor (Matt. 6:3), to pay taxes (Matt. 22:17), and to show gratitude and love (Matt. 26:6-13).

In the apostolic church a community of sharing developed: "All who believed were together and had all things in common; they would sell their possessions and goods and distribute the proceeds to all, as any had need" (Acts 2:44-45). This spontaneous and voluntary act was a temporary economic practice to meet a unique crisis. Though brief, the procedure reflects the Christian spirit of love and sharing in early Christianity.

Paul the apostle did not challenge the economic injustices of the Graeco-Roman world, for he anticipated the imminent end of the present age (1 Cor. 7:31). However, he did expound economic **principles** in his letters, urging Christians to earn their livelihood by honest work (Eph. 4:28), to shun idleness (2 Thess. 3:10), and to share with the needy (Eph. 4:8; Rom. 12:8, 13).

The teachings of the Scriptures concerning money and the materialities of life are uncomfortably clear. God created everything that is and all belongs to God. Christians are responsible to be good stewards of our material resources, using them for God's glory and to meet human need. Honesty is a Christian **virtue** that should characterize believers in personal finances as well as business transactions.

Property and possessions, therefore, are not inherently evil. However, wealth is viewed with extreme suspicion in the Bible because of the potential danger of trusting in riches rather than in God. Prosperity should never be considered a sign of God's favor, nor should poverty be considered God's curse upon the sinful.

Economic justice is a major point in the messages of the prophets. Dishonest business practices, economic exploitation, and the tendency of the powerful to oppress the weak are condemned. God's preferential option for the poor is a recurring theme in the Bible. "The Exodus is but the beginning of a long list of canonical witnesses to God's special care for the poor, the hungry, the oppressed, the exploited, the suffering. Text after text echoes the theme of Ps. 12:5, 'Because the poor are despoiled, because the needy groan, I will now rise up, says the LORD; I will place them in the safety for which they long.'"[21]

Richard Foster summarized the heart of the biblical revelation: "The dark side of money inevitably leads to greed, which leads to vengeance, which leads to violence. The light side of money inevitably leads to generosity, which leads to magnanimity, which leads to shalom. The great **moral** question of our time is how to move from greed to generosity, and from vengeance to magnanimity, and from violence to shalom. . . . simplicity points the way."[22]

Economic Attitudes of the Church through the Centuries

Over the centuries the Christian church has expressed both radical and ultraconservative attitudes toward economic issues. The biblical pattern parallels the judgment of history—no economic system can be labeled the "Christian" strategy.[23]

Early Church Struggles. The first three centuries of Christian history reveal the initial attempts of the church to discover the mind of Christ. Historian Ernst Troeltsch contended property was the first social problem with which the church had to deal.[24] The initial response of the early church mainly echoed the biblical appeals to beware of riches, help the poor, and follow the Old Testament traditions on almsgiving and usury.

The *koinonia* ethic of sharing reflected in the Book of Acts (2:44-45) was adopted by some of the church fathers, especially in the communal life of the monastics. But most Christians living "in the world" soon adjusted to the idea of private property, fulfilling their spiritual duties through benevolence.

The fullest treatment of wealth was the homily by Clement of Alexander titled "The Rich Man's Salvation." Written in response to Polycarp and others who wrote that riches were a spiritual barrier to salvation, Clement (in a prosperous environment) defended wealth and calmed the fears of well-to-do Christians.[25]

Thomistic Teachings. During the latter part of the medieval period, Thomas Aquinas discussed economic concepts in his *Summa Theologica.* Quoting **natural law**, Thomas defended the right to private ownership of property, which should be used for the common good. The Roman Catholic theologian condemned usury, theft, robbery, and cheating in business, and he supported a "just price" theory, restitution, and charity for the poor.[26]

Reformation Revolutions. The Reformation introduced two leaders, Luther and Calvin, who viewed economics as central to the Christian life. Like Aquinas, Luther supported the right to private ownership of property, but not because of natural law; Luther believed the fallen nature of humanity required it. As a conservative reformer, Luther believed serfdom was necessary but condemned communal ownership because it discouraged industry.[27]

Luther had deep compassion for the poor and organized a "community chest" for their welfare and education. Both Luther and Calvin attacked the practice of usury because the moneylender collected profits without risk or labor. Lending ought to be free. At the same time, both reformers allowed moneylending on certain commodities, as long as reason and charity prevailed, and if the rate limit was 4 to 6 percent per year.[28]

Whereas Luther was socially conservative, Calvin was radical, intellectual, urban, and more at home among traders and merchants in the business world. Calvin's dream was to create a "sanctified society" in Geneva—a city submissive to the rule of God in all its civic, commercial, and political affairs. While Lutherans sought to return to feudal, rural simplicity, "Calvin sought to discipline commercial life by those very virtues of hard work, high responsibility, thrift and diligence, which the emerging industrial economy required."[29]

The Reformation contributed greatly to feudalism's march into **capitalism.** Both Calvin and Luther restored the biblical doctrine of "calling" (*vocatio*). Since the fourth century the church had taught that only the religious were "called" by God to enter the superior life of the monastery. In contrast, the two reformers preached that all forms of constructive work in the world—

butcher, baker, or priest—are stations assigned by God: "All work is taken up into the religious sphere; there is no distinction between sacred and profane. For the first time in the history of Christianity, the dignity and value of work as work are fully insisted on. . . . Idleness is the worst of sins."[30]

Yet Luther and Calvin differed on one important point. While Luther dignified every line of work, he taught that Christians should serve *in* the same vocation as their forebears. John Calvin disagreed. He believed God called a Christian to serve *through* his or her vocation in whatever line of work a person was best suited. Calvin's contribution was to free people from following their parents' occupation, moving vocation from inheritance to achievement.[31] Max Weber linked the rise of capitalism with Calvin's economic virtues of honesty, frugality, diligence, and prudence.[32]

Modern Adjustments. The Industrial Revolution of the nineteenth century spawned many economic changes. Mechanization generated new factories and new products. Railways spanned the continent. Trade expanded and wave after wave of new immigrants arrived, providing cheap labor. For a few the change brought prosperity, but for the working classes it meant backbreaking toil, long hours of labor, exploitation of women and children, inadequate education and health benefits, and poverty. The Social Gospel Movement was an attempt by churches to solve the many social problems created by the Industrial Revolution.

The classical economic theory of *laissez faire* stimulated the development of capitalism, a system of production for private profit regulated by the forces of supply and demand in a free market.[33] Capitalism's method is competition, its motive is profits on investments, its end is the accumulation of wealth, and private property is its basic right.

Cases for and against "free enterprise" capitalism have been argued constantly.[34] Critics of capitalism note these weaknesses: (1) economic considerations take precedence over human needs; (2) serious inequalities develop between owners and workers; (3) the profit motive fosters a spirit of materialism; and (4) social catastrophes like mass unemployment are common.

Proponents of a free market system stress these strengths of capitalism: (1) increased productivity; (2) higher standards of living; (3) greater occupational freedom; (4) emphasis on individual initiative; (5) opportunity for economic achievement; and (6) the support of philanthropy, education, and science.

Despite these merits, in contemporary America we have moved to stabilize the economy by limiting the capitalistic system—today we have a modified welfare state. Although private ownership is dominant, since midcentury the government has legislated many social policies that provide economic benefits to workers: progressive income tax, Social Security, federal grants and loans, minimum wage, improved working conditions, public housing, and fair distribution of the nation's wealth.[35]

The modified welfare state is not without its own dangers. Government interference and control often stifle business and discourage entrepreneurship. A growing government bureaucracy soon develops many of the problems it sought to cure: runaway inflation, insensitivity to human need, inefficiency, financial waste, and administrative "red tape." Enforcing government policies and regulations is another difficult and costly problem. The most serious danger of bureaucratic control of the economy is the temptation to depend upon the government to solve all social problems, thereby discouraging private enterprise.

Relying heavily on the biblical revelation, the church has struggled to develop a Christian position on economics. Two ethical principles stand like twin mountain peaks rising above the rest: love and justice. Yet how do these ethical ideals apply to specific areas like property and wealth, borrowing and benevolence, or work and wages? The devil is in the details! One thing is certain: "It is the function of religion to teach society to value human life more than property, and to value property only insofar as it forms the material basis for the higher development of human life."[36]

As we noted in the beginning, the key word for personal Christian responsibility in economics is stewardship. John Wesley defined Christian stewardship in a straightforward sentence: "Gain all you can, save all you can, give all you can."[37]

But what about social justice? The community of believers must not overlook the implications of the gospel for the economic practices of social institutions. Christians should foster and support specific social policies that reflect the Christian values of compassion, sharing, equality, and justice for all.

Hunger and Poverty

In a speech to a college audience, former President Jimmy Carter said economic discrimination—rich versus poor—is "the most insidious form of discrimination" and "the most troubling ethical problem faced today." Carter defined the rich as people who have a home and at least a chance of getting medical care, an education, a good job, and a better life for their children, who live in a safe community and feel the justice system is on their side, and that their decisions can make a difference, at least in their own lives.[38]

By this definition, most Americans are rich. But we live in a hungry world. One out of five deaths on our globe is from hunger. Each year 15 to 20 million persons die of starvation or hunger-related illnesses—14 million of them are children under the age of five. Each minute, twenty-four people die of hunger.[39] If one hundred jumbo jets, each loaded with four hundred infants and children, crashed every day, the world would be horrified. Yet each day 40,000 children awaken to die of malnutrition or simple infection, with virtually no press attention.[40] Take a look at our impoverished world:

- More than one billion people (one of six persons) are chronically hungry and live in absolute poverty.
- Worldwide, five million children die annually from diarrhea and 100,000 children become blind due to a lack of vitamin A.
- In Latin America, malnutrition is the primary cause of 60 percent of the deaths of children under the age of five.
- A child born in most African and Asian countries is ten times more likely to die before the age of five than a child born in the U.S.A., Japan, or Sweden.
- More people have died from hunger in the past five years than have been killed in all the wars, revolutions, and murders in the past 150 years.
- By the year 2000, authorities estimate more than two billion people will suffer from malnutrition.[41]

We also live in a nation where hunger and poverty exist. In the United States, more than 39 million persons endure below the poverty level of $7,263. Another 30 million are sinking toward it.[42]

The poor are everywhere—in urban ghettos, in cities abandoned by industry, in crowded housing projects, and in rural settings. About 40 percent of America's hungry live in rural areas as tenants, sharecroppers, migrants, or native Americans.[43]

Children are the poorest Americans. More than one-third of the 15 million poor children in the U.S. live in families where at least one parent is employed full-time.[44] The elderly are also at risk to hunger. An estimated 3.3 million citizens over the age of sixty-five have incomes below the poverty line. The most visible poor are the homeless—estimates range from 500,000 to 3 million persons, 28 percent of whom are families. Another group is the working poor, about 1.2 million Americans who have full-time, minimum-wage jobs and still live in poverty.[45]

Yet hunger and poverty are more than statistics. Each figure represents people—children without food or health care, parents unable to escape the despair of daily survival, and families who feel powerless to change their hopeless future.

Causes of Hunger and Poverty. An initial response to hunger and poverty is to demand that food production increase. However, food is available. Enough grain is produced annually to provide every person on earth with three thousand calories per day. The real causes are more complex and multidimensional.[46]

A major reason for hunger at home and abroad is unequal distribution and consumption of food. For example, the wealthier 30 percent of the world consumes more than 50 percent of the world's food. Three primary reasons for this inequity are overeating (Americans consume 3,200 calories per day), a meat-rich diet (it takes seven pounds of grain to produce one pound of steak), and wasteful habits (food thrown away would feed thirty-four million persons).

Another contributing factor is war. When international or civil war invades a nation, economic growth declines, food production is disrupted, people are displaced, and most of the population experience hunger and poverty.

Economic decisions and policies also create hunger. Unfair taxes, inadequate welfare practices, global consumer patterns, and international debt are major contributors. For example, poor nations often must produce food and other resources for foreign consumption to service debts, stifling their economic growth.

Environmental factors, such as droughts or flooding, may bring crop failure and famine. Overgrazing, overcultivation, and deforestation turn productive lands to wastelands.

Overpopulation is another element many people think causes hunger and poverty. Economic insecurity often leads poor parents to have more children for their workforce. The result is too many mouths to feed and increased destitution.

The most important cause of world hunger is the poverty perpetrated by inadequate and faulty economic and political systems. Impoverishment is perpetuated by systems of government that allow the rich to exploit the poor, where farmland is owned by a few landowners who export resources to affluent nations, and where exorbitant amounts are spent on arms and the military to the neglect of basic needs.

For the church of Jesus, the greatest danger is an attitude of apathy and indifference. Because the problem of poverty and hunger is enormous and complex, Christians can easily become discouraged and give up. Although no quick-fix solutions exist, a number of individual and corporate actions from the Christian community can make a significant difference.

A Christian Response. Ghandi once remarked, "The world has enough for every person's need, but not enough for every person's greed." A basic question facing every believer is lifestyle.

Indeed, if I am a "rich" Christian living in an affluent society on a planet populated by millions who are poor and hungry, what are my options? John Stott has suggested three choices for Christians: to become poor, to stay rich, or to cultivate generosity, simplicity, and contentment.[47] Although some have taken vows of poverty and others have justified wealth, the last option is the one upheld in the Scriptures.

Although Jesus was not destitute, His life exemplified simplicity and contentment—Christ had no home and very few possessions (Matt. 8:20). He taught from a borrowed boat, rode into Jerusalem on a borrowed donkey, spent His last evening in a borrowed room, and was buried in a borrowed tomb. Although Jesus did not call His followers to divest themselves of all their possessions, He did challenge us to renounce covetousness, materialism, and luxury, and to care for the poor.

Paul's word to the rich is informative: "As for those who in the present age are rich, command them not to be haughty, or to set their hopes on the uncertainty of riches, but rather on God. . . . They are to do good, to be rich in good works, generous, and ready to share" (1 Tim. 6:17-18). Warning the rich of the danger of pride and materialism, the apostle does not tell them to become poor but to be generous, willing to share.

In 1974 the International Congress on World Evangelization adopted part of the Lausanne Covenant, which called upon Christians to cultivate a simple lifestyle. This prompted an International Consultation on Simple Lifestyle in 1980 to elucidate the implications of the 1974 statement. Under the concept of "simplicity," the document resolved to "renounce waste and oppose extravagance in personal living, clothing and housing, travel and church buildings" and added these distinctions: "We also accept the distinction between necessities and luxuries, creative hobbies and empty status symbols, modesty and vanity, occasional celebrations and normal routine, and between the service of God and slavery to fashion."[48]

The biblical basis for a simplified lifestyle as a means of sharing with the poor and hungry has been well documented by Ron Sider in *Rich Christians in an Age of Hunger*.[49] For affluent American Christians to adopt a personal lifestyle that is free from the burden of materialism and opulence is difficult. Ethicist David R. Wilkinson has proposed that First World Christians:

- Have intellectual and spiritual honesty in interpreting the Bible's teachings on economics and justice.
- Avoid confusing the "American way" with God's way and laissez-faire economics with God's will.
- Beware of the trap of legalistic **asceticism**—the call to simple living is not an escape from the world.[50]

In speeches to students, Tony Campolo often states it more bluntly: "If Jesus had $40,000 and knew there were starving people in the world, would He buy a BMW?" The simple lifestyle is an outward expression of an inward reality. Christians are to seek the kingdom of God and the righteousness of God first, knowing everything else will find its proper order (Matt. 6:33).

But what specifically can we do about hunger and poverty in America? Robert Parham names four important actions: (1) change the public **prejudice** toward the poor; (2) develop a positive attitude toward poor children; (3) reform welfare and strengthen antipoverty programs; and (4) make the tax system fairer.[51]

A Swahili language proverb states, "Drop by drop the bucket fills." What individuals and churches do about hunger and poverty may seem to be "just a drop in the bucket," but drop by drop, the bucket fills. Churches can play a unique role through:

- Education—create awareness and knowledge about hunger and poverty by organizing study groups and task forces.
- Participation—cooperate with international and domestic relief organizations to provide food, serve meals, distribute clothing, and respond to disasters.
- Contributions—give regularly to hunger relief projects and church mission boards that feed people and help people feed themselves.
- Advocacy—work for the support of the poor as Christian citizens by influencing government policies, such as salvaging the

sixty million tons of food that spoils each year in American farm fields, unharvested and uneaten.

Ghandi also said, "He who has more than he needs is a thief." In Jesus' parable of the rich man and Lazarus, God stands clearly on the side of poor Lazarus and against the wealthy Dives, who never noticed the beggar at his gate (Luke 16:19-31). As we leave our affluent homes to drive in our luxury cars to enter our multimillion dollar church complexes, do we notice the beggar on our doorstep? God does.

POLITICAL ETHICS

To talk about "political ethics" or to use the word *politics* with "church" immediately raises red flags and howls of protest. "Religion and politics don't mix," is the common cry. The fear is that Christian involvement in politics will corrupt both church and state.

Our initial need is to define what we mean by "political" and to determine the true function of the state. The nature, origin, and authority of government have been widely debated by church leaders throughout Christian history.

What is the God-ordained role of government and what responsibilities do Christians have to the state? Traditionally the church has urged citizens to submit to the authority of government and obey its decrees. For many Christians the safest position has seemed to be to refrain from all sociopolitical action. At times, however, faithfulness to God has required believers to resist the authority of unjust governments. In recent years the church has called its members to transform society by infusing Christian principles into political life.

Politics can be defined in two major ways. The broad definition of politics refers to the life of the city (*polis*) and the responsibilities of the citizen (*polites*). In this sense, politics is the whole of our life in human society, it is "the art of living together in community."[52]

A narrow definition, however, views politics as the adoption of certain policies that are enforced through legislation. This meaning tends to identify the state with the rulers and the power delegated to them by the government.[53] From this viewpoint, the state stands for or symbolizes constituted authority, the authority to maintain

law and order.[54] "The state is the institution in which the ultimate
social authority and power are located, authority and power which
are necessary to maintain order and to give conscious direction to
the life of society."[55]

Christians have generally accepted political authority as both
necessary for human society and ordained by God for human good.
This positive attitude toward the state does not imply the legitimacy of any specific government in power, and even less the
uncritical acceptance of specific policies or actions. The normal
Christian response has been twofold: to just political authority, a
tradition of submissive acceptance and prophetic critique; to
unjust governments, courageous and principled opposition.[56]

Biblical Teachings

Christian thinking about the state was influenced by the Old Testament descriptions of the political kingdoms of Israel and Judah.
The power and authority of Hebrew kings was always limited by
the theocratic ideal—Israel's true ruler was Jehovah. The Old Testament record also reveals another important conclusion: no form
of government was ideal for the Jews. Before the coming of Christ,
God's people existed under patriarchy, theocracy, monarchy, and
as a vassal state.

The New Testament begins with the story of Jesus, whose life
was significantly impacted by political powers. Jesus was born in
Bethlehem because of a decree by Caesar Augustus about taxation
(Luke 2:1-7), lived among Jewish people during Roman occupa-
tion, and ended His public ministry when Roman soldiers crucified
Him by order of the governor, Pontius Pilate (John 19:12-24).

A controversial question that must be asked is whether Jesus was
involved in politics. Two divergent views have emerged. For the
most part, biblical scholars have assumed Jesus was not political.
"He never formed a political party, adopted a political programme
or organized a political protest. He took no steps to influence the
policies of Caesar, Pilate or Herod."[57] Ethicists note that Jesus presented no political theory; indeed, the political order received only
incidental reference in His teaching. However, scholars are quick to
point out that in Jesus' example and attitude are principles for political relations.[58]

In contrast to those who believe Jesus avoided politics, a few
scholars point out that Jesus' ministry was political in the broader
sense of the word. The chief proponent of this position is John
Howard Yoder, who in his *The Politics of Jesus* found it impossible

to evade the question of Jesus' involvement in politics. The Mennonite professor contends that Jesus' life and ministry was in constant conflict with the political forces of His day, forces that are still with us—government, institutional religion, and nationalism.[59]

However, direct teachings from Christ about political life are rare. Jesus did make two key statements which recognized the authority of the state and its legitimate functions to maintain order and peace, to collect taxes, and to establish a monetary system (Matt. 17:24-27; 22:15-22).

In the first passage, collectors of the temple tax asked Peter if his Master paid the levy. Simon impulsively said, "Yes, he does" (Matt. 17:25), planning later to clear the matter with Jesus. At that time the annual half-shekel tax, required of every male Jew over twenty (Exod. 30:11-16), was paid to Rome, not Jerusalem. Refusal to pay could serve as proof of rebellion to the authority of Rome.

When told of the incident, Jesus' response was the declaration of a principle: "What do you think, Simon? From whom do kings of the earth take toll or tribute?" (Matt. 17:25). As kings are free from toll (*tele*, "local tax") or tribute (*kensos*, "head tax"), so the Son of God is rightfully exempt. Nevertheless, the willingness to relinquish personal rights is basic to the way of Christ. Jesus' act of paying the tax through the miracle that followed supported His claim of divine authority as well as the state's right to tax citizens.[60]

The best-known words of Jesus concerning government came in answer to a question from Pharisees and Herodians who intended to entrap Him: "Is it lawful to pay taxes to the emperor, or not?" (Matt. 22:17). Jesus knew their evil intent: if He declared the tribute unlawful, the Herodians could charge Him with treason. If Christ stated the poll tax was lawful, patriotic Jews would reject Him. Jesus responded by calling for the coin used to pay tax and asked, "Whose head is this, and whose title?" After they answered, "Caesar," Jesus replied, "Give therefore to the emperor the things that are the emperor's, and to God the things that are God's" (Matt. 17:20-21).

Jesus' command upheld the validity of political authority and recognized our responsibilities to God and government. In that answer, Jesus "lays down the fundamental principles which must guide his disciples in those future crises in which human authority and divine authority—State and Church—make conflicting claims."[61]

In a real sense, therefore, Jesus' life and teachings were "political." Although Jesus lived under an imperial dictatorship that ruled through vassal kings, Jesus always taught respect for the authority of existing political powers (Mark 12:17). At the same time, Christ offered an alternative to the status quo. The kingdom of God which Jesus announced and proclaimed was a radically new social order, whose values and standards challenged the old order of a fallen community.[62] As Lord and King, Jesus challenged Caesar, the Sanhedrin, and all other worldly powers—for that reason He was accused of sedition and was executed.

However proud the apostle Paul was of his Roman citizenship—he once used it to appeal to Caesar—he wrote to Philippians living in a Roman colony that the Christian's true citizenship was in heaven: "But we are a colony of heaven" (3:20, Moffat). Paul also believed that Christians should make no use of pagan law courts and was upset with believers in Corinth who turned to heathen judges rather than the judgment of "saints" (1 Cor. 6:1).

Nevertheless, Pauline writings reflect an optimism about the state that none of the other New Testament writers share.[63] The classic text about the legitimacy of government and Christian responsibility is found in Romans 13:1-7. Victor Paul Furnish calls this moral instruction a problem passage that "should not be regarded as a sacred cow or a white elephant."[64]

According to this text, political authorities are God's instruments of order in society, functioning to protect the lawful and to restrain evildoers (Rom. 13:1-4). Since government has a God-given role which even pagans can fulfill, political rulers are entitled to respect and cooperation from all citizens. Because the state is God's servant, it is the duty of Christians to pay taxes and honor those in authority (Rom. 13:6-7).[65]

The divine origin of the state does not call Christians to uncritical obedience to any form of government. The New Testament sets the outside limits within which political ethics moves; it warns at the same time against anarchism and against the unlimited state. Paul's appeal to be subject to governing powers, reinforced by Simon's call for submission (1 Pet. 2:13-17), is balanced by Peter's warning, "We must obey God rather than any human authority" (Acts 5:29). The attempt to harmonize these passages has dominated Christendom since the time of Constantine.[66]

Christians were soon to discover that the ruler could be a "terror" to good people, as well as to evil. Not long after Paul was executed by the Roman government, emperor worship as a symbol of the state was inaugurated. Refusal by Christians to acknowledge any human ruler as "Lord" led to widespread persecution. John's writings, penned at the close of the first century, reveal a changed attitude of Christians toward the state. The Roman Empire, God's instrument in Romans 13, has now become the "beast" in the service of Satan in Revelation 13!

Church and State in Christian History

The early church withdrew from political life. In the face of totalitarian claims by Roman imperial power, early Christians refused to swear allegiance to the state. "Many of the martyrs of the early church died for this reason: because of their acknowledgment of the lordship of Christ they could not participate in the political religion which absolutized the Roman State."[67]

The importance of the events that changed Christianity from a persecuted sect to the dominant religious force in Roman civilization would be difficult to overstate. The judgment that Constantine effected "the greatest revolution in mind and manners that has been known among men"[68] may be such an exaggeration, but the transformation of the Roman Empire after 313 did profoundly change Western history.

The Edict of Milan not only granted recognition and freedom to Christians; it marked the beginning of a union of religious faith with cultural and political power. Each subsequent generation has had to struggle with the question raised by the Constantinian reversal: "How can the purity of faith be safeguarded against cultural idolatries?"[69]

For the next millennium the relation of the church to the state was characterized by identification and domination. At least in theory, the church and state were partners, although the church normally occupied the controlling role. At various times both the church and the state have sought to master the other and to dominate all of life. Those who identified the church with the state held an optimistic view of the social order based on natural law. The underlying idea of the state church was the assumption that the whole nation was Christian, a concept that continues in most of Europe today.[70]

Sectarian Christianity, along with Luther and traditional Lutheranism, held a more negative view of the state. Sectarian believers tended to condemn the whole world of nature and culture as irrevocably evil and beyond redemption, an "eschatological dualism" that either combined religion and politics (Puritans), or more often, relegated religion entirely to the inner life.[71]

The Reformation of the sixteenth century was another watershed in Christian history, but the changes were primarily theological. Lutheran and Calvinistic leaders are commonly called **Magisterial Reformers** because they believed the magistrate (state power) should defend and protect the church, as well as depend on the church to keep certain records (birth, marriage, death).[72] These reformers did not depart very far from the Roman Catholic position concerning church and state. Both Luther and Calvin thought in "terms of the *corpus christianum*,"[73] believing the church should be the **conscience** of the state and the state should enforce the "spiritual" advice of the church.[74]

Another group of reformers (often ignored or belittled) were the *Radical Reformers*, small groups of "believers" like the Anabaptists and the Mennonites. As sectarian Christians, the Radical Reformers emphasized personal decision and voluntarism, opposed the concept of Christendom, and believed true faith could not be obliged or coerced. In God's plan, church and state had different functions and should be separate. Other reformers accused these groups of anarchy, but the Radical Reformers believed the state was to be obeyed, unless its demands conflicted with the believer's conscience.[75]

Both the Roman Catholic Church and the Protestant reformers wanted only their churches in the territories they advised; thus groups like the Anabaptists and Mennonites were forced to flee westward to Canada, the United States, and South America. Some contact was made between English Baptists and the Mennonite-Anabaptists in Holland during the early seventeenth century. This influence was significant for the development of **religious liberty** and separation of church and state in the new world. Along with a wide diversity of religions in the American colonies, many minority groups flourished there. Baptists, who were strong in New England, Pennsylvania, and Virginia, contended consistently for religious freedom and made a major contribution to the provision for separation in the Constitution.[76]

Thomas Jefferson and James Madison "cut the pattern" for religious liberty in America. Jefferson's famous phrase "a wall of separation between church and state" first appeared in a letter from the Virginia statesman to the Baptists of Danbury in 1802.[77] The belief that Jefferson and Madison intended the First Amendment to the

Constitution to erect such a wall of separation is supported in Madison's "Memorial and Remonstrance Against Religious Assessments" drafted in 1784 and Jefferson's "Bill for Establishing Religious Freedom" passed in 1786 by the Assembly of Virginia.[78]

Many contend the First Amendment does not mean or necessitate **separation of church and state** but only forbids the establishment of a single church or special favors to that church. It does not prohibit, they say, state aid to religion in general.[79] To this, a church-state scholar retorts: "The contention is false. The history of the First Amendment and the specific declaration of James Madison, its chief author, disprove it. The First Amendment prohibits, not only ecclesiastical monogamy, but also ecclesiastical polygamy."[80]

In modern times, the legitimacy of governments has been called into question when unjust states or totalitarian rulers have set themselves against God. The two types are closely connected, but the latter was the focus of the Barmen Declaration (1934), when "the Confessing Church in Germany rediscovered and reasserted the sole lordship of Christ as the basis for opposing the totalitarianism of the Nazi State."[81] The former type is best seen in the liberation theology of Latin America and other Third World countries where Christians opposed unjust political, social, and economic structures.

Implications for Christian Citizenship

In the political sphere, the state is the highest authority, but it always stands under the judgment of God. The primary duty of the state is to maintain law and order in society, and in so doing, minister to the life of its citizens. "The government, more than any other human agency, is given the responsibility by God for justice. . . . to ensure the basic rights of living in community."[82]

A cardinal Christian belief is the conviction that each person is created in God's image (Gen. 1:27), which is the basis for the twin doctrines of freedom and responsibility. These two principles have profound implications for political life. Although the state is the servant of God for human good, it is temporal and limited. Government belongs to the fallen order of society; political power may be a threat to freedom and justice. To enable the state to fulfill its God-given functions, Christians must be responsible citizens.

Another related conviction is that Christians are citizens of two worlds. In one realm the people of God are a "colony of heaven" (Phil. 3:20, Moffatt), citizens in a spiritual kingdom whose primary loyalty is to God (Luke 20:25). In the other realm we are also citizens of a nation, a temporal government. The temptation for believers is to so separate life into the "spiritual" and the "secular" that we abdicate our civic responsibilities. In the Sermon on the Mount, Jesus stressed that kingdom disciples are "salt" and "light" in the world (Matt. 5:13–14). As salt retards corruption and light dispels darkness, so Christians are to penetrate and transform the moral darkness and decay in society through their personal influence. As one minister put it, "My citizenship may be in heaven, but I vote in Cooke County."

Both in forms of organization and in scope of activity, the political is one of the most changeable aspects of life. In addition, no static blueprint for a "Christian" government exists in the Bible or Christian theology. "Forms of government are human inventions, not prescribed by God, and contemporary representative democracy is a recent invention, which became possible in specifically modern circumstances."[83]

However, we do possess God-ordained principles and purposes for social life, whatever the political structure. To shape and lead society toward peace, justice, and other moral values is legitimate, although using coercive political power to do so is not. Employing the state's authority to evangelize, subsidize, or enforce belief is never God's way. Constantine tried it in the fourth century and failed. As Christianity became the politically established religion, the "Dark Ages" descended upon Europe.

In a democratic society, Christian citizenship requires a person to understand the structure of government, actively participate in political life, and do so from a Christian perspective. "A person who takes his Christian citizenship seriously is one who applies the gospel to his world through responsible involvement in the political process."[84] In addition to the civic duties outlined earlier in the teachings of the Bible, Christians can also heed these practical suggestions:[85]

- Be intelligent: study the democratic process to understand how government works.
- Participate: vote, lobby, campaign, support good candidates, and get involved at all levels.
- Influence: work for peace, justice, equality, freedom, truthfulness, and other social and moral values.
- Serve: running for public office is not only allowable; it is imperative for Christians to serve in government.

- Oppose: any person or movement that denies basic human rights or supports policies contrary to God's will.
- Test: examine all political movements who want your support, to be sure they are not counter-Christian. Remember that politics and power are intertwined.

Christians in a democratic society have the constitutional right to be involved at every level of government.[86] More importantly, Christians have the biblical responsibility to influence and transform society toward the will of God. "Christian citizenship is a mandate, not an option, nor an elective, for all who take seriously their call to discipleship by our Lord Jesus Christ."[87]

Issues in Political Ethics

Few areas in Christian ethics have created more divergent opinions than issues in political ethics. Individual believers and the church have struggled to develop a consistent Christian response to social problems like crime and punishment, gun control, **civil disobedience**, war, and church-state relations.

As well as being controversial, political issues are among the most crucial problems facing American society at the close of the century. Complex church-state questions have multiplied during the last decade—**civil religion**, prayer in public schools, government-sponsored religious displays, tuition vouchers for private schools, licensing and regulation of church ministries, and tax exemptions for ministers and churches, to name a few.

None is easy to comprehend. The average Christian feels ill-equipped to deal with dilemmas so complicated. Even ministers confess a reluctance to declare a "Christian" position on these ethical questions. In order to apply biblical principles and Christian values to political concerns, a careful study of the subject is usually required. Although our brief introduction does not allow a full treatment of any issue, we will attempt to analyze a few significant areas, as well as point the reader toward numerous helpful resources.

Crime and Punishment. Criminology and penology are popular subjects in American universities today, as political leaders and law enforcement agencies struggle with the problem of increasing crime and overcrowded prisons.[88] Followers of Christ often feel ambivalent in dealing with crime and criminals—how does a Christian support fair and impartial justice while at the same time maintaining compassion for the lawbreaker? For example, is the purpose of incarceration punishment or rehabilitation?

A subject of much debate and discussion in recent years has been the death penalty.[89] The United States is one of the few democratic societies in the world that has not abolished **capital punishment**.[90] From 1976 to 1995, there have been 288 executions nationally, two-thirds of them in five states: Texas (97), Florida (33), Virginia (26), Louisiana (22), and Georgia (20).[91] As the number of executions surges, Christians remain divided on the death penalty's morality and purpose.

The prevalence of violence in American society has diminished the deterrence argument for capital punishment—simple retribution is the more common defense today. Christians on both sides of the issue cite scriptural support. Those who favor it, like Carl F. H. Henry, quote passages they believe uphold God's justice (Gen. 9:6).[92] Opponents of capital punishment, like Lewis Smedes, contend the New Testament (especially the example of Jesus) supercedes the Old Testament and stresses love and forgiveness (Matt. 5:38–48; John 8:1–11).[93]

Charles Colson is among those who maintain the Scriptures neither mandate nor prohibit the death penalty. Although Colson favors capital punishment in principle (in extreme cases), he has grave reservations about the way the penalty is administered.[94]

The question of equal justice is a major one. One study cites twenty-three persons executed this century whose guilt was later disproven or in doubt. Another forty-eight inmates have been able to prove their innocence while on death row. Unfair treatment, racial and class bias, and inadequate representation for the poor have all been documented as proof of injustice.[95] *Time* magazine reported, "Execution in the U.S. is a horrifying lottery in which who dies is determined less by the crime that is committed than by politics, money, and **race**."[96]

Religious Liberty. The struggle for religious liberty in Christian history was narrated earlier. These lessons of the past should have informed American colonists that the "fondness of magistrates to foster Christianity has done it more harm than all the persecutions ever did."[97] Yet few remembered.

One of the distinctive achievements of the American Revolution was the guarantee of religious liberty. However, our ancestors almost missed it. Thomas Jefferson referred to its passage as "the severest contest in which I have ever been engaged."[98] Patrick Henry opposed it, as did George Washington and James Monroe.

Jefferson went off to France leaving James Madison to battle for its passage. Rigorous debate ensued.

Madison and George Mason, heirs of the **Enlightenment,** furnished the brain power for lobbying. The religion of the revivals, however, supplied the troops. The role of Baptists in this story is one of the grand moments in Baptist history. Everyone in the colonies knew preachers like John Clarke, Roger Williams, Isaac Backus, and others who had been jailed or beaten for preaching the gospel.[99]

A Baptist minister named John Leland played a major role by stumping across southwestern Virginia denouncing state support for religion.[100] Virginians knew well the danger of religious persecution and passed the Virginia Statute for Religious Freedom, which denied tax support to churches, set out the separation of church and state, and guaranteed the free exercise of religion. Most important of all, the document became the foundation for the First Amendment.

Religious liberty is based on the belief of "soul freedom"—that each person as created by God has the freedom to accept or reject religious belief without government interference. Many believe the fullest expression of religious freedom is impossible without the related doctrine, separation of church and state. In a letter to Danbury Baptists, Jefferson first stated that there exists "a wall of separation between Church and State."[101] By "separation" is meant that neither church nor state should be controlled by the other or dependent upon the other, although each should be open to the other's views so that respect and influence flow between the two.

Many church-state scholars point out that religious liberty is both freedom "from" and freedom "to" and "for." T. B. Maston contends the fullest religious freedom would include at least: (1) freedom of conscience, (2) freedom of worship, (3) freedom of association, (4) freedom of propaganda, (5) freedom from civil disability (right to vote, hold office), (6) freedom from discrimination against any and all religions, and (7) freedom of the church from financial, political, or other control.[102]

The twin doctrines of religious freedom and separation of church and state do not mean separation of God from government—no mortal could do that, for God is omnipresent. Nor does it mean separation of religion and politics—no mortal should do that, for religious faith must influence political life. "Church-state separation is the recognition that the institutions of church and state are separate and distinct. Each is important. Each is divinely ordained. But each has its own peculiar role to play in society, and neither controls the other. . . . The state is God's answer to the chaos of anarchy; . . . The church is the conscience of society."[103]

Civil Religion. Because of the complex relationships between church and state in American history, civil religion has become a controversy of considerable scholarly attention.[104] In its simplest form, civil religion "is the use of commonly-accepted religious sentiments, concepts, and symbols by the state for its own purposes."[105] This action is often unconscious, a blurring of religion and patriotism and of religious values and national values. In the American context, with our historic experience, civil religion resembles Christianity, makes use of its symbols, but does not identify with any particular faith. For many citizens, it is their only real religion.[106]

According to a report in *Christianity Today*, the 1991 Southern Baptist Convention "took on the flavor of a five-day 'God and Country' rally."[107] One leader decried the elaborate wedding of patriotism and religion as "an orgy of civil religion" and "a shocking departure from Baptist sensitivity to the appropriate role of religion in political life." However, another leader countered, "When it comes to God and country, it can never be overdone."[108]

What is wrong with this display of patriotism? Does it violate the First Amendment or "crack" the historical wall of separation between church and state? The great danger of civil religion is the temptation to confuse God and government. To confess "Jesus is Lord," as did the early church, was to risk the wrath of Rome, for loyalty to the emperor meant, "Caesar is Lord." The threat is more subtle today.

Historians note that President Eisenhower, though he had little interest in formal religion, was the patron of civil religion. His era included a proposed Christian amendment to the constitution (1951), a "God's Float" in his inauguration (1953), adding "under God" to the Pledge of Allegiance (1954), and the adoption of "In God We Trust" as the national motto (1956).[109]

One might ask, "What's wrong with that? Shouldn't America be 'one nation under God'?" Opponents of this synthesis warn that civil religion is based on four major fallacies:

1. The assumption that the U.S. is a Christian nation.

2. The confusion of God and country.

3. The belief in "manifest destiny," that America is God's chosen nation, a unique creation of divine providence.

4. The manipulation of God for national ends and purposes, pronouncing God's blessings on political agendas.

In such a scheme God is reduced to a tribal deity, rather than the God of the prophets who judges all nations.

In recent years the proponents of civil religion have been identified with conservative politics and the Religious Right movement. Religious leaders Jerry Falwell, Pat Robertson, and Ralph Reed have become major voices in American political life, espousing what some term "right-wing" morality and politics.[110] In 1995, a progressive evangelical group organized to offer "a different kind of politics that emphasize spirituality rather than ideology. . . . The Religious Right has been such a strong and singular media voice on matters of politics and morality that even the word 'Christian' now has been associated with a very particular brand of very conservative Republican politics."[111]

Fifteen years ago Billy Graham stated, "Liberals organized in the 1960s and conservatives certainly have a right to organize in the 1980s, but it would disturb me if there was a wedding between religious fundamentalists and the political right. The hard right has no interest in religion except to manipulate it. . . . It was a mistake to identify the kingdom of God with the American way of life."[112]

The idea of America being "under God" does not imply privilege, but accountability. God is our judge. Patriotism is far more than a religious feeling expressed in pious phraseology or pep-rally cheers. True patriotism is the recognition that the "nation whose God is the LORD" (Ps. 33:12) is the country that learns "to do justice, and to love kindness, and to walk humbly with your God" (Mic. 6:8).

War and Peace. War is perennial. Peace is temporary. The world seems addicted to conflict between nations. A renowned sociologist has observed that the Western world has suffered 967 major interstate wars from 500 B.C. to 1925, averaging a war every two and one-half years.[113] Within the lifetime of one generation, Americans have been engaged in two world wars, two devastating battles in Korea and Vietnam, and numerous military operations in places like Panama, the Persian Gulf, and Bosnia. Since the disintegration of the U.S.S.R., most Americans assume the world is at peace. However, the truth is that "wars and rumors of wars" (Matt. 24:6) continue to the present moment.[114]

The biblical picture seems ambivalent—both the "red horse" of war and the "dove" of peace appear.[115] War between tribes and nations is common in biblical history. In the Old Testament, Israel goes forth to battle the enemies of God, often as an act of Jehovah's judgment of godless nations (Josh. 8:1-2). In the Gospels, however, Jesus calls His disciples to a life of peace; kingdom citizens are characterized by a spirit of forgiveness, nonretaliation, and love for enemies (Matt. 5:38-45). The resolution of these two biblical pictures is very difficult.

One thing is certain: the Bible does project a realistic view of war, its causes and consequences. Wars are inevitable because nations are motivated by greed, self-interest, and sin (Matt. 24:6-7; Rom. 1:28-32; James 4:1). Though nations choose war, God promotes peace (Ps. 120:6-7) and does not take sides in war (Josh. 5:13-14). The history of warfare in the Bible reveals its cost—the destruction of human life, property, resources, and moral and spiritual values.

The biblical attitude toward war, however, is mixed. Many passages in the Scriptures seem to defend war and picture Jehovah as a God of war. The Mosaic law governing warfare implies God directs Israel to wage war (Deut. 20:1-20). Jehovah even used wars to judge Israel (2 Kings 18:11-25; 24:1-4). Israel's "wars of extermination" fulfilled God's command to "utterly destroy" the enemies in the land (Deut. 7:2; 13:15-18; Josh. 11:20).[116]

A few passages in the New Testament are used to defend war. Jesus' forceful expulsion of the moneychangers from the temple, especially His use of the "whip," is commonly quoted to justify armed conflict (John 2:13-16). Opponents argue that (1) the passage does not indicate Jesus used the whip; or (2) if He did, it may have been upon the animals only; and (3) none of this justifies war or the loss of human life.

Another text used to defend war is Jesus' command to His disciples, "And the one who has no sword must sell his cloak and buy one" (Luke 22:36). On the surface this charge seems to dispute Jesus' reprimand to Simon Peter, "Put your sword back into its place; for all who take the sword will perish by the sword" (Matt. 26:52). Most biblical scholars call the command to buy a sword a speech metaphor that meant, "Be prepared for danger ahead."[117]

Opponents of war question the claim that war may be God's will, noting the biblical ideal is a world at peace. God is a God of peace

(Rom. 15:33), who is committed to establishing peace (1 Chron. 22:9). The prophets predicted history was moving toward a golden age of peace (Isa. 2:4; 11:6-9; Mic. 4:3) and a Messiah who would be the Prince of Peace (Isa. 9:6). King David was not allowed to build the temple because he was a man of war (1 Chron. 22:6-8; 28:3). The first heralds of Jesus Christ announced He came to bring peace to the world (Luke 2:14; Acts 10:36).

Few would protest the idea that war seems contrary to the life, spirit, and teachings of Jesus, especially as explained in His nonresistance imperatives (Matt. 5:38-42). Jesus' personal example of nonresistance to violence, "when He did not return abuse" (1 Pet. 2:23), perfectly illustrated His teachings.

In the New Testament, Christians are clearly identified as "peacemakers," not warriors, in the kingdom of God (Matt. 5:9). God's reign of peace in the hearts of believers is the foundation for peaceful relationships (Rom. 5:1; Phil. 4:7). If Christians allow the peace of Christ to rule their lives (Col. 3:15), they will love even enemies (Matt. 5:44), live peaceably with all persons (Rom. 12:18), and work diligently for peace (Rom. 14:19).

Defenders of a limited use of military force contend these teachings apply only to personal relationships and not to the responsibilities of citizens to government. Thus, early disciples who served in the military were not condemned (Acts 10), and New Testament writers freely used military terms and metaphors to describe spiritual conflict (2 Tim. 2:3; Eph. 6:10-20).

How then did Christians sort out these biblical variations? The early church concluded love and killing were incompatible, consequently no Christian should serve in the Roman army.[118] Leaders in the early church were opposed to war not only because of the shedding of blood, but also because obedience to the emperor conflicted with faithfulness to God, the conduct of soldiers was contrary to Christian ethics, and as "aliens in a foreign land," Christians felt no loyalty toward the state.[119]

By the time of Constantine the tide had turned—the cross became a military emblem! In 314 a church canon made military service open to Christians, and by 416 non-Christians were forbidden to serve in the army.[120] Augustine (345-430) had an uneasy conscience about war, stating the wise person would wage nothing but a just war, and then only with deep sorrow. This attitude continued throughout the Middle Ages, perhaps influencing Aquinas (1224-74) to work out a philosophical-theological basis for the moral justification of war, enlarging on Augustine's three conditions: just authority, just cause, and rightful intention.[121] Also during the Middle Ages the Crusades recaptured the Holy War tradition, glorifying armed conflict.

Luther's dualism led him to contend that the Christian, as a citizen, should obey the state and go to war. Like Luther, Calvin viewed civil authority as God's instrument to administer God's judgment on sinful persons. The reformer defended war, under certain conditions, and the Christian's participation in it.

Out of these traditions have evolved four major Christian positions concerning war:[122]

1. Pacifism—Christians are called to peacemaking, which excludes participation in war.[123]
2. Just War—In a sinful world, a defensive war is justified under certain conditions.[124]
3. Holy War/Preventive War—War is glorified as one way to achieve God's purposes in human history, especially to prevent acts of aggression or injustice.[125]
4. Nonresistance—Christians may participate in war, but only as noncombatants.[126]

Many Christians term themselves "Nuclear Pacifists," stating the level of destruction in modern warfare due to nuclear weapons questions the justification of war for any reason.[127]

War is evil. No one questions that. War kills, maims, and destroys. At best, war making is a failure of peacemaking. The call from God is a call to peace—peace with God, with ourselves, with our families, and with others. To be peacemakers in a warring world is a major task.[128]

Peace is more than the absence of war. The biblical word for *peace* is *shalom*—it means wholeness and health, prosperity and security, political and spiritual well-being. The peace of the Bible is never a negative peace; it is always a positive effort to create a new sense of harmony.

True peace means belonging—belonging to God and to others. True peace involves justice—seeing to it that each person has what is his or her due. True peace is first and foremost community—it is people learning to live together in community.

In *Making Peace in the Global Village*, Robert McAfee Brown wrote, "Concern for *shalom*, or peacemaking, doesn't just involve keeping us out of war (though it obviously includes that); it also involves seeing to it that people have enough to eat; that they are not undernourished or malnourished; that they can go to bed at night without fear that someone will spirit them off to prison; that the society will be so planned that there is food enough to go around; that the politics of the country (and of the world) are so arranged that everybody's basic needs are met. Otherwise, no *shalom*."[129]

Christians who have experienced God's peace can never abandon the biblical vision of peace, justice, and hope. Peacemaking is an effort of faith. Faith makes peace possible. In the face of persistent hostility and increasing violence, Christians must pursue peace in the name of Him who is the Prince of *Shalom*.

FOR THOUGHT AND DISCUSSION

1. Compare the views of the early church, Thomas Aquinas, Luther, Calvin, and John Wesley on money and wealth.
2. Discuss the validity of the statement by President Jimmy Carter that economic discrimination is the most troubling ethical problem facing the world today.
3. In light of world hunger, develop a list of proposals for churches and for Christians to alleviate this problem.
4. Respond to the statement "Churches should keep out of politics because religion and politics don't mix."
5. Explain the historical struggle of Baptists and other groups for religious liberty.
6. Debate this proposition: "The Bible supports capital punishment as a legitimate function of government."
7. Compare and contrast a Christian understanding of patriotism, civil religion, and war.

CONCLUSION

From the beginning we have emphasized that Christian ethics is both a discipline and a practice—studying about the Christian life is prelude to living it. The Greek philosophers were right: the purpose of philosophy is to answer the question, "What would a life worth living look like?"

In the first half of this book, we focused on the discipline of ethics, studying the "grounds, goals, and guidelines for Christian character and conduct." Before we are able to apply Christian ethics to relevant issues, we must first understand the nature of biblical authority, the role of Christian tradition, the function of theological insights, and the process of moral decision making.

Foundations are important. Without deep theological roots, ethics is like floating seaweed, carried in every direction by the changing winds and tides of culture.

Equally important is the practice of Christian ethics. Christian belief without ethical behavior is not genuine faith. Jesus' most scathing denunciations were directed toward persons who were orthodox in doctrine but deficient in duty. Christ called them hypocrites (*hupokrites*, "actors"). Though they claimed to be theologically correct, their ethical conduct contradicted biblical religion.

In the Christian faith, theology and ethics are married. However you say it—creed and conduct, belief and behavior, or doctrine and duty—the two are one. Biblical faith has always included ethical behavior because the God of the Bible is by nature moral. Jehovah commanded Israel: "You shall be holy, for I the LORD your God am holy" (Lev. 19:2).

The gospel proclaimed by Jesus was more than a new theology; it was an invitation to become a new people. The first Christians were called people of "the Way" (Acts 9:2) because they lived by different ethical standards—a righteous life in a community faithful to God. The "Way" they followed was the one taught and lived by Jesus of Nazareth, the Son of God.

The key feature of Jesus' ethic is this: every truth He taught was illustrated by His life—Jesus perfectly exemplified His ethic. No religious leader ever did that; no Christian is able to do that. However, the degree to which our Christian life matches our religious profession proves the genuineness of our faith. This was the point made by the apostle James: "What good is it, my brothers and sisters, if you say you have faith but do not have works? . . . faith apart from works is barren" (James 2:14, 20).

As we conclude this introduction to the study of Christian ethics, how do we put what we have learned into practice? This is the final question of this book and the real test of any study of Christian ethics. We conclude by challenging you the reader to live your Christian faith in today's world, for the meaning of the Christian life is in the living of it.

As disciples of Jesus Christ and members of His "body," believers occupy a dual role in the world—the role of "salt" and "light" (Matt. 5:13-14). Through social action, the Christian community preserves the world from moral decay and dispels moral darkness. Through social ministry, the body of Christ brings healing and hope to the victims of immoral behavior.

What God expects of every one of us is a life worth living. For Christians this means a life that glorifies God by walking just as Jesus walked (1 John 2:6)—Walking in The Way.

GLOSSARY

Abortion: The termination of pregnancy by expulsion from the womb of an embryo or fetus, usually before the viability of the fetus.

Absolutes/Absolutist: The contention that moral norms allow no exceptions, are universally binding, and must be obeyed.

Agape: The unique Greek word for that love which is entirely devoid of self, an out-going love of others. In the Bible, *agape* describes God's love and the highest of human love.

AIDS: Acquired immunodeficiency syndrome is a disorder that is a collection of many abnormalities caused by a virus known as human immunodeficiency virus (HIV).

Anti-Semitism: Having or showing prejudice against Jews.

Artificial Insemination: A reproduction technology procedure that replaces human fertilization by heterosexual intercourse, collecting the sperm of the husband (AIH) or a donor (AID) and inseminating the female with the sperm.

Ascetic/Asceticism: From the Greek word *askesis* (which means practice or discipline), referring to the practice of living a life of self-denial and contemplation based on the belief that the physical/material world is innately evil.

Authority: The power or right to give commands, enforce obedience, and make final decisions. Authority is the guiding factor in ethical decision making. For Christian ethics, the ultimate authority is Jesus Christ as revealed in the main objective authority, the Bible.

Bioethics/Biomedical Ethics: The application of ethics to the biological sciences, medicine, health care, and related areas, as well as the public policies directed toward them.

Capitalism: An economic system in which the price mechanism, working through supply and demand in competitive markets, provides the dominant mode of economic decision making for both production and distribution.

Capital Punishment: The form of human punishment that deprives the individual of his or her existence, usually justified on the grounds of deterrance or retribution.

Categorical Imperative: Immanuel Kant's distinction between hypothetical imperatives, which command an action as a means to a given end, and categorical imperatives, which command an act as good in itself and thus universally necessary.

Character: That basic moral orientation that gives unity and direction to our lives by forming our habits, patterns, and dominant convictions.

Christian Ethics: The study and practice of the grounds, goals, and guidelines for human character and conduct as determined by the will of God revealed in Jesus Christ and empowered by the Holy Spirit.

Church-State Separation: The recognition that church and state are distinct and have separate roles to fulfill; neither should be controlled by or dependent on the other.

Civil Disobedience: A form of dissent and resistance to an unjust law, which is justified if the dissent is public, nonviolent, and submissive to the sanctions of the law.

Civil Religion: The use of commonly accepted religious concepts, sentiments, or symbols by the state for its own purposes.

Conscience: The sum total of one's moral knowledge as taught by family and culture. Conscience is not a legislator, but a judge of norms already established.

Consequentialism: Another term for teleological ethics, which contends that good or evil is determined solely by the end result or consequences of an action.

Constantinianism: A coined term referring to Constantine's establishment of Christianity as the state religion; the word denotes any form of cultural support of religion.

DNA: Deoxyribonucleic acid is an essential component of all living matter and a basic material in the chromosomes of the cell nucleus; it contains the genetic code for heredity.

Decalogue: Literally "ten words," the Ten Commandments revealed to Moses on Mount Sinai (Exod. 20:1-17).

Deontology/Deontological: From *dei* meaning "necessary," this ethic of obligation stresses the duty to obey absolutes. Goodness or rightness is inherent in the act itself.

Descriptive Ethics: The morality of particular societies or groups—a description of what is, not what ought to be.

Enlightenment: An era (1600-1800) in Western intellectual history sometimes called the Age of Reason, characterized by an emphasis on nature, autonomy, harmony, and human ability.

Epicureanism: Founded by the Greek philosopher Epicurus, this negative form of hedonism taught that the goal of life was to avoid pain and mental anguish.

Ethical Relativism: Since norms vary from culture to culture, the view that no universal absolutes exist and all ethics are relative.

Ethics: The science of human conduct, the systematic examination of the moral life based on human reason. A normative study, ethics focuses on what "ought" to be.

Ethnocentricism: The attitude that one's own group, nation, or culture is superior to all others.

Ethos: The characteristic and distinguishing attitudes, habits, and beliefs of an individual or group.

Etiquette: Conventional forms, manners, and ceremonies established as acceptable for social relationships.

Eugenics: From the Greek word meaning "wellborn," the term describes a branch of study that focuses on improving the human race by judicious matching of "superior" genes.

Euthanasia: Literally an "easy" or "gentle death," usually denoting the painless death of the terminally ill. Euthanasia may be active (inducing death) or passive (not prolonging life), as well as voluntary (living will), involuntary, or compulsory.

Exception Clause: The phrase "except for unchastity" (Matt. 19:9), an exception in Jesus' statement about marriage and divorce, which some scholars believe was a later textual addition.

Feminization of Poverty: A recently coined phrase based on the discovery that three-fourths of the world's poor are women and their dependent children.

Genetic Counseling: An informational process between a qualified counselor and individuals or families at higher risk to transmit genetic disorders.

Genetic Engineering: The manipulation of genetic material in an attempt to modify the structure of an organism or aid in the transmission of genetic information, including gene splicing, cloning, and artificial reproduction technologies.

Genetics: Human genetics involves the study of human variability in terms of its causes and effects. Modern genetics includes genetic screening, counseling, prenatal diagnosis, and treatments for genetic disorders.

Gnosticism: A system of belief derived from Greek philosophy and Oriental mysticism which influenced early Christianity. Claiming a special knowledge *(gnosis)*, Gnostics often expressed a deep aversion to the material world, sometimes leading to the extremes of asceticism or libertinism.

Greater Good: The higher norm choice, in hierarchicalism, when two absolute moral norms come into unavoidable conflict.

Hedonism: The teleological theory that contends any action that brings individual pleasure is good, and any action that brings pain is bad.

Hermeneutical: The study of the principles of biblical interpretation.

Hierarchicalism: Also termed "graded absolutism," the theory contends when two or more absolute norms come into unavoidable conflict, the choice of the higher norm, the "greater good," is morally right.

Hippocratic Oath: An ethical code of the medical profession attributed to Hippocrates, taken by medical students.

Homosexual/Homosexuality: A definite preferential erotic attraction to members of the same sex, which may (but not necessarily) include sex relations. The term may apply to orientation or behavior.

Human Genome Project: A government-funded project to identify and map every gene on the twenty-three pairs of chromosomes in humans, which includes about 100,000 genes in three billion base pairs.

In Vitro Fertilization: Literally "in glass" fertilization (IVF), the process whereby a woman's egg is removed by laparoscopy and fertilized with sperm in a laboratory.

Kingdom of God: God's reign or righteous rule over the lives of persons in His spiritual kingdom—a present reality that has a future culmination.

Laissez Faire: Literally "let do," the practice of letting people act without interference, usually applied to noninterference from government in business and industry.

Legalism: A system of ethics in which strict rules seek to govern ethical behavior.

Lesser Evil: A method of dealing with conflicting absolutes by choosing an unavoidable evil. Though less than ideal, the choice is often the best possible one in our fallen world.

Magisterial Reform: One of three major reforms during the Reformation, represented by Luther and Calvin, which promoted many theological changes, but continued the belief that the magistrate (the state) should defend and protect the church.

Modernism/Modernity: The Western cultural mentality associated with the Enlightenment, which began in the seventeenth and eighteenth centuries in Europe and climaxed in the mid-twentieth century. The key features are the supremacy and objectivity of human reason, the reliability of science and technology, and the inevitability of progress.

Moral Philosophy: See Ethics.

Morals: From *mores* (Latin), originally meaning "custom" or "habit." Although used interchangeably with "ethics," in this text the term refers to right and wrong conduct as actually practiced—what "is" rather than what "ought" to be.

Mores: Folkways that are considered conducive to the welfare of society that, through observance, develop the force of law.

Natural Law: Certain discoverable laws or norms that are written into the created nature of the world and persons, which reveal the ends and purposes of humanity.

Norm: A law for living—a rule, commandment, or guideline defined by some recognized authority.

Pacifism: Means "making peace" and is the advocacy of personal nonparticipation in war or violence of any kind, with an endeavor to find nonviolent means of resolving conflict.

Paradigm: A pattern, example, or model.

Philosophical ethics: Synonymous with the term *ethics*, the phrase refers to the study of right and wrong conduct as determined by the authority of human reason.

Philosophy: The word means "love of wisdom" and refers to the study of the principles underlying conduct, thought, knowledge, and the nature of the universe.

Postmodernity: The collapse in the last half of the twentieth century of the grand narratives of the Enlightenment—reason, technology, progress—and the emerging cultural movement that questions all certainties.

Prejudice: A preconceived judgment formed before the facts are known, often leading to irrational attitudes and practices.

Prescriptive Ethics: Also termed normative ethics, the approach "prescribes" norms or standards for the good life.

Prima Facie Duty: Meaning "on first appearance," this phrase refers to a basic duty required of everyone, all other things being equal.

Principle: The statement of a value. Broad moral guidelines that are more foundational and universal than rules.

Principlism: Sometimes called "conflicting absolutism," this ethical methodology emphasizes the application of ideals or principles in contextually sensitive ways.

Professional Ethics: The study of the standards of competence and responsibility attached to professionals and their vocation.

Race: An ambiguous concept developed in the nineteenth century that attempts to classify humans according to physical criteria; however, the infinite number of genetic and cultural differences among humans has led many to reject the term.

Racism: The belief that certain groups or races are innately inferior and certain groups are innately superior.

Radical Reformers: One of three reform movements during the Reformation, mainly Anabaptists and Mennonites, who upheld personal faith, voluntary discipleship, believer's baptism, and the separation of church and state.

Relational Ethics: A recent ethical approach that focuses on personalist arguments, contending the fitting or responsible moral decision considers human beings and what happens to persons as the key to ethics.

Religious Liberty: The freedom granted by God to each person to accept or reject religious belief without government coercion or interference.

Reproduction/Reproduction Technology: The development in medicine of procedures that offer hope to couples who have been unable to bear a child, including surgery, artificial insemination (AI), in vitro fertilization (IVF), and gamete intro-Fallopian transfer (GIFT).

Sexism: The economic exploitation and social domination of members of one sex by the other.

Situation Ethics/Situationism: Also called contextualism, a teleological system of act-oriented ethics, which gives the individual the freedom to decide the best result in concrete moral contexts, according to some fundamental principle.

Stereotype: A fixed conception of inherent traits or behavior patterns of certain people or groups, which allows no individuality.

Stoicism: A philosophical school that taught that the cosmos and every person reflected a rational God, who is everywhere and in everyone. Stoicism emphasized self-discipline, equality, and living in accordance with Nature.

Teleology/Teleological: Also called consequentialism, this method contends that good or evil is determined solely by the "end" or "goal" *(teleos)* of the action.

Torah: From the root meaning "to teach," used initially to refer to all regulations for humanity in the Old Testament, but later came to mean the first five books, the Law of Moses.

Traditionalism: A deontological approach that holds the right or the good is the customary, the cultural and religious traditions of a group.

Utilitarianism: Also termed social hedonism, this approach contends the right moral choice is the one that brings the greatest good to the greatest number.

Value: A highly appraised and worthwhile ideal of a person or a society; most norms are the expression of a value.

Vice: An evil or bad action, habit, or characteristic, often in contrast to virtue.

Virtue: A certain moral quality, habit of the heart, or behavior trait that is good and leads toward excellence of character.

ENDNOTES

PREFACE

1. Larry L. Rasmussen, "A People of the Way, Part 2," *Auburn Views* 1 (fall 1994): 8.

2. T. B. Maston was Professor of Christian Ethics at Southwestern Baptist Theological Seminary from 1943 until his retirement in 1963. Well known and widely respected for his teaching and writing, Maston's greatest influence revolved around his personal example. [See "Foreword" in the reprint of Maston's *Why Live the Christian Life?* (New Orleans: Insight Press, 1996), vii-ix.]

3. H. B. Workman, "Abelard," *Encyclopedia of Religion and Ethics*, vol. 1, ed. James Hastings (Edinburgh: T. & T. Clark, 1908), 15.

4. Soren Kierkegaard, *On Authority and Revelation* (Princeton, N.J.: Princeton University Press, 1955), xx.

INTRODUCTION

1. CBS *Sixty Minutes*, November 10, 1991.

2. Edward Leroy Long Jr., *A Survey of Christian Ethics* (New York: Oxford University Press, 1967), 40.

3. Bruce C. Birch and Larry L. Rasmussen, *Bible and Ethics in the Christian Life: Revised and Expanded Edition* (Minneapolis: Augsburg, 1989), 23.

4. Ibid., 22.

5. James Wm. McClendon Jr., *Systematic Theology: Ethics* (Nashville: Abingdon, 1986), 1:41–45, who also emphasized that he is not arguing against the logical order of theology.

6. As did Frederick Schleiermacher, who considered this question and stated he could have begun his classic *Glaubenslehre* with ethics or doctrine. Yet he never completed his ethics section, though he lived to be sixty-six.

7. Stanley Hauerwas and William Willimon, *Resident Aliens* (Nashville: Abingdon, 1989), 24.

8. My colleague Fisher Humphreys correctly reminded me that theological ideas of God's kingdom, of God's grace, and of a new community of Jews and Gentiles were marks of the early church. I still contend, however, that the earliest believers first lived their faith and then reflected upon it.

9. Stephen Charles Mott, *Biblical Ethics and Social Change* (New York: Oxford University Press, 1982), 110.

10. Anonymous *Epistle to Diognetus* 5, 6; translated from J. Donaldson, *History of Christian Literature and Doctrine* (London: Macmillan, 1864).

11. Tertullian, *Apology*, 39.

12. Cited in Robert C. Solomon, *Ethics: A Brief Introduction* (New York: McGraw Hill, 1984), 25.

13. Emil Brunner, *The Divine Imperative* (Philadelphia: Westminster Press, 1947), 86.

14. T. B. Maston, *Biblical Ethics* (New York: World Publishing Co., 1967), 145.

15. L. H. Marshall, *The Challenge of New Testament Ethics* (London: Macmillan, 1946), 31.

16. R. E. O. White, *Christian Ethics* (Atlanta: John Knox Press, 1981), 378.

17. Birch and Rasmussen, *Bible and Ethics*, 141.

18. See Stanley Hauerwas, *A Community of Character* (Notre Dame: University of Notre Dame Press, 1981) for a constructive theory of the narrative formation of Christian character in the Christian community.

19. C. H. Dodd, *Gospel and Law* (New York: Columbia University Press, 1951), 3–4.

20. Interview of Steven E. Ambrose on NBC's *Today* program of April 27, 1994.

21. See Lewis B. Smedes in *Choices* (San Francisco: Harper & Row, 1986) for an outstanding overview of decision making.

22. Richard Higginson, *Dilemmas: A Christian Approach to Moral Decision Making* (Louisville: W/JKP, 1988), 27.

23. See Richard Bondi's *Leading God's People: Ethics for the Practice of Ministry* (Nashville: Abingdon, 1989) for an excellent discussion of this responsibility.

24. See "The Minister's Vocation: Career or Profession?" (chapter 1) in Joe E. Trull and James E. Carter, *Ministerial Ethics: Being a Good Minister in a Not-So-Good World* (Nashville: Broadman & Holman, 1993).

25. Bondi, *Leading God's People*, 137–40.

26. White, *Christian Ethics*, 42–43.

27. Found in *The Ante-Nicene Fathers*, translations edited by Alexander Roberts and James Donaldson (Grand Rapids: Eerdmans Publishing Co., 1950).

28. T. B. Maston, *To Walk as He Walked* (Nashville: Broadman, 1985).

29. Robert C. Maynard, "Bagging Biaggi, teaching ethics," *New Orleans Times-Picayune*, 3 March 1987, A-23.

30. Michael Levin, "Ethics Courses: Useless," in *Update*, November 1990, 3.

31. "Can Ethics Be Taught?" *Issues in Ethics*, October 1987, 3.

32. Ibid. See also Mary M. Wilcox, *Developmental Journey* (Nashville: Abingdon, 1979).

33. Sydney Allen, "Teaching Ethics Is Vital," *Update*, November 1990, 4. See also other articles in this same issue on the debate.

CHAPTER ONE

1. J. Philip Wogaman, *Christian Ethics: A Historical Introduction* (Louisville: W/JKP, 1993), 16.

2. Augustine, *Confessions*, 3.4f, 7.9f.

3. Robert Baker, *A Summary of Christian History,* (Nashville: Broadman Press, 1959), 33.

4. Robert C. Solomon, *Ethics: A Brief Introduction* (New York: McGraw Hill, 1984), 26.

5. Wayne G. Boulton, Thomas D. Kennedy, and Allen Verhay, eds., *From Christ to the World* (Grand Rapids: Eerdmans, 1994), 1.

6. Aristotle, *Politics,* 1.2.

7. Aristotle, *Nichomachean Ethics,* 2.5-9.

8. Wogaman, *Christian Ethics*, 21, states these nonbiblical sources never exerted as much influence as the Bible itself.

9. "What Is Ethics?" *Issues in Ethics*, October 1987, 2.

10. Dedicated to his son Nicomachus, Aristotle probably did not personally write this compilation of his notes, though most scholars believe the material is his.

11. Aristotle, *Nicomachean Ethics*, 2.1.

12. Nolan B. Harmon, *Ministerial Ethics and Etiquette* (Nashville: Abingdon, 1928), 193–200.

13. R. M. Hare, "Ethics," *The Westminster Dictionary of Christian Ethics*, eds. James F. Childress and John Macquarrie (Philadelphia: The Westminster Press, 1986), 206.

14. See W. D. Hudson, ed., *The Is/Ought Question* (London: Macmillan, 1972).

15. Solomon, *Ethics*, 12.

16. *National and International Religion Report* 8 (21 February 1994): 2.

17. Michael Bayles, *Professional Ethics* (Belmont, Calif.: Wadsworth Publishing Co., 1989), 18.

18. John S. Feinberg and Paul D. Feinberg, *Ethics for a Brave New World* (Wheaton, Ill.: Crossway Books, 1993), 19.

19. John Macquarrie, "Free Will and Determinism," *The Westminster Dictionary of Christian Ethics*, 237.

20. The classical expression of this tension occurred between Augustinianism and Pelagianism in the fourth century.

21. Feinberg and Feinberg, *Ethics for a Brave New World*, 19–22.

22. Robin Gill, *A Textbook of Christian Ethics* (Edinburgh: T & T Clark, 1985), 8.

23. William M. Tillman Jr., *Understanding Christian Ethics* (Nashville: Broadman Press, 1988), 28–29.

24. Richard Higginson, *Dilemmas* (Louisville: John Knox Press, 1988), 42.

25. W. D. Ross, *The Right and the Good* (Oxford: Oxford University Press, 1946), 19–21.

26. Immanuel Kant, *Critique of Practical Reason and Other Writings in Moral Philosophy* (Chicago: University of Chicago Press, 1949), 80.

27. Ibid., 87.

28. Higginson, *Dilemmas*, 45.

29. The story is told in the book and film *The Hiding Place*; this is a vivid contrast to Kant's essay "On a Supposed Right to Tell Lies from Benevolent Motives," in which he argued to tell the truth in all situations.

30. See Higginson, *Dilemmas*, 228–33, and William Frankena, *Ethics* (Englewood Cliffs, N.J.: Prentice-Hall, 1963), 13–45.

31. Edward Leroy Long Jr., *A Survey of Recent Christian Ethics* (Oxford, England: Oxford Press, 1982), 32–46.

32. H. Richard Niebuhr, *The Responsible Self* (New York: Harper and Row, 1963).

33. Emil Brunner, *The Divine Imperative* (Philadelphia: Westminster Press, 1947), 86.

34. T. B. Maston, *Why Live the Christian Life?* (Nashville: Broadman Press, 1974), 9-11.

35. Boulton et al., *From Christ to the World,* 3.

36. Albert C. Knudson, *The Principles of Christian Ethics* (New York: Abingdon, 1953), 16-31.

37. Maston, *Why Live the Christian Life?* 10.

38. Ibid., 7.

39. Henlee H. Barnette, *Introducing Christian Ethics* (Nashville: Broadman Press, 1961), 3-4.

40. Higginson, *Dilemmas,* 55-77.

41. Aquinas defined conscience *(synderesis)* as "the mind of man making moral judgments."

42. Max L. Stackhouse, *Public Theology and Political Economy* (New York: University Press of America, 1991), 4-15.

43. Boulton et al., *From Christ to the World,* 5.

CHAPTER TWO

1. Wayne G. Boulton, Thomas Kennedy, and Allen Verhey, eds., *From Christ to the World* (Grand Rapids: Eerdmans, 1994), 15.

2. James M. Gustafson, "The Place of Scripture in Christian Ethics: A Methodological Study," *Interpretation* 24 (1970): 430-55.

3. Lisa Sowle Cahill, "The New Testament and Ethics: Communities of Social Change," *Interpretation* 44 (October 1990): 383.

4. Ibid., 383-84.

5. J. Philip Wogaman, *Christian Ethics: A Historical Introduction* (Louisville: W/JKP, 1993), 2.

6. W. S. Bruce, *The Ethics of the Old Testament* (Edinburgh: T. & T. Clark, 1909), 16.

7. T. B. Maston, *Biblical Ethics* (Cleveland: World Publishing Co., 1967), 34.

8. Bruce C. Birch and Larry L. Rasmussen, *Bible and Ethics in the Christian Life* (Minneapolis: Augsburg Publishing House, 1976), 11-16.

9. Birch and Rasmussen, *Bible and Ethics,* rev. and exp. ed., 1989, 10.

10. T. B. Maston, *Why Live the Christian Life?* (Nashville: Broadman, 1974), 47, to whom I am indebted for this summary.

11. Maston, *Biblical Ethics,* 287.

12. Ibid., 282.

13. Josephus and others divide the Decalogue 5/5, interpreting the Fifth Commandment as a vertical duty to honor the God of your parents.

14. Several evangelical writers [see Norman Geisler, *Christian Ethics: Options and Issues* (Grand Rapids: Baker, 1989), 116] contend that what Jesus named as the "greatest and first commandment" is a "higher moral law" than the "second." Without debating the supreme priority of loving God, to declare love for neighbor as a "lower moral law" is to risk implying that pietism is superior to ethical obedience, a mistake often made in biblical and Christian history.

15. Lindsay Dewar, *An Outline of New Testament Ethics* (Philadelphia: The Westminster Press, 1959), 203.

16. J. I. Packer, "The Reconstitution of Authority," in *Readings in Christian Ethics*, ed. David K. Clark and Robert V. Rakestraw (Grand Rapids: Baker Books, 1994), 1:92.

17. Birch and Rasmussen, *Bible and Ethics* rev. and exp. 1989, 141.

18. Ibid., 142.

19. Edward Farley and Peter C. Hodgson, "Scripture and Tradition," in *Christian Theology*, ed. Peter C. Hodgson (Philadelphia: Fortress, 1985), 62.

20. I first heard this concept from J. W. McGorman, Professor of New Testament at Southwestern Seminary.

21. Henlee H. Barnette in his classic text, *Introducing Christian Ethics* (Nashville: Broadman Press, 1961), devotes an entire chapter (10) to the "Ethics of the Holy Spirit."

22. Richard Higginson, *Dilemmas* (Louisville: Westminster/John Knox Press), 233.

23. Maston, *Why Live the Christian Life?*, 100–101.

24. Clark, David K. and Robert V. Rakestraw, ed. (Grand Rapids: Baker, 1994), 1:180.

25. Stanley Hauerwas, *A Community of Character* (Notre Dame: University of Notre Dame Press, 1981), 69–70.

26. "SBC conference focuses on biblical interpretation," *Baptist Message*, 5 May 1988, 1.

27. I am indebted to Ebbie Smith's *Syllabus for the Study of Christian Ethics* (Fort Worth: Alphagraphics, 1984), 58–62, for the compilation of these principles.

28. See Birch and Rasmussen's discussion, "The Importance of Exegesis," in *Bible and Ethics*, rev. and exp. ed., 166–71.

29. For examples, see Paul Wooley, "The Relevance of the Scripture," in *The Infallible Word* (Grand Rapids: Baker, 1970), 195.

30. Bernard Ramm, *Protestant Biblical Interpretation* (Grand Rapids: Baker, 1970), 185–92.

31. Gordon D. Fee and Douglas Stuart, *How to Read the Bible for All Its Worth* (Grand Rapids: Zondervan, 1982), 65.

32. Ibid., 66–70.

33. Ibid., 68.

34. Smith, *Syllabus*, 62.

CHAPTER THREE

1. Henlee H. Barnette, *Introducing Christian Ethics* (Nashville: Broadman Press, 1961), 12.

2. See Rodney Clapp, "Democracy as Heresy," *Christianity Today*, 20 February 1987, 17-23.

3. T. B. Maston, *Biblical Ethics* (Cleveland: World Publishing Co., 1967), viii.

4. Walter Kaiser, "How Can Christians Derive Principles from the Specific Commands of the Law?" in *Readings in Christian Ethics*, ed. Clark and Rakestraw 1:192-201.

5. W. H. Bellinger Jr., "The Old Testament: Sourcebook for Christian Ethics," in *Understanding Christian Ethics*, ed. William M. Tillman Jr., (Nashville: Broadman, 1988), 39-40.

6. Waldemar Janzen, *Old Testament Ethics: A Paradigmatic Approach* (Louisville: W/JKP, 1994).

7. Bellinger, "The Old Testament," 41.

8. See Clinton Gardner, *Biblical Faith and Social Ethics* (New York: Harper & Row, 1960), 24-28, and Barnette, *Introducing Christian Ethics*, 12-16, for a discussion of some of these themes.

9. The Greek word Paul used to explain the purpose of the law, *pedagoga*, was a title for the slave who gave moral instruction.

10. An example of the last explanation is Moses' accommodation of divorce (Deut. 24:1-4), which Jesus called an "allowance" (Matt. 19:8).

11. James Muilenburg, *The Way of Israel: Biblical Faith and Ethics* (New York: Harper, 1961), 59.

12. A. R. Osborn, *Christian Ethics* (Oxford: University Press, 1940), 42.

13. Barnette, *Introducing Christian Ethics*, 19.

14. Cited by D. H. Field, "Ten Commandments," *Encyclopedia of Biblical and Christian Ethics*, ed. R. K. Harrison (Nashville: Thomas Nelson, 1987), 407.

15. For an excellent exegetical study of the last six commandments and their application to contemporary ethical issues, see Lewis Smedes, *Mere Morality* (Grand Rapids: Eerdmans, 1983).

16. Maston, *Biblical Ethics*, 30-31.

17. Ibid., 34.

18. John Patterson, *The Goodly Fellowship of the Prophets* (New York: Ch. Scribner's Sons, 1950), 3.

19. Barnette, *Introducing Christian Ethics*, 28–29.

20. Ibid., 26.

21. Norman H. Snaith, *The Distinctive Ideas of the Old Testament* (London: Epworth Press, 1944), 59.

22. Muilenburg, *Way of Israel*, 98–106.

23. H. Wheeler Robinson, *Inspiration and Revelation in the Old Testament* (Oxford: Clarendon Press, 1946), 241.

24. Bellinger, "The Old Testament," 55.

25. See Barnette, *Introducing Christian Ethics*, 36, and Robinson, *Inspiration*, 246.

26. See Helmut Gollwitzer, *Song of Love: A Biblical Understanding of Sex* (Philadelphia: Fortress, 1979).

27. Barnette, *Introducing Christian Ethics*, 40.

28. Ibid., 42.

29. Thomas D. Lea, "Living to the Glory of God: The Ethics of the New Testament," in *Understanding Christian Ethics*, 60–61.

30. Richard N. Longnecker, *New Testament Social Ethics for Today* (Grand Rapids: Eerdmans, 1984), 1–9.

31. Barnette, *Introducing Christian Ethics*, 42.

32. L. H. Marshall, *The Challenge of New Testament Ethics* (London: Macmillan, 1960), 4.

33. In Shaw's preface to *Androcles and the Lion*, as quoted by Marshall, *The Challenge*, 5.

34. See Maston, *Biblical Ethics*, 165–75; Barnette, *Introducing Christian Ethics*, 44–46; and E. F. Scott, *The Ethical Teachings of Jesus* (New York: Macmillan Co., 1924), 17–24, for discussions of these characteristics.

35. Marshall, *The Challenge*, 6.

36. Joseph Klausner, *Jesus of Nazareth* (New York: Macmillan Co., 1925), 389.

37. Marshall, *The Challenge*, 12.

38. Ibid., 200.

39. Lindsay Dewar, *An Outline of New Testament Ethics* (Philadelphia: The Westminster Press, 1959), 73.

40. Maston, *Biblical Ethics*, 169–71.

41. Reinhold Niebuhr, *An Interpretation of Christian Ethics* (New York: Harper, 1935), 113, and John Knox, *The Ethic of Jesus in the Teaching of the Church* (Nashville: Abingdon, 1961), 18.

42. Maston, *Biblical Ethics*, 173, includes Georgia Harkness and T. W. Manson, to which could be added Henlee Barnette, *Introducing Christian Ethics*, 46; and R. E. O. White, *Biblical Ethics* (Atlanta: John Knox Press, 1979), 57.

43. Quoted in Barnette, *Introducing Christian Ethics*, 46.

44. Maston, *Biblical Ethics,* 174.

45. Ibid., 147–48.

46. Dispensationalists look forward to a restoration of an earthly king-dom, but more common is the temporal understanding of the kingdom as the final reign of God in eternity.

47. Stephen C. Mott, *Biblical Ethics and Social Change* (New York: Oxford University Press, 1982), 87.

48. White, *Biblical Ethics,* 78.

49. The Synoptic Gospels refer to the kingdom thirty-four times in Mat-thew, sixteen times in Mark, and thirty-two times in Luke.

50. Marshall, *The Challenge,* 31.

51. White, *Biblical Ethics,* 84–108, where he applies kingdom principles to all social relationships.

52. D. J. Moos, "Sermon on the Mount," *Encyclopedia of Biblical and Christian Ethics,* ed. R. K. Harrison (Nashville: Thomas Nelson, 1987), 373–76.

53. Barnette, *Introducing Christian Ethics,* 50.

54. Quoted by Moos, "Sermon on the Mount," 374.

55. John R. W. Stott, *The Message of the Sermon on the Mount* (Downers Grove, Ill.: InterVarsity Press, 1978), 22–24.

56. Moos, "Sermon on the Mount," 374.

57. Stott, *The Message,* 24.

58. C. A. A. Scott, *New Testament Ethics* (Cambridge: University Press, 1936), 75.

59. Victor Paul Furnish, *The Moral Teaching of Paul* (Nashville: Abing-don, 1979), 11–29.

60. Waldo Beach and H. Richard Niebuhr, *Christian Ethics: Sources of the Living Tradition* (New York: The Ronald Press, 1955), 44.

61. C. H. Dodd, *Gospel and Law* (New York: Columbia University Press, 1951), 5.

62. See Barnette, *Introducing Christian Ethics,* 69–73 and Maston, *Bibli-cal Ethics,* 189–202.

63. James S. Stewart, *A Man in Christ* (New York: Harper & Bros., 1935).

64. Karl Barth, *The Epistle to the Romans* (London: Oxford University Press, 1933), 436.

65. A. M. Hunter, *Interpreting Paul's Gospel* (London: SCM Press, 1954), 47.

66. Barnette, *Introducing Christian Ethics,* 76–77, who terms this "Pauline realism." The words used by Paul to describe human nature are *body, soul, flesh, spirit, mind, heart,* and *bowels.*

67. Quoted in White, *Biblical Ethics,* 137.

68. Ibid., 109.

69. Maston, *Biblical Ethics*, 215–17.

70. Edward W. Bauman quoted in Maston, *Biblical Ethics*, 224.

71. White, *Biblical Ethics*, 209–12.

72. Ibid., 204.

73. Barnette, *Introducing Christian Ethics*, 82.

74. White, *Biblical Ethics*, 193.

75. Of more than twenty basic works, only Henlee Barnette, *Introducing Christian Ethics* (87–95), devotes a chapter to the subject. A few, like Richard Higginson, *Dilemmas* (232), write a few paragraphs, but most say nothing.

76. Barnette, *Introducing Christian Ethics*, 87, to whom I am indebted for this overview.

77. Ibid., 94.

78. Quoted by W. A. Elwell, "New Testament Ethics," *Encyclopedia of Biblical and Christian Ethics*, 277.

CHAPTER FOUR

1. Kenneth Scott Latourette, vol. 1 of *Beginnings to 1500, A History of Christianity* (New York: Harper & Row, 1953), 228.

2. See Ernst Troeltsch, *The Social Teaching of the Christian Churches*, vols. 1 and 2 (Louisville: W/JKP, 1931, 1992).

3. H. Richard Niebuhr, *Christ and Culture* (New York: Harper & Row, 1951), 1–44.

4. Ibid., xii.

5. Along with Troeltsch and Latourette, see also C. J. Cadoux, *The Early Church and the World* (Edinburgh: T. & T. Clark, 1925); R. E. O. White, *Christian Ethics: The Historical Development* (Atlanta: John Knox Press, 1981); and J. Philip Wogaman, *Christian Ethics: A Historical Introduction* (Louisville: W/JKP, 1993).

6. T. B. Maston, *Christianity and World Issues* (New York: MacMillan, 1957), 1–2.

7. Troeltsch, *Social Teaching*, 1:132.

8. Maston, *Christianity and World Issues*, 3.

9. Aristides, *Apology*, 15, 16, in J. Stevenson, *A New Eusebius* (London: SPCK, 1970), 56.

10. W. E. H. Lecky, *History of European Morals* (New York: D. Appleton, 1880), 1:428–63.

11. White, *Christian Ethics*, 13.

12. S. Angus, *The Environment of Early Christianity* (New York: Charles Scribner's, 1914), 38.

13. White, *Christian Ethics*, 14.

14. Ibid., 15.

15. Cited by James Orr, *Neglected Factors in the Study of the Early Progress of Christianity* (London: Hodder and Stoughton, 1899), 200.

16. Cadoux, *Early Church*, 611.

17. White, *Christian Ethics*, 52.

18. Ibid., 52-80.

19. Troeltsch, *Social Teaching*, 1:115.

20. Waldo Beach and H. Richard Niebuhr, *Christian Ethics: Source of the Living Tradition* (New York: The Ronald Press, 1955), 79, 94-98.

21. White, *Christian Ethics*, 57.

22. Ibid., 59.

23. Tertullian, *Apology*, 30.1-4, 3.2.1.

24. Origen, *Against Celsus*, 8.68.

25. R. H. Bainton, *Christian Attitudes to War and Peace* (London: Hodder and Stoughton, 1961), 68.

26. White, *Christian Ethics*, 71.

27. Ibid., 77-78.

28. Maston, *Christianity and World Issues*, 6.

29. Philip Yancey, "Jesus and the Virtue Squad," *Christianity Today*, 6 February 1995, 104.

30. Walter Hobhouse, *The Church and the World in Idea and in History* (London: Macmillan, 1910), 112.

31. Latourette, *Beginnings to 1500*, 326.

32. Hobhouse, *Church and the World*, 124.

33. Maston, *Christianity and World Issues*, 9.

34. Beach and Niebuhr, *Christian Ethics: Sources of the Living Tradition*, 142.

35. Ibid., 148.

36. See Anton C. Pegis, *Basic Writings of Saint Thomas Aquinas*, 2 vols. (New York: Random House, 1945).

37. Thomas Aquinas, *Summa Theologica*, 2:1, Q.3, art.8.

38. White, *Christian Ethics*, 135.

39. Bob E. Adams, "The Church and the World," in *Understanding Christian Ethics*, ed. William Tillman Jr. (Nashville: Broadman Press, 1988), 108.

40. Wogaman, *Christian Ethics: A Historical Introduction*, 108.

41. Adams, "Church and the World," 109-13.

42. Ibid., 114-15. For example, television evangelist Pat Robertson enticed presidential candidates Phil Gramm, Bob Dole, Newt Gingrich, and William Bennett to appear at his Christian Coalition convention in Washington, D.C., in September 1995.

43. Maston, *Christianity and World Issues*, 10.

44. The book (endnote 3) was an expanded form of a series of lectures delivered in 1949, which Niebuhr indicated were based on "Troeltsch's analysis of the encounters of church and world" (endnote 2). Niebuhr substituted five main types of responses for Troeltsch's three and attempted "to understand this historical relativism in the light of theological and theocentric relativism" (xii).

45. The author is indebted to Charles M. Swezey and Douglas F. Ottati of Union Theological Seminary in Virginia for these insights.

46. Niebuhr, *Christ and Culture*, 45–86.

47. Maston, *Christianity and World Issues*, 17, who names this the "rejection or withdrawal strategy."

48. Niebuhr, *Christ and Culture*, 55.

49. Tertullian, *Apology*, 38; *On Idolatry*, 10, 11, 19.

50. Stanley Hauerwas and William H. Willimon, *Resident Aliens* (Nashville: Abingdon Press, 1989), 12.

51. Niebuhr, *Christ and Culture*, 66.

52. Tertullian, *Prescription Against Heretics*, 7.

53. Niebuhr, *Christ and Culture*, 77.

54. Ibid., 79.

55. Ibid., 81.

56. See Latourette, *History of Christianity*, 2:822, for an example of this fallacy in George Fox's radical reform of Christianity, the Society of Friends.

57. Niebuhr, *Christ and Culture*, 83–115.

58. Wogaman, *Christian Ethics: A Historical Introduction*, 228.

59. Niebuhr, *Christ and Culture*, 91–100.

60. Ibid., 103.

61. Ibid., 107.

62. Ibid., 120–48.

63. Clement, *The Instructor*, 2.1.2.

64. Niebuhr, *Christ and Culture*, 130–131.

65. Maston, *Christianity and World Issues*, 21, adds that this ethical dualism holds within one strategy both the withdrawal and the accommodation approach.

66. Niebuhr, *Christ and Culture*, 143.

67. Ibid., 149–89.

68. Ibid., 150.

69. Martin Luther, *Works of Martin Luther* (Philadelphia: Board of Publication United Lutheran Church, 1931), 4:265–66.

70. Niebuhr, *Christ and Culture*, 171.

71. Ibid., 187.

72. Ibid., 188.

73. Ibid., 190–229.

74. Ibid., 190.

75. See especially his *Confessions,* books 13, 27, 31, 33, and his *City of God*, books 12, 14, 18, 19.

76. Maston, *Christianity and World Issues,* 24, and *Why Live the Christian Life?* (Nashville: Broadman Press, 1974), 174 ff.

77. John Bennett, *Christian Ethics and Social Policy* (New York: Scribner's, 1946), 60.

78. See *Moral Man and Immoral Society* (New York: Scribner's, 1932).

79. John Bennett, *Christian Ethics and Social Policy,* 77, suggests that "a middle axiom is more concrete than a universal ethical principle and less specific than a program that includes legislation and political strategy."

80. Maston, *Why Live the Christian Life?,* 185

CHAPTER FIVE

1. Martin E. Marty, "The Judeo Christian Looks at the Judeo Christian Tradition," *The Christian Century*, 8 October 1986, 858.

2. My colleague Fisher Humphreys has correctly reminded me that Christian decision making existed before the Enlightenment and was altered by this movement, which included five new emphases: (1) individuals are more basic than community; (2) reason is more dependable than faith; (3) people need to be free from the authorities of church and state; (4) an optimism toward the future; and (5) the inevitability of progress. For our purposes, however, the major impact on decision making in the twentieth century has come from movements during the previous two centuries.

3. J. Philip Wogaman, *Christian Ethics: A Historical Introduction* (Louisville: Westminster/John Knox Press, 1993), 147.

4. Wayne E. Ward and W. Boyd Hunt, "Liberalism," *Encyclopedia of Southern Baptists* (Nashville: Broadman Press, 1958), 2:785.

5. William Hordern, *A Layman's Guide to Protestant Theology* (New York: Macmillan, 1968), 79.

6. *The Christian Century* became the title of the primary journal of theological liberalism.

7. A phrase used by H. Richard Niebuhr to describe the many variations of the "Christ-of-Culture" theme in recent Christian history [*Christ and Culture* (New York: Harper & Row, 1951), 9].

8. Wogaman, *Christian Ethics: A Historical Introduction*, 195.

9. Ibid.

10. Charles H. Hopkins, *The Rise of the Social Gospel in American Protestantism: 1865-1915* (New Haven: Yale University Press, 1940), 175.

11. Wogaman, *Christian Ethics: A Historical Introduction*, 197-202. A professor of church history at Rochester Theological Seminary from 1897 until his death in 1918, Rauschenbusch was deeply influenced by an eleven-year ministry in the slums of New York City. His most influential works were *Christianity and the Social Crisis* (1907), *Christianizing the Social Order* (1912), and *A Theology for the Social Gospel* (1917).

12. Sherwood E. Wirt, "Social Gospel," *Baker's Dictionary of Christian Ethics*, ed. Carl F. H. Henry (Grand Rapids: Baker Book House, 1973), 637.

13. John Bennett, "A Changed Liberal—But Still a Liberal," *The Christian Century*, 8 February 1939, 179-81.

14. R. E. O. White, *Christian Ethics: The Historical Development* (Atlanta: John Knox Press, 1981), 309-10.

15. Stanley L. Grenz and Roger E. Olson, *Twentieth-Century Theology* (Downers Grove, Ill.: InterVarsity Press, 1992), 287.

16. C. T. McIntyre, "Fundamentalism," *Evangelical Dictionary of Theology*, ed. Walter A. Elwell (Grand Rapids: Baker Book House, 1984), 433.

17. T. P. Weber, "Niagara Conferences," *The New Dictionary of Theology*, eds. Joseph Komonchak, Mary Collins, and Dermot Lane (Collegeville, Minn.: The Liturgical Press, 1987), 773.

18. Wayne E. Ward, "Fundamentalism," *Encyclopedia of Southern Baptists*, 2:515. However, Carl F. H. Henry in "Fundamentalist Ethics," *The Westminster Dictionary of Christian Ethics*, eds. James Childress and John Macquarrie (Philadelphia: The Westminster Press, 1986), 241, attributes the five points to the 1895 Niagara Conference, while C. T. McIntyre, "Fundamentalism," 433, and others cite The General Assembly of the Northern Presbyterian Church in 1910 as the originator. George Marsden clarifies the confusion, noting the 1910 Presbyterian General Assembly adopted a five-point declaration of essential doctrines, which became the basis of what (with premillenialism substituted for the authenticity of miracles in point five) were long known as the "five points of fundamentalism" [*Fundamentalism and American Culture* (New York: Oxford University Press, 1980), 117].

19. Henry, "Fundamentalist Ethics," 241.

20. William Dinges, "Fundamentalism," *The New Dictionary of Theology*, 412.

21. Hordern, *Layman's Guide*, 65.

22. Grenz and Olson, *Twentieth-Century Theology*, 287.

23. Ward, "Fundamentalism," 516.

24. Carl F. H. Henry, *Christian Personal Ethics* (Grand Rapids: Eerdmans, 1957), 258.

25. Henry, "Fundamentalist Ethics," 241. For example, many fundamentalists defended racial segregation and discrimination on biblical grounds.

26. Carl F. H. Henry, *The Uneasy Conscience of Modern Fundamentalism* (Grand Rapids: Eerdmans, 1947).

27. Joseph C. Hough Jr., "Rules and Ethics of Sex," in *Moral Issues and Christian Response*, 3rd ed., ed. Paul T. Jersild and Dale A. Johnson (New York: Holt, Rinehart, and Winston, 1983), 92–94.

28. S. D. Anderson, "Social Concern, Evangelical," *Encyclopedia of Biblical and Christian Ethics*, ed. R. K. Harrison (Nashville: Thomas Nelson Publishers, 1987), 387.

29. Ibid.

30. Ibid., 389. Other possible reasons for evangelical withdrawal from efforts at social reform include reactions to the Prohibition Movement, the controversy over evolution, and the political turmoil of the Al Smith presidential campaign.

31. Grenz and Olson, *Twentieth-Century Theology*, 287–88.

32. Ron Sider has organized "Evangelicals for Social Action," and Jim Wallis publishes the magazine *Sojourners*.

33. Anderson, "Social Concern, Evangelical," 390.

34. Norman L. Geisler, *Christian Ethics: Options and Issues* (Grand Rapids: Baker Book House, 1989), 97–111.

35. Ebbie C. Smith, *Syllabus for the Study of Biblical Ethics* (Fort Worth: Alphagraphics, 1984), 106.

36. T. B. Maston, *Biblical Ethics* (New York: World Publishing Company, 1967), viii.

37. T. B. Maston, *Why Live the Christian Life?* (Nashville: Broadman Press, 1974), 154.

38. D. Glenn Saul, "The Ethics of Decision Making," in *Understanding Christian Ethics*, ed. William M. Tillman Jr. (Nashville: Broadman Press, 1988), 83.

39. The pattern is illustrated throughout Maston's *Biblical Ethics*.

40. This relationship between norms, values, and principles is discussed in chapter 2.

41. Most Bible commentaries note that prostitutes in Corinth did not wear the long *yashmak* veil, and shorn heads for women were a mark of disgrace.

42. J. Philip Wogaman, *Christian Moral Judgment* (Louisville: Westminster/John Knox Press, 1989), 72–97.

43. D. Glenn Saul, "Ethics of Decision Making," 86–87, describes Henlee Barnette, renowned Southern Baptist ethicist, as a "contextual principled-agapist" who believed principles give direction like a compass.

44. Paul Ramsey, *Deeds and Rules in Christian Ethics* (New York: Charles Scribner's Sons, 1967).

45. Paul Ramsey, *Basic Christian Ethics* (Louisville: Westminster/John Knox Press, 1950, 1993).

46. Ibid., xxviii.

47. Edward Leroy Long Jr., *A Survey of Recent Christian Ethics* (New York: Oxford University Press, 1982), 25.

48. Geisler, *Christian Ethics: Options and Issues*, 98.

49. Theologians and ethicists disagree about the "lesser evil" choice being sinful. Richard Higginson, for example, believes that viewpoint makes too ready an equation between evil and sin. "If one has made a well-informed conscientious decision and believes that it is clearly the better alternative, I do not see why one ought to feel sinful about it" [*Dilemmas* (Louisville: W/JKP, 1988), 139]. My position, however, is better voiced by Anglican Peter Hinchliff: "The fact that one has not been truthful does not mean that a lie is as good as the truth. And one ought to acknowledge that fact by admitting that one's action has not been wholly right, wholly ideal. One is still a sinner in need of forgiveness because the untruth, if willingly embraced, might make one a kind of person other than the ideal to which one is committed" [*Holiness and Politics* (London: Darton, Longman & Todd, 1982), 111-12].

50. Kenneth Scott Latourette, *A History of Christianity: Reformation to the Present* (New York: Harper & Row, 1953, 1975), 1420.

51. Grenz and Olson, *Twentieth-Century Theology*, 64.

52. Ibid., 63.

53. Ibid., 64.

54. Emil Brunner, *Dogmatics*, vol. 1 of *The Christian Doctrine of God*, trans. Olive Wyon (London: Lutterworth, 1949), 45.

55. The primary journal in America of neoorthodox ethics has been *Christianity and Crisis*, which ceased publication in 1993.

56. Edward Leroy Long Jr., "Modern Protestant Ethics," *The Westminster Dictionary of Christian Ethics*, 387.

57. William C. Spohn, *What Are They Saying about Scripture and Ethics?* (New York: Paulist Press, 1984), 12.

58. Ibid., 27-35. Barth's ethics are found in three major sections of his *Dogmatics*: 2.2, 3.4, and 4.2.

59. Spohn, *What Are They Saying?*, 35.

60. Emil Brunner, *The Divine Imperative* (New York: The Macmillan Co., 1937), 291 ff.

61. Long, "Modern Protestant Ethics," 384.

62. Rudolf Bultmann, *Jesus and the Word* (New York: Charles Scribner's Sons, 1958), 103.

63. Dietrich Bonhoeffer, *The Cost of Discipleship* (New York: Macmillan Publishing Co., 1963), 73.

64. Ibid., 96.

65. H. Richard Niebuhr, *The Responsible Self* (New York: Harper & Row, 1963).

66. Spohn, *What Are They Saying?* 14.

67. Wogaman, *Christian Ethics: A Historical Introduction,* 229.

68. Grenz and Olson, *Twentieth-Century Theology,* 99.

69. Reinhold Niebuhr, *Moral Man and Immoral Society* (New York: Scribner's, 1932).

70. Wogaman, *Christian Ethics: A Historical Introduction,* 218.

71. Ibid.

72. Reinhold Niebuhr, *The Children of Light and the Children of Darkness* (New York: Scribner's, 1944), xiii.

73. Grenz and Olson, *Twentieth-Century Theology,* 157.

74. Although many other names (like Harvey Cox) were associated with the movement, these two were the main voices.

75. *Time* magazine featured a cover story entitled "Is God Dead?" in 1965, followed by numerous magazine and newspaper articles.

76. Thomas J. J. Altizer and William Hamilton, *Radical Theology and the Death of God* (Indianapolis: Bobbs-Merrill, 1966), 27–28.

77. John A. T. Robinson, *Honest to God* (Philadelphia: Westminster, 1963), 7–8.

78. Paul Lehmann, *Ethics in a Christian Context* (New York: Harper and Row, 1963), 124.

79. Paul Lehmann, "Contextual Ethics," *Dictionary of Christian Ethics,* (1967), 73.

80. Joseph Fletcher, *Situation Ethics: The New Morality* (Philadelphia: The Westminster Press, 1966), 17–39. Fletcher identified Brunner, Barth, Bonhoeffer, Bultmann, H. R. Niebuhr, James Gustafson, Lehmann, and others as situationists.

81. The method is usually termed "act-agapism," but it can also be called "act-utilitarianism," for love is applied directly to judgments in situations, rather than to rules.

82. Joseph Fletcher, "Situation Ethics," *Toward Authentic Morality for Modern Man* (Nashville: Christian Life Commission, 1970), 18.

83. White, *Christian Ethics,* 364, 366.

84. Ramsey, *Deeds and Rules,* 152.

85. Although Fletcher made contributions to the field of biomedical ethics, his methodology was difficult to apply to social systems—personal medical decisions might rely on situationism, but most bioethical questions require guiding principles and interaction between various medical voices and health values (see chap. 9).

86. James Childress, "Situation Ethics," *The Westminster Dictionary of Christian Ethics*, 586.

87. Richard John Neuhaus, "Who, Now, Will Shape the Meaning of America?" in *Moral Issues and Christian Response*, 4th ed., ed. Paul Jersild and Dale Johnson (New York: Holt, Rinehart, and Winston, 1988), 41.

88. Jerry Falwell, "An Agenda for the Eighties," *Moral Issues and Christian Response*, 4th ed., 23–29.

89. McIntire, "Fundamentalism," 435.

90. Joe E. Trull, "One Nation Under God," *Baptist Message*, 30 April 1992, 6.

91. John Bennett, "Assessing the Concerns of the Religious Right," *Moral Issues and Christian Response*, 4th ed., 34.

92. Ibid., 35.

93. Neuhaus, "Who, Now, Will Shape the Meaning of America?" 42.

94. Norman Geisler, *Ethics: Alternatives and Issues* (Grand Rapids: Zondervan, 1971).

95. Educated at Wheaton College and Detroit Bible College, Geisler has taught at Detroit, Trinity College, Dallas Theological Seminary, and was dean at Falwell's Liberty University.

96. Long, *A Survey*, 29.

97. Geisler, *Ethics*, 115–20, lists seven principles of higher values: persons more than things; infinite person more than a finite one; complete person more than an incomplete one; etc.

98. McIntire, "Fundamentalism," 435.

99. Gustavo Gutierrez, *A Theology of Liberation: History, Politics, and Salvation* (Maryknoll, N.Y.: Orbis Books, 1973).

100. In a speech delivered on March 16, 1988, titled "The Spirituality of Liberation Theology."

101. Gutierrez, rev. ed., xvii–xlvi.

102. Dennis P. McCann, "Liberation Theology," *The Westminster Dictionary of Christian Ethics*, 349.

103. Ibid., 350.

104. Ibid.

105. Grenz and Olson, *Twentieth-Century Theology*, 271.

106. James Wm. McClendon Jr., *Biography as Theology* (Philadelphia: Trinity Press International, 1974).

107. James Wm. McClendon Jr., *Systematic Theology: Ethics* (Nashville: Abingdon Press, 1986), 41–45.

108. Stanley Hauerwas, *The Peaceable Kingdom* (Notre Dame: University of Notre Dame Press, 1983), 4.

109. Stephan S. Bilynskyj, "Christian Ethics and the Ethics of Virtue," *Covenant Quarterly* 45 (August 1987): 127.

110. Ibid., 129.

111. Bruce C. Birch and Larry L. Rasmussen, *Bible and Ethics in the Christian Life,* rev. and exp. ed. (Minneapolis: Augsburg Fortress, 1989), 17-34.

112. Saul, "Ethics of Decision Making," 90.

113. Stanley Hauerwas and William H. Willimon, *Resident Aliens* (Nashville: Abingdon Press, 1989), 11-12.

114. Stanley Hauerwas, *A Community of Character* (Notre Dame: University of Notre Dame Press, 1981), 10.

115. Lecture delivered by Charles Swezey, Professor of Christian Ethics at Union Theological Seminary in Virginia, October 1991.

116. Vernon Elmore, "The Lesson in Life," *Broadman Comments, 1971* (Nashville: Broadman, 1970), 178-79.

117. Ray Higgins, *Turn Right: A Christian's Guide for Making Better Decisions* (Nashville: Baptist Center for Ethics, 1994), 10-17.

118. See Higgins, *Turn Right,* 34; Higginson, *Dilemmas,* 228; and Lewis Smedes, *Choices: Making Right Decisions in a Complex World* (New York: Harper & Row, 1984).

119. Lewis Smedes, *A Pretty Good Person* (San Francisco: Harper & Row, 1990), 3.

120. Darrell Reeck, *Ethics for the Professions: A Christian Perspective* (Minneapolis: Augsburg, 1972), 47.

121. See Smedes, *Choices,* 36-41, for a full discussion.

122. Ibid., 31.

123. Higgins, *Turn Right,* 36.

124. Smedes, *Choices,* 43-44.

125. Ibid., 89-90.

126. Higginson, *Dilemmas,* 55-69.

127. Smedes, *Choices,* 89.

128. Higgins, *Turn Right,* 41-42.

129. Ibid., 91-92.

130. Niebuhr, *The Responsible Self,* 47-68.

131. Smedes, *Choices,* 114.

132. Reeck, *Ethics for the Professions,* 55.

133. Smedes, *Choices,* 81.

CHAPTER SIX

1. Liddell's life story is told by D. P. Thomson in *Scotland's Greatest Athlete: The Eric Liddell Story* (Crief, Scotland: Research Unit, 1970).

2."The numbers tell of a nation in trouble," *Baptist Message*, 9 March 1995, 4.

3. Unless otherwise indicated, the statistics that follow describing social trends are gleaned from *Statistical Abstract of the United States* published annually by the U.S. Bureau of the Census, Washington, D.C., and "Snapshot of a Changing America," *Time*, 2 September 1985, 16–18.

4. In 1950 the nuclear family comprised about 70 percent of American homes. The figure has progressively dropped to 40 percent in the 1970s, 28 percent in 1985, and about 7 to 10 percent in 1995.

5. "Understanding Generations," *Baptist Standard*, 19 October 1994, 4.

6. Tom Sine, "Shifting into the Future Tense," *Christianity Today*, 17 November 1989, 18–21.

7. Paul Sadler, "Top Ten Issues Facing Churches," *Ethics Report* 11 (Fall 1994): 7.

8. "What's on Southern Baptists' minds?" *Baptist Message*, 14 March 1993, 5.

9. Joe E. Trull, "If Gold Rusts . . . Southern Baptists and Ethics Today," *The Theological Educator* (Spring 1990): 151–64.

10. Carl F. H. Henry's classic work on ethics is titled *Christian Personal Ethics* (Grand Rapids: Eerdmans, 1957). However, since the emergence of the Religious Right in the 1970s, many evangelicals have become more involved in applying moral convictions to public policy, though the agenda is often politicized.

11. T. B. Maston, *Biblical Ethics* (New York: World Publishing Co., 1967), 205–9.

12. Stanley Hauerwas, "Virtue," *The Westminster Dictionary of Christian Ethics*, ed. James F. Childress and John Macquarrie (Philadelphia: The Westminster Press, 1986), 648.

13. Paul Griffin Jones II, "Our Addictive Society," *Salt and Light* 8 (January/February 1995): 1.

14. Ibid.; and "Out in the Open," *Time*, 30 November 1987, 80-90.

15. "Abstinence from Alcohol on the Increase in the U.S.," *Salt and Light* 8 (January/February 1995): 4.

16. NBC News Report, 13 April 1992.

17. Normally "hard drugs" are classified in four categories: narcotics (opium derivatives such as heroin); depressants (alcohol); stimulants (cocaine); and hallucinogens (marijuana).

18. Jones, "Our Addictive Society," 1.

19. "Churches, parents urged to respond to rise in teen drug use," *Baptist Message*, 15 September 1994, 3.

20. "Survey—drug use among youth on the rise," *Baptist Message*, 28 March 1996, 4.

21. Deb Riechmann, "Poll: Student support for abortion drops," *The New Orleans Times-Picayune*, 8 January 1996, A-4.

22. Laurie A. Lattimore, "Beer on campus," *Word and Way*, 1 July 1993, 7.

23. J. H. Thayer, *A Greek-English Lexicon of the New Testament* (New York: American Book Co., 1889), 442, and other lexicographers point to its frequent use in the Septuagint as a translation for *yayin*.

24. Henry George Liddell and Robert Scott, *A Greek-English Lexicon*, 5th ed. (Oxford: Clarendon Press, 1864), 976. Also see Arndt and Gingrich, *A Greek-English Lexicon of the New Testament* (Chicago: University of Chicago Press, 1957), 564.

25. Davis,"Wine," in *Illustrated Davis Bible Dictionary* (Nashville: Royal Publishers, 1973), 868.

26. Once in derision Jesus was called *oinopotas*, a "wine drinker" (Matt. 11:19).

27. The law also prohibited eating grapes (6:3), cutting hair (6:5), and having contact with a dead body (6:6).

28. Kenneth L. Gentry Jr., *The Christian and Alcoholic Beverages* (Grand Rapids: Baker, 1986), 63–67.

29. I am indebted to my colleague Dr. Dennis Cole, Professor of Biblical Archaeology, for these insights.

30. Researchers writing in the British Medical Association Journal reported red and white table wine, straight and diluted, do a better job of killing food-borne bacteria that cause diarrhea than several other medicines, noting the ancient "Greeks and Romans found that if they had a big meal and they didn't drink wine, they were more likely to get diarrhea" ["Study Finds Wine. . . ," *New Orleans Times-Picayune*, 22 December 1995, A-18].

31. Many denominations provide excellent resources, such as "Alcohol Awareness: A Guide for Teenagers and Their Parents" and "Drug Awareness: A Guide for Youth and Youth Leaders" published by the Christian Life Commission of the SBC, 901 Commerce St., Nashville, TN 37203-3696.

32. "Louisiana Loophole," *New Orleans Times-Picayune*, 19 February 1995, A-12.

33. Dr. Vernon J. Bitner of the Institute for Christian Living has adapted "The Twelve Steps" used by Alcoholics Anonymous to treat alcoholics—see "Taking the Twelve Steps to Church," *Christianity Today*, 9 December 1988, 31.

34.William Safire, "Gambling Plank," *New Orleans Times-Picayune*, 16 September 1995, B-7.

35. John Zipperer, "Against All Odds," *Christianity Today*, 14 November 1994, 58, who compares the $330 billion wagered in 1992 to $132 billion of sales reported by the largest U.S. corporation (GMC), $154 billion in

assets claimed by the largest life insurance company (Prudential), $214 billion in assets reported by the largest commercial bank (Citicorp), and $316 billion in total U.S. corporate profits.

36. Leslie Ansley, "Bet on more gambling," *USA Weekend*, 10 February 1995, 18.

37. Quoted by C. Lacy Thompson in "Snake eyes?," *Baptist Message*, 8 September 1994, 6. Louisiana is a prime example of Goodman's observation, as riverboat gambling, land-based casinos on Indian lands, video-poker in restaurants and bars, and a land-based casino in New Orleans were approved without public action, often against public opinion, and by legislators who received "campaign contributions" of $1,066,747 from the gambling industry in 1993 and 1994.

38. Mark Winfield, "Casinos Win Big," *Baptists Today*, 10 March 1994, 12.

39. Reported in *Action Alert,* published by the National Coalition Against Legalized Gambling, 540 Palisade Drive, Orem, UT 84058. The year 1995 was a rough one for the gambling industry—along with voter rejection in several states, many conservative politicians attacked gambling on moral grounds; and in New Orleans (viewed by many as the best-case scenario for gambling) Harrah's temporary casino filed Chapter 11 bankruptcy and scaled back its original projections of $823 million by 35 percent to $425 million for the permanent casino.

40. HR 497 is sponsored by Rep. Frank Wolf (R-VA), HR 462 by Rep. John LaFalce (D-NY), and S 704 by Sen. Paul Simon (D-IL). The House bill passed on March 5, 1996, and Sen. Paul Simon said he has been assured the bill will soon be brought up in the Senate and the president will sign it into law.

41. Thompson, "Snake eyes?," 6.

42. Ibid.

43. Ken Camp, "Gambling cost catastrophic, economist tells lawmakers," *Baptist Press*, 17 February 1995, 6. A two-year study in Maryland showed gambling already costs that state $1.5 billion every year in lost work production, unpaid taxes, bankruptcies, public defenders, crime fighting, and other additional services.

44. "Relying on gambling is taking a long chance," *USA Today*, 6 April, 1994, 12A. Texas, for example, sets aside $500,000 per year from lottery profits for compulsive gambling assistance programs and puts a hot-line number on every lottery ticket.

45. Zipperer, "Against All Odds," 58.

46. Ibid.

47. Ken Camp, "Gambling games in your child's stocking?" *Baptist Standard*, 20 December 1995, 12.

48. Corley Petersen, "Gambling with Our Kids' Future," *The Wall Street Journal*, 28 December 1995, A-6.

49. "Youth gambling addicts growing with industry," *The Clarion-Ledger*, 9 January 1994, 15-A.

50. Quoted in John Allen in "The Social Impact of Gambling," a position paper deliverd at Glorieta Conference Center, 26 July 1995, 22.

51. "Letters," *Biloxi Sun Herald*, 5 August 1989, 2.

52. James Muilenburg, "Isaiah," *Interpreter's Bible* (Nashville: Abingdon Press, 1956), 5:751-52.

53. Quoted in Ross Coggin, ed., *The Gambling Menace* (Nashville: Broadman, 1966), 25.

54. Zipperer, "Against All Odds," 59.

55. Braidfoot, *Gambling: A Deadly Game* (Nashville: Broadman Press, 1985), 33. who also notes an MIT math professor figured the odds of winning the Massachusetts lottery were better—one in 1.9 million—yet the chances of winning were like being dealt four royal flushes, all in spades, and then leaving the poker table to meet four complete strangers who had the same birthday.

56. Presented in a position paper at Glorieta (NM) Conference Center, 26 July 1995.

57. Churches have had to determine their policy toward members who gamble, who are employed directly and indirectly by the gambling industry, and who donate winnings to the church—the last issue has often created divisions in the church, sometimes leading to the termination of the pastor or the exclusion of members.

58. U.S. Department of Health and Human Services, *HIV/AIDS Surveillance Report* 7, 1 (Atlanta: CDC, June 1985), 5, 14. An NBC news story (31 January 1996) reported more than 600,000 infected persons in the U.S., but a predicted decrease of 40,000 infected in 1996.

59. William M. Tillman Jr., *AIDS: A Christian Response* (Nashville: Convention Press, 1990), 36.

60. "Top Statistics of 1995," *Baptist Message*, 11 January 1996, 5.

61. Daniel Q. Haney, "AIDS risk to middle class may be exaggerated," *New Orleans Times-Picayune*, 17 April 1994, A-21.

62. The *New York Times* broke the story on September 8, 1992, followed by an NBC *Today* feature and a television report on *Dateline* by Jane Pauley. Numerous newspaper articles have focused on the Allen family, including a feature in *USA Today* (28 November 1995, 13-A).

63. The entire story is told by Jimmy Allen, Scott's father, in *Burden of a Secret* (Nashville: Moorings, 1995).

64. The history of the epidemic is chronicled by Harold Ivan Smith in Michael Malloy, ed., *Am I My Brother's Keeper? The AIDS Crisis and the*

Church (Kansas City: Beacon Hill Press, 1990), 1-26; and Earl E. Shelp and Ronald Sunderland in *AIDS and the Church: The Second Decade* (Louisville: Westminster/John Knox Press, 1992), 33-55.

65. Malloy, *Am I My Brother's Keeper?* 27-43; Allen, *Burden of a Secret,* 221-32.

66. The CDC reports (*USA Today*, 28 December 1995, D-1) the risk of getting AIDS from a blood transfusion is rare—between 1-in-83,000 and 1-in-122,000—due to improved screening techniques. Approximately 99.5 percent of infection occurs through other sources.

67. "AIDS: Facing Facts, Confronting Fears, Ministering to People," Texas Baptist Christian Life Commission (333 N. Washington, Dallas, TX 75246), 2, a resource booklet and videotape presentation designed to help churches and individuals begin an AIDS ministry, as well as a sample "Infectious Disease Policy."

68. See Wendell W. Hoffman and Stanley J. Grenz, *AIDS: Ministry in the Midst of an Epidemic* (Grand Rapids: Baker Book House, 1990); "AIDS: Facing Facts, Confronting Fears, Ministering to People," a twenty-four-page booklet and videocasette by the Texas Baptist Christian Life Commission, 333 N. Washington, Dallas, TX 75246; "The Face of AIDS" a videotape presentation about a ministerial student who contracted AIDS through tainted blood, with an explanation of the disease by a medical doctor from Sex and Family Education, 1608 13th Ave. South, Suite 112, Birmingham, AL 35205; and the National AIDS Hotline, 1-800-342-AIDS.

69. One such program adopted by many denominations is "True Love Waits," which guides youth to make commitments about sexual purity.

70. A model church policy is contained in the AIDS booklet (Texas CLC) listed above.

71. Howard W. Roberts, *Approaching the Third Millennium* (Greenville, S.C.: Smith & Helwys, 1992), 44.

72. Lewis Smedes, *How Can It Be All Right When Everything Is All Wrong?* (San Francisco: Harper & Row, 1982).

73. Resources include Robert Parham, *Loving Neighbors Across Time: A Christian Guide to Protecting the Earth* (Birmingham: New Hope, 1991); Richard D. Land and Louis A. Moore, eds., *The Earth Is the Lord's: Christians and the Environment* (Nashville: Broadman & Holman, 1992); Dick Austin, *Hope for the Land: Nature in the Bible* (Louisville: John Knox Press, 1988); and Wesley Granberg-Michaelson, *Ecology and Life: Accepting Our Environmental Responsibility* (Waco: Word Books, 1988).

74. See "An Evangelical Declaration on the Care of Creation," a statement released in 1993 by the Evangelical Environmental Network, 10 E. Lancaster Ave., Wynnewood, PA 19096-3495.

75. Discussed in a paper, "Evangelicals and the Environment," prepared by Jonathan R. Wilson of Westmont College for the Society of Christian Ethics meeting in January 1996.

76. Ibid., 6–7.

77. Parham, *Loving Neighbors*, xi.

78. "Side effects of the tube," *New Orleans Times-Picayune*, 18 September 1995, D-4.

79. "Help for Television Viewers: Awareness/Action Guide," Christian Life Commission, 901 Commerce, Nashville, TN 37203; William F. Fore, *Television and Religion: The Shaping of Faith, Values, and Culture* (Minneapolis: Augsburg Publishing House, 1987); Neal Bernard, ed., *The Mass Media* (St. Paul: Greenhaven Press, 1988).

80. Dennis M. Campbell, *Doctors, Lawyers, Ministers: Christian Ethics in Professional Practice* (Nashville: Abingdon, 1982), 31.

81. Darrell Reeck, *Ethics for the Professions: A Christian Perspective* (Minneapolis: Augsburg, 1984), 24.

82. See Joe E. Trull and James E. Carter, *Ministerial Ethics: Being a Good Minister in a Not-So-Good World* (Nashville: Broadman & Holman, 1993), 9–16. The final chapter evaluates the value of a code of ethics, including various examples in the appendices.

83. Garth M. Rosell, "Grace Under Fire," *Christianity Today*, 13 November 1995, 31.

CHAPTER SEVEN

1. Surveyed were 1,500 youth ages 12–18 from the Nazarene, Evangelical Covenant, Church of God, Free Methodist Church, Lutheran Church-Missouri Synod, Grace Brethren Church, Wesleyan Church, and the Salvation Army.

2. "Study Shows Church Kids Are Not Waiting," *Christianity Today*, 18 March 1988, 54–55.

3. Robert Byrd, "Students sexually active, survey finds," *New Orleans Times-Picayune*, 4 January 1992, 1.

4. "Adolescent Sexual Activity on Rise," *New Orleans Times-Picayune*, 18 March 1993, B-7.

5. Unless indicated otherwise, statistics are gleaned from the annual reports of the U.S. Bureau of the Census, *Statistical Abstract of the United States*, Washington, D.C.

6. James F. Childress, "Platonic Ethics," *The Westminster Dictionary of Christian Ethics*, eds. James F. Childress and John Macquarrie (Philadelphia: The Westminster Press, 1986), 477.

7. E. R. Hardy, "Asceticism," *The Westminster Dictionary*, 44.

8. Lisa Sowle Cahill, "Sexual Ethics," *The Westminster Dictionary*, 581.

9. Ibid., 582–83.

10. Stanley Grenz, *Sexual Ethics: A Biblical Perspective* (Dallas: Word Publishing Co., 1990), xvii.

11. Ibid., xix.

12. John Leo, "The Revolution Is Over," *Time*, 9 April 1984, 74.

13. Tim Stafford, *The Sexual Christian* (Wheaton, Ill.: Victor Books, 1989), 14–23.

14. Libby Potts, "Sexuality: Reflecting Who We Are," in *Understanding Christian Ethics*, ed. William M. Tillman Jr. (Nashville: Broadman, 1988), 186.

15. Tim Stafford, "Great Sex: Reclaiming a Christian Sexual Ethic," *Christianity Today*, 2 October 1987, 29–33, which provides the basic outline for this section.

16. Many biblical scholars argue the Hebrew word *adam* (related to *adamah*, "earth") could be accurately translated "earth creature," a human being without maleness or femaleness.

17. Stafford, "Great Sex," 30.

18. Walter C. Kaiser Jr., *Toward Old Testament Ethics* (Grand Rapids: Zondervan, 1983), 195–99.

19. Stafford, "Great Sex," 32.

20. Charles Gore, *The Sermon on the Mount* (London: John Murray, 1928), 64–65.

21. W. Robertson Nicoll, ed., *The Expositor's Greek Testament*, vol. 1, *The Synoptic Gospels*, by Alexander Bruce (Grand Rapids: Eerdmans, 1967), 110. See also John Jefferson Davis, *Evangelical Ethics* (Phillipsburg, N.J.: Presbyterian and Reformed Publishing Co., 1985), 98–99.

22. Stafford, "Great Sex," 32.

23. Lewis Smedes, *Sex for Christians* (Grand Rapids: Eerdmans, 1976), 128–29.

24. Stafford, "Great Sex," 32.

25. Guy Greenfield, "Paul and the Eschatological Marriage," *Southwestern Journal of Theology* 26 (Fall 1983): 32–48.

26. Andres Nygren, *Agape and Eros*, trans. Philip S. Watson (Philadelphia: Westminster Press, 1953).

27. D. H. Field, "Love," *New Dictionary of Christianity Ethics and Pastoral Theology*, eds. David J. Atkinson, David F. Field, et al. (Downers Grove, Ill.: InterVarsity Press, 1995), 12.

28. Smedes, *Sex for Christians*, 94.

29. James Nelson, "The Liberal Approach to Sexual Ethics," in *From Christ to the World: Introductory Readings in Christian Ethics*, eds. Wayne

Boulton, Thomas Kennedy, and Allen Verhey (Grand Rapid: Eerdmans, 1994), 357–58.

30. Elton and Pauline Trueblood, *The Recovery of Family Life* (New York: Harper and Row, 1953), 54.

31. William Wylie, *Human Nature and Christian Marriage* (New York: Association Press, 1958), 65.

32. Stafford, "Great Sex," 34.

33. "Lesbian writes to fight misunderstanding," *New Orleans Times-Picayune*, 30 December 1994, E-8.

34. Chaplain Ray, "What the Bible Says to Homosexuals," published by International Prison Ministry, Box 63, Dallas, TX 75221.

35. Judd Marmor, ed., *Homosexual Behavior: A Modern Reappraisal* (New York: Basic Books, 1980), 5.

36. Herant A. Katchadourian, *Fundamentals of Human Sexuality*, 4th ed. (New York: Holt, Rinehart, and Winston, 1985), 330–31.

37. A. C. Kinsey, W. B. Pomeroy, et al., *Sexual Behavior in the Human Male* (Philadelphia: Saunders, 1948). Many critics noted Kinsey's data seemed biased.

38. Paul Cameron, "A Case Against Homosexuality," *Human Life Review* 4 (1978): 20.

39. Marmor, *Homosexual Behavior*, 7.

40. Delia M. Rios, "Gays, lesbians show up in small number in polls," *New Orleans Times-Picayune*, 7 October 1994, A-6. An earlier series of studies at the University of Chicago found the gay population to be 2 to 3 percent ("Report alarms homosexuals," *New Orleans Times-Picayune*, 16 April 1993, A-10).

41. Stanton L. Jones, "The Loving Opposition: Speaking the Truth in a Climate of Hate," *Christianity Today*, 19 July 1993, 23.

42. Grenz, *Sexual Ethics*, 199.

43. Robert L. Spitzer, "The Diagnostic Status of Homosexuality in DSM-III: A Reformulation of the Issues," *American Journal of Psychiatry* 138, no. 2 (1981): 210.

44. D. S. Bailey, *Homosexuality and the Western Christian Tradition* (London: Longman, Green and Co., Ltd., 1955); John Boswell, *Christianity, Social Tolerance, and Homosexuality* (Chicago: University of Chicago Press, 1980); Robin Scroggs, *The New Testament and Homosexuality* (Philadelphia: Fortress Press, 1983).

45. Letha Scanzoni and Virginia Mollenkott, *Is the Homosexual My Neighbor?* (San Francisco: Harper & Row, 1978).

46. Albert Truesdale Jr., "AIDS: Facing the Issue of Homosexuality," in *Am I My Brother's Keeper?* ed. Michael Malloy (Kansas City: Beacon Hill Press, 1990), 61. See also Smedes, *Sex for Christians*, 62–73; Tony Campolo,

Twenty Hot Potatoes Christians Are Afraid to Touch (Dallas: Word Publishing Co., 1988), 112.

47. Victor Paul Furnish, *The Moral Teaching of Paul* (Nashville: Abingdon Press, 1985), 53.

48. Ibid., 68–69.

49. See Truesdale, "Facing the Issue of Homosexuality," 74–87; Grenz, *Sexual Ethics*, 204; and Davis, *Evangelical Ethics*, 114–22.

50. Bailey, *Homosexuality and the Western Christian Tradition*, 4.

51. Don Williams, *The Bond That Breaks: Will Homosexuality Split the Church?* (Los Angeles: BIM, 1978), 47.

52. Ibid., 57.

53. John Hart and Diane Richardson, eds., *The Theory and Practice of Homosexuality* (London: Routledge and Kegan Paul, 1981), 5.

54. Katchadourian, *Fundamentals*, 349–53.

55. Malloy, *Am I My Brother's Keeper?* 62–65; Davis, *Evangelical Ethics*, 110–11; "Born or Bred," *Newsweek*, 24 February 1992, 46–53; and Stanton Jones, "Homosexuality According to Science," in *The Crisis of Homosexuality*, ed. J. Isamu Yamamoto (Wheaton: Victor Books, 1990), 103–14.

56. Elizabeth R. Moberly, *Homosexuality: A New Christian Ethic* (Greenwood, S.C.: Attic Press, 1983), 2–6. Another Christian psychiatrist, Dr. Joseph Nicolosi, espouses this approach which he calls "Reparitive Therapy."

57. Evelyn Hooker, "Sexual Behavior: Homosexuality," *International Encyclopedia of the Social Sciences*, ed. David L. Sills (New York: MacMillan, 1968), 14:225.

58. Arthur Caplin, "Gay Ethics: Biology No Basis," *Saint Paul Pioneer Press*, 14 October 1992, D-1.

59. Jeffrey S. Siker, "How to Decide? Homosexual Christians, the Bible and Gentile Inclusion," *Theology Today* 51 (July 1994): 222–23.

60. Grenz, *Sexual Ethics*, 219–20.

61. Bailey, *Homosexuality and the Western Christian Tradition*, 168.

62. Jones, "The Loving Opposition," 24–25.

63. See Tim Stafford, "Ed Dobson Loves Homosexuals," *Christianity Today*, 19 July 1993, 22, for a story about the ministry of one pastor and his church; and Guy Charles, "The Church and the Homosexual," in *The Secrets of our Sexuality* (Waco, Tex.: Word Books, 1976).

64. See Bob Davis, "The Exodus Story: The Growth of Ex-Gay Ministry"; and Ronald Enroth, "Ministry Outside the Church," in *Crisis of Homosexuality*, 45–59, 77–87.

65. Tamar Lewin, "Ozzie, Harriet are just a myth, new report says," *New Orleans Times-Picayune*, 30 May 1995, A-7.

66. Statistics gleaned from the annual reports of the U.S. Bureau of the Census, *Statistical Abstract of the United States*, Washington, D.C.; and Mark Winfield, "America headed for anarchy or revival, Barna warns," *Baptist Press*, 28 February 1996, 3–4.

67. Joann S. Lublin, "Family Values," *The Wall Street Journal*, 28 December 1995, A-1.

68. Tamar Lewin, "Surprise! Sex steady, best in marriage," *New Orleans Times-Picayune*, 7 October 1994, A-1.

69. Terri Lackey, "Adultery can involve other than just sexual infidelity," *Baptist Message*, 19 October 1995, 4.

70. "Adultery Still Exception, Not Rule," *Christianity Today*, 22 November 1993, 42.

71. Howard A. Snyder, "Will Promise Keepers Keep Their Promises," *Christianity Today*, 14 November 1994, 20.

72. Terri Lackey, "True Love Waits Goes Through the Roof in Atlanta," *Baptist Messenger*, 7 March 1996, 13. Information is available at 1-800-LUV-WAIT.

73. Used elsewhere in Scripture, mostly in reference to God, the word does not connote subordination or inferiority, but strength.

74. Initially God created "the earth creature," named only with the generic term for all humankind, *ha adam*, indicating relation to the soil (*ha adamah*), as translated by Phyllis Trible, *God and the Rhetoric of Sexuality* (Philadelphia: Fortress Press, 1978), 16–21.

75. Henlee H. Barnette, *Introducing Christian Ethics* (Nashville: Broadman Press, 1961), 112.

76. John Stott, *Decisive Issues Facing Christians Today* (Grand Rapids: Fleming H. Revell, 1990), 289.

77. E. Neufield, *Ancient Hebrew Marriage Laws* (New York: Longman Green and Co., 1944), 176.

78. Herbert Danby, trans., *The Mishna* (Oxford: Oxford University Press, 1985), Gittin 9:3.

79. John Jefferson Davis, *Evangelical Ethics*, 95.

80. According to Davis, *Evangelical Ethics*, 95, the strict school of Rabbi Shammai taught that a wife who went out with her hair unbound, spinning in the street or talking to a strange man, was guilty of immodest behavior.

81. *The Mishna*, Gittin 10. Both Philo (De. spec. leg. 3,30) and Josephus (Ant. 4.253) knew of the Hillelite view and agreed with it.

82. William Barclay, *The Daily Study Bible Series*, vol. 2, *The Gospel of Matthew* (Philadelphia: The Westminster Press, 1975), 196.

83. R. C. H. Lenski, *The Interpretation of St. Matthew's Gospel* (Columbus, Ohio: Wartburg Press, 1943), 230–35, notes the English translations

tend to overlook the passive forms of the verbs *moicheuthenai* and *moichatai* in 5:32 and 19:9.

84. The variations in Mark's account are explained in part by the fact that Jesus' words occur "in the house" (v. 10) and that Mark's Gospel was written to a Gentile audience, where the legal status of women was somewhat different.

85. Nicoll, *Expositor's Greek Testament*, 110.

86. The explanations for its omission include: (1) an interpolation (later addition)—the verse is a class B or C reading, meaning it is in some of the older manuscripts, but not in others; (2) an addition by Matthew to tone down or clarify Jesus' words; (3) a redaction, part of the editing process; (4) statements made by Jesus on more than one occasion; or (5) words actually spoken by Jesus, but Mark and others chose not to include them, assuming everyone understood sexual unchastity was grounds for divorce. See Barnette, *Introducuing Christians Ethics* 115-16.

87. Carroll D. Osburn, "The Present Indicative in Matthew 19:9," *Restoration Quarterly* 24 (1981): 193-203. An example of the gnomic present is found in Matthew 7:17, "Every good tree bears (*poiei*) good fruit"; i.e., it is characteristic of a good tree to bear good fruit, though not continuously throughout the year.

88. Clifton J. Allen, ed., *The Broadman Bible Commentary*, vol. 10, *Acts-1 Corinthians*, by Raymond Bryan Brown (Nashville: Broadman Press, 1970), 330.

89. Archibald Robertson and Alfred Plummer, *The First Epistle of Saint Paul to the Corinthians* (Edinburgh: T. & T. Clark, 1914), 140.

90. Note the similar language of Paul in affirming the right of a widow to remarry; she is "bound" to her husband only while he lives—after he dies, she is "released" to remarry.

91. Davis, *Evangelical Ethics*, 102, who himself disagrees with this view.

92. See *Apostolic Constitutions*, 6.17 and *Apostolic Canons*, 16 (17).

93. Davis, *Evangelical Ethics*, 104-105; see also Ed Glasscock, "The Husband of One Wife Requirement in 1 Tim. 3:2," *Bibliotheca Sacra* 140, no. 559 (1983): 249-253.

94. This section is an adaptation of the author's article "Is the Head of the House at Home? (Eph. 5:21-6:9)," *Theological Educator* 54 (Fall 1996): 83-94.

95. The theme of the conference and the title of the workbook, led by the director of Great Hills Ladies' Retreat Ministry from Austin, Texas.

96. "The Joy of Submission," a workbook published by the Allendale Baptist Church, Austin, Texas.

97. John and Letha Scanzoni, "Changes in Marital Gender Roles—Authority to Affirmation," in *The Secrets of Our Sexuality*, ed. Gary Collins (Waco: Word Books, 1976), 22.

98. Letha Scanzoni and Nancy Hardesty, *All We're Meant to Be* (Waco: Word Books, 1974), 110.

99. See Ebbie C. Smith, *Syllabus for the Study of Biblical Ethics* (Fort Worth: Southwestern Baptist Theological Seminary, 1984), 186-205, for examples of the authority-submission pattern (Bill Gothard, Marabel Morgan, Tim LeHaye, Jay E. Adams, Larry Christenson, George Knight III, Jack R. Taylor, C. C. Ryrie) and the equality-partnership pattern (D. S. Bailey, Howard and Charlotte Clinebell, Dwight H. Small, Gladys M. Hunt, Paul K. Jewett, David and Vera Mace, John and Letha Scanzoni).

100. James R. Beck, "Is There a Head of the House in the Home?" *Priscilla Papers* 2 (Fall 1988): 1.

101. An extensive discussion of this subject can be found in chapter 8, "Human Equality: Gender and Race," under the topic of "The New Testament World."

102. Cited in William Barclay, *The Letter to the Galatians and Ephesians* (Philadelphia: Westminster Press, 1956), 199-200.

103. Ibid., 202.

104. Beck, "Head of the House," 61-63.

105. John Howell, *Equality and Submission in Marriage* (Nashville: Broadman Press, 1979), 57-62.

106. See "The Battle of the Lexicons," *Christianity Today*, 16 January 1987, 44.

107. Gilbert Bilezikian, *Beyond Sex Roles* (Grand Rapids: Baker Book House, 1990), 215-52.

108. Berkeley and Alvera Mickelsen, "The 'Head' of the Epistles," *Christianity Today*, 20 February 1981, 20. The comprehensive lexicon of the Greek language compiled by Liddell, Scott, Jones, and McKenzie lists nearly twenty-five possible meanings of *kephale* ("head") but does not include our common English usage of "authority over," "leader," "director," or "superior." The commonly used lexicon of Arndt and Gingrich also gives little or no support for such a meaning.

109. Ibid., 21.

110. Mickelsen, *"Head' of the Epistles,"* 21-22; Bilezikian, *Beyond Sex Roles*, 23.

111. Mickelsen, 22. See also Richard S. Cervin, "Does *kephale* ("head") Mean 'Source' or 'Authority Over' in Greek Literature?: A Rebuttal," doctoral paper, University of Illinois; published by Christians for Biblical Equality, St. Paul, Minn.

112. Joannis Chrysostom, *S.P.N. Joannis Chrysostomi, Archiepiscopi Constantinopolitani, Opera Omnia Quae Existant*, Patrologiae Cursus Completus, Series Graece, ed. J. P. Migne, no. 61 (Paris: Garnier Fratres, 1862), 215-16.

113. Bilezikian, "Hierarchist and Egalitarian Inculturations," *Journal of the Evangelical Theological Society* (December 1987), 424.

114. Frank Stagg, *New Testament Theology* (Nashville: Broadman Press, 1962), 298.

115. See Diana S. Richmond Garland and Diane L. Pancoast, *The Church's Ministry with Families* (Dallas: Word Publishing, 1990).

CHAPTER EIGHT

1. Cited in a news story, *Baptist Standard*, 16 June 1993, 3.

2. Ronald Preston, "Equality," *The Westminster Dictionary of Christian Ethics*, ed. James F. Childress and John Macquarrie (Philadelphia: The Westminster Press, 1986), 199-200.

3. "Christians for Biblical Equality," published by CBE at 122 W. Franklin Ave., Suite 218, Minneapolis, MN 55404.

4. Advertisement in *Christianity Today*, 13 January 1989, 40-41, which lists the Council at P.O. Box 1173, Wheaton, IL 60187.

5. Ibid. The statement also included a list of thirty Council members and twenty-one Board of Reference persons.

6. John Piper and Wayne Grudem, eds., *Recovering Biblical Manhood and Womanhood* (Wheaton: Crossway Books, 1991). Only 3 of the 26 essays and 25 of the 566 pages are by women.

7. Timothy C. Morgan, "RE-Imagining Labeled 'Reckless,'" *Christianity Today*, 18 July 1994, 49.

8. James R. Edwards, "Earthquake in the Mainline," *Christianity Today*, 14 November 1994, 38-43, who asked, "What other language besides 'heresy' is appropriate where the Incarnation and Trinity were derided, where Scripture was contradicted, and where a goddess named Sophia was actively promoted?"

9. Katherine Kersten, "How the Feminist Establishment Hurts Women," *Christianity Today*, 20 June 1994, 22.

10. Kersten, 22, who notes Simone de Beauvoir's 1954 book, *The Second Sex*, was the first indicator of the new feminism, followed by Betty Friedan's *The Feminine Mystique*, Germaine Greer's *The Female Eunuch*, and Kate Millett's *Sexual Politics*.

11. Margaret A. Farley, "Feminist Ethics," *Westminster Dictionary*, 229-31.

12. See Elizabeth Achtemeier's "Why God Is Not Mother," *Christianity Today*, 16 August 1993, 16-23.

13. Recent works representing evangelical feminism include Sheri Adams, *What the Bible Really Says About Women* (Macon, Ga.: Smith & Helwys, 1994); Rebecca Merrill Groothuis, *Women Caught in the Conflict: The Culture War Between Traditionalism and Feminism* (Grand Rapids: Baker Books, 1994); Stanley Grenz, *Women in the Church: A Biblical Theology of Women in Ministry* (Downers Grove, Ill.: InterVarsity Press, 1995); and Rebecca Merrill Grothuis, *Good News for Woman: A Biblical Picture of Gender Equality* (Grand Rapids: Baker Books, 1977).

14. Cited in a news report by Wesley G. Pippert, *Christianity Today*, 4 May 1979, 48.

15. Willard M. Swartley in *Slavery, Sabbath, War, and Women* (Scottdale, Pa.: Herald Press, 1983) used these four case issues to teach biblical interpretation.

16. Ruth A. Tucker, *Women in the Maze* (Downers Grove, Ill.: InterVarsity Press, 1992), 35-36. Tucker added that although the Danvers Statement affirmed the first couple were "equal before God as persons," a drafter of the statement explained that in authority relationships "it is absolutely appropriate to say that the man images God and that the woman does not."

17. Bruce Metzger notes in the introduction to the NRSV that "in references to men and women, masculine-oriented language should be eliminated as far as this can be done without altering passages that reflect the historical situation of ancient patriarchal culture" (ix).

18. Morar M. Murray-Hayes, "Emancipation of Women," *Encyclopedia of Biblical and Christian Ethics*, ed. R. K. Harrison (Nashville: Thomas Nelson, 1987), 129-31. Leon Kass also made this point in "Man and Woman: An Old Story," *First Things*, November 1991, 17.

19. Barth contends that one cannot say "Man" without having to say male or female and also male and female, *Church Dogmatics* 3, no. 2 (Edinburgh: T. & T. Clark, 1956), 280.

20. Paul K. Jewett, *Man as Male and Female* (Grand Rapids: Eerdmans, 1975), 24.

21. John R. W. Stott, "Homosexual Marriage," *Christianity Today*, 22 November 1985, 21.

22. Raymond C. Ortland Jr., "Male-Female Equality and Male Headship," in *Biblical Manhood and Womanhood*, 102, 104.

23. Tucker, *Women in the Maze*, 37-38.

24. Shari Shubert, "Women's Roles: What Does the Bible Say," *Word and Way*, 25 February 1993, 7. This interview of six conservative seminary professors also noted the word translated "rule" means "iron-fisted domination," the same word used to describe the rule of Pharoah in Exodus.

25. Evelyn and Frank Stagg, *Women in the World of Jesus* (Philadelphia: Westminster Press, 1978), 55.

26. William Barclay, *The Letters to Timothy, Titus, and Philemon* (Philadelphia: Westminster Press, 1975), 66.

27. Ibid., 67.

28. William Barclay, *The Letters to the Galatians and Ephesians* (Philadelphia: Westminster, 1954), 201.

29. Barclay, *Letters to Timothy*, 67, where he notes they were called the *Melissae*, which means "the bees."

30. Charles C. Ryrie, "Women, Status Of," *Baker's Dictionary of Christian Ethics*, ed. Carl F. H. Henry (Grand Rapids: Baker, 1973), 712.

31. The majority of the best Greek manuscripts omit John 7:53–8:11; however, many authorities believe the story is authentic and was added because of its lasting value.

32. Letha Scanzoni and Nancy Hardesty, *All We're Meant to Be* (Waco: Word Books, 1974), 37.

33. Significantly, both Greek terms are used in 1 Timothy 3:1–13 to describe the ministry of pastors/bishops and deacons.

34. A. T. Robertson, *Word Pictures in the New Testament* (Nashville: Broadman Press, 1931), 4:425–26.

35. See Manfred T. Brauch, *Hard Sayings of Paul* (Downers Grove: InterVarsity Press, 1989).

36. See Richard and Catherine Kroeger, *I Suffer Not a Woman: Rethinking 1 Timothy 2:11–15 in Light of Ancient Evidence* (Grand Rapids: Baker, 1992), and Andreas J. Kostenberger, Thomas R. Schreiner, and H. Scott Baldwin, eds., *Women in the Church: A Fresh Analysis of 1 Timothy 2:9–15* (Grand Rapids: Baker Books, 1995) for contrasting viewpoints.

37. See "The Problem of Cultural Relativity" in Gordon Fee and Douglas Stuart, *How to Read the Bible for All Its Worth* (Grand Rapids: Zondervan, 1982), 65–70.

38. Rosemary Ruether thinks that even more significant than Jesus' treatment of women and violation of Jewish taboos was His model of ministry, "The waiting on tables, the lowly role of women and servants, . . ." *New Women New Earth* (New York: Seabury Press, 1975), 65.

39. Philip Schaff, *History of the Christian Church* (Grand Rapids: Eerdmans, 1979), 2:398.

40. "Women's Ordination: The Hidden Tradition," A BBC-TV Production in association with Reel Spirit Productions, 55 min., 1992, videocassette.

41. Murray-Hayes, "Emancipation of Women," 130.

42. Tucker, *Women in the Maze*, 155–56.

43. Ibid., 160–61.

44. See Margaret Troutt's *The General Was a Lady* (Nashville: A. J. Holman Co., 1980).

45. Murray-Hayes, "Emancipation of Women," 130.

46. T. B. Maston, 20 September 1973, Broadman Ministers' Tape, Baptist Sunday School Board, Nashville, Tennessee.

47. Position paper on "Puzzles" written by Diane C. Prayter in an Introduction to Christian Ethics class at New Orleans Baptist Theological Seminary.

48. *Statistical Abstract of the U.S.—1991*, Washington, D.C.: U.S. Bureau of the Census, 385.

49. "Snapshot of a Changing America," *Time*, 2 September 1985, 16.

50. Stephan A. Grunlan, *Marriage and the Family: A Christian Perspective* (Grand Rapids: Zondervan, 1984), 138-39.

51. Ibid.

52. Kroeger, *I Suffer Not a Woman*, 119-25. For a traditionalist interpretation, see Andreas J. Kostenberger, et al.

53. Richard and Catherine Kroeger, "May Women Teach?" *The Reformed Journal* 30 (October 1980): 14-18.

54. Quoted by Richard Ostling in "The Second Reformation," *Time*, 23 November 1992, 53.

55. Ibid.

56. Mark Winfield, "Baptist women gaining ground in ministry roles," *Word and Way*, 25 February 1993, 5.

57. Gilbert Bilezikian, "No Limits to Ministry," *Discipleship Journal* (September/October 1993), 71.

58. Ibid.

59. Marjorie Warkentin, *Ordination: A Biblical-Historical View* (Grand Rapids: Eerdmans, 1982), 41.

60. Quoted by Glen Kehrein in "Breaking Down Walls," *Focus on the Family*, December 1994, 12.

61. Billy Graham, "Racism and the Evangelical Church," *Christianity Today*, 4 October 1993, 27.

62. A news story on the NBC *Today* program of 23 April 1996.

63. Gunnar Myrdal, *An American Dilemma* (New York: Harper & Bros., 1944), xivii.

64. F. W. Bridger, "Race," *New Dictionary of Christian Ethics and Pastoral Theology*, eds. David Atkinson, David Field, et al. (Downers Grove, Ill.: InterVarsity Press, 1995), 716.

65. Classification of major racial groups range from nine (Stanley Garn) to thirteen (W. C. Boyd) to thirty (C. S. Coon) to thirty-four (Theodosius Dobzhansky), as noted by George Simpson and J. Milton Yinger in *Racial and Cultural Minorities* (New York: Harper & Row, 1965), 37.

66. Robert S. Byrd, "Discoveries Contradict Notion of Separate Races," *New Orleans Times-Picayune*, 13 October 1996, A-4, who notes, "Thanks to spectacular advances in molecular biology and genetics, most scientists now reject the concept of race as a valid way to divide human beings into separate groups."

67. Ashley Montagu, "The Concept of Race," *American Anthropologist*, October 1962, 925.

68. D. Elizabeth Thoms, "Racism," *Encyclopedia of Biblical and Christian Ethics*, 342.

69. Henlee H. Barnette, *Introducing Christian Ethics* (Nashville: Broadman Press, 1961), 21-22.

70. Simpson and Yinger, *Racial and Cultural Minorities*, 13.

71. Ibid., 14.

72. Cited by Barnette, 129.

73. Thomas Sowell, *Ethnic America: A History* (New York: Basic Books, Inc., 1981), 185, who notes that by the middle of the seventeenth century, 10,000 slaves per year were transported to America, reaching a peak of 60,000 per year a century later.

74. David Brion Davies, *The Problem of Slavery in Western Cultures* (Cornell University Press, 1966), 31.

75. Commenting on the evil of slavery, John Stott notes the horror of it was that "it regarded adult men and women as tools, animals or children" (*Deciding Issues Facing Christians Today* [Grand Rapids: Baker Book House, 1995], 210).

76. The speech is recorded in Coretta Scott King's *My Life with Martin Luther King, Jr.* (London: Hodder & Stoughton, 1969), 249.

77. Cited by Stott, 212.

78. James H. Cone, *Martin and Malcolm and America: A Dream or a Nightmare* (Maryknoll, N.Y.: Orbis, 1991), ix.

79. "Affirmative Action," which requires an appropriate quota of minorities be employed to compensate for past deficiencies in education and opportunity, is under serious political attack.

80. "Losing Ground," *Newsweek*, 6 April 1992, 20-22.

81. In March of 1991, during an arrest, Rodney King (a black) was beaten by white officers of the Los Angeles Police Department. The trial and acquittal of all of the policemen in 1992 precipitated rioting, looting, destruction of property, and attacks upon passing motorists in south Los Angeles, all of which was witnessed by millions around the country via television.

82. M. F. Ashley Montagu, *Man's Most Dangerous Myth: The Fallacy of Race*, 5th ed. (Oxford: Oxford University Press, 1974), 420.

83. For a full discussion of the contention, see T. B. Maston's *The Bible and Race* (Nashville: Broadman Press, 1959), 105-17.

84. See R. E. O. White, *Christian Ethics* (Atlanta: John Knox Press, 1981), 57-60, for the efforts of the early church to come to terms with slavery.

85. Maston, *The Bible and Race*, 12.

86. Ibid., 16-17.

87. Ibid., 53-57, for a key chapter, "You Are a Samaritan."

88. Donald R. Potts, "Samaria, Samaritans," *Holman Bible Dictionary*, ed. Trent Butler (Nashville: Holman Bible Publishers, 1991), 1225.

89. David Smith, *The Days of His Flesh* (London: Hodder & Stoughton, n.d.), 73-74.

90. Jews normally did not talk with a woman in public, not even a wife, sister, or mother. Likewise, pious Jews did not socialize with sinners. However, the greatest wonder of this conversation was that Jesus conversed with a Samaritan.

91. A. T. Robertson, *Word Pictures in the New Testament* (Nashville: S. S. Board of the S.B.C., 1932), 5:155.

92. Documentation of the entire story is contained in a publication, "The Birmingham Confession," produced by the Baptist Peace Fellowship, 499 Patterson St., Memphis, TN 38111.

93. Ibid. The Baptist Peace Fellowship of North America subsequently developed "The Birmingham Confession," a statement delivered to the Sixteenth Street Baptist Church on July 31, 1993.

94. John Dart, "Christians repent for old sins," *New Orleans Times-Picayune*, 15 July 1995, D-10.

95. "Pentecostals Renounce Racism," *Christianity Today*, 12 December 1994, 58.

96. *1995 Southern Baptist Convention Annual* (Nashville: Executive Committee of the SBC, 1995), 80-81.

97. A call from Baptist World Alliance leaders in 1995 ["Cancer of racism threatening society," *Baptist Message*, 4 January 1996, 1].

98. "Will Promise Keepers Keep Their Promises?" *Christianity Today*, 14 November 1994, 20.

99. The story is told by Pulitzer Prize winner Robert Coles in the illustrated children's book, *The Story of Ruby Bridges* (New York: Scholastic Inc., 1995). Her walk also inspired the 1964 Norman Rockwell painting, *The Problem We All Live With*. Today Ruby Bridges Hall works in the same school, encouraging parental involvement in education and directs the Ruby Bridges Educational Foundation.

100. John C. Raines, "Righteous Resistance and Martin Luther King, Jr.," *The Christian Century*, 18 January 1984, 53.

101. Martin Luther King, Jr., *Why We Can't Wait* (New York: Mentor Books, 1964), 76-95.

CHAPTER NINE

1. John F. Kilner, Nigel M. de S. Cameron, and David L. Schiedermayer, eds., *Bioethics and the Future of Medicine: A Christian Appraisal* (Grand Rapids: Eerdmans, 1995), ix.

2. V. R. Potter, *Bioethics: Bridge to the Future* (Englewood Cliffs, N.J.: Prentice-Hall), 1971.

3. James F. Childress, "Bioethics," *The Westminster Dictionary of Christian Ethics*, eds. James F. Childress and John Macquarrie (Philadelphia: Westminster Press, 1986), 61, who observes that the *Encyclopedia of Bioethics* (1978) also adopts this definition.

4. Paul Ramsey, "The Nature of Medical Ethics," in *The Teaching of Medical Ethics*, eds. Robert Veatch, Willard Gaylin, and Councilman Morgan (Hastings-on-Hudson, N.Y.: Institute of Society, Ethics and the Life Sciences, 1971), 14.

5. Ibid., 14–28.

6. Thomas A. Shannon, ed. *Bioethics: Revised* (Ramsey, N.J.: Paulist Press, 1976, 1981), 1.

7. Ibid.

8. The 50,000 to 100,000 genes that make up the human genome are the genetic endowment that lies in the nucleus of every human cell. To study 100,000 of these genes, 23 times 2 of those chromosomes, and three billion of another of these 'letters,' is to study what goes on in each of the body's three trillion cells, the encyclopedia-length recipe for making a human being.

9. Dr. Victor A. McKusick of Johns Hopkins, quoted by Martin E. Marty, "The Human Genome Project," *Context* 22 (1 December 1990): 1.

10. Ibid., 3–5, where Marty also discusses the areas directly impacted: eugenics, control and privacy, justice, international affairs, law, abortion, insurance, and employment discrimination.

11. David Neff, "The Eugenic Temptation," *Christianity Today*, 19 November 1990, 23.

12. Daniel B. McGee, "Issues of Life and Death," *Understanding Christian Ethics*, ed. William M. Tillman Jr. (Nashville: Broadman Press, 1988), 227–234.

13. Ibid., 228.

14. Marty, "Human Genome Project," 3.

15. McGee, "Life and Death," 229–34.

16. R. A. Higginson in "Ethics of Medical Care" [*New Dictionary of Christian Ethics and Pastoral Theology*, ed. David Atkinson, et al. (Downers Grove, Ill.: InterVarsity Press, 1995), 93] observes that in its original form the oath involved swearing by pagan gods, but it has proved readily adapt-

able to other religious settings and has had enduring effect upon Western medicine.

17. Edmund Pelegrino, "The Metamorphosis of Medical Ethics," *Journal of the American Medical Association* 269 (3 March 1993): 1158-62.

18. Based on Aristotelian views about the nature of the soul and the time of "ensoulment," later Christian theologians like Thomas Aquinas believed the embryo was "animated" in successive stages from vegetative to animal to human soul.

19. Higginson, "Ethics of Medical Care," 93-94.

20. Daniel Callahan, "Religion and the Secularization of Bioethics," *Hastings Center Report: Special Supplement* 20 (July/August): 2-4.

21. Joseph Fletcher, *Morals and Medicine* (Princeton: Princeton University Press, 1954).

22. Allen Verhey and Stephen E. Lammers, "Rediscovering Religious Traditions in Medical Ethics," *Theological Voices in Medical Ethics* (Grand Rapids: Eerdmans, 1993), 1.

23. Leroy Walters, "Religion and the Renaissance of Medical Ethics," in *Theology and Bioethics: Exploring the Foundation and Frontiers*, ed. Earl E. Shelp (Dordrecht, Holland: D. Reidel Publishing Co., 1985), 3.

24. David H. Smith, "On Paul Ramsey: A Covenant-Centered Ethic for Medicine," in *Theological Voices*, 7-29.

25. Allen Verhay, "On James M. Gustafson: Can Medical Ethics Be Christian?" in *Theological Voices*, 30-56.

26. Immanuel Jacobovits, *Jewish Medical Ethics* (New York: Block, 1959).

27. Verhay and Lammers, *Theological Voices*, 2-3, list numerous Protestant, Roman Catholic, and Jewish contributors to the religious tradition concerning issues of medical care.

28. Callahan, "Secularization of Bioethics," 3.

29. Verhay and Lammers, *Theological Voices*, 3.

30. Callahan, "Secularization of Bioethics," 4.

31. Jeffrey Stout, *Ethics after Babel: The Language of Morals and Their Discontents* (Boston: Beacon Press, 1988), 60-81.

32. Alasdair MacIntyre, *After Virtue: A Study in Moral Theory* (Notre Dame: University of Notre Dame Press, 1981), 49-75.

33. Verhay and Lammers, *Theological Voices*, 4-5.

34. Ibid., 2.

35. Loreen A. Herwaldt, "Daniel versus Saul: Toward a Distinctly Christian Biomedical Ethics," in *Bioethics and the Future of Medicine*, 30.

36. Paul Ramsey, *The Patient as Person* (New Haven: Yale University Press, 1970), xi.

37. Nigel M. de S. Cameron, "The Christian Stake in Bioethics: The State of the Question," in *Bioethics and the Future of Medicine*, 5.

38. Ibid.

39. James M. Gustafson, *Theology and Christian Ethics* (Philadelphia: United Church Press, 1974), 141.

40. Ian Thompson, M.D., of Edinburgh, Scotland, argues that the personal moral responsibility of the doctors in making difficult moral decisions in clinical practice makes moral intervention from church or state, lay groups, or commercial interests "both irrelevant and impertinent" ["The Implications of Medical Ethics," *Journal of Medical Ethics* 2 (1976): 14].

41. Paul D. Simmons, *Birth and Death: Bioethical Decision Making* (Philadelphia: The Westminster Press, 1983), 28-29.

42. Higginson, "Ethics of Medical Care," 97. For example, see "What the Bible Teaches about Abortion" [Nashville: Christian Life Commission of the SBC, 1989] for numerous examples of the misuse of texts.

43. Ibid.

44. Edward Leroy Long Jr., *A Survey of Recent Christian Ethics* (New York: Oxford University Press, 1982), 101-4. See also Tom L. Beauchamp and James F. Childress, *Principles of Biomedical Ethics* (New York: Oxford University Press, 1979), 236.

45. Herwaldt, "Daniel versus Saul," 30-31.

46. See Henlee H. Barnette, *Exploring Medical Ethics* (Macon, Ga.: Mercer University Press, 1982), 22, who explains this methodology which he terms "Contextual Principled-Agapism." Others identified by some as principlists are T. B. Maston and Paul Ramsey.

47. Barnette, 26-30, notes the "Golden Rule" is really a "Golden Principle" for medical ethics.

48. Higginson, "Ethics of Medical Care," 94.

49. P. Helm, "Double Effect," in *Dictionary of Christian Ethics*, 318.

50. D. W. Vere, "Death and Dying," in *Dictionary of Christian Ethics*, 284-85.

51. Higginson, "Ethics of Medical Care," 95.

52. D. J. Atkinson, "Life, Health, and Death," in *Dictionary of Christian Ethics*, 87-92.

53. Higginson, "Ethics of Medical Care," 95.

54. E. D. Cook, "Consent," in *Dictionary of Christian Ethics*, 252-53.

55. Higginson, "Ethics of Medical Care," 98.

56. P. Helm, "Confidentiality," in *Dictionary of Christian Ethics*, 248-49.

57. Smith, "Paul Ramsey," in *Theological Voices*, 24-28.

58. Higginson, "Ethics of Medical Care," 96.

59. Ramsey, *The Patient as Person*, 160-64.

60. Higginson, "Ethics of Medical Care," 96.

61. Ibid., 98.

62. Higginson (98) lists the four most common models of justice: the egalitarian, the differential, the meritocratic, and the redistributive.

63. P. Helm, "Abortion," in *Encyclopedia of Biblical and Christian Ethics*, ed. R. K. Harrison (Nashville: Thomas Nelson, 1987), 1.

64. Ibid., where Helm described these methods: crude insertion of a rod, an electric current or drugs, curettage (scraping of the womb), "suction" method, hysterotomy, and the saline method.

65. "American Abortion Rates Down—Again," *Baptist Message*, 23 January 1997, 10. The article notes the number of abortions per one thousand women also dropped to twenty-one.

66. David E. Early, "Late-term abortions debated," *New Orleans Times-Picayune*, 24 September 1995, A-16. In congressional hearings over a controversial bill that would ban late-term abortions (H.R. 1833 and S.B. 939), estimates ranged from six hundred to thousands.

67. C. J. Cadoux, *The Early Church and the World* (Edinburgh: T. & T. Clark, 1925), 445. Although the Greeks permitted abortion by whatever methods were available, the Hippocratic Oath forbade physicians to procure them.

68. Foy D. Valentine, "Critical Issues: Abortion" (Nashville: Christian Life Commission of the S.B.C., 1985), 6–7. The orthodox tradition does allow a qualified permission for abortion (*Mishnah* of Tractate Oholoth [7:6]).

69. Cadoux, *Early Church*, 283, 599.

70. Aristotle's view that human life began with the infusion of the soul into the body was the basis for two theological positions: Tertullian upheld "creationism," the belief that the soul came into existence at the same time as the body; Thomas Aquinas thought the soul was infused into the body at forty days for the male and ninety days for the female [Valentine, "Critical Issues," 7–8].

71. The principle of "double effect" does allow an abortion to save the life of the mother, but the choice between the life of the mother and fetus is considered the same, some insisting two deaths are better than one murder. A mother who refuses abortion and dies may be granted the reward of "martyrdom" by the church.

72. E. Clinton Gardner, "The Sacredness of All Human Life," *Engage/Social Action*, February 1974, 18.

73. Paul T. Jersild and Dale A. Johnson, eds., *Moral Issues and Christian Response*, 5th ed. (Orlando: Harcourt Brace Jovanovich, 1993), 337.

74. For a full discussion of the various views on personhood of the fetus, see Lewis B. Smedes, *Mere Morality* (Grand Rapids: Eerdmans, 1983), 127–34.

75. In the case of identical twins (1 in 300), genetic individuality does not exist for up to fourteen days, and it is possible for twins or triplets to be recombined into one individual, which is why research in embryology and infertility uses fourteen days as a cut-off point for experimentation on embryos.

76. Cook, 131.

77. Shirley L. Barron, "Searching for Life's Beginning," *Christianity Today*, 11 November 1991, 41.

78. Cook, 132.

79. Patricia Wilson-Kastner, Beatrice Blair, and Paul D. Simmons, "Abortion: A Pro-Choice Perspective," in *Moral Issues and Christian Response* (4th ed.), 352-53.

80. John Jefferson Davis, *Abortion and the Christian* (Phillipsburg, N.J.: Presbyterian and Reformed Publishing Co., 1984), 40-62; John MacArthur, "The Biblical Position on Abortion," *Masterpiece*, March/April 1991, 18.

81. Smedes, *Mere Morality*, 127-28, who also points out that the passages are not meant to be scientific statements—Psalm 139:15; Jeremiah 1:5; and Job 10:10 ("milk" means semen) are metaphoric poetry.

82. Davis, *Abortion and the Christian*, 49-52, discusses all positions including a third view by Meredith Kline: a case of negligent manslaughter.

83. J. H. Hertz, *The Pentateuch and Haftorahs* (London: Soncino Press, 1978), 309, 527.

84. Bob Terry, "The Bible—A Witness to Life," a paper delivered at the Christian Life Conference, Nashville, Tenn., 31 August 1987.

85. Cook, 132.

86. Dietrich Bonhoeffer, *Ethics* (New York: Macmillan, 1955), 176.

87. Cardinal Bernardin of Chicago is credited with the term "seamless garment ethic," which proposes a true "pro-life" position on all life and death issues: abortion, euthanasia, war, capital punishment, and hunger. Evangelical leaders of JustLife (Ron Sider, et al.) also embrace this ethic.

88. *Good Morning America*, ABC Television, 11 February 1996.

89. Jersild and Johnson, "Euthanasia/Suicide," 356.

90. Nigel M. de S. Cameron, "Euthanasia," in *Dictionary of Christian Ethics*, 357.

91. P. D. Toon, "Euthanasia," in *Encyclopedia of Biblical and Christian Ethics*, 138.

92. Already Dr. Jack Kevorkian has received national publicity over his "death machine," which allows the terminal patient to assist in his or her own death [See Dr. Jack Kevorkian, *Prescription Medicine: The Goodness of Planned Death* (Buffalo: Prometheus Books, 1991)].

93. Cameron, "Euthanasia," 357.

94. During the 1980s the medical profession in Holland supported voluntary euthanasia. Though not formally legalized in that country, the practice of inducing death through chemical toxins has general medical and social acceptance there.

95. Cameron, "Euthanasia," 358.

96. Richard Doerflinger, "Assisted Suicide: Pro-Choice or Anti-Life?" in *Moral Issues and Christian Response*, 363-70.

97. Cameron, "Euthanasia," 357, who points to the modern hospice movement as an example.

98. McGee, "Life and Death," 240.

99. Smedes, *Mere Morality*, 154.

100. Robert N. Wennberg, *Terminal Choices* (Grand Rapids: Eerdmans, 1989), 229.

101. See Thomas A. Shannon, *What Are They Saying about Genetic Engineering?* (New York: Paulist Press, 1985).

102. D. G. Jones, "Genetic Engineering," *Dictionary of Christian Ethics*, 403-4.

103. Barnette, *Exploring Medical Ethics*, 92, from which many of the definitions are gleaned.

104. Jones, "Genetic Engineering," 404.

105. Ibid., 405.

106. Barnette, *Exploring Medical Ethics*, 95-96.

107. Gina Kolata, "Scientist Reports First Cloning Ever of Adult Mammal," New York Times, 24 February 1997, 1.

108. D. B. Fletcher, "Reproductive Technologies," *Dictionary of Christian Ethics*, 733. In the U.S., about 22,000 babies are available for two million prospective adoptive couples.

109. Some countries require legal contracts, while in others the practice is illegal. Legal difficulties occur when surrogates are reluctant to give up the baby or deformed infants are rejected.

110. J. K. Anderson, "Genetic Engineering," in *Encyclopedia of Biblical and Christian Ethics*, 166.

111. The first "test-tube baby" was born in 1978 in Britain; many thousands have been born since.

112. Fletcher, "Reproductive Technologies," 733.

113. Anderson, "Genetic Engineering," 166.

114. Ibid., 166-67.

115. Fletcher, "Reproductive Technologies," 734.

116. Barnette, *Exploring Medical Ethics*, 81-90.

117. C. S. Lewis, *The Voyage of the Dawn Treader* (London: G. Bles, 1960), 75.

118. Cameron, *Bioethics and the Future of Medicine*, 4.

119. Ibid., 11–12.

CHAPTER TEN

1. Roy McCloughry, "Basic Stott," *Christianity Today*, 8 January 1996, 25.

2. Ibid., 29.

3. Max L. Stackhouse, *Public Theology and Political Economy* (Lanham, Md.: University Press of America, 1991), 95.

4. T. B. Maston, *Christianity and World Issues* (New York: The Macmillan Co., 1957), 208.

5. Stackhouse, *Public Theology*, 96–97.

6. Reinhold Niebuhr, *An Interpretation of Christian Ethics* (New York: Harper & Row, 1935, 1963), 112.

7. John Stott, *Decisive Issues Facing Christians Today* (Grand Rapids: Revell, 1984, 1990), 2–6, who discusses "The Evangelical Heritage of Social Concern," noting Wesley and a host of evangelical leaders supported penal and parliamentary reform and campaigned against the slave trade, dueling, drunkenness, gambling, cruel animal sports, and the mistreatment of children.

8. Quoted by Donald W. Dayton in *Discovering an Evangelical Heritage* (New York: Harper & Row, 1976), 24.

9. Stott, *Decisive Issues*, 6–10, and David O. Moberg, *The Great Reversal* (Philadelphia: Lippincott, 1972), 184.

10. Carl F. H. Henry, *The Uneasy Conscience of Modern Fundamentalism* (Grand Rapids: Eerdmans, 1947).

11. Stott, *Decisive Issues*, 9–10.

12. See Jerry Falwell's "An Agenda for the Eighties," in *Moral Issues and Christian Response*, 4th ed., Paul Jersild and Dale Johnson (New York: Holt, Rinehart, & Winston, 1988), 23–29.

13. Emil Brunner, *The Divine Imperative* (Philadelphia: Westminster Press, 1947), 86.

14. A. B. Cramp, "Economic Ethics," *New Dictionary of Christian Ethics and Pastoral Theology*, ed. David J. Atkinson, et al. (Downers Grove, Ill.: InterVarsity Press, 1995), 116–21.

15. John C. Bennett, et al., *Christian Values and Economic Life* (New York: Harper, 1954), 183.

16. Richard J. Foster, *The Challenge of the Disciplined Life: Money, Sex, and Power* (San Francisco: Harper & Row, 1985).

17. Ibid., 20–23.

18. See also Matthew 6:19; 19:24; Luke 6:30; and 12:33.

19. Foster, *Money, Sex, and Power,* 28.

20. Ibid., 37.

21. Bruce C. Birch, *Let Justice Roll Down: The Old Testament, Ethics, and Christian Life* (Louisville: W/JKP, 1991), 121.

22. Foster, *Money, Sex, and Power,* 86.

23. Henlee H. Barnette, *Introducing Christian Ethics* (Nashville: Broadman Press, 1961), 147.

24. Ernst Troeltsch, *The Social Teaching of the Christian Churches* (Louisville: W/JKP, 1931, 1992), 1:115.

25. Waldo Beach and H. Richard Niebuhr, *Christian Ethics: Sources of the Living Tradition* (New York: The Ronald Press, 1955), 75.

26. Barnette, *Introducing Christian Ethics,* 148.

27. R. E. O. White, *Christian Ethics: The Historical Development* (Atlanta: John Knox Press, 1981), 172–74.

28. Karl Holl, *The Cultural Significance of the Reformation,* trans. Karl and Barbara Hertz and John H. Lichtblau (New York: Meridian Books, 1959), 81–92.

29. White, *Christian Ethics,* 202.

30. W. R. Inge, *Christian Ethics and Modern Problems* (London: Hodder and Stoughton, 1930), 232.

31. Darrell Reeck, *Ethics for the Professions: A Christian Perspective* (Minneapolis: Augsburg, 1982), 34–35.

32. Max Weber, *The Protestant Ethic and the Spirit of Capitalism,* trans. Talcott Parsons (New York: Charles Scribner's Sons, 1930).

33. S. Dex, "Capitalism," *New Dictionary of Christian Ethics,* 213–14.

34. Barnette, *Introducing Christian Ethics,* 153.

35. Ibid., 154.

36. Walter Rauschenbusch, *Christianity and the Social Crisis* (New York: Macmillan, 1907), 372.

37. John Wesley, "The Use of Money," in *Sources of the Living Tradition,* 372–79.

38. Greg Warner, "Discrimination of rich versus poor is world's worst problem," *Florida Baptist Witness,* 12 November 1992, 10.

39. Paul Griffin Jones, "I Was Hungry...?" *Salt and Light* 4 (August 1990): 1.

40. "Hunger: The Daily Disaster," *Christianity Today,* 19 November 1990, 49.

41. "A Look at Your Hungry World," produced by the Research and Planning Office, Foreign Mission Board of the S.B.C., Richmond, Virginia.

42. Washington, D.C.: U.S. Department of Commerce, Bureau of the Census, 1995, *Statistical Abstract of the United States: 1995,* 480–81.

43. Jones, "I Was Hungry . . .?" 1. The 1.2 million American Indians living in the U.S. have a per capita income of $1,470, the lowest of any population group.

44. Anita Manning, "Third of U.S. Kids Live with Working Poor," *USA Today*, 4 June 1996, 1. The number is up 30 percent since 1989 and challenges the stereotype that poor families are primarily young mothers on welfare.

45. Robert Parham, *What Shall We Do in a Hungry World?* (Birmingham: New Hope Press, 1988), 38–44.

46. "Issues and Answers: Hunger" (Nashville: Christian Life Commission of the S.B.C., 1993), 4–6.

47. Stott, *Decisive Issues*, 241–48.

48. *An Evangelical Commitment to Simple Lifestyle*, Exposition and Commentary by Alan Nichols (Lausanne Occasional Papers, No. 20, 1980), as published in *Lifestyle in the Eighties*, ed. Ron J. Sider (Philadelphia: Westminster, 1982), 35–36.

49. Ron Sider, *Rich Christians in an Age of Hunger: A Biblical Study* (Downers Grove, Ill.: InterVarsity Press, 1984).

50. David R. Wilkinson, "Christian Life-Style: Toward a Responsible Economic Ethic," in *Perspectives on Applied Christianity*, eds. William M. Tillman Jr. (Macon, Ga.: Mercer University Press, 1986), 92–95.

51. Parham, *What Shall We Do?* 47–48.

52. Stott, *Decisive Issues*, 11.

53. Dietrich Bonhoeffer (*Ethics*, trans. Neville H. Smith [New York: Macmillan, 1956], 297) makes a distinction between "state" (the ruled and the rulers) and "government" (rulers only).

54. Maston, *Christianity and World Issues*, 208.

55. John C. Bennett, "State," *The Westminster Dictionary of Christian Ethics*, eds. John F. Childress and John Macquarrie (Philadelphia: The Westminster Press, 1986), 602.

56. R. J. Bauckham, "Politics," *New Dictionary of Christian Ethics*, 669.

57. Stott, *Decisive Issues*, 11.

58. Barnette, *Introducing Christian Ethics*, 161.

59. John Howard Yoder, *The Politics of Jesus* (Grand Rapids: Eerdmans, 1972). Yoder notes that Jesus rejected the revolutionary way of the Zealots, the withdrawal response of the Essenes, and the accommodation approach of the Sadducees.

60. Clifton J. Allen, ed., *The Broadman Bible Commentary*, vol. 8, *Matthew*, by Frank Stagg (Nashville: Broadman Press, 1969), 180.

61. H. D. A. Major, *The Mission and Message of Jesus* (New York: E. P. Dutton & Co., 1938), 148.

62. Stott, *Decisive Issues*, 11.

63. Barnette, *Introducing Christian Ethics*, 162.

64. Victor Paul Furnish, *The Moral Teaching of Paul: Selected Issues* (Nashville: Abingdon, 1985), 115.

65. In one of his last letters, Paul urged Christians to pray for governmental leaders (1 Tim. 2:1–2).

66. Bennett, "State," 602–3.

67. Bauckham, "Politics," 670.

68. A. Cleveland Coxe, "Elucidations," in *The Ante-Nicene Fathers* (Grand Rapids: Eerdmans, 1976 [1885]), 3:58.

69. J. Philip Wogaman, *Christian Ethics: A Historical Introduction* (Louisville: W/JKP, 1993), 45.

70. Maston, *Christianity and World Issues*, 216–17.

71. Ibid., 217.

72. Bob Adams, "The Church and the World," in *Understanding Christian Ethics*, ed. William M. Tillman Jr. (Nashville: Broadman Press, 1988), 109–10.

73. William A. Mueller, *Church and State in Luther and Calvin* (Nashville, Broadman Press, 1954), 127.

74. Luther and Lutheranism have a more negative view of the state, a dualistic interpretation of "two kingdoms," which taught the state's main function was to provide a dike against sin.

75. Ibid., 111–12.

76. Maston, *Christianity and World Issues*, 220. Many other currents and trends, such as the Great Awakening and the intellectual and political atmosphere of that day, contributed to the adoption of the separation theory.

77. Anson Phelps Stokes, *Church and State in the United States* (New York: Harper, 1950), 27.

78. Maston, *Christianity and World Issues*, 222.

79. In the past, Roman Catholic writers made this claim, but recently many evangelicals (even some Baptists) have proposed this theory in their quest to restore a "Christian" America.

80. Frank Swancara, *The Separation of Religion and Government* (New York: Truth Seeker Co., 1950), iv.

81. Bauckham, "Politics," 670.

82. Stephen Charles Mott, *Biblical Ethics and Social Change* (New York: Oxford University Press, 1982), 192.

83. Bauckham, "Politics," 671.

84. William H. Elder III, "Politics and Christian Discipleship," in *Understanding Christian Ethics*, 123.

85. Elaboration upon these suggestions are found in Elder, 140–43, and "Citizen Christians: Their Rights and Responsibilities," Nashville: Christian Life Commission of the S.B.C., 1990).

86. A Gallup Poll reported 54 percent of Americans believe churches should speak out on political and social issues, an increase from 40 percent in 1965 ["Poll: White Protestants are key force in politics," *New Orleans Times-Picayune*, 25 June 1996, A-7].

87. Elder, "Politics and Christian Discipleship," 143.

88. At the end of 1994, a record 5.1 million Americans were either behind bars or on probation or parole, 2.7 percent of the population.

89. The book (and award-winning movie) *Dead Man Walking: An Eye-witness Account of the Death Penalty in the United States* by Sister Helen Prejean (New York: Random House, 1993) has motivated many Christians to rethink their position on the subject.

90. Examples of abolition include Canada, Mexico, Britain, Australia, Germany, Italy, Spain, Switzerland, France, Brazil, and the Scandinavian countries. Most nations that permit the death penalty—such as China and Iraq—are infamous for human rights violations.

91. Randy Frame, "A Matter of Life and Death," *Christianity Today*, 14 August 1995, 50.

92. Ibid., 52.

93. Lewis Smedes, *Mere Morality* (Grand Rapids: Eerdmans, 1983), 118-24.

94. Frame, "Matter of Life and Death," 52.

95. Jersild and Johnson, *Moral Issues,* 231-38.

96. A news report in *Time*, 2 March 1987, 21.

97. John Leland as quoted by James Dunn in "Reflections," *Report from the Capital*, October 1986, 15. The historical account that follows is largely based on information in this article.

98. Ibid.

99. Robert G. Torbet, *A History of the Baptists* (Philadelphia: The Judson Press, 1950), 252-61, 480-81.

100. Torbet, 259, notes that Thomas Jefferson is said to have worshiped in Leland's church and enjoyed his friendship.

101. Saul K. Padovor, *The Complete Jefferson* (New York: Duell, Sloan & Pierce, 1943), 518-19.

102. Maston, *Christianity and World Issues,* 234.

103. Oliver S. Thomas, "Church and State: Matthew 22:15-22," in *The Theological Educator* 36 (Fall 1987), 35-36.

104. Two works that direct the reader to the voluminous literature on the topic are Russell E. Richey and Donald G. Jones, eds. *American Civil Religion* (New York: Harper & Row, 1974); and Robert D. Linder and Richard V. Pierard, *Twilight of the Saints: Biblical Christianity and Civil Religion in America* (Downers Grove, Ill.: InterVarsity Press, 1978).

105. Richard V. Pierard, "One Nation Under God: Judgment or Jingoism?" in *Christian Social Ethics*, ed. Perry C. Cotham (Grand Rapids: Baker Book House, 1979), 81.

106. Robert N. Bellah, "Civil Religion in America," *Daedalus* 96 (Winter 1967): 1–21.

107. Richard Leigh Walker, "Conservatives Reign at Convention," *Christianity Today*, 22 July 1991, 40.

108. Ibid. During a speech by Colonel Oliver North, the audience was given small American flags to wave in response.

109. Pierard, "One Nation Under God," 82–99.

110. See Ralph Reed, *Politically Incorrect: The Emerging Faith Factor in American Politics* (Nashville: Word, 1995); and Michael Cromartie, *Disciples and Democracy: Religious Conservatives and the Future of American Politics* (Grand Rapids: Eerdmans, 1995).

111. Pam Parry, "Progressive evangelicals offer alternative to Religious Right," *Baptist Press*, 24 May 1995, 4. While applauding the Religious Right for making America conscious "that political issues are at the heart of the Christian faith," the group regretted "the use of the Christian label for a brand of religion which has abandoned prophetic justice and compassion for the poor, the elderly and our children."

112. Billy Graham, "Moral Majority," *Parade Magazine*, 1 February 1981, 5.

113. Pitkim A. Sorokin, *Society, Culture, and Personality* (New York: Harper & Bros., 1947), 496–97.

114. In 1993 the Peace Academy founded by President Jimmy Carter reported monitoring 112 wars in the world.

115. For example, Isaiah's hope, "These shall beat their swords into plowshares, and their spears into pruning hooks" (2:4) is directly contradicted by Joel's command, "Beat your plowshares into swords, and your pruning hooks into spears" (3:10).

116. This ethical problem is discussed in chapter 3.

117. Clifton J. Allen, *The Broadman Bible Commentary*, vol. 9, *Luke*, by Malcolm Tolbert Nashville: Broadman Press, 1969), 170.

118. C. J. Cadoux, *The Early Church and the World* (New York: Charles Scribner's Sons, 1925), 275, where he notes there is no evidence of Christian soldiers before A.D. 200, except those converted while in the military.

119. Maston, *Christianity and World Issues,* 251.

120. Cadoux, *Early Church,* 588–89.

121. Maston, *Christianity and World Issues,* 252–53.

122. Robert G. Clouse, *War: Four Christian Views* (Downers Grove, Ill.: InterVarsity Press, 1981, 1991).

123. Christian pacifist Myron S. Augsburger [Clouse, *War,* 81-97] contends Christians must live in the world by Jesus' ethic of nonviolent resistance as a witness to the Christian way. John H. Yoder and Stanley Hauerwas make similar proposals.

124. Arthur F. Holmes [Clouse, *War,* 117-35] explains that war is a necessary evil allowable only when it meets the rules of (1) just cause, (2) just intention, (3) last resort, (4) formal declaration, (5) limited objectives, (6) proportionate means, and (7) noncombatant immunity.

125. The Crusades and the Islamic Jihad represent extreme forms of this tradition which views war as service to God; preventive war is waged in anticipation of aggression to prevent a greater evil [see Harold O. J. Brown in Clouse, *War,* 152-68].

126. Herman A. Hoyt [Clouse, *War,* 29-57] rejects physical violence as a method of accomplishing any purpose, although spiritual responses such as nonresistance are a Christian obligation.

127. Vernon Grounds, ed., *Nuclear Arms: Two Views on World Peace* (Waco: Word, 1987) and D. J. Atkinson, "Just War Criteria," *Encyclopedia of Biblical and Christian Ethics,* ed. R. K. Harrison (Nashville: Thomas Nelson, 1987), 216.

128. See Glenn Stassen, *Just Peacemaking: Transforming Initiatives for Justice and Peace* (Louisville: Westminister/John Knox Press, 1992).

129. Robert McAfee Brown, *Making Peace in the Global Village* (Philadelphia: The Westminster Press, 1981), 14.